The Army of Ptolemaic Egypt 323 to 204 BC

The Army of Ptolemaic Egypt 323 to 204 BC

An Institutional and Operational History

Paul A. Johstono

Pen & Sword
MILITARY

First published in Great Britain in 2020 by
Pen & Sword Military
An imprint of
Pen & Sword Books Ltd
Yorkshire – Philadelphia

Copyright © Paul Johstono 2020

ISBN 978 1 47383 383 8

The right of Paul Johstono to be identified as Author of this work has been asserted by him in accordance with the Copyright, Designs and Patents Act 1988.

A CIP catalogue record for this book is
available from the British Library.

All rights reserved. No part of this book may be reproduced or transmitted in any form or by any means, electronic or mechanical including photocopying, recording or by any information storage and retrieval system, without permission from the Publisher in writing.

Printed and bound in the UK by TJ Books Ltd, Padstow, Cornwall.

Pen & Sword Books Limited incorporates the imprints of Atlas, Archaeology, Aviation, Discovery, Family History, Fiction, History, Maritime, Military, Military Classics, Politics, Select, Transport, True Crime, Air World, Frontline Publishing, Leo Cooper, Remember When, Seaforth Publishing, The Praetorian Press, Wharncliffe Local History, Wharncliffe Transport, Wharncliffe True Crime and White Owl.

For a complete list of Pen & Sword titles please contact

PEN & SWORD BOOKS LIMITED
47 Church Street, Barnsley, South Yorkshire, S70 2AS, England
E-mail: enquiries@pen-and-sword.co.uk
Website: www.pen-and-sword.co.uk

Or

PEN AND SWORD BOOKS
1950 Lawrence Rd, Havertown, PA 19083, USA
E-mail: Uspen-and-sword@casematepublishers.com
Website: www.penandswordbooks.com

Contents

Acknowledgements		ix
List of Plates		xi
Introduction		xix
Maps		xxvii
Chapter 1:	The Ptolemaic Army at Raphia	1
Chapter 2:	Ptolemy the Satrap, Ptolemy the King	18
Chapter 3:	The Antigonid Wars, 315–285 BC	47
Chapter 4:	Origins of Soldiers in the Ptolemaic Army	77
Chapter 5:	The Age of Midas, Part I	108
Chapter 6:	The Age of Midas, Part II	138
Chapter 7:	Ptolemy III and the Third Syrian War	162
Chapter 8:	Ptolemy III and the Purported Decline of the Ptolemaic Army	200
Chapter 9:	The Fourth Syrian War and the Battle of Raphia	227
	Conclusions	263
Notes		281
Bibliography		311
Index of Personal Names		333
General Index		337

To Brasidas, Berenike, and Laenus,
Whose mother wisely vetoed these first names.

Acknowledgements

Many of the ideas studied in this book arose from questions posed or formulated in studies years ago with Joshua Sosin and Alex Roland at Duke. They challenged me to establish what I could prove, what I suspected, and what held explanatory power. The book contains many suggestions and conjectures, all admitted, and I hope the reader may find some convincing and useful. Some portions of the book were rewritten from sections of my 2012 dissertation. Many other ideas studied in the book arose in the course of providing historical guidance for the Europa Barbarorum series, and many thanks go both to the EB team and to all those who played EB. I am thankful for the wisdom and advice of far better scholars than I, especially Everett Wheeler, Wayne Lee, Kristen Neuschel, Lee Brice, Tim Howe, and many, many others. A work like this depends on the excellent scholarship of too many talented papyrologists and other classicists to name here; I only hope some of the work adds to the field.

Thanks also go to my family; to Phil Sidnell; to David Preston, Kyle Sinisi, Michael Livingston, Kelly DeVries, Scott Buchanan, and Keith Knapp, excellent scholar-friends from The Citadel and Charleston; to Daniel Bessner and Fahad Bishara; to my matriculating cohort from Duke in '05; to my new colleagues at Air Command & Staff College, who have welcomed an ancient historian into their midst; and to many other friends and colleagues who have helped and encouraged me along the way, in Greenville, in Durham, in Charleston, and now in Alabama.

Much of my research depended upon a host of online resources. All maps made use of the tools at the Ancient World Mapping Center. The hundreds of papyri cited in the text can be examined online through the Papyrological Navigator, at papyri.info. Online resources like these, Trismegistos, the Packhum Epigraphy database, and the Thesaurus Linguae Graecae were enormous helps to this work, but I also spent a lot of time in museum archives and in the Duke Library Special Collections working on parts of this project. Except where I have offered my own translations, I have followed public domain translations broadly accessible through sites like Perseus, Lacus Curtius, Attalus, and Livius. What errors there are in this book are mine alone.

List of Plates

1. Gold issues of the first four Ptolemies.
1a. Stater of Ptolemy I. MET DP.16199.004. The reverse face of the gold stater, which dates from the first decade of the monarchy, depicts the deified Alexander (7.1 grams). (*Public domain*)
1b. Trichryson (*pentadrachm*) of Ptolemy II. ANS 1944.100.64172. These heavier issues, three times the value of the quadriga staters (17.8 grams), mostly date to Ptolemy II's wars of the 270s BC. This type prominently displays a Galatian shield, hearkening to Ptolemy's destruction of his seditious Galatian mercenaries. (*Public domain*)
1c. Mnaieon (*oktodrachm*) of Ptolemy II. ANS 1967.152.620.obv. The jugate bust royal couple issues, depicting the Ptolemaic Sibling-Gods, were issued from near the end of the First Syrian War until at least the end of the Chremonidean War. (*Public domain*)
1d. Mnaieon of Ptolemy IV. MET inv. 30.115.21. This gold issue dates from the time of the Fourth Syrian War, and depicts a deified Ptolemy III with a radiant crown and aegis. It may have been the – or one of the – issues given out in the soldier bonuses after the victory at Raphia, just as it may also have been used to pay officers during the war. (*Public domain*)
2. Stele of a Macedonian cavalryman, Alexandria Museum inv. 10228. The deceased, mounted on a rearing horse, rides to the left. The horse furniture is all in dark leather, with a deep scarlet-brown riding blanket. Reins in his left, a *xyston* in his right, the rider is helmetless, with a fine chlamys in saffron yellow and purple stripe flowing behind him, like the Companions in Alexander's army. His long chiton wraps along his upper legs, and he may wear greaves. His armour appears to be in the style of a linen corselet, with two rows of ptergyes plainly visible (as well as the scabbard for his sabre), but its colour suggests it could be a bronze corselet like the one associated with Philip II. The attendant running behind him may carry his helmet. (*Photograph A. Lecler,* ©

CEAlex archives, with thanks for this and others to Marie-Dominique Nenna)

3. Stele of an *Agema* officer, Alexandria Museum inv. 10689. The deceased, whom I identify as an officer of one of the units of the Ptolemaic *agema*, stands with a long spear, presumably a sarissa, gripped above eye level in his left arm. His red helmet is in the Phrygian style, with a silvered Atticizing visor, a horsetail crest and two feathers, akin to the helmets of elite infantry officers on the Agios Athanasios frieze in Macedonia. His chiton is also red, a chlamys over his arm white. He wears greaves and a bronze muscled cuirass with bronze pteryges. A rimless shield, the approximate size of the ideal "8-palms" Macedonian shield, was bronze with traces of red paint. He is the very model of a Ptolemaic elite infantry officer. (*Photograph A. Pelle,* © *CEAlex archives*)

4. Stele of the Thessalian Polyoktos, Alexandria Museum inv. 10233. Two men in armour grasp hands, with a boy attending the man on the left. The left figure wears a muscled cuirass in bronze over a long white chiton, and a conical helmet that may be iron. The man on the right wears a white corselet, presumably of linen, with two or possibly three rows of long ptergyes, over a deep scarlet chiton, and a chlamys in a dark ochre yellow. (*Photograph A. Lecler,* © *CEAlex archives*)

5. Stele of the Thessalian Lykinos, Alexandria Museum inv. 18824. The deceased extends his hand to a son or boy attendant. Lykinos wears a tanned corselet, perhaps leather, with two rows of pteryges and a reddish stripe on his belly. He wears a saffron yellow chlamys, a violet chiton and tanned boots. The boy stands behind a nearly rimless and very convex reddish-bronze shield, in proportion to the standing man, estimated at about 1 metre in diameter, etched with a twenty-four-ray star. The shield appears large for a phalangite, but otherwise matches much closer with the Macedonian shield than with any cavalry shield, leaving Lykinos' military status doubtful. (*Photograph A. Lecler,* © *CEAlex archives*)

6. Stele of a Ptolemaic soldier, Musée Archaeologique Nationale inv. 31232. The deceased stands leaning on a spear in his right hand, gripped at shoulder height. He wears a bronze muscled cuirass and a long yellow chiton, with an even longer chlamys draped over his left shoulder, brown, with a light blue-green stripe at the end. Behind his right leg are the traces of a sizeable shield, possibly painted at one time with a face or an eagle. (© *MAN (France) / Loïc Hamon, with thanks to Françoise Aujogue*)

7. Stele of a Ptolemaic soldier, Alexandria Museum inv. 19110. The deceased, probably an officer, stands between two attending boys. He wears a white corselet, presumably of linen, with deep red shoulder harness and a deep red stripe across his belly. A chlamys is over his shoulder, and a sword, with dimensions indicative of a cavalryman's *kopis*, hangs in its scabbard on a baldric by his left. He grasps a spear low in his left hand, cradling it along his left forearm as it extends over his shoulder. Barely visible by his left leg is a small round shield, at scale to the man in the general range of 60cm, with twelve- or twenty-four-ray starburst. (*Photograph A. Lecler, © CEAlex archives*)
8. Stele of the Bithynian Dionysios, Alexandria Museum inv. 20919. The infantryman depicted here is typical of the *thureophoros* panoply that proliferated in the Hellenistic period. The shield – a narrow oval a metre tall, flat, with a prominent vertical rib – was borrowed from the Galatians over the course of the third century BC. Dionysios' attendant wears his conical hat or helmet and carries the shield and two javelins. Dionysios carries a heavier spear himself and wears a brown chiton with a thick vertical stripe in white or cream, and a wreath upon his head. Dionysios may be typical of many mercenaries in Ptolemaic service by the late third century. (*Photograph A. Lecler, © CEAlex archives*)
9. Stele of the Galatian Bitos, Metropolitan Museum inv. 04175. Many Galatian *stelai* have been found in the necropolises of Alexandria. The stele of Bitos, son of Lostoieko, is a good example. We see the nearly body-length *thureos*, more lens-shaped than pure oval, with a round bronze thimble boss. The red-bearded Galatian warrior wears the typical woad blue cloak. The pommel of a sword, belted high on his right waist, is barely visible, and his right hand holds a spear. Like many Galatians, he presents ready for military service, nude under the woad-dyed cloak, which might be thrown back or off before combat. (*Public domain*)
10. Stele of the Galatian –atos, Metropolitan Museum inv. 04176. A second Galatian soldier. Many of the preceding stelae were erroneously identified as Galatians by overzealous scholars a century ago, but this figure presents another good example. The soldier is again nude save for a long woad blue cloak. He has a dark moustache, but many other details are lost. A sword with typically La Tene trilobate pommel seems visible at his right waist, suiting Celtic fashion. An attendant holds a long, narrow *thureos*, lavishly decorated with triplet red crescents on each end, blue and yellow fields, and a white boss and spine. (*Public domain*)

11. Limestone mould/model for Ptolemaic bronze shields, Allard Pierson Museum inv. 7879. The model shield may have been used as a mould for bronze covers for Macedonian *peltai* shields, for use in the phalanx. It is at least reversed as a mould should be. It features the inscribed dynastic name – PTOLEMAIOY – indicating the state (the king) owned these shields. The seven arcs and stars in the outer band are very consistent with other Macedonian shields. The Gorgoneion was a common *episema*, but the Ptolemies likely made use of many others. On these shields, see Anderson (1967) and Liampi (1988). (*Image courtesy of Collection Allard Pierson, Amsterdam, with thanks to René van Beek*)
12. Back of limestone shield mould/model, Allard Pierson Museum inv. 7879. The other side of the theorized mould features a rosette mixed with pellets and ringed, with five pellets on one side. The purpose of this design is less clear. (*Image courtesy of Collection Allard Pierson, Amsterdam, with thanks to René van Beek*)
13. Ptolemaic shield medallion, Museum für Byzantinische Kunst inv. 4377. This small medallion was made in imitation of a Ptolemaic pikeman's shield. The triple arcs and pellets are reminiscent of designs on the Pydna monument. Eight sets of arcs is less common, but appears on the Lyson and Kallikles tomb and on the smallest of three shields on the frieze in the Agios Athanasios tomb. The shield blazon is archetypally Ptolemaic: Zeus's eagle gripping the thunderbolt. (© *Staatliche Museen zu Berlin, Skulpturensammlung und Museum für Byzantinische Kunst, Photo: Antje Voigt, with thanks to Cäcilia Fluck*)
14. Hadra hydria with shield, Metropolitan Museum inv. 90967. This cinerary urn, presumably for a deceased mercenary who had served at Alexandria, was manufactured and painted at Alexandria. It depicts a rimmed bronze shield (the standard Greek aspis) with a gorgoneion device, comparable to that on the shield mould from Memphis. (Public domain)
15. Terracotta Bes as warrior, Paul Perdizet, *Les terres cuites grecques d'Égypte de la collections Fouquet*, 1921. Pl. XLI. Many terracotta figures of the grotesque god Bes have been found from Ptolemaic and Roman times. These examples depict Bes, as is often the case, in elements of Hellenistic military costume. Neither Bes wears body armour, but each wields a sword and carries a Macedonian shield. The Bes typically wears a triple-crested or five-feathered helmet. One wields a *kopis* slashing sword, the other a sword much like the Celtiberian gladius, while standing atop a Galatian shield as a trophy. (Public domain)

16. Bes as a shielded cavalryman, SzM inv T 505. The depiction of Bes on horseback is quite rare. This Bes appears in heavy armour, on rearing horse, with a large round shield, reminiscent of the appearance of Macedonian cavalry on monuments from the late third and early second centuries. (© *László Mátyus, Museum of Fine Arts, Budapest, with thanks to Csaba Bodnár*)
17. Stele of Somtutefnakht, National Naples Archaeological Museum inv 1035. The stele tells in hieroglyphs how the priest and warrior – a role that was not at all atypical for the Egyptian aristocracy, even during the Ptolemaic period – served in the temple in Herakleopolis but also fought in a great battle, probably Issus, against Alexander's army. (*Photograph Berthold Werner, Wikimedia Commons, CC BY-3*)
18. The Perdiccas pediment from the Alexander sarcophagus, Istanbul Archaeological Museum. This scene from the famous Alexander sarcophagus, most commonly reckoned that of Abdalonymos king of Sidon, is usually thought to depict the assassination of Perdiccas after the failure to cross the Nile near Memphis. Wounded men on the sides of the scene may be part of the retreat from the Nile. (*Courtesy of Egisto Mannini*)
19. Macedonian cavalryman from the Alexander sarcophagus, Istanbul Archaeological Museum. This scene, from the same sarcophagus, depicts a battle between Alexander's Macedonians and the Persian army, perhaps the Battle of Gaugamela. The rider on the right of the scene is one of Alexander's *hetairoi* in typical Boeotian helmet, while his scarlet chlamys identifies him as a member of the elite royal *il* of Companions, like Ptolemy himself until his elevation to *somatophylax*. (*Courtesy of Stephen Zucker, used with permission*)
20. Statue base for Honours to Ptolemy I (*I.Milet.* 7.244). The surviving dedication is for Ptolemaios son of Laagos, Macedonian, and so pre-dates Ptolemy I's acclamation as king. It most likely belongs to Ptolemy's campaign in the area in 309/308 BC. The dedication is of Ptolemy I, but to Apollo. The middle lines, which undoubtedly praised Ptolemy, have been effaced. The most likely culprits for the erasure are the agents of the Antigonids. (*Author's photograph*)
21. Bronze bust of Ptolemy III, Museo archeologico di Firenze. This depicts Euergetes as Herakles, with lion skin tied around his neck, a depiction that was also employed on silver coins during the Third Syrian War (see 23b). (*Photograph Francesco Bini, CC BY-SA-3.0*)

Ptolemy III as Pharaoh, Neues Museum Berlin. Here the depiction is Euergetes in Egyptian style. The young Pharaoh wears the traditional nemes headdress. It may belong to the period of his euergetisms and the end of the revolt, or as late as the time of the Canopus decree. (*Photograph Miguel Cuesta, CC BY-SA-4.0*)

23. Coins of Euergetes and the Third Syrian War.
23a. Year 2 Soter-series Tetradrachm from Joppa. ANS 1944.76348. Representative of the enormous issues of silver tetradrachms from numerous Phoenician mints in support of the war effort in Asia. The Soter tetradrachm had also been minted extensively during the Second Syrian War, and mints at Joppa, Sidon, Tyre and Ptolemais-Ake produced large numbers from Year 2 (246/245 BC) to Year 5 (242/241). (*Public domain*)
23b. Ptolemy III Tetradrachm from Ephesus. ANS 1992.35.1. An excellent example of the issues put out from Ephesus after its capture. Unlike the Soter series, these depict Ptolemy III himself, young, with filet and lion-skin cloak. It probably dates to about 245 or 244 BC. (*Public domain*)
23c. Year 4 Mnaieon of Arsinoe II from Joppa. ANS 1944.100.76346. Representative of the heavy production of gold coins of Arsinoe II in the Phoenician mints during the fighting phase of the Third Syrian War. (*Public domain*)
23d. Year 5 Soter Tetradrachm from Sidon. ANS 1944.100.76361. The eagle on the obverse practically preens Ptolemaic victory in the war as of 242/241 BC. Year 5 was the last year that saw heavy minting activity in silver tetradrachms at the Phoenician mints, correlating with the conclusion of the war. (*Public domain*)
23e. Berenice II Mnaieon-and-a-half. ANS 1967.152.562. One of the larger gold coins produced in the Hellenistic era, these Berenice II issues seem to be marked to Year 5, although they could date later. Such a large denomination coin in irregular size suggests efforts to stabilize the Ptolemaic economy in Egypt coming out of both a major war and dangerous famines. (*Public domain*)
24. Alexandria, French Imperial sketching. From *Recueil des observations et des recherches qui ont été faites en Égypte pendant l'expédition de l'armée française,* 1809, Carte générale des côtes, rades, ports, ville et environs d'Alexandrie. NYPL b14212718-1268199. This depiction shows the outlines of ancient Alexandria according to surveyors with Napoleon's expedition in 1801, including the contemporary city built

upon the silted Heptastadion, the Fatamid walls around Rhakotis and the remains of the far larger Ptolemaic and Roman city, including the stadium in the southwest, the ruins of the Brucheion and Lochias royal neighbourhoods by the eastern seaboard and the disposition of Alexandria between Lake Maraeotis and the sea. (*Public domain*)

25. Alexandria in the Late Ptolemaic era. Drawn from the plan of Otto Puchstein *c.*1890. Viewed with the preceding sketching it is possible to get a clearer idea of the layout and scale of Hellenistic Alexandria, although this depiction may not have been as accurate for third-century BC Alexandria. (*Wikimedia Commons*)

Introduction

On 22 June 217 BC, one of the largest pitched battles in world history took place just inland from the Mediterranean coast at Raphia, near the border between Egypt and the Gaza Strip. The reported strengths of the two field armies that faced off that day totalled more than 143,000 men, who clashed in nearly equal numbers across a front that may have stretched up to 3 miles. To the south was Ptolemy IV, king of Egypt, and on the north was Antiochus III, king of the Seleucid Empire. The two kings commanded larger field armies than Alexander ever did: Ptolemy's was the third largest Hellenistic army ever fielded for battle, that of Antiochus probably the sixth or seventh largest.[1] Only Philippi in 42 BC, Ipsos in 301 BC and Gaugamela in 331 BC could be spoken in the same breath in terms of the total number of combatants. Even the Romans only fielded armies of the same magnitude at Philippi (on both sides), Cannae and perhaps on a couple of occasions in the civil wars of the Late Republic or in the Year of the Four Emperors.[2] Ptolemy's army at Raphia was certainly one of the ten largest armies fielded in the Western world in antiquity; and unlike most of the other largest armies in antiquity, the Ptolemaic army emerged victorious from its day of battle.

The Ptolemaic army does not generate enormous interest for its campaign record; in fact it is often denigrated. It attracts what interest it does mainly because of the source record available: thousands of papyri and inscriptions from Egypt and elsewhere. These sources make it possible to talk with authority about aspects of the Ptolemaic army that, for other armies, lie in the realm of conjecture alone. Because the battlefield and operational record of the Ptolemies has been denigrated, it has often been neglected. The result is that disproportionately more has been written about the ethnic makeup, economic activities and social life of Ptolemaic soldiers than about the army as an operational institution.[3] This work seeks to offer some corrections of that tendency with an account of the Ptolemaic army that is at times institutional, operational, material and social. This sort of multi-dimensional military history is not only possible, but also necessary, when dealing with the Ptolemaic army, because it was at all times a military body structured for armed conflict, a colonizing and occupying presence mainly in Egypt, and a reflection and auxiliary of the monarchic project of the Ptolemies themselves.

We know about the armies that fought at Raphia because of the account Polybius recorded at least fifty years later, drawing from at least two unnamed accounts that were composed much closer to the battle. For Polybius, the campaign at Raphia was a brief acme for the Ptolemaic kingdom and its armies. The kingdom's slow moral decline was arrested for one of the great military encounters of antiquity, only for a steeper decline – in terms political, economic and military, as well as moral – to set in precipitously afterwards, and even as a result of the campaign. Polybius' sour view of Ptolemaic affairs has cast a shadow over all subsequent treatments of the Ptolemaic army.

Similarly, the attraction of a parabolic narrative for the Ptolemies – the grandeur and success of the first two kings, the corruption and failures of those who followed – has so dominated the baseline for discussing Ptolemaic military and political affairs as to have become a presupposition.[4] It makes an easy and memorable story. Aside from narrative value, it also reflects an idea – current in Polybius' day and endorsed by him – that there was a half-life for Greek virtue in a place like Egypt. This sense, that what made Greeks a great people in the Classical age would necessarily degrade when exposed to "Eastern" qualities like subservient populations, wealth, ease and despotism, makes it impossible for the Ptolemaic narrative to be anything other than one of decline. This cultural and ethnic bigotry appeared in numerous sources, and while the correlation has been demolished, the narrative derived from it has not been. One of the chief contributions I hope to make through this book is to challenge not only some aspects of the decline narrative, but also of the Golden Age of the early Ptolemies.

In order to develop a history of the Ptolemaic army that is free of a presuppositional framework of 'glory-then-decline', it is necessary to field an analytical framework for the history that follows. The remainder of this introduction lays out the analytical and methodological framing for the study, uses the army that took the field at Raphia to offer a very brief introduction to the overall force and lays out the chapters to follow.

The Framework

The Ptolemaic army was always functioning to fulfil three missions. First, the army was an extension and expression of the king's power in areas under

Ptolemaic rule, and especially Egypt. It began fulfilling this mission under Alexander and continued it under the Ptolemies. This particular function should be set against the common Greek and Macedonian conception of the army as an extension of the people. In Egypt, the army was primarily the regular expression of the state's claim to a monopoly on violence, and the advance of state power over the length and depth of the land. The settlement of soldiers in cities or in the countryside, the posting of garrisons or construction of forts, even the economic and judicial measures taken with regard to the soldiers were all ways of making the army an extension of Ptolemaic authority.[5] Most Ptolemaic soldiers, especially those from the Greek world – but also Egyptians and North Africans – were privileged compared to the native, civilian populace of Egypt. Their privilege helped them represent Ptolemaic power and incentivized them as agents of the Ptolemies. Incorporation of Egyptian groups with their own political or social weight – the aristocratic priesthoods or the old warrior classes – figured not only as a way to access new reserves of manpower, but also as a path to negotiating an expansion of Ptolemaic authority.[6]

The army was also the enforcement of royal power in armed conflict, as an army of conquest or defence in interstate warfare, but also as a force for relief, coercion and security in the Ptolemaic 'empire', the collection of regions and cities under Ptolemaic rule, occupation or influence.[7] The Ptolemaic army was a product of military traditions, Hellenistic military doctrine, and the personnel and equipment available to the Ptolemies.[8] The Ptolemaic army emphasized, for war campaigns, the royal army. This was a natural product of all three factors influencing Ptolemaic military activity. The Hellenistic approach to doctrine tended to emphasize the capacity for the kingdom's combined arms force – well-organized, well-equipped and well-disciplined – to achieve battlefield victory, especially under the leadership of a competent general, ideally the king himself. To be included in the royal army was a privilege. Thus the royal army was not merely the contingent collection of soldiers brigaded into the royal army at one or another time; it was the permanent collection of specific units mobilized together for big wars. Accident and contingency could change the makeup of royal armies – mercenary components in particular would necessarily vary – but an important part of the Ptolemaic or any Hellenistic army was the permanence, through mobilization and demobilization cycles, of the royal army. The Ptolemaic army was also far more than the royal army: hosts of soldiers served in lesser roles, filling garrisons in permanent or rotational service, in Egypt and abroad. The collection of needs and wants for Ptolemaic military activity, at the level of the royal army or the far-flung garrison, always exerted influence over the institutions and activities of Ptolemaic forces.

Finally, the army was a reflection of Ptolemaic identity and a component of the Ptolemaic kingship.[9] Its institutions, culture and activities were a product of and a contribution to the very character of the Macedonian monarchy in Egypt. Ptolemaic kingship emulated Alexander's kingship and aspects of traditional Macedonian kingship, all filtered through Hellenistic memory and perspective. But the Ptolemies also incorporated elements of Egyptian and Near Eastern monarchies. Macedonian soldiers reflected and affirmed the Macedonian character of the monarchy, while Egyptian soldiers and acts of largesse to Egyptian temples or priesthoods forged associations with the Pharaohs of old. The importance of the units of the royal army reflected both the demographic realities of the Ptolemaic position and the importance of the king-general, whose brilliance – he was to be the heir of Alexander, after all, a great burden on any commander – combined with warrior élan to garner victories. Having a phalanx armed in the Macedonian manner, and Macedonians in the phalanx, fitted the cultural sense of Hellenistic monarchy, especially in the era covered in this text. Cultural expectation and aspiration contributed, in some cases, just as much to the history of the Ptolemaic army as operational imperatives.

These three functions – colonizing and occupying Ptolemaic territory, carrying out armed operations in armies and garrisons, and reflecting the character of the monarchy – worked in rough harmony in Ptolemaic history. Evaluating their relative priority in different eras is often a challenge, and there are few clear indications that the Ptolemies or their chief agents recognized the tensions between the three primary roles of their army. A study of the development, or rise and decline, of the Ptolemaic army must give some attention to the interplay between these functions.

In analyzing the army, there are also several categories of analysis that are useful: the operational, institutional, material, social and political. The Ptolemaic army, especially in wartime, can be studied through an operational lens, but outside of the Battle of Raphia itself, or the last Ptolemaic wars against the Caesars, rarely has been. The operational perspective examines the army operating in its environment, its use of fortifications, use of natural terrain, logistical networks, varied missions and performance in combat. The Ptolemaic army is, because of the source material available, easier to study in institutional terms. The army was a collection of institutions. The fundamental aspect of the institutional study is the organization of the army by divisions, units and command structure, but also includes the mechanisms that existed to recruit, equip, train, mobilize, pay and provision the army. The material category considers the arms and armour, food and drink of the Ptolemaic soldier, the everyday and exceptional, technical and technological, individually or state-supplied elements that set apart a trained man as a soldier. Because the Ptolemaic army fulfilled two significant functions aside from its war-fighting function, and was always performing those other functions, attention should be paid to the social and political status and activities of Ptolemaic soldiers or the Ptolemaic army.

The final aspect of the framework for this study is chronological. The study addresses the Ptolemaic army under the first four kings, all of whom were named Ptolemy. Ptolemy I Soter founded the dynasty, and as satrap then king ruled from 323–282 BC. Ptolemy II Philadelphus began co-rule with his father in 285 BC and ruled until 246 BC. Together, their reigns represent over half of the period covered in this study, and the era often recognized as the golden age of Ptolemaic rule and for the Ptolemaic army. Ptolemy III Euergetes succeeded his father and ruled until 222 BC. Ptolemy IV Philopator then ruled until his death in 205 BC. When he died his son was still a child, and the country and its military establishment were in a serious crisis. The study ends with Ptolemy IV for two reasons. In him and his predecessors there is sufficient material to study the narrative of the climax and decline of the Ptolemaic army. Furthermore, the period from Ptolemy V onward, unlike that prior to it, featured dynastic conflicts, sometimes a divided monarchy, and recurrent domestic revolts and seditions. These added numerous complications and could not be accommodated satisfactorily in the constraints of the present study. The study, therefore, proceeds chronologically, from king to king. Each chapter, however, addresses the development of the three main functions of the army and devotes some consideration to each of the categories of analysis.

The Army at Raphia as a Window

The army that Ptolemy IV Philopator marshalled at Raphia numbered more than 75,000 men (Plb. 5.79.2). The varied contingents provide an opportunity to break down the structures of the Ptolemaic army and introduce the reader to some of the main categories and terms that will feature in the remainder of this study. The account in Polybius does not make most of these connections, but by reading the Polybian account alongside other sources – chiefly documentary papyri from Egypt – it is possible to connect Polybius' fairly short description of an army at one battle to the dispersed, peacetime army across more than a hundred years of Ptolemaic history and thousands of individual documentary texts.

Polybius described the army from the left wing to the right wing at Raphia, but also described the same contingents earlier as part of Ptolemaic preparations for war. The two passages are from his *Histories*, book 5, sections 65 and 82. The king was on the left, along with most of the elite units in the army. On this wing there were 3,000 cavalry: 700 from the palace squadron and 2,300 recruited from Egypt and Libya. There were forty African elephants and their crews, and 3,000 Cretan light infantry. Then there were 5,000 elite infantrymen, comprising 3,000 from the royal *agema* and 2,000 called *peltastai*. These elite infantry linked the left wing to the centre, the infantry phalanx. The infantry phalanx had four contingents. First were 3,000 infantry from Libya armed in the Macedonian manner – that is, as phalangites – then 25,000 Macedonian phalangites, 20,000 Egyptian phalangites and finally 8,000 Greek mercenaries. These mercenaries linked the centre to the right wing, where there were 6,000 Galatians and Thracians marshalled together, thirty-three more elephants and 2,000 cavalry, identified as Greeks and other mercenaries. In all there were 5,000 cavalry, 70,000 infantry and seventy-three elephants.

Within these diverse groups, there were at least three distinct terms of service in the Ptolemaic army: professional soldiers, military settlers and foreign mercenaries. Professional soldiers spent much of their year in active service of some sort. They were often called *misthophoroi* (mercenaries), but resided permanently in Egypt. Many were semi-professionals, military settlers who also performed regular, paid service. Some Ptolemaic professionals were elite troops, including units of the royal guard, while others were paid regulars of the army. Some were the sons of military settlers, other professionals or Alexandrians. Some professional regiments seem to have been raised in wartime and then disbanded at the conclusion of hostilities. The line between the professionals and foreign mercenaries was blurred in some cases. Both received wages (*misthoi*), but the professionals often held higher status and were associated with some sense of permanent residence, although there was not enough of a sense of citizenship in the Ptolemaic army to make this a clear marker between professionals and mercenaries. Because the Ptolemaic army was always recruiting, many foreign mercenary soldiers could take up residence in Egypt, and with that transition some would also have switched into other types of military roles, professional or settled. In general, though, the mercenaries lived outside Ptolemaic dominions, or at least outside Egypt, prior to their service in the Ptolemaic army. Many mercenaries were Greek, but many others – perhaps most – were Hellenized but not Greek. Individual mercenaries, and occasionally whole units, who were drawn into the permanent institutions of the Ptolemaic army generally did so through joining the other class of Ptolemaic soldiers: the settlers.

The largest class of soldiers in the Ptolemaic army was that of the military settlers. Settlers, or *katoikoi*, possessed land allotments, or *kleroi*, and from that term for allotments the settlers were often called *klerouchoi*, or cleruchs, in Ptolemaic documents. In the earlier Ptolemaic period, officers were probably among the first to receive allotments, and many officers may have attained allotments as rewards well in advance of the general settlement of their soldiers. But as time went on, more and more of the regular army acquired land. In return for their land allotments, the cleruchs owed military service to the Ptolemies. The precise conditions of the arrangement are incompletely attested and varied over time, place and branch of service, but short-term, small-unit mobilizations seem to have been the norm in peacetime. Whole regiments may have only been called up in times of war. In that sense it may be helpful to think of the cleruchs as a kind of reservist force. At the same time, it seems clear that some cleruchs had more burdensome active-duty obligations, and their regular paid service seems to have correlated to smaller land allotments in most cases. Ptolemaic bureaucratic documents often referred to the allotments by a unit of area measurement called the *aroura*, which was equivalent to 0.68 modern acres. Egyptian soldiers and police had fairly small allotments (5 to 10 *arouras*), when they had them at all, infantry had medium-sized allotments (sixteen to thirty), and cavalry larger allotments (seventy to 100). Officers sometimes had far larger allotments.

Throughout Ptolemaic history, it was probably traditional to try to position a son on the allotment of his father to take up his military duty, but this succession rule was not codified for many years. It was unquestionably in place at the time of the Battle of Raphia. The sons of cleruchs, unless they were citizens of one of the two Greek cities in Egypt – Alexandria and Ptolemais – were called *epigonoi*, and until the day they took their father's place (if they ever did), they were eligible for conscription into short-term, paid service. The Ptolemies expanded the ranks of the cleruchs by settling mercenaries from abroad, granting allotments to wartime professional soldiers at the conclusion of their service, giving land to aged-out veterans or even settling prisoners of war. These settlers were the backbone of the Ptolemaic army.

This work is divided into chronological and thematic chapters. The first chapter delves more deeply into Polybius' description of the Ptolemaic army at Raphia to present a short study on the organization and makeup of the Ptolemaic army. The next two chapters relate to the establishing of the Ptolemaic army and Ptolemaic kingdom under Ptolemy I Soter. The second chapter deals with Ptolemy's role as an opponent to the Perdiccan faction, an antagonism from the days of Alexander that grew in scale and ferocity after Alexander's death. The third chapter looks at Ptolemy's wars with Antigonus the One-Eyed, his assumption of the crown and his fairly stable reign. Chapter four is a study of the men who served in the Ptolemaic army and its various units, and especially where they originated. The next two chapters examine the reign of Ptolemy II Philadelphus. While Philadelphus does not have a martial reputation, the fifth chapter examines the martial activities of his reign, which was marked as much by war as by wealth and advancement in the arts and sciences. Chapter six is a study of the institutional development of the Ptolemaic army, and especially the cleruchy, during Ptolemy II's reign. The seventh and eighth chapters consider aspects of the army in the reign of Ptolemy III Euergetes. The first is primarily operational, a study of the army in the Third Syrian War; the second is institutional and social, a consideration of organizational and legal reforms. The ninth chapter returns to the story of the Fourth Syrian War and the Battle of Raphia, as well as the affairs and reforms of the Ptolemaic army early in the reign of Ptolemy IV Philopator. This chapter tests a narrative of continuity as an alternative to the glory-then-decline narrative. Between these two narratives, Raphia can either appear as the culmination of decades of military development or a brief, short-lived recovery of Ptolemaic glory. The final chapter and conclusion of this volume evaluates the Ptolemaic army relative to the three missions, considers the ways those missions changed after the reigns of the first four Ptolemies, and argues that that changing relationship holds explanatory power for the ways the Ptolemaic army evolved in the second century BC.

Maps

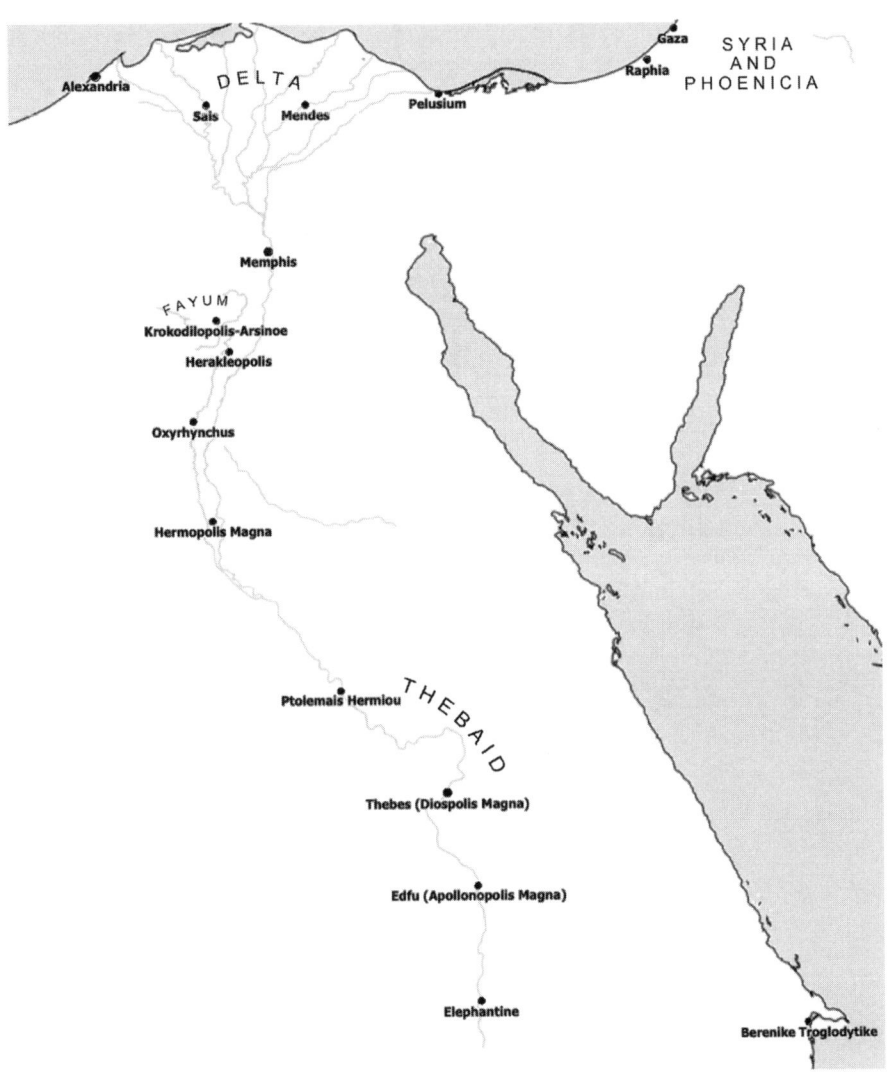

1. Ptolemaic Egypt

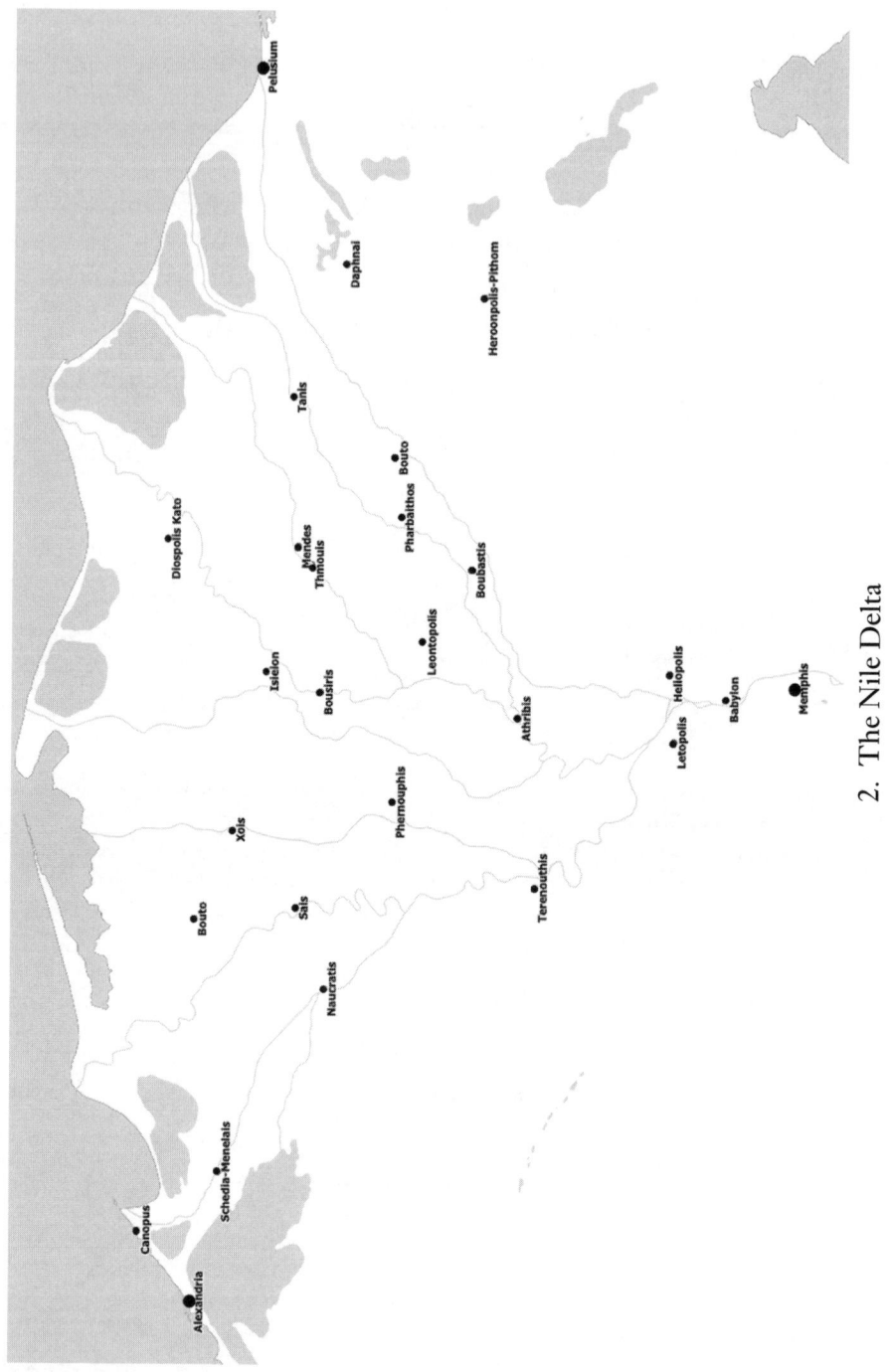

2. The Nile Delta

3. Seleucid Syria

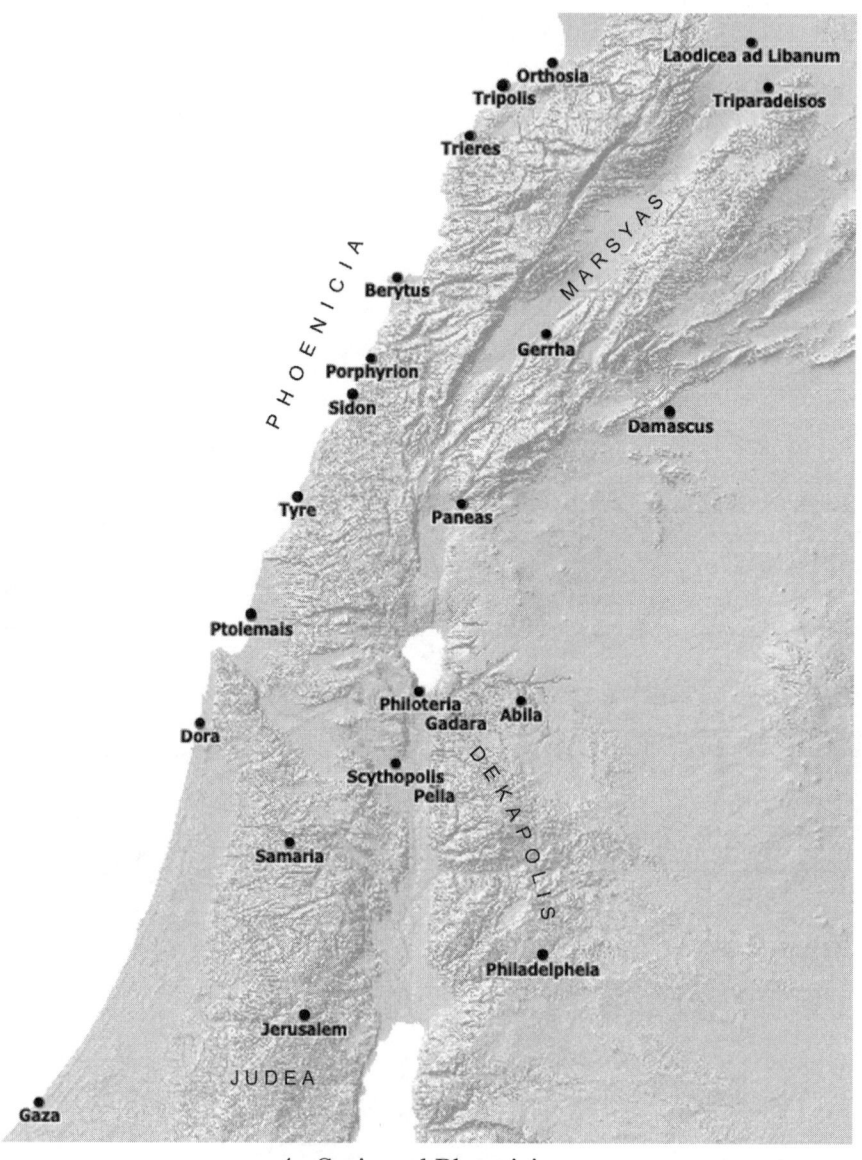

4. Syria and Phoenicia

5. The Aegean to Cyprus

Chapter 1

The Ptolemaic Army at Raphia

A Brief Institutional History

The aforementioned Battle of Raphia was among the largest engagements in all of ancient history and a decisive victory for the Ptolemaic army. Fought in 217 BC, it assured the Ptolemaic recovery of the kingdom's province of 'Syria and Phoenicia', that stretched from the area around Gaza in the south to the Dekapolis region in the Transjordan to the east, and around Tripolis in Phoenicia, the northern end of the Bekaa and probably Damascus in the Syrian plain. This chapter is not so much a discussion of the battle or the larger Fourth Syrian War, both of which shall be treated in more detail later in this book. In a study of the Ptolemaic army, the surprising thing is that, in spite of nearly 300 years of military campaigns and numerous significant engagements, Raphia is the only battle for which we possess a detailed breakdown of the Ptolemaic army. Polybius' 'autopsy' of the Ptolemaic army in Book 5, chapter 65, of his *Histories* contains more detail than all the other descriptions combined. In reconstructing the structures of the Ptolemaic army – the regular units, national units, elite units, infantry, cavalry and mercenaries, settlers, reservists, allies and professionals – no other narrative account can come remotely close to what is offered in Polybius 5.65 and 5.82.

The singularity of the Raphia account for the history of the Ptolemaic army is an artefact of the contingency of source preservation. Only a few fragments survive from the histories of the third century BC, and of Polybius' surviving books, none contain what were surely at least similarly detailed descriptions of the Ptolemaic forces at the battles of Panion in 200 BC or Kasios and Pelusium in 169 BC. By comparison, three detailed descriptions survive for the Seleucid army and six for the Antigonid army. On the other hand, the documentary evidence from Egypt, especially from papyri, makes it possible to flesh out Polybius' description of the Ptolemaic army at Raphia in ways that surpass the many descriptions of the other kingdoms' armies.

2 The Army of Ptolemaic Egypt 323 to 204 BC

The purpose of this chapter is to examine the army as described in Polybius, using documentary evidence in places to supplement, correct and extend the information from the eminent Hellenistic historian.

Let us begin with the two passages in question. Polybius described the Ptolemaic preparations for war as a massive military reform, but the documentary evidence reveals that narrative to be deeply problematic. In fact, the army at Raphia, apart from a couple of elements – chiefly the Egyptian phalanx – would have been much the same army if it had marched from Egypt a decade earlier. Aside from the reform narrative, the two passages describe, first, the various contingents of the army as it coalesced in Egypt, and second, their positions in the battle line at Raphia:

> 'Eurylochos of Magnesia commanded a body of about three thousand men known as the Royal Agema, Sokrates the Boeotian had under him two thousand peltasts, [3] Phoxidas the Achaean, Ptolemaios the son of Thraseas, and Andromachos of Aspendos exercised together in one body the phalanx and the Greek mercenaries, [4] the phalanx twenty-five thousand strong being under the command of Andromachos and Ptolemaios and the mercenaries, numbering eight thousand, under that of Phoxidas. [5] Polykrates undertook the training of the Royal Cavalry, about seven hundred strong, and the cavalry from Egypt and Libya; all of whom, numbering about three thousand, were under his command. [6] It was Echekrates the Thessalian who trained most admirably the cavalry from Greece and all the mercenary cavalry, and thus rendered most signal service in the battle itself, [7] and Knopias of Allaria too was second to none in the attention he paid to the force under him composed of three thousand Cretans, one thousand being Neocretans whom he placed under the command of Philon of Cnossus. [8] They also armed in the Macedonian fashion three thousand Libyans under the command of Ammonios of Barce. [9] The total native Egyptian force consisted of about twenty thousand heavy-armed men, and was commanded by Sosibios, [10] and they had also collected a force of Thracians and Gauls, about four thousand of them from among settlers in Egypt and their descendants, and two thousand lately raised elsewhere. These were commanded by Dionysios the Thracian.' (Polybius, *Histories* 5.65)

> '[1] The kings, after remaining encamped opposite each other for five days, both resolved to decide matters by a battle. [2]

The moment that Ptolemy began to move his army out of camp, Antiochus followed his example. Both of them placed the phalanxes of the picked troops armed in the Macedonian fashion confronting each other in the centre. [3] Ptolemy's two wings were formed as follows. Polykrates with his cavalry held the extreme left wing, [4] and between him and the phalanx stood first the Cretans, next the cavalry, then the Royal Agema, then the peltasts under Sokrates, these latter being next those Libyans who were armed in the Macedonian manner. [5] On the extreme right wing was Echekrates with his cavalry, and on his left stood Gauls and Thracians, [6] and next them was Phoxidas with his Greek mercenaries in immediate contact with the Egyptian phalanx. [7] Of the elephants forty were posted on the left where Ptolemy himself was about to fight, and the remaining thirty-three in front of the mercenary cavalry on the right wing.' (Polybius, *Histories* 5.82)

The Left Wing

The 3,000 cavalry on the left wing represent two groups. The first, the palace squadron (or 'cavalry around the palace'), numbered 700, and they held the far left. The number 700 is an unusual total for a royal squadron. Alexander's royal squadron was probably about 200 strong at the start of his campaign, and was eventually increased to 300. Several of the Successors fielded similar numbers, and in Hellenistic Macedonia the Antigonid kings several times led royal squadrons 300 or 400 strong. Documentary sources partially resolve the odd size of the palace cavalry: this body of 700 cavalrymen was not one elite unit, but several elite cavalry units brigaded together. Some of the units are known because of their settlement zones in Middle Egypt; others are known from members of the units active at Alexandria or in the countryside. Some of the attested elite cavalry were in the cavalry *peri Aulēn* ('at the palace') or in the 'royal squadron', *Basilikē ilē*, and the cavalry unit called the *Archaion Agema* (the 'veteran guards') seems to require that there was also an *Agema*, or 'Guards' squadron to feed the ranks of the veterans. The veterans may have functioned as a reserve unit, even in wartime. This surmise is possible because in the middle of the Third Syrian War, the hipparch (cavalry commander) of the *Archaion Agema* was still in Egypt while much of the army was in Asia (*P.Cair.Zen.* 3.59347). The Palace Squadron, the Royal Squadron and the Guard Squadron – three distinct units – probably comprised the whole 700 at Raphia. Narrative sources referred to a unit of 'bodyguards', or *somatophylakes*; whether these were identical with the whole unit or one of its components is unclear.[1] Perhaps one – which is impossible to say – was 300 strong, and the other two about 200 apiece. At least some of them were cleruchs, since neighbourhoods of the Herakleopolite nome, a province of Middle Egypt just above (or south of) Memphis, were named *Agema*, *Peri Aulēn* and *Archaioi* (although this latter name may not have appeared until the middle of the second century BC). Many guard cavalrymen whose names survive were Alexandrian citizens. Even as cleruchs, their elite status probably afforded them the means to live at Alexandria part of the year, and at least some of them were posted to the palace as part of the royal guard.

They, like most of the cavalry at Raphia, probably fought in the fashion of Argead Macedonian cavalry, with finely wrought armour protecting their chests, helmets in Boeotian or other cavalry styles, a *xyston* thrusting spear about 12ft long and a cavalry sabre (see plate 2 fig. 2, plate 11 fig. 19). Some may have worn greaves for leg protection; others may have worn boots. Their tactical disposition probably reflected the existence of three distinct units, although Polybius offered no details on that sort of thing in his account. It is easiest to imagine the three units, and 700-rider brigade, in a simple linear formation. If Polycrates of Argos, who commanded at Raphia, was a poor battlefield leader, then that is a possibility. Linear cavalry phalanxes probably became more common with the rise of cataphract cavalry, who relied on mass, but few if any of the Ptolemaic elites would have been so heavily armoured. Instead of a linear formation, the Ptolemaic guard cavalry may have used a wedge formation, more like the classical dispositions of Alexander and his successors. The 300-rider unit probably anchored the elite squadrons in its own linear formation, perhaps five or ten ranks deep with sixty or thirty files. If the Ptolemies were using the classical cavalry dispositions, the other two units screened the anchor unit to their front and to their outside (left) flank. This formation would be sensible for a less aggressive or even defensive battle plan, and we know that Antiochus was the real aggressor on the field. The unit arrayed on the front may have formed up in wedge formation, with the unit leaders stepping off ahead of file leaders to create a chevron wedge. More likely, the four individual platoons (called *ilai*) within the unit formed their own wedges of fifty to sixty men, arrayed much like bowling pins, permitting individual unit commanders within the elite unit to lead their men as necessary. Platoon wedges would also have permitted the screening contingent to wheel about more easily as they initiated combat. The unit on the flank was probably formed up in a sort of column, with multiple squared platoons in column or an oblique line. The purpose of both screening units was to blunt or break up a determined charge by the Seleucid cavalry, while giving the anchor unit opportunity to respond into gaps or charge across the whole front against a more vulnerable Seleucid formation.

Alongside the 700 palace cavalry were 2,300 cavalry, whom Polybius described as those from Libya and the '*enchorioi* cavalry', that is, the cavalry from Egypt. Polybius' word choice could be misleading; *enchoric* things are 'native', so many commentators on Polybius' account have identified these cavalry as Egyptians. But in that passage (5.64–65), Polybius was building a contrast between Greek soldiers and officers recently arrived from the Greek world, in whom 'Hellenic martial ardour' was still alive (5.64.5), and the Greek inhabitants of Egypt, who in his view had gone native and lost their martial spirit. For that reason, it seems most likely Polybius was actually describing cleruch cavalry. The documentary record reinforces this interpretation: there is little or no evidence for Egyptian cavalry throughout the third century, but there is abundant evidence for far more than 700 cavalry cleruchs, and the vast majority of those attested were not in units of the royal guard. The cavalry cleruchs were a landed aristocracy in Egypt. They controlled estates that were three to four times larger than the allotments given to infantry, equivalent to 50–70 acres of land. Many owned houses in the country on or near the allotment plus houses or apartments in nome (province) capitals or the big cities of Egypt like Memphis and Alexandria. By the time of Raphia, there were no less than twelve hipparchies of cleruch cavalry in Ptolemaic Egypt, and probably more, although they were not all at full strength.[2] These, plus additional cavalry from the Cyrenaica in Libya, likely comprised the whole of the 2,300 heavy cavalry posted to the left wing.

The organization of the hipparchies, and the manpower they represented, merits a little more discussion. Cavalry units were created from smaller units that doubled until reaching the size of the hipparchy, or of even larger units. Cavalry units may have, at different times, used a base file of varying depths, from five to eight or more. Thus a standard cavalry company (*ilē*) numbered fifty to sixty-four troopers. Either way, four of these companies formed a hipparchy, led by a hipparch, with 200–256 men. Thus, ten or more cleruch hipparchies in Egypt represented theoretical strength of at least 2,000 cavalrymen, and probably more like 2,500. This comes to about the right order of magnitude for the force at Raphia. Nine hipparhcies of 256 men comes to almost exactly 2,300 troopers. At least one of the hipparchies was probably from the Cyrenaica region, which might suggest there were eight cleruch hipparchies settled in Egypt. These were probably the cleruchs called the *hekatontarouroi hippeis*, or 100-aroura cavalry, in the documentary evidence. Five hipparchies of these troops had all or most of their settlements in the Fayum basin, just west of the Nile, and at least two additional hipparchies had lands in the provinces just east and south-east of the Fayum basin in the Nile valley, the Herakleopolite and Oxyrhynchite nomes.

Most of the regular cavalry would have fought in the traditional Macedonian style, but it is possible that several of the hipparchies had, by Raphia, been re-equipped as shielded cavalry (see plate 9 fig. 16). If any were, they were probably the five new 'ethnic hipparchies', which were only formed in the late 230s BC. They were named for different national groups – Macedonians, Thessalians, Thracians, Mysians and Persians – but there is no evidence their personnel or armament were matched to those peoples. Mounted use of a fairly large round or oval shield became popular among Italians and Gauls in the fourth century, and grew in popularity among Greek and Macedonian troopers throughout the third century. Units formed in the 230s and 220s BC may have reflected the broad adoption of shielded cavalry across much of the Mediterranean.[3] If so, they probably carried two or more types of cavalry shield. One popular cavalry shield was very similar to the Greek hoplite's *aspis* in initial appearance, but was flatter and assuredly lighter. Another popular cavalry shield was the cavalryman's *thureos*. The *thureos* was a flat shield, usually oval or sub-rectangular in shape, with a prominent spine running up the front. They were held at the centre of the spine, like the Roman *scutum*, which was itself an innovation upon the standard *thureos* design. The cavalry *thureos*, however, was usually round rather than oval, and could be quite large. It was popularized in southern Italy and became very common across the Mediterranean world by the late third century. The use of a cavalry shield did not compel a cavalryman to fight in a particular style. Ptolemaic shielded cavalry may have still carried a *xyston* lance, or a shorter spear like the hoplite's *dory*, more nimble and manageable for a rider holding reins and a shield in their other hand. It is also possible they carried javelins or dual-use spears (*lonchai*). They may have tended to wear somewhat lighter armour as well. By comparison, we know from papyri that several troopers in the regular hipparchies went about purchasing cataphract gear prior to the war, including *cheires*, laminated armour for a rider's arms, which would have been unnecessary if they carried shields. If the ethnic hipparchies were the only shielded cavalry, then most or all of the left-wing cavalry were unshielded, because the ethnic hipparchies were understaffed and may have been placed on the right wing. At the battle, these 2,300 cavalry were posted right of the Cretans and palace cavalry units, but left of the guard infantry.

The Cretans, 3,000 strong, filled in the space between the two cavalry formations. The Cretans were arguably the most famous mercenary people of the Hellenistic age. Some 2,500 Cretans were in the Seleucid army at Raphia, and at least a few thousand more were serving in other armies at the same time. Of those at Raphia, 1,000 were so-called 'Neo-Cretans', organized and trained separately from the regular Cretans. The meaning of the term has stymied interpreters, because Polybius and those in his day clearly knew what it meant and so never explained it. There are several possible interpretations, and it is difficult to get further than presenting them. First, the Neo-Cretans could have been from a particular class of the Cretan population or from particular cities on Crete, comparable perhaps to the Spartan Neodamodeis.[4] Second, they could have been Cretans carrying a non-traditional set of equipment.[5] By tradition, Cretans were archers, but they also had a penchant for close-quarter combat. A painted stele dedicated to a deceased Cretan mercenary, Chalkokedes of Lyttos, found at Demetrias in Thessaly, shows the Cretan accompanied by a servant carrying his gear.[6] Chalkokedes carried his own bow and wore a helmet, but the servant carried a curious oval shield of small size, a curved dagger and a pair of javelins. It seems plausible that the standard Cretan mercenary carried bow, javelins, light shield and short sword anyway, but it is possible the terminology of 'Neo-Cretans' distinguished the peltast armament from that of the archers. Finally, the Neo-Cretans may not have been Cretans at all, but other soldiers armed and trained like Cretans.[7] This last interpretation fails, for at Magnesia in 190 BC, Antiochus III's Neo-Cretans were posted next to Cilicians and Carians armed like Neo-Cretans. Surely, if Neo-Cretans were non-Cretans armed like Cretans, there would be no point distinguishing the Neo-Cretans from the Cilicians and Carians. Some of the Cretans in the Ptolemaic army at Raphia may have been military settlers (at least one Cretan infantry cleruch is attested in the documentary record), but many or most would have been mercenaries. About 1,000 Cretans served in the Alexandrian garrison (Plb 5.36.4) and others served elsewhere in the Ptolemaic empire, like Cyprus. Still more may have been recruited for the campaign itself, hired by recruiters on Crete or through contracts established between Cretan cities and Hellenistic powers, through which contracts the Cretan cities supplied units of mercenaries when needed.

These contracts were not true alliances, but they represented a way for both parties to stake a claim on good-paying jobs and top-flight mercenaries.

In advance of the Cretans and across the front of some of the horse were forty of the seventy-three African elephants. These elephants had been hunted and captured from the African coasts of the Erythraean (Red) Sea and as far south as the Horn of Africa.[8] They were big bush elephants, and the Ptolemaic parties that hunted them were small armies in their own right. They transported captured elephants to Egypt, using them in a number of campaigns as an alternative to Indian elephants. Like Indian elephants, the African bush elephants were large enough to fit a tower on their backs, and men with pikes, javelins or bows could be posted in the towers to assist in combat. A driver, or mahout, guided the elephant in battle, so between the personnel in the towers and the mahout most elephants probably carried three 'crew'. In the Hellenistic period, there does not seem to have been a consensus on the appropriate tactical use of elephants. They could be posted like guard towers along a front to help stabilize a line, gathered in close order to carry out their own offensive actions or used as a screen. At Raphia, the Cretans may have been interspersed with the elephants on the left wing, or they may have gone unaccompanied into battle against Antiochus' Indian elephants.

The Centre

The Ptolemaic centre, the phalanx, comprised six different contingents. Two infantry units came after the Cretans: the 3,000-strong *agema* and 2,000 peltasts. In Alexander's army, the infantry *agema* had been a special unit within the elite hypaspist corps. In late Classical Greece down to Alexander's day, peltasts were skirmisher infantry below the rank of hoplites. In the Hellenistic period, the *agema* came to mean something much closer to Alexander's whole hypaspist corps, while peltasts, in some contexts, took on a much-elevated sense. In Antigonid Macedonia, for example, the '*agema* of the Macedonians' and 'peltasts' were two units that together could be called the *agema* or the peltasts, and numbered 5,000 in all. They were the elite infantry of the Macedonian army. In the days of Philip V, at least, the peltasts were younger men, and the *agemata* somewhat older. In Ptolemaic Egypt, a similar system may have prevailed. Polybius nearly always meant elite troops when he wrote of peltasts, and their presence alongside the royal *agema* in the Ptolemaic army also points toward their elite role there. The two units together made the Ptolemaic elite 5,000, the same as in

Macedonia. The Seleucid elite division, often called the Silvershields, was twice as large, which may have reflected the size of the Seleucid Empire and its maintenance of two royal spheres, from Antioch to the west and Seleukeia to the east.

The Ptolemaic *agema* is visible in the documentary record, but a unit called 'peltasts' is not. Because the documentary record relates mainly to activity in the countryside of Egypt rather than at Alexandria, it tends to tell us more about cleruchs than about professional soldiers. It may be that the Ptolemaic peltasts were professional troops, young men from elite families, some of whose fathers may have still been in primary control of a family allotment. It is also possible that the Ptolemies did not actually call them peltasts at all. A soldier attested in a papyrus from 252 BC, Dionysios, was a paid professional (called *taktomisthos*) serving in the 'palace guard', confirming there was a standing body of elite troops at the palace; whether these were analogous to Polybius' peltasts or cavalry troops is unclear (*P.Lond.* 7.1986). Another man from the same text was an Alexandrian citizen and member of the *agema*. In nearly all cases, the *agema* soldiers who have appeared in papyri seem to have been cleruchs. But there are not very many, which might mean either most were settled in parts of Egypt where the documentary record is poor or the settled *agema* soldiers were an exception to the rule. Even the available documentary evidence could be read several ways. On the one hand, the several attested officers were all Macedonians and all cleruchs. It is conceivable, then, that most soldiers in the *agema* were full-time soldiers and Macedonians, but only their officers received large estates as a reward for service. On the other hand, four non-Macedonian soldiers in the *agema* are attested (*P.Petr.2* 16 and 18, *P.Lond.* 7.1986), the first three in close proximity to infantry officers of the *agema*, and two of those were identified as 100-aroura cleruchs. If they were from the cavalry *agema* and just coincidentally appeared in witness lists next to infantry *agema* officers, the former conclusions could hold. If they were from the infantry *agema*, as their proximity to the officers suggests, then many from the infantry *agema* were settled, received large allotments like the settler cavalry and were ethnically diverse rather than uniformly Macedonian. If all 3,000 soldiers in the royal *agema* were cleruchs with 100 arouras apiece, they would represent one of the largest land-holding populations in all Ptolemaic Egypt, equivalent to the cavalry. The paucity of evidence for the royal *agema* suggests that is implausible, but not impossible, because so much of our evidence comes from just a few regions of Egypt. The royal *agema* and peltasts did not train for Raphia alongside the phalangite units. This suggests they may have fought with different equipment. At the battle, the routed Ptolemaic elephants were able to push through them without difficulty, which likewise suggests they were not protected by rows of pikes. In later Ptolemaic history, the court guard units were called *lonchophoroi* and *machairophoroi* (spearmen and swordsmen). Perhaps the *agema* and peltasts also carried *lonchai* (dual-use spears) and swords as early as Raphia. For shields, the *agema* may have retained the hoplite's aspis, while the peltasts undoubtedly carried Macedonian *peltai*, the smaller aspis that was compatible with the use of sarissa pikes, but also functional for light infantry. Their armour probably matched their status: expensive and showy (see plate 3 fig. 3).

After the guard units came the phalanx, which comprised 3,000 Libyans, 25,000 Macedonians, 20,000 Egyptians and 8,000 Greek mercenaries. These 56,000 represented more than two-thirds of the entire Ptolemaic army at Raphia. The 3,000 Libyans were 'armed in the Macedonian manner', which means they were pikemen (for that weapon kit, see the discussion of the Macedonian phalanx below). They were probably Greeks from the cities of Cyrenaica rather than actual Libyans. Their military tradition would transfer to pike training more readily, and moreover, their citizen status might explain their prestigious position linking the guard units to the Macedonians. Their commander was a native of Barke, one of the city-states of Cyrenaica. Numerous Cyreneans and others from Cyrenaica migrated to Ptolemaic Egypt, often as soldiers. It is conceivable that just as many Libyan Greeks were fighting in other units of the Ptolemaic army as the 3,000 fighting in one body. Cyrenaica was an extension of the Egyptian homeland, more secure than other regions from attack, and apart from a few decades in the third century, it was generally under firm Ptolemaic control until Ptolemy Apion willed it to the Roman Republic in 96 B.C.

The largest single contingent in the army, according to Polybius, was the 25,000-strong Macedonian pike phalanx. These wielded the sarissa in classic Hellenistic Macedonian style, as Polybius describes:

'When it has closed up for action, each man, with his arms, occupies a space of three feet in breadth, and the length of the pikes is according to the original design sixteen cubits, but as adapted to actual need fourteen cubits, from which we must subtract the distance between the bearer's two hands and the length of the weighted portion of the pike behind which serves to keep it couched – four cubits in all – it is evident that it must extend ten cubits beyond the body of each hoplite when he charges the enemy grasping it with both hands. The consequence is that while the pikes of the second, third, and fourth ranks extend farther than those of the fifth rank, those of that rank extend two cubits beyond the bodies of the men in the first rank, when the phalanx has its characteristic close order as regards both depth and breadth, as Homer expresses it in these verses: "Spear crowded spear, Shield, helmet, man press'd helmet, man, and shield; The hairy crests of their resplendent casques Kiss'd close at every nod, so wedged they stood." [XIII.131] This description is both true and fine, and it is evident that each man of the first rank must have the points of five pikes extending beyond him, each at a distance of two cubits from the next. From this we can easily conceive what is the nature and force of a charge by the whole phalanx when it is sixteen deep.' (*Histories* 18.29.2–30.1).

The sarissa was a weapon for mass infantry formations rather than individual or small-unit combats. It was a long pike, as long as 20ft by the middle Hellenistic period, and had to be held with two hands. Most historians doubt whether the sarissa was ever regularly as much as 16 cubits, an astounding 24ft! Many suspect the sarissa actually lengthened over time, from closer to 15ft in Alexander's day to 20ft around the time of Raphia.[9] The pikeman, or phalangite, sacrificed agility and most individual initiative to help create a human bulwark, a vast and deep close-order formation arrayed behind row upon row of spear points. Macedonian-style phalanxes often arrayed sixteen or even thirty-two ranks deep. At a charge, the sarissa points could pierce shields, armour and flesh, and in defence against frontal attacks the pugnacious pikes kept even the most determined enemy at bay. The Macedonians first began using the sarissa under Philip II, and pike phalanxes were instrumental in nearly all of Alexander's victories. Polybius referred to Ptolemaic troops with sarissas at least twice, in his accounts of Raphia and the later Battle of Panium, but the word has yet to be discovered in a Ptolemaic papyrus. Most likely, the Ptolemaic kings kept sarissas in royal armouries and they were not part of the weaponry kept at hand by Ptolemaic soldiers in Egypt. The phalangites carried the Macedonian shield, a concave shield a little more than 2ft in diameter (see plate 7 fig. 11, plate 8 fig. 13). It could be held like a Greek aspis, affixed to the forearm, but the use of a telamon, a strap passed over the shoulder, freed phalangites to use both hands to wield the cumbersome sarissa. The soldiers would have generally worn helmets and carried the short machaira swords that they also wore in the countryside of Egypt. At least the officers and men of the front rank would have had body armour and greaves, but whether these were standard for the entire phalanx is not in the surviving evidence. Helmet, shield and weapons were probably the normal kit of many regular phalangites.

The soldiers in the pike phalanx were Macedonians, at least in theory. Polybius never calls them or the Seleucid phalanx Macedonians in the text, but all other pike-armed troops, he said, were 'armed in the Macedonian manner', so the tacit assertion is that these were Ptolemy's Macedonians. For him, phalangites were, unless qualified, practically synonymous with Macedonians. The Macedonians conquered the Persian Empire with Alexander, and to a degree viewed the empire as something of a shared possession. Macedonian troops helped legitimize the Successor kings after Alexander's death, and their skill at arms helped carve out their kingdoms. Ptolemy I never had much access to strong sources of Macedonian manpower. It should be a little surprising, then, to see 25,000 Macedonians at Raphia. In the same era, the Macedonians serving in the phalanx in Macedon itself were never more than 16,000. The presence of 25,000 Macedonian phalangites offers an impression of the Macedonian character of the Ptolemaic monarchy, but in truth the phalanx was not nearly so monolithic as their depiction at Raphia implies.

The main part of the Ptolemaic phalanx was, by the time of Raphia, an infantry cleruch class called the *triakontarouroi Makedones*, the 'thirty-aroura Macedonians', a label that noted their possession of somewhere around 20 acres of farmland and their identity as Macedonians. The identity was useful for all involved, as will be clear later, but for many soldiers it was certainly fictive. The infantry settlers were organized in thousand-man regiments, called *chiliarchiai*, several of which are attested in documentary evidence. The highest attested, however, is the seventh regiment. It is likely that the Ptolemies, in emulation of Hellenistic military doctrine, built their phalanx up to 16,000 men, so papyri may some day reveal the sixteenth regiment or some of the eight in between. But the phalanx at Raphia was of 25,000 men, suggesting the addition of a third wing (a little more than 8,000 men) to the formation. Thus at least one-third of the phalanx, and up to two-thirds, came from some source other than the Macedonian cleruchs. One certain source of these phalanx soldiers is the civilian sons (*epigonoi*) of Macedonian and other cleruchs. Thousands of soldiers' sons were enrolled for service in the Second Macedonian War, and many were also verifiably signed up for the phalanx in the Fourth Syrian War, and were subsequently recategorized as 30-aroura Macedonians. The only other significant potential source is the units of paid infantry that were in active Ptolemaic service. Documentary sources provide evidence for numerous regular (that is, paid) or mercenary units active in Egypt and Alexandria. These units seem to have generally been organized in *syntagmata* of 250 or 500 men rather than 1,000-strong chiliarchies, but there may also have been considerable variety within the classes of mercenary and active-duty troops.[10] Many in the countryside were semi-professional units in which the soldiers also possessed small land allotments. Their role at Raphia – however many participated in the campaign, versus those who garrisoned the country – must have been in either the main phalanx or the mercenary phalanx. The sheer size of the main phalanx – 25,000 – at least suggests that many of the paid regulars and semi-professionals from Egypt were added to the phalanx for the major campaign. The most important lesson here is that the large block of 25,000 phalangites was actually numerous components, among which the settler Macedonians comprised merely the largest and best-established contingent.

While increasing the size of the main phalanx by half again was a major feat for the Ptolemaic military, the addition of a second phalanx of 20,000 Egyptian soldiers is far more famous. Egyptian soldiers had played roles in the Ptolemaic army from the early days of the dynasty, but until Raphia had always followed one of two distinct paths: Hellenization and incorporation into main units was one probable route, the argument for which will appear later in this text, and the other was to retain Egyptian character and serve mainly in unglamorous roles. Egyptians served in the Ptolemaic navy in very large numbers, as both rowers and marines. Otherwise, the *machimoi* (the old warrior class in Egypt) and some other specialized classes of Egyptians helped garrison frontier posts, held small land allotments in return for service as guards and police, and may have held roles for the army as archers or other light infantry. It is possible a few small Egyptian contingents filled honoured posts at court too. Most of the Egyptian *machimoi* soldiers held 5 arouras, just under 3½ acres. The inferior status of *machimoi* changed shortly before Raphia, when Ptolemy IV's advisors made the unprecedented decision to train thousands of Egyptian soldiers as phalangites. They were nearly as large as the whole main phalanx, and presumably were armed in similar panoply. After Raphia, the *machimoi* and other Egyptian soldiers played more significant, but not always positive, roles in the Ptolemaic army and its affairs and operations.

Next to the Egyptian phalanx were the 8,000 Greek mercenaries. Polybius called them Greek, but it seems very likely many were Hellenizing more than Hellenic. Some would have been newly hired troops, while others were parts of mercenary garrisons in Egypt and abroad. One large source of mercenaries would have been the Alexandrian garrison. Shortly before the war, Cleomenes of Sparta had estimated that 3,000 of the mercenaries in the Alexandrian garrison were Peloponnesians, while the other main mercenary contingents were from 'Syria and Caria' (Plb. 5.36.5). Cleomenes may have been exaggerating the number of Peloponnesians a little, and in mentioning contingents from Syria and Caria he certainly excludes other Greeks from the mainland and soldiers from all across the Anatolian coast, but Syria and Caria – on either arm of the north-east Mediterranean littoral – provide some indication of the origin point for a large part of the mercenary garrison of Alexandria. By 'Syria' we should probably understand Judeans in particular, among others, while 'Caria' is likely a shorthand expression for coastal Anatolia, from Caria east to Cilicia. In the first century, Caesar, in a propagandistic description of the Ptolemaic field army, emphasized the Syrian and Cilician origins of many Ptolemaic professionals (BC 3.110). The Ptolemies also recalled mercenary garrisons from overseas (Plb. 5.63.8). Many of these would not have been particularly large, and it is possible that the Ptolemaic generals only recalled detachments of troops from the largest garrisons, such as Cyprus, Cyrene and Ephesos. In any case, it seems very likely that a large majority of the 8,000 mercenaries were already in Ptolemaic service prior to the Fourth Syrian War and the Battle of Raphia, and that, despite Polybius' wording, a significant proportion of them were Mediterranean rather than truly Greek.

The mercenaries trained for the battle alongside the other phalanx units, which has led to a common interpretation that they, too, were phalangites. But Polybius never wrote that they were armed in the Macedonian manner, and while they were posted at the link between the centre and the right wing, in the battle they advanced far ahead of the pike phalanx to launch their attack. This suggests that they were in more flexible armament. It is conceivable that several different panoplies were exhibited among these mercenaries: some were probably carrying the *thureos*, flat oval shields of wood, which exhibited a prominent vertical spine, comparable to a Roman *scutum* and popularized in the Greek world by the Galatians. Men with the *thureos* were called *thureophoroi*, and might carry javelins, a spear and sword, while those who carried that shield and wore heavy armour were called *thorakitai* (see plate 5 fig. 8). Some of the Greek mercenaries may have still been kitted as hoplites, with aspis, spear and sword (see plate 4 figs. 5–6). Yet others could have carried the lighter equipment of peltasts. Among 8,000 men from different parts of the Hellenistic world, diversity is more likely than uniformity.

The Right Wing

Next to the 'Greek' mercenaries were 6,000 Galatians and Thracians, who bridged the gap between the phalanx and the cavalry stationed on the right. These are an interesting contingent in several respects. First, Polybius says that 4,000 were raised from the settlers and their descendants in Egypt (Plb. 5.65.10), a clear reference from his source material to the cleruch settlers and *epigonoi*. I have already conjectured that *epigonoi* were recruited for service in the main phalanx, and the conscription of Galatian and Thracian *epigonoi* for service alongside their fathers and brothers makes that only more likely. Second, 2,000 more were recruited elsewhere. Polybius says they were recruited 'lately', but that could mean either for the Fourth Syrian War or during one of the wars late in the reign of Ptolemy III. Whether the new recruits were Galatians or Thracians is not clear. Thracians are certainly more numerous in the documentary evidence, but those Thracians also almost always served in standard Hellenistic units rather than ethnically distinct, national contingents. Finally, the Galatians and Thracians fought in related but distinct styles. Both were probably making use of the oval *thureos* as their primary shield, and the Thracians in particular probably made heavy use of javelins. The Galatians were famous for their long, woad-blue cloaks and for slinging them over their shoulders to reveal their nude body in the moments before battle (see plate 6 figs. 9–10). The Galatians carried double-edged and sometimes pointed longswords for close-quarters combat; the Thracians probably used single-edged *machaira* swords or curved *sica* from their homeland. Both were famous for a furious charge, and must have been lightly armoured at the battle because of their incredible mobility, accompanying cavalry in a rapid march around the flank of the foe.

The cavalry that led the Galatians and Thracians around the Seleucid flank, and the last contingent in the Ptolemaic army at Raphia, were the mercenary horsemen. Theirs was the decisive performance in the battle, and so they are truly last but not least. They were 2,000 strong. Polybius described two brigaded bodies, with 'the cavalry from Greece and the whole body of the mercenary cavalry' (Plb. 5.65.6). One may interpret each of these groups in different ways. The cavalry from Greece could signal either mercenary troops recently recruited from the Greek world or the military cavalrymen of Greek origin settled in Egypt. If they were mercenary cavalry, one might expect to see no differentiation between these cavalry from Greece and the mercenary cavalry with whom they were brigaded, and wonder why Polybius (or his source) differentiated them. However, the regular Ptolemaic army included a division of cavalry called the *misthophoroi hippeis*, or mercenary cavalry. They are well known from documentary sources in Egypt itself. They were not foreign mercenaries; most or all had allotments of land, but also served for pay, which is what *misthophoroi* means: wage-bearing. It is entirely possible that the Polybian text refers to this group of cavalry by their institutional title, creating a confusing reading for modern interpreters. That is, the 'cavalry from Greece' may have been the true mercenaries, while the 'mercenary cavalry' were semi-professional settlers from Egypt (see plate 3 fig. 4).

The *misthophoroi hippeis* in the Ptolemaic army were an affluent, active body of cavalry distinct from the guard and settler cavalry. A partial census from the Fayum basin records that there were 1,426 adult males in the households of the *misthophoroi hippeis* settled in that region about the middle of the third century BC (*P.Count* 1). Because they were affluent, their households were large, so the 1,426 men may have corresponded to only 400–600 actual troopers. The Ptolemies liked to use the mercenary cavalry on their elephant hunts, which means there are numerous sources on their activities that are unlike the regular business of the documentary evidence. Their commanders were often well established at the Ptolemaic court, and many of their officers were Alexandrian citizens. Several of the famed 'hunting grounds' on the Red Sea were named after the commanders of several of the attested units of mercenary cavalry: Eumenes, Lichas and Pythangelos (Strabo 16.4.13–15). Many of the commanders of the mercenary horse had children who were honoured as annual priests in the Ptolemaic cults. The mercenary cavalry seem to have operated in the same social milieu as the Alexandrian officers and royal guardsmen from the *Petrie Wills* papyri. There were several hipparchies of mercenary cavalry in the Fayum and at least a few others in the rest of Egypt, and it is certainly conceivable they contributed half of the manpower of the cavalry on the right wing, or about 1,000 troopers. The best papyrological evidence is for the mercenary hipparchy of Eteoneus, mainly during the reign of Ptolemy III. If the men from that unit are a good indication for the whole class, the rank-and-file generally received 80 arouras as military settlers, with additional compensation for their active-duty service. So while their allotments were smaller than those of the regular cavalry, they may have been wealthier. Their participation in elephant hunts also meant they did regular military service, giving them more experience than the regular settler cavalry.

The cavalry from Greece who fought alongside the Ptolemaic 'mercenary' cavalry were, most likely, mercenaries in the conventional sense, drawn to Egypt from the Greek world by promises of good pay and other rewards. Ptolemaic recruiters had, as mentioned before, gone out to hire additional troops. It should not be a surprise if some of these were able to serve as cavalry. And yet there is also the possibility that some of them were from the 'ethnic hipparchies'. The best-attested of these, and perhaps the only one that was fully staffed, was the hipparchy 'of the Thessalians and other Greeks'. If they were not posted with the 100-aroura cavalry to complete the contingent on the left wing, then the few hundred of them in the Ptolemaic army were presumably posted with the semi-regular cavalry and foreign mercenaries on the right wing. What this could mean, however, is that in the final tally of 5,000 Ptolemaic cavalry, it should be considered very likely that approximately 4,000 of them were soldiers from the regular Ptolemaic army.

This is by no means a comprehensive account of the Ptolemaic army in its particulars, even of the force at Raphia, but a review of the various components: settler, guard and mercenary cavalry, elite, Macedonian, Egyptian and foreign infantry, cleruchs, mercenaries and *epigonoi*. These components – their strengths and weaknesses, the conditions of their recruitment and service – play significant roles in understanding the history of the Ptolemaic army.

Chapter 2

Ptolemy the Satrap, Ptolemy the King

Imagine Ptolemy son of Lagos, an up-country Macedonian of nearly 60 years, standing upon a dais at the Lochias of Alexandria, palace grounds under construction at the growing foundation in Egypt, surrounded by officers of his army and soldiers of his guard. With shouts of acclamation they hail him as king, who had been satrap of Egypt. But the Argead family, to whom he had professed a kind of loyalty, had been exterminated over the preceding years, and now – in 305 BC – only the generals were left to struggle for power and legitimacy over Alexander's empire. In truth, Ptolemy had acted autonomously for years. Ptolemy's main rival, Antigonus, had been acclaimed and crowned a year earlier after a magnificent victory over Ptolemy's navy near Cyprus. The Hellenistic king was made through military prowess. It was a component of Alexander's legacy that could be appropriated in a way outright Argead lineage could not, and a straightforward reflection of the simple truth that military power defined state formation in the generation after Alexander's death. In those days, 'neither nature nor justice gave kingdoms to men, but kingdoms went to those able to lead an army and handle affairs intelligently'.[1] Thus Ptolemy, with his own signal victory, became king as well and inaugurated the longest-lived royal dynasty of the Hellenistic era.

Ptolemy's victory, for all its importance, was dubious. It lay more in not losing than in winning, and marks one of the rare instances where defensive victories sufficed for acclamation. In October 306 BC, Antigonus had marched from Syria with a massive army, intent on subjugating Ptolemy and Egypt. We know of the campaign almost exclusively from the account of Diodorus of Sicily, a first-century BC historian whose reliability often depends much on the sources at his disposal. In this case, his chief source was probably Hieronymus of Cardia, a very competent historian who spent much of his career at the court of Antigonus. According to Diodorus, Antigonus had nearly 90,000 men in his army, making it the largest army fielded by any of the Successors in the entire Hellenistic era.

Antigonus the One-Eyed was the strongest of the Successors, and while he was showing his age, his son and heir Demetrius had proven quite capable as his lieutenant. Demetrius commanded the Antigonid fleet in the campaign. Ptolemy's army took defensive positions at Pelousion, the Pharaonic fortress of Sin, and looked to hold the eastern branch of the Nile Delta. On that campaign there is more later in this chapter, but in a conflict that involved more skirmish and manoeuvre than battle, Ptolemy prevented Antigonus from launching an effective attack. Antigonus, rather than unleash a doomed assault or completely exhaust his supplies, chose to withdraw. While Antigonus was playing a less disastrous turn at Napoleon's retreat from Moscow, Ptolemy claimed Egypt as *doriktetē gē* (spear-won land), the prerequisite for his accession, which took place some months after the conclusion of the campaign.[2]

Ptolemy ruled as king from 305–284 BC, when he passed the main responsibilities of rule over to one of his sons, also named Ptolemy, who became Ptolemy II Philadelphus. The state founded and built up under these kings was among the largest and wealthiest of the ancient Mediterranean, maintained through political skill, trade and military power. The army of Ptolemy I, first as satrap and then as king, was necessary to the founding and survival of Ptolemaic rule, and essential to the structure of the Ptolemaic state. Ptolemy was a talented general, building his army practically from scratch. Evidence from his reign is rarely very detailed, thus reconstructing the recruitment of the army, the development of military institutions and the operational history of Ptolemy can be difficult tasks. This chapter covers the history of Ptolemy in the army of Alexander, and his army-building and campaigning through to the end of his reign.

Ptolemy in Alexander's Army

Ptolemy crossed to Asia with Alexander in 334 BC. He was probably a member of the aristocratic Royal Squadron of the Companion Cavalry at the time, a suitable place for a close companion of Alexander. The history he later wrote of the campaign was the favoured source of Arrian, whose record of the campaign is the most complete, detailed and sober that we possess. Arrian believed that Ptolemy – as one who had been on the entire campaign, and as a new king whose credibility might depend on an accurate accounting of facts – was an eminently trustworthy source. It is probably wise to take a shrewder view of Ptolemy's devotion to pure truth. One detail that probably comes from Ptolemy, who as a cavalryman near Alexander would have been in his company at the great battles, highlights his problematic nature as a source: Alexander and his guard, during the pursuit phase after the Battle of Issus, crossed a gully at speed because it had been made passable by a mass of corpses. On the one hand, there is some obvious exaggeration in play, but on the other, it at least suggests some of Ptolemy's memory of his Issus experience in the company of the king during the pursuit.

The historical traditions say that his father, Lagos, was not particularly notable, which probably means he was from the lower nobility of Eordaea rather than the royal house of the Eordaean petty kingdom before it was absorbed into Macedonia. There were also rumours – unquestionably spread and quite likely invented by Ptolemy's own agents later in his life and after his death – that his mother was pregnant when she married Lagos, and Ptolemy's true father was King Philip II himself. Whatever his origin, he was a friend of Alexander in his youth and was one of his companions exiled after the Pixodarus affair (Pixodarus was a satrap of Caria who offered his daughter in marriage to an illegitimate son of Philip, but Alexander jealously sought her hand for himself and was punished when his father discovered his scheming). He returned home and to Alexander's side after the death of Philip, and joined Alexander's campaign. The Royal Squadron rode to battle in the immediate company of Alexander. The twenty-five fallen men commemorated with statues after the battle at the Granicus River were probably all members of the Royal Squadron, rather than men from the whole of the Companions. As a member of the Royal Squadron, Ptolemy was almost certainly involved in the most dangerous and decisive actions at the Granicus River, Issus and Gaugamela. But most of that can only be inferred, for Ptolemy only became a chief player in 330 BC.

Ptolemy gained one of the seven prestigious spots in the Somatophylakes, the Bodyguards, in 330 BC after Alexander executed one of the guards, Demetrius, on suspicions that he was involved in a conspiracy against his life. Before then, only Arrian's description of the battle at the Persian Gates gives Ptolemy a command role any earlier in the campaign. Ptolemy was hardly mentioned before that time. In Arrian's account, Ptolemy led an infantry fixing force in the mountain operations at the Gates, but this seems unlikely. The other sources do not mention Ptolemy at all, and Curtius' version suggests, more plausibly, that the commander of the hypaspists, Philotas son of Parmenion, had command in the role Arrian ascribed to Ptolemy. Philotas was executed soon after, so it may be a bit of Ptolemaic propaganda accepted too readily by Arrian. Ptolemy was the fifth replacement in the Bodyguards since the start of the campaign. He quickly became one of

Alexander's favourite officers, and remained in the Somatophylakes until Alexander's death. Ptolemy, in his capacity as a Bodyguard, played a significant role in a couple of the conspiracies and tragedies of Alexander's campaign in Central Asia. Not much later than the capture of Bessus, Ptolemy tried to usher Cleitus the Black out of Alexander's presence when both had become drunk and violent, but Cleitus returned to the king's presence and was slain there (Arr. 4.8.9). Ptolemy's attempt to keep the peace failed, and so only appeared in Aristobulus' account, not Ptolemy's own. Later, he was the contact for informants in the conspiracy of the Pages (Arr. 4.13.7). Some accounts – probably the history of Clitarchus – put Ptolemy with Alexander when he was wounded among the Mallians, and include a story about Alexander finding an antidote to a poisonous wound inflicted on Ptolemy by a Brahmin arrow. These may have been inventions; the former, at least, Arrian tells us Ptolemy denied ever happening, since he was in command of a division of the army in another place when Alexander was wounded.

Ptolemy, as one of the Bodyguards, took on a role something like a staff officer. He fought alongside the king in battle and stayed with him on campaign, but also commanded independent detachments and took on a variety of missions. Thus in 312 BC, prior to the Battle of Gaza, the illustrious advisors of Demetrius – nearly all veteran officers from Alexander's campaign – described Ptolemy as 'nearly the greatest of Alexander's generals' who 'not only campaigned with him, but often commanded whole armies', and remained, the whole time down to 312 BC, 'undefeated' in person (Diod. 19.81.5). Ptolemy's first independent command, unless Arrian's story at the Persian Gates has merit, was the pursuit of Bessus Artaxerxes in 329 BC. Two of Bessus' lieutenants had agreed to surrender him to Alexander, and Alexander gave Ptolemy a division of the army to make a rapid march to their position (Arr. 3.29.7). Ptolemy's force comprised three hipparchies from the Companions, the new contingent of hippakontistai – mounted javelin-men who probably hailed from the Iranian plateau – a chiliarchy of hypaspists, a taxis from the phalanx, the specialized Agrianian light infantry and some of the archers. The division bore similarities to the elite divisions that often accompanied Alexander himself on forced marches, and may have numbered 4,000–5,000 in all.[3] Ptolemy's force covered a ten-day march in just four days. Ptolemy's account claimed that he then surrounded and captured Bessus before leading him back to Alexander. Aristobulus, who was also on the campaign and wrote a history of it, said␣Bessus' officers had already put him in chains to lead back to Alexander themselves, making Ptolemy's mission little more than escort duty.[4]

Ptolemy held numerous other military duties on the campaign, especially during the invasion of India. At the siege of the Rock at Choriene, Ptolemy led one-third of the army in siege-work relays, combat-engineering under Alexander's supervision (Arr. 4.21.4). In the invasion of Aspasia, Ptolemy was one of several prominent officers injured in aggressive attacks with an advance force under Alexander's personal command (Arr. 4.23.3). Ptolemy must have proved himself to this point, because he increasingly received brigade commands to operate independently. Then Alexander gave Ptolemy operational control over half the cavalry, one-third of the hypaspists, the Agrianes, two chiliarchies of the archers and the infantry battalions of Philotas and Philip for offensive actions against the Aspasians and Guraei (Arr. 4.24.10). The infantry battalion of Philotas was probably a Macedonian phalanx battalion, but that of Philip may have been an auxiliary battalion. At the Rock of Aornos in Assaceni territory, Alexander gave Ptolemy command of a light infantry force comprising the Agrianes, the *epilektoi* of the hypaspist corps and other ranged troops to make a march through difficult terrain and seize a position commanding the fortifications at Aornos. Ptolemy took, fortified and held the position long enough for more of Alexander's forces to join him there. He commanded sections of the army in the march down the Indus, including at one point 'three chiliarchies of the hypaspists' – that is, all but the king's guard units – and led an army division in the march across Gedrosia. After Hephaestion's death, he and Alexander led detachments of the army in the campaign against the Cossaeans of Media (Arr. 7.15.3). These commands gave Ptolemy plentiful experience commanding brigades of soldiers with multiple functions and learning to use them in complementary ways. They also afforded him a strong network of relationships with officers and soldiers who served under his leadership.

In one of these brigade commands, Ptolemy carried out what was arguably the single greatest combat exploit of any of the Ptolemies. In the pursuit of the Aspasians, a tribe dwelling between the Hindu Kush and the upper Indus River, Ptolemy was operating with a small force of cavalry and hypaspists under his personal command. The terrain was difficult and there was thick forest. Ptolemy and his band tracked the military commander of the Aspasians to a small hillock. There he dismounted from his horse, made his way to the top of the hill and engaged the commander in single combat. Arrian relates that 'in close quarters the Indian struck Ptolemy through his cuirass to the breast, but the cuirass checked the blow. Ptolemy slashed him right through the thigh, struck him down, and despoiled him' (Arr. 4.24.4).

His victory in single combat against an enemy commander was one of just a couple of such encounters in Alexander's campaign, but these sorts of heroic duels became more popular in the Successor era. Eumenes could claim a similar victory in single combat, Seleucus had two and Pyrrhus would later have one as well.

After Alexander died, Ptolemy seems to have worked to secure a strong position for himself and an aristocratic management of what was at the time the largest empire the world had ever known (Curtius 10.6.13–16). He may have set his sights on Egypt from the beginning. He would not have had a real chance to become regent himself at Babylon, but Egypt was a plum prize for any of Alexander's officers who anticipated that peace and cooperation would not persist. The attractions of Egypt in that sense were many. First of all, it was easily defended. Unlike almost other satrapies of any significance, it possessed secure flanks and rear: there would be no other satrap in Africa, and aside from the coast the only land access to Egypt was across the narrow coastal plain from Palestine, and even a commander of minimal competence could command access to Egypt from the fortifications at Pelusium. Other satrapies had wealth that could at least compete with Egypt's (its second attraction) – Babylonia, Media and Persia – but they could not rival its security. Second, one might note its resources: productive mines, some of the most fertile agricultural land in the world, a large population and significant trade opportunities. Finally, while Egypt was fairly secure, it was nonetheless in an influential position. With the Nile Delta and the city of Alexandria on the Mediterranean coast, Egypt was off the Royal Highway from Asia Minor to the Iranian Plateau, but by sea could directly influence the rest of the Mediterranean littoral and the Aegean world. The Macedonian infantry and the Companions came to blows over succession and the regency, but Ptolemy made sure he secured Egypt.

The Satrap of Egypt

Ptolemy visited Egypt with Alexander after the Battle of Issus, and probably accompanied him to the oracle of Ammon at the Siwa oasis as a member of the Royal Squadron of the Companion cavalry, which was the only cavalry unit in his company (Arr. 3.1.4). For several months, Ptolemy witnessed first-hand the natural strengths and enticements of Egypt, the country he later ruled. The power of the region was generally well understood in his day without visiting the country. A Macedonian officer in Persian service, Amyntas, had attempted to seize the country after Issus, but was killed by the Persian garrison, which had probably already decided to surrender to Alexander without further fighting. Ptolemy likely witnessed the foundation of Alexandria, the great city off the western (Canopic) mouth of the Nile. That city, which came to be the capital of the Ptolemaic dynasty and arguably the greatest city of the Hellenistic world, Alexander founded as a testament to his achievements. Plutarch called it a Greek *polis* (*Alex.* 26.4), Justin labelled it a Macedonian colony (*Epit.Trog.* 11.11.13), but just what Alexandria already was in the days of Alexander is difficult to say. It was a monumental foundation, by any account: while it used a similar Hippodamian grid plan to other Hellenistic foundations, its city blocks were more squared than most and more than three times larger.[5] Its construction proceeded in stages for years to come, and if Alexander did leave settlers for that famous city, his dispositions went unmentioned in the main histories. The *Alexander Romance*, which is not generally very reliable, was written by an Alexandrian in the Roman era for the Alexandrian people. It provides unique details of the founding, some of which may or may not be reliable (Ps-Call. 1.31–32). For example, it says that the populations of the dozen or so villages at the site where Alexandria was built were temporarily relocated but permitted to return and reside in the city, at least some of them as full Alexandrian citizens. These villages would presumably have been involved in fishing and trade in particular, and may have included both Egyptian and broadly Mediterranean populations. The greatest of the villages, it says, was Rhakotis, which in the Ptolemaic era and even in that author's day was the name for the Egyptian quarter in western Alexandria (see plates 15–16). Rhakotis seems to mean 'the construction site', and so presumably was the name given to the settlement during construction rather than one of the names of the pre-Alexandrian villages. On the other hand, the text also relates that two men, Eurylochos and Melanthion, had authority over the relocated villagers and had a public square in Alexandria named for them. Frazer suspected an element of truth in this passage: Eurylochos was a common name in Macedonia in the fourth century BC, and Melanthion broadly Greek; rather than village chieftains, as the *Romance* puts it, they may have been in charge of Greek and Macedonian settlers who became some of the first Alexandrians.[6] Alexandria was built on a massive scale and incorporated many new settlers to Egypt, but like so much in Ptolemaic history, it appeared newer and more Greek than it truly was.

When Alexander left Egypt, he was headed toward his climactic battle with Darius, but he nevertheless left substantial forces in Egypt and divided them among many commanders. The extensive – and exceptional – divisions Alexander made surely reflect his awareness of the strength of Egypt (Arr. 3.5). Curtius tells us he left 4,000 of his soldiers in Egypt (Curt. 4.8.4). He settled garrisons in Memphis and Pelusium under Macedonian officers drawn from his Companions. The men of the garrisons were probably, as elsewhere, Macedonians unfit for future campaigning. There may have been a few hundred of them. Perhaps they had been among the 4,500 wounded at Issus or among the many others wounded in the sieges of Tyre and Gaza. By comparison, Alexander settled 700 older or wounded Macedonians as the garrison in the citadel of Babylon, and 1,000 more at Susa (Curt. 5.2.16). In each case their responsibility was not to be the primary army of occupation, as they were too few. Rather, they secured vital defensive positions, may have acquired roles in training new soldiers and likely benefited from nearby estates as sources of revenue. For other military roles, Alexander also left mercenaries (*xenoi*), presumably Greek or Thracian, in the garrisons under other commanders, both Greek and Macedonian.[7] Then he established a separate army of occupation and left two Macedonian officers, Peukestas and Balakros, to command them, and put another Macedonian, Polemon, in charge of the fleet of Egypt, with thirty ships under his command. Most of the men in the field army and fleet were probably mercenaries from the Aegean world. He also left a band of exiles from Chios under a guard at Elephantine (Arr. 3.2.1). Political and economic affairs he left in the hands of still more subordinates, so that in all there were thirteen high-ranking civil and military officials sharing power over Egypt. In this way he attempted to ensure that no one man could exert control over all of Egypt. The sources on Alexander's campaign make few mentions of Egyptian affairs after that point, but the following two things are relatively clear.

First, one of Alexander's civil officials, Cleomenes of Naukratis, came to wield considerable power over the country. Naukratis was a Greek city-state not far from the site where Alexander had ordered the construction of Alexandria. As the chief financial official, he concentrated the revenues collected in the nomes (provinces) of Egypt. As governor of the western districts, he also oversaw the construction of Alexandria. He was by all accounts a self-aggrandizing, shrewd and acquisitive man, and through his middling position eventually acted as if he were the satrap of Egypt. The pseudo-Aristotelian *Economicon*, purportedly written about 320 BC, told how Cleomenes, in a time of famine in the Mediterranean, forbade grain exports from Egypt in order to further stoke prices, while he sold his own grain at triple the normal price. When the nome governors reported they could not pay their taxes without exporting grain, he permitted export, but charged an export duty to the Egyptians so that their overseas price would be as high as his own, but their profits were undercut by the duties, which filled his coffers. The *Economicon* contains several other stories of ways Cleomenes raised funds through double-crosses and extortion (2.1352). Demosthenes' *Against Dionysodorus* confirms this picture. The case against Dionysodorus probably took place in early 322 BC, while Athens was engaged in the Lamian War against Macedonian rule. Demosthenes argued against Dionysodorus and several of his business partners, all of whom were subordinates of 'that Cleomenes who was then ruling Egypt' (56.7). They had taken money from Athenians to buy grain in Egypt and return it to Athens for sale, but instead sold the grain in Rhodes, where their own profits were better. Cleomenes, Demosthenes said, had made a practice of buying up the grain market and then reselling at his inflated price. In all these things Cleomenes increased his stature in Egypt, dispatched fortunes to Alexander, built Alexandria along the coast and still set aside a treasure counted at 8,000 talents (Diod. 18.14.1). Complaints against him eventually reached Alexander, but Cleomenes' willingness to placate the king so soon after the loss of Hephaestion earned him a pardon. When Alexander died, he was clearly the head of Egyptian affairs, even if he still lacked the title of satrap.

Second, the garrisons or field armies left in Egypt engaged in a recruitment and training programme for youths enlisted in Egypt. We know this only from an entry in the *Suda*, a Byzantine collection of short excerpts from classical authors arranged like an encyclopaedia. Under *basileoi paides*, or Royal Pages, the *Suda* recorded that Alexander ordered 6,000 Royal Pages in Egypt thoroughly trained in Macedonian warfare (B'154).[8] Some of their recruits may have been Greeks, Carians, Judeans or others residing in Egyptian settlements, but because of the size of the cohort it seems likely, even necessary, that most of the Pages were drawn from the local Egyptian and Libyan populations.[9] The programme sounds very similar to that which produced the *Epigonoi* from the Iranian plateau, an army of 30,000 Iranian youths trained in Greek language and Macedonian arms (Diod. 18.108.1–3). Alexander ordered the training of the *Epigonoi* in 329 BC and they were ready for service by 324 BC.[10] As for the Egyptian Pages, the narrative sources do not mention them at all. Detachments of auxiliary forces joined Alexander's main force from lesser regions like Lydia, Caria, Lycia and Syria. No source actually clarifies if or when the Egyptians joined Alexander, but if they were trained about the same time as the *Epigonoi* or the Royal Pages of Macedon, they might have joined the army in about 326 BC. It just so happens that two accounts of Alexander's campaign, those by Diodorus of Sicily and Quintus Curtius Rufus, mention large reinforcements to his army at that time. Diodorus mentions 30,000 infantry and 6,000 cavalry, without breaking down the large army's individual contingents (Diod. 17.95.4), while Curtius mentions Mesopotamian and Thracian contingents with a total of 12,000 men (Curt. 9.3.21). If both were relating parts of an accurate account, perhaps the Egyptian Pages were part of this army. This would also explain how there were Egyptians in the army a few months later, when they were among the leading groups enrolled as sailors for the Indus river fleet (Arr. 6.1.6). The other possibility, favoured by Hammond, is that these 6,000 men were added to the other military contingents in Egypt.[11]

What do these observations mean for the satrapy Ptolemy claimed after Alexander's death? It had an established and robust system for revenue collection and a large treasury. Cleomenes' 8,000 talents could have sufficed to equip and field large military forces for several years, if only Ptolemy could get his hands on the treasury. Cleomenes, for all his wealth, was in an awkward position: he lacked an official capacity remotely comparable to his exercised power, and there is no indication he ingratiated the dozen other authorities of Egypt to his hold on power. Perdiccas, suspicious of Ptolemy, made sure Cleomenes was titled *hyparchos* to Ptolemy as satrap, making him lieutenant governor, but Ptolemy rapidly removed him from the picture, availing himself of the pretext provided by Cleomenes' abuses of power (Paus. 1.6.3). Egypt was in many ways a land of potential rather than real power: our sources do not mention any military forces awarded to Ptolemy to take with him to Egypt. He must have gained some, but mainly he would depend on the troops already there and any clients he could attract to his person before he left Babylon for Egypt. One of the men he attracted to his side was Ophellas, wealthy enough to have served as one of the thirty trierarchs of the Indus river fleet (Arr. *Ind.* 18.3). He had the Royal Pages in his company after Alexander's death, and may have also drawn several of those young elites into his service (Curt. 10.7.16). Diodorus (18.14.1) reports that Ptolemy was able to attract 'a multitude of friends' to his camp. It seems likely that he rode to Egypt with an entourage rather more like an aristocratic officer corps than an actual army.

If we trust the *Suda* passage, Ptolemy had in his favour a tradition and infrastructure from Alexander's lifetime to Hellenize Egyptians and arm them like Macedonian soldiers. If some or all of the 6,000 graduates joined

Alexander's army in 326 BC, as seems likely for at least some of the class, and if a new group of Egyptian Royal Pages were then trained (which needs further examination), the second group should have been ready for military service about 320 BC. The first attested training programme for local auxiliaries was the one operating in Lydia, which sent its first reinforcements in 330 BC (Arr. 3.25.4), then sent more in 324 BC (Arr. 7.23.1), providing strong evidence that multiple cohorts could be raised from a single province. Lycia and Pamphylia together sent reinforcements in 328 BC (Curt. 7.10.11), and Antigonus' possession of at least 3,000 Lycian and Pamphylian phalanx soldiers in the Diadochi Wars suggests a second class was trained there as well and retained by the satrap when Alexander died (Diod. 19.29.3). In the usual rendering of the history of the Ptolemaic army, Egyptian soldiers appear as Egyptian units in insignificant or limited roles until Ptolemy IV's advisors raised 20,000 Egyptians as pikemen in the Fourth Syrian War. The account in the *Suda* suggests, first, that Egyptians were playing a larger role much earlier. It also suggests, however, that through their Hellenizing experience at the military academy in Egypt, they may be less visible in our surviving sources than the culturally Egyptian troops that fought at Raphia.

The Army of the Satrap

Ptolemy rode to Egypt, removed Cleomenes, secured the treasury and established his unquestioned hold on one of the wealthiest territories in the entire Macedonian Empire, or in the entire world at the time. Diodorus, whose source was probably Hieronymus of Cardia, reported that Ptolemy transitioned into his satrapy more easily than any other major figure (Diod. 18.14.1). Only an oblique reference in a late source gives any hint of difficulty. Lucan's *Hippias* records that Sostratos of Knidos was a military engineer for Ptolemy, and helped him conquer Memphis without violence by redirecting the flow of the Nile (*Hipp.* 2). Sostratos also designed the Pharos lighthouse and served the first two Ptolemies. Some have interpreted Lucan's reference as evidence that Cleomenes attempted to prevent Ptolemy's entrance into Memphis and Ptolemy avoided a fight by Sostratos' engineering stratagem.[12] While a tempting possibility, it is difficult to say more. Perdiccas' royal army certainly lacked a comparable level of engineering ability during his invasion of Egypt in 320 BC. Ptolemy had wealth and a large following of Friends (*Philoi*), aristocratic veterans of Alexander's campaigns who brought their experience, wealth and networks to Ptolemy's side. And yet, he had no real army. Ptolemy felt certain of a challenge from Perdiccas, so one of his first priorities, after securing Egypt, was to build his army. Perdiccas, even after detachments were sent off with the new satraps and generals across the empire, could, if it came to that, march on Egypt with an army of at least 30,000 and as many as 40,000 men that included, by historians' estimates, between 5,000 and 9,000 veteran Macedonians.[13]

The army Ptolemy built was eventually able to defend Egypt and campaign in the Mediterranean. It comprised soldiers in three categories: those he started with, those he recruited and those he gained through victories. Of these he started with, it seems safe to assume that the 4,000 soldiers, or replacements for those who passed away or out of service, were still in Egypt. The progress in construction work at Alexandria may also have attracted some other Greeks to the country. Ptolemy's entourage on the journey to Egypt may have numbered as many as a few thousand, but it seems safe to say it included no very large contingent of Macedonians, and may not have had any organized tactical unit at all. If Perdiccas had invaded Egypt immediately – that did not occur for nearly three years – Ptolemy would have been badly outnumbered. Diodorus said he started hiring mercenaries immediately. With 8,000 talents in his treasury and a wealthy province, he could have hired and paid handsomely more men than he could muster. One thousand mercenary infantry on a ten-month pay schedule with a well-compensated officer corps may have cost between 60 and 80 talents per year, although Ptolemy probably could have kept costs down by encouraging soldiers to purchase their food and drink from his own vendors. If he lowered his costs to 50 talents per year per 1,000 men, the 8,000 talents alone could have kept 16,000 mercenaries on hand for ten years. Egyptian dynasts had often raised between 5,000 and 20,000 mercenaries from the Greek and Aegean world as recently as a generation earlier,[14] so it is not unlikely Ptolemy could attract just as many to an Egypt under Greek rule.

The most effective way for Ptolemy to lower the costs of mercenary soldiers was to draw them out of pure mercenary service. The best way to accomplish this was to entice them into Egyptian residency and convert some of their wages into permanent benefits in the form of lands, revenues or status. In 306 BC, Demetrius, the son of Antigonus, captured 3,000 Ptolemaic soldiers on Cyprus. When he attempted to enrol them in his own army, they deserted back to the Ptolemaic side because, according to Diodorus, 'their belongings were in Egypt' (Diod. 20.47.4). The word for belongings is *aposkeuē*, which could refer to campaign baggage, but in this sense almost certainly means more. Ptolemy, through lavish spending or giving, managed to attract many of his mercenaries into serving him and inhabiting Egypt on a semi-permanent or permanent basis. The city of Alexandria probably functioned as one of the primary vehicles for accomplishing that transition. We know that Alexandria was still mostly a construction site when Alexander died, and that it was a splendid, populous city early in the reign of Ptolemy II Philadelphus, so it must have grown rapidly in the forty years Ptolemy son of Lagos ruled. We know from later Ptolemaic history that many Alexandrian citizens with military connections also had land in the countryside. This system of combined privileges almost certainly had roots in the era of Ptolemy the satrap.

Aside from Alexander's garrison, Ptolemy's Friends and followers, and however many mercenaries he could hire, the satrap could also raise soldiers from the Egyptian and Libyan populations of Egypt. Egyptians had served the Persian Empire, especially in its navy (Hdt. 7.89). Alexander left thirty triremes in Egypt under his officer Polemon; as many as 6,000 Egyptians would presumably have been pressed into service to man these and other ships. Most of the Egyptian population did not come from a strong military tradition. In the last period of Egyptian self-rule, most of its army were militia soldiers at best.[15] Nonetheless, a smaller military aristocracy and military class did exist in some parts of Egypt at the time of Alexander's conquest, and they could and did contribute to the Ptolemaic army.[16] A stele at Herakleopolis in Middle Egypt records the safe return of an elite Egyptian soldier after the Battle of Issus (see plate 10 fig. 17).[17] Somtutefnakht was from a family of priest-soldiers in Herakleopolis. The priest-soldier class, in Egypt, might better be termed a priest-officer class. Most Egyptian warriors were not part of the religious establishment. Somtutefnakht was in the company of the satrap of Egypt, Sabaces, and was probably part of the satrapal guard or a commanding officer when he 'saw thousands around him slaughtered' at Issus. Sabaces was among those killed, but Somtutefnakht returned 'by land and by sea' to Egypt. The inscription that describes his experiences may predate Alexander's arrival in Egypt, but he typifies the sort of aristocratic soldier Ptolemy likely courted to stabilize his rule of Egypt and build his army.

Not only did Egyptians like Somtutefnakht represent augmentation to the army and influence in Egypt, but their role as priests also helped Ptolemy establish secure access over a network of strong fortifications. The temples of Egypt are often squat complexes with thicker walls than most cities and fortresses. The Ptolemies seldom bothered to build new fortifications in Egypt, unless they were building them as part of temple construction.[18] The temples of Egypt made excellent strongpoints for Ptolemaic garrisons in the country or for Ptolemaic defensive bases against invaders. Good relations with the priestly classes helped assure a secure hold of some of the most impressive fortifications in the Mediterranean. This policy may be one Ptolemy son of Lagos adopted from his predecessors. The aforementioned notice from Peukestas about staying clear of the priest's quarters makes the most sense if part of the garrison of Memphis was housed in the sprawling temple complex. Greek soldiers were also garrisoned at an Egyptian temple in Athribis, north of Memphis off the Canopic (western) branch of the Nile. A cult statue for a wealthy Egyptian, Djedhor, describes his benefactions to the temple of Iat-Maat, which consisted in large part in removing the garrison from the temple.[19] The text describes him granting land to the soldiers to get them out of the temple, but they continued residing there, so he relocated them to the south of the Athribite nome. The incidents may have taken place over several years, but seem likely to belong to the era when Ptolemy was satrap. Both of Djedhor's interactions with the soldiers probably required approval from Ptolemy, who was willing to remove soldiers from a fortified holy precinct in order to gain the good will of the Egyptians at Athribis.

Ptolemy had to be open-handed to establish his army. He could start with Alexander's garrison forces, Cleomenes' auxiliaries (the Jewish population resident in Egypt had served him as soldiers, for example), his own friends and followers, and any Egyptians available, whether from the Page programme or from troops who had formerly been available to serve the Persians, both in garrisons and on campaign. Collectively, these probably numbered less than 10,000. Beyond these, Ptolemy relied on recruiting mercenaries or gaining troops through conquest. Thus for the next decade or so, military action, which depended on the troops he could acquire, was also one of the best ways for Ptolemy to increase his army. His able generalship helped compensate for his low numbers, and led to a series of campaigns that increased the size of his army for the next fifteen years.

The Campaigns of Ptolemy the Satrap

The Conquest of Cyrene

The first military venture of Ptolemy's rule was into Cyrenaica in 322 BC. The previous year a mercenary captain, Thibron, led an army of 6,000 men to Cyrene. He and most of his soldiers were veterans of Alexander's campaign. They were invited by exiles from Cyrene and Barke, the largest cities in the Cyrenaican Pentapolis. Thibron's campaign, after initial successes, stalled. He gained Apollonia, the harbour city of Cyrene, and defeated the Cyreneans in a battle, but could not capture the city and some of his own men mutinied and joined the Cyreneans. Thibron managed to bring the cities of Barke and Hesperis into an alliance, and hired another 2,500 veteran mercenaries in Greece. A grand battle in early 322 BC went in Thibron's favour, and he laid siege to Cyrene. Amid the siege, the Cyreneans went through a democratic revolution, and many from the aristocracy, after being ejected from the city, fled to Ptolemy's court. Ptolemy sent one of his leading Friends, Ophellas, back to Cyrene with a 'considerable force' by land and by sea (Diod. 18.21.7).

Ophellas' campaign ended Thibron's attempt to carve out a kingdom and added all of Cyrenaica to Ptolemy's satrapy. It is only possible to tease out some elements of the campaign. The size of Ophellas' force, his alignment with the aristocratic Cyreneans and the success of his opening moves compelled the democratic Cyreneans to reconcile with Thibron. Thibron and the democrats then fought Ophellas in pitched battle and were defeated. Thibron tried to escape, but Arrian tells us he was captured by Libyans and turned over to Epikydes of Olynthos, Ophellas' garrison commander at Teucheira, one of the lesser cities in Cyrenaica. The presence of Epikydes and his garrison at Teucheira is a significant detail. Thibron had earlier besieged, captured and garrisoned that city,

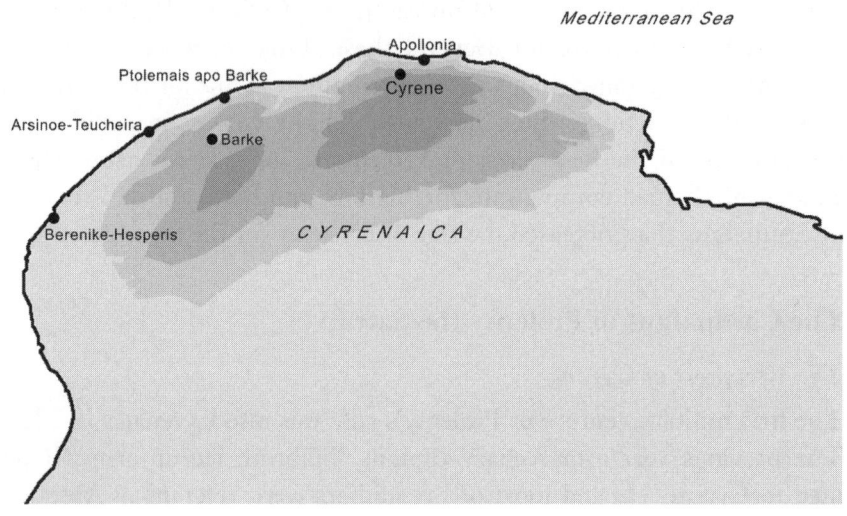

The Cyrenaica.

which was on the coast in western Cyrenaica. It seems that some part of Ophellas' forces – perhaps his naval arm – had made an indirect attack away from Cyrene, while Thibron was caught up facing Ophellas' main force, which had probably put in at Apollonia to the north-east of Cyrene. Securing Teucheira meant Ophellas' men were in easy striking distance of Barke and were between Hesperis and Thibron. Capturing Teucheira may well have taken those two other cities out of the war and given Ophellas improved odds against Thibron. It is worth bearing in mind that Thibron, even without his allies or the Cyrenean democrats, should have had some 6,000 veteran soldiers under his command, and as many as 8,500. Ptolemy had probably not yet been in Egypt a full twelve months when he dispatched Ophellas, but must have been able to send him with a force of nearly 10,000 men. It would not be surprising if many of the defeated mercenaries were subsequently enrolled in Ophellas' army in Cyrenaica or Ptolemy's armies back in Egypt. Thibron, however, was tortured and killed.

The defeat of Thibron did not finally pacify Cyrenaica. Arrian described the Cyreneans – the democratic faction – refusing to cooperate with Ophellas, and it is possible Barke and Hesperis were troublesome as well. Photius' epitome of Arrian reports that Ptolemy himself embarked on his own campaign at that point (*Met'Al.* 1.19), but Diodorus and the Parian Marble both put Ptolemy's intervention later, probably after Perdiccas' invasion. Most likely Ophellas stayed in Cyrenaica, suppressing unrest and installing garrisons in the cities for more than a year before Ptolemy's visit. Ophellas was probably the founder of Ptolemais-from-Barke, a new Cyrenaican city up the coast from Teucheira, at the site of inland Barke's harbour.[20] Ophellas may have used it as his base to govern Cyrenaica.[21] Barke rapidly declined in prominence, suggesting Ophellas relocated many Barkans to the new settlement site. At least some of the settlers were from Hesperis (*SEG* 9.362); others may have been from Cyrene as well. The large numbers of Cyreneans who served as cleruchs in the Ptolemaic army suggests that another of the ways Ophellas (or Ptolemy) pacified the region was by transplanting some populations to Egypt, enrolling them in the Ptolemaic army and granting them estates along the Nile. Cyreneans are found in the documentary evidence throughout Egypt, from Alexandria to Elephantine, but the heaviest concentration of them appears to have been in the Oxyrhynchite nome, the province between Herakleopolis and Hermopolis in Middle Egypt. The cavalry units stationed there, and the civilian population of *epigonoi* – sons of cleruchs – or other soldiers, not yet mobilized for service themselves, were heavily Cyrenean, with a scattering of men from Barke, Hesperis and

Libya. By the addition of Cyrenaica, Ptolemy added thousands of men to his army (Just. *Epit.* 13.8.1) and gained a populous Greek region from which he could recruit still more.

The Body of Alexander

In 321 BC, as Ophellas was wrapping up his successful campaign in Cyrene, a large procession, accompanied by a small army, set forth from Babylon. The commander of the procession was a Macedonian nobleman named Arrhidaios, and its purpose was to transport the body of Alexander to its final resting place. The escort – whom Pausanias called Macedonians, and the *Heidelberg Epitome* described as a 'large, filled up *doryphoria* [bodyguard]' – was neither a mean police force nor a purely ceremonial troop (FGrH 155 2). Perdiccas' intent was certainly to have the body taken to Macedon (*Met'A* 1.25, also Paus. 1.6.3). Whether that was Alexander's will or the consensus of the Macedonians is not entirely clear. Arrhidaios spent nearly two years at Babylon overseeing the construction of Alexander's magnificent coffin and the hearse that carried it, making his departure some time in spring 321 BC. He, his soldiers and the procession around Alexander's magnificent coffin travelled from Babylon toward Syria. They moved at a processional pace, not a military one, so it probably took a month to reach Syria. It is an indication of the general indecision about the body's destination and the importance of the body of the great Alexander that Perdiccas sent two of his senior officers, Dokimos and Polemon, with troops to Syria to oversee Arrhidaios. But Ptolemy went to Syria himself, and took an army with him (Diod. 18.28.3). At Damascus, Arrhidaios snubbed Perdiccas' agents and 'deserted' to Ptolemy (*Met'A* 24.1). This was Ptolemy's first campaign command since the death of Alexander, and while it gave him an opportunity to test his growing army in the field, it was presumably more about posturing than violence. Ptolemy's display of concern for the body of Alexander, by coming to Syria himself, impressed many observers (Diod. 18.28.4–5), and his military force dissuaded Dokimos and Polemon from attempting to force the procession to continue toward Macedon. A single word in an isolated fragment of the Vatican palimpsest of Arrian tells us that, whether by posturing or actual blows, Perdiccas' agents were forced to 'retreat' from Damascus or its environs (*Met'A* 24.1). The cortège would have moved very slowly, and Polemon in particular attempted to 'hinder' Arrhidaios, so one should not imagine a rapid break for Egypt. Rather, Arrhidaios' procession had to lumber down passable roads, and Ptolemy's forces were probably required to counter Polemon's attempts to set up blocking positions. Ptolemy's brazen and armed intervention, the diversion of Alexander's body and the rebuff of Perdiccas' agents assured eventual military action against the satrap of Egypt.

Ptolemy escorted Alexander's body and coffin to Egypt, and it was kept in Memphis until he had prepared a suitably grand site in Alexandria. Whether Arrhidaios and his forces stayed in Egypt at that point is not clear. Hammond concluded that their 'desertion' suggested they did, which makes sense. He also proposed that the army included the same units of Alexander's guard that were depicted beside his chariot in a painted scene on the carriage that held his coffin (Diod. 18.27.1) and in the immediate company of Alexander in the descriptions of his court at the end of his reign (Poly. 4.3.24, Ath. 539E): the Persian *melophoroi* hypaspists and the *agema* of the hypaspists, each at least 500 but likely 1,000 strong.[22] If he were right, Arrhidaios not only brought Alexander's body to Egypt, but some of the best soldiers in the whole Macedonian world, making the incident a real military and propaganda coup. Unfortunately, we cannot know if they went to Egypt with Ptolemy, nor if they were the escort with Arrhidaios or in what numbers. Hammond's conclusion would require, first, that the *agema* of the hypaspists was not counted among the 3,000 Silvershields or reconstituted after their discharge; and second, that they did not remain in the presence of the new king, Philip Arrhidaeus. The latter is more problematic, and I suggest that, in selecting an honour guard for the great Alexander, Arrhidaios likely travelled with detachments from these or perhaps other famous regiments.

The arrival of Arrhidaios and the troops in the company of the cortège marked the beginning of a recruiting burst for Ptolemy. Diodorus describes Ptolemy's immense success at this particular moment in recruiting soldiers to his side: '[M]en, because of his graciousness and nobility of heart, came together eagerly from all sides to Alexandria and gladly enrolled for the campaign, although the army of the kings was about to fight against that of Ptolemy' (Diod. 18.28.5). This particular line sounds like it came straight from the text of an admirer of Ptolemy, so it merits some critical analysis. Perhaps the satrap's noble heart did bring a few brave souls to Egypt to stand at his side against Perdiccas and the royal army, but his graciousness, in the form of open coffers, may have been more winsome. The infusion of manpower between Ptolemy's acquisition of Alexander's body and Perdiccas' invasion of Egypt was instrumental in Ptolemy's eventual success. We do not know how many came, but Diodorus' account implies it was a considerable number. Diodorus states that they 'gladly enrolled for the campaign', but the truth may lie in the other direction. While it was obvious that Perdiccas harboured ill will for Ptolemy and an attack on Egypt might come at some point, the flashpoint in the Successor era was not in Egypt. The war everyone anticipated was instead that between Antipater and Craterus on one side and Perdiccas and the royal army on the other.[23] That war drew the attention of the Greek world and all Asia Minor, as the soldiers of Macedon were 'armed against its own vitals, and turned the sword from warring against the enemy to the effusion of civil blood, being ready, like people in a fit of madness, to hack its own hands and limbs' (Just. 13.6.17). Anyone wishing to avoid the terrible clash of Macedonian armies could make for Egypt, where, in 321 BC at least, it seemed they could await with Ptolemy the outcome of the larger conflict between Perdiccas and Antipater.

Perdiccas and the First Invasion of Egypt

> 'The king did battle with the satrap of Egypt and ... the troops of the king were slaughtered.' – *BCHP* 3.23

It just so happened that Perdiccas preferred to attack Ptolemy first, trusting his lieutenants, with a large part of the royal forces, to hold the line in Asia Minor. Perdiccas began his march toward Egypt about the end of the winter of 320 BC with 'the majority of the royal army' (Diod. 18.29.1). Eumenes had more than 20,000 men from the royal army in his force at the Hellespont, Alcetas seems to have had about 10,000 with him in southern Anatolia, Dokimos had a small army with 'some of the leading Macedonians' for his armed conquest of Babylonia (*Met'A* 24.3) and Aristonous the Bodyguard had at least 1,300 for an expedition against Ptolemy's allies on Cyprus (*Met'A* 24.6).[24] Perdiccas seems likely, then, to have led an army of about 30,000, or at most 40,000. In spite of Ptolemy's successes in expanding his own forces, it seems very likely that he would be outnumbered on the order of two-to-one.

The main narrative for Perdiccas' campaign is Diodorus 18.33–37. It is detailed, but has numerous faults. Justin's *Epitome* adds nothing that is not already in Diodorus' account, and Photius' *Epitome* of Arrian adds only a few, relatively minor details, e.g., Perdiccas' departure point for the campaign was Damascus in Syria (*Met'A* 1.28). Perdiccas wintered in Pisidia or Cilicia, so he must have moved out to Damascus in the first months of 320 BC. Perhaps he took that route to prolong the dispatch of Dokimos and to impress upon Laomedon, the satrap of Syria, the importance of his future loyalty, having failed to stop Ptolemy and Arrhidaios the previous year. The Babylonian *Diadochi Chronicle* helps situate the invasion of Egypt in the summer of 320 BC and confirms that the king's army did battle with the satrap of Egypt and lost.[25]

Perdiccas, in spite of his numbers and the presence of the royals, nonetheless faced an uphill battle if it came to subjugating Ptolemy and Egypt by force. The gateway to Egypt was at Pelusium as an army travelled from Syria and Phoenicia, and provisioning an army en route to Pelusium was no easy task. There were no fields at hand, few ready storehouses to plunder and little fresh water. We know that Perdiccas had a navy at hand during the campaign, and some of his naval power may have been employed to resupply his army by sea, limiting its potential for offensive operations. The main fortifications at Pelusium were on the eastern bank of the Pelusiac branch of the Delta, but by opening sluices, canals and hollows on the south and east of the fortifications were filled and it became an island. Ptolemy had occupied it and numerous other positions along the Pelusiac branch. He was forced to disperse his army across a fairly large front, and kept some of his best troops around him as a reaction force. If Perdiccas crossed the Pelusiac branch, he would be better situated to supply his army, but Ptolemy would still be able to reposition his forces to take advantage of other chokepoints.

The action at Pelusium began with politics, and never really came to arms. Arrian related an attempt by Perdiccas to call Ptolemy to account, perhaps before the Macedonians or the kings. He brought 'numerous charges', but Ptolemy 'publicly refuted them' so as to make them 'appear ill-founded' (*Met'A* 1.28). Arrian's words, if we can follow Photius this closely, suggest that Perdiccas' accusations were a mixture of truths and falsehoods, overwrought in an attempt to silence opposition and force Ptolemy into submission. What might Perdiccas have charged? Ptolemy had hired mercenaries for a satrapal army after Alexander had ordered all satrapal mercenaries disbanded. He had executed or otherwise killed Cleomenes of Naukratis. He had interfered in Cyrenaica and suborned the Cypriots. He had taken an army into another satrapy to hijack the coffin and body of Alexander, and had interfered there with agents of the royal army. He had done all of those things, and Ptolemy's proofs of his innocence suggest he was also accused of things less true, perhaps that he had participated in a conspiracy against the life of Alexander or the new kings, that he conspired to proclaim himself king or had funded and fomented Greek rebellion against Macedon.

The juridical strategy failed, and his army wished to end the campaign then and there (*Met'A* 1.29).

Perdiccas' next attempt was to prepare an attack on Pelusium. Diodorus says only that his men were working to 'clear out an old canal, and the river broke out violently and destroyed his work' (Diod. 18.33.2). The region around Pelusium, up to the very walls of the fortress, had numerous embankments and canals, some of which could be used to create moats around the fortifications.[26] In 343 BC, Lacrates diverted the water filling a canal around part of Pelusium, filled in the emptied moat and launched attacks across it (Diod. 16.49.1). Perdiccas' men were most likely clearing out a secondary canal so they could similarly drain the moats around Pelusium. The early, unanticipated release of water would have destroyed equipment and perhaps drowned workers. At the same time, if the canal was not sufficiently cleared yet, it would not have diverted enough water to dry out the moats below the walls. We might contrast Perdiccas' failed siege engineering with the report of Ptolemy's successful siege engineering when he took Memphis in 323 BC. Perdiccas' men were unimpressed, and Diodorus reports that a large-scale desertion took place then and there, noting even that many of the Friends in the royal army went over to Ptolemy.

After the failures around Pelusium, Perdiccas launched two more attacks. There is a problem with Diodorus' account because he separated each attack by a night march and the second attack occurred near Memphis, more than 100 miles from Pelusium. There must have been several full days of marching involved, rather than the failed action at Pelusium and two more battles in three consecutive days. His strategy, at least, can be discerned. By undertaking night marches, he was seeking to get ahead of Ptolemy and around his flank, crossing the river before Ptolemy could defend the crossing. It was not a bad operational concept. Ptolemy had already been compelled to divide much of his army among many fortifications up and down the eastern Delta. One of the largest contingents was probably at Pelusium, which had 5,000 men as its garrison in 343 BC, and so may well, at a similar garrison, have quartered something like one-in-four or one-in-five Ptolemaic soldiers. Furthermore, Ptolemy himself was active down in the vicinity of Pelusium with his reaction force. Perdiccas could steal a march and bring heavy force to bear at whatever point he chose, and Ptolemy would be hard-pressed to react in time.

Perdiccas launched an attack on a position called the Camels' Fort. This fort is otherwise unknown, and many historians writing on the subject have placed it near Memphis, because after another overnight march

Perdiccas could attack Memphis. But the attack on the Camels' Fort also supposedly came after an overnight march, so by the same reasoning it should be near Pelusium. A quick forced march up to the vicinity of Memphis would suggest that the Camels' Fort action took place in the vicinity of Heliopolis, a city with a fortified temple and a Persian fort. Unfortunately, Heliopolis is also on the eastern side of the Pelusiac branch, so no river crossing would have been required. It would also be quite strange for Diodorus to refer to an attack near Heliopolis solely through an obscure reference to a Camels' Fort. I suggest we should look for the Camels' Fort closer to Pelusium. There are several pre-Ptolemaic sites, mainly fortified temples, that make interesting candidates. A place called the Camels' Fort should – if the name meant anything – have been attractive for overland traffic toward either the Red Sea or Sinai. Ancient Daphne, or Tapanhes, was the largest old site in the area, and Ptolemaic forces used it as a garrison later in the dynasty.[27] Its fortifications were mainly on the west bank, and it was nearly 30 miles overland from Pelusium, making it a reach for even the best troops – and impossible for the elephants – to cover in an overnight forced march.[28] Halfway between Daphne and Pelusium are two fortifications in close proximity to one another. The Tell-Hebua fort is actually two impressive fortifications located on opposite banks of the Pelusiac branch at the entrance to a paleo-lagoon, and the fort at Abu Saifa sat 5 miles south on a promontory between the paleo-lagoon and the El-Ballah Lakes.[29] Both sites were well-fortified, and occupation by soldiers during the time of Ptolemy I has been confirmed archaeologically at Abu Saifa.[30] Both sites could function as departure points for camel trade to the east. Abu Saifa would not actually have gotten Perdiccas across the Pelusiac branch, so perhaps Tell-Hebua has the better merit.[31] If he had to skirt the lagoon his forced march would have had to cover about 16 miles to Tell-Hebua and 18 to Abu Saifa. Tell-Hebua, with a fort on the east bank and a larger fort on the west bank, is probably the best candidate for the Camels' Fort.

Diodorus says that the Indian elephants led the attack on the Camels' Fort, with the hypaspists alongside (Diod. 18.33.6). The latter may have been the famed Silver-Shields, unless a new corps of hypaspists was active with the royal army.[32] Either seems possible. Diodorus describes Perdiccan troops crossing the river, then forming up and fighting across a narrow strip between the shore and the walls. Ptolemy's forces, probably his cavalry chiefly, were able to reach the fort and add their numbers and experience to the defence. Those around Ptolemy were the 'best' in his army, and many would have been the Friends and veterans of Alexander's campaign who

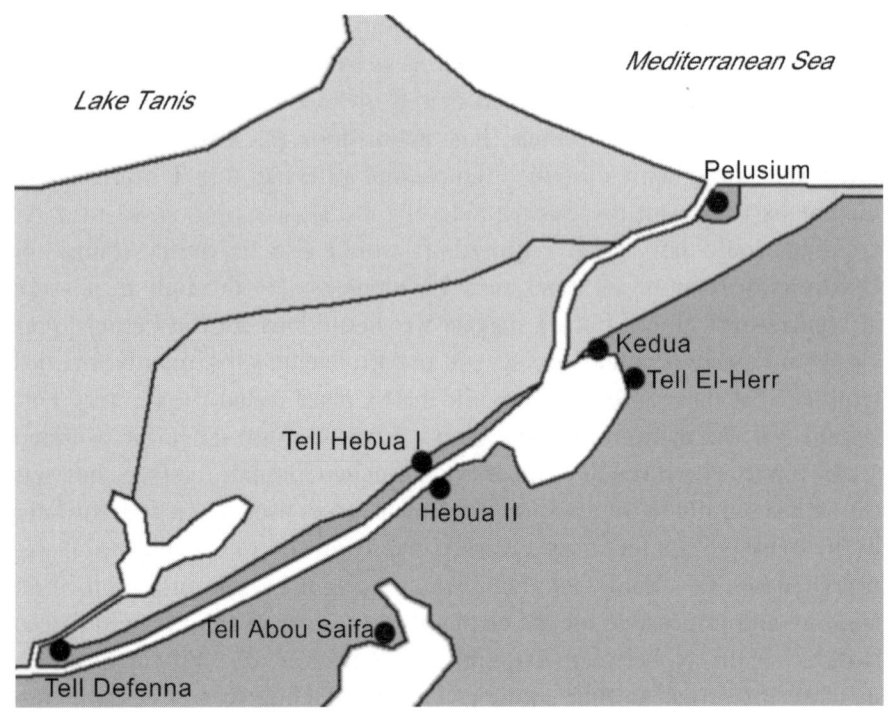

Pelusium and the Approaches to Egypt.

first accompanied the satrap to Egypt. Their numbers and valour helped dull the Perdiccan attack. Diodorus' source is nearly hagiographic toward Ptolemy in its entire account of the campaign, and describes him fighting at the fore atop the walls, blinding the leading war elephant with a sarissa and casting men down from their assault ladders (Diod. 18.34.2). In this passage Ptolemy fulfils the requirements of a good Hellenistic general: modelling valour, encouraging his men and personally exceeding what he demanded of his subordinates. Units of the royal army took turns assaulting the fort, but could not dislodge Ptolemy and his men, who were also most likely reinforced throughout the day. The attack on the Camels' Fort may have been the occasion for Ptolemy's use of a stratagem: some of his horsemen, and some hands, drove the army's pack animals behind Ptolemy's force-marching column, raising up an enormous cloud of dust and convincing the Perdiccan attackers that Ptolemy had a large army marching to relieve the beleaguered defenders.[33]

Perdiccas abandoned the attack on the Camels' Fort after taking heavy losses and failing to turn Ptolemy's flank. If the fight at the Camels' Fort was when Ptolemy used the pack animal stratagem, Polyaenus recorded that

Ptolemy managed to capture many of the attackers. Perdiccas broke camp after nightfall and again tried to steal a march: '[B]reaking camp at night, he marched secretly and came to the place that lies opposite Memphis' (Diod. 18.34.6). Historians have sometimes read Diodorus as saying that he reached Memphis by the next morning, but the text does not have to be read that way. Rather, he emphasized secrecy, so perhaps Perdiccas travelled a bit further off the Pelusiac branch, hoping to gain some initiative from keeping Ptolemy guessing about his whereabouts. If the Camels' Fort was at or in the vicinity of Tell-Hebua, then it was still about 100 miles to Memphis. With the war elephants and the royal court, the march may have taken about a week.

Perdiccas' army launched an attack across the Nile toward Memphis, miles upstream of the branching of the Delta. The Nile then and now splits in two in the vinicity of Memphis, forming small 'islands' on the eastern edge of the Nile flood plain. Most of the modern ones near Memphis are fairly small, but several large ones exist in the vicinity of Cairo, a few miles downstream. In 320 BC, there was an island near Memphis 'large enough to hold with safety a camp of a very large army' (Diod. 18.34.6). Ptolemy's army won its second victory in the Battle of the Nile, but according to Diodorus this owed more to hydromechanics than operational art or individual valour. The vanguard of Perdiccas' army made it to the island across a neck-deep ford, but the progress of thousands of men steadily carried off silt from the ford, and the last men to cross did so swimming. As the ford disappeared, Perdiccas ordered his vanguard to return to the east bank, and they swam across, but 2,000 drowned or were eaten by crocodiles, including several unnamed 'illustrious officers' (Diod. 18.35.1–36.1). This loss was said to have been suffered 'without a blow from an enemy' (Diod. 18.36.2). Arrian, however, says that Ptolemy defeated Perdiccas in two battles (*Met'A* 1.28), and the *Diadochi Chronicle* says, in a line that describes the end of Perdiccas' invasion, that 'the army of the king did battle with the satrap of Egypt and ... the troops of the king were slaughtered' (*BCHP* 3.23–24). Their testimony suggests that something is missing from Diodorus' version of events. Perdiccas' decision to recall some of his best soldiers after the ford had become impassable was an astounding mistake if their possession of the island went unopposed. Perhaps Ptolemy's riverine force was able to launch an attack against the vanguard, fighting from ships or even landing troops on the island, or the ford from the western side toward Memphis was more reliable and he managed to cross to the island with his own troops. Either way, the sources are in harmony that Ptolemy made an attack on Perdiccas' stranded vanguard and forced their hazardous retreat.

Perdiccas' army became mutinous after the defeat on the Nile, and within a day or two several leading officers, accompanied by Macedonian Companion cavalry, assassinated Perdiccas (see plate 11 fig. 18). Ptolemy capitalized on the situation to continue recruiting hundreds and perhaps thousands of men into his own army, but did not attempt to seize control of the entire royal army for himself. He appointed allies – Arrhidaios from his army, Peithon from the royal army – as guardians for the royals, provided food and gifts for the royal army and helped prepare its return to Syria. The *Heidelberg Epitome* relates that Ptolemy 'took over as much of Perdiccas' army as he wanted' (FGrH 155.4), but if true he must not have wanted too many, for the royal army remained formidable. Numerous Macedonians were almost certainly among the officers and men of leading units who had deserted to Ptolemy or been captured by him in various engagements during the campaign. Those Ptolemy took in after the campaign may have included some of the satrapal auxiliaries or men from the *Epigonoi*. Perhaps they even included some of the surviving men from the first class of Egyptian Royal Pages. He probably did not add more than several thousand to his army during the campaign. He had little need to: the defeat of Perdiccas and his alliance with Antipater put Ptolemy in a fairly secure position, and he must have hoped that Arrhidaios and Peithon would secure his permanent influence in the royal camp. In Syria, the royal army met with the Macedonian army marching down under Antipater and the combined forces met in council at Triparadeisos. There, Peithon and Arrhidaios resigned the guardianship and it was passed on to Antipater. In council they reassigned satrapies, reapportioned forces in the army and declared supporters of slain Perdiccas to be enemies of the Macedonians. That declaration spurred several more years of warfare, chiefly between Antigonus and Eumenes. They affirmed Ptolemy's possession of Egypt and Cyrene, but Diodorus adds that Ptolemy was already 'holding it by virtue of his own prowess, as if a prize of war' (Diod. 18.39.5). The Greek emphasizes Ptolemy's *andreia*, translated as prowess but communicating courage and charisma as well, and the holdings as *doriktēton*, spear-won.[34] Diodorus, or his source, read back from Ptolemy's later kingship the budding of royal aspirations in his army's successful defence of Egypt in 320 BC.

The Ptolemaic Army During the Second Diadoch War, 319–316 BC

Ptolemy came off well in the settlement at Triparadeisos, and the locus of conflict shifted to the Royalist campaign against the remnants of the

Perdiccan faction. Ptolemy had no role to play in that war, which was fought mainly in Asia Minor. Instead, Antigonus had command of the royal army, a position bestowed on him by Antipater. The Perdiccan faction included a number of leaders in Asia Minor – Attalus, Alcetas and Eumenes chief among them. Ptolemy used the action in other quarters to begin shoring up an outer network of defences for Egypt, mainly in Syria and Cyprus. Strengthening his hand as satrap of Egypt necessarily required preying upon other loyal governors, but he could justify his actions as part of the war against the Perdiccans, and the instability of the time made arms the root of legitimacy.

In 319 BC he occupied Syria and Phoenicia, which had been under the authority of the satrap Laomedon. Appian records he launched the campaign with his fleet first, and tried and failed to bribe the satrapy from Laomedon (Syr. 52). Invasion followed, for Diodorus says he dispatched a significant army under one of his Friends, Nikanor, to seize Syria and Phoenicia from its rightful satrap. The identity of this Nikanor is impossible to establish, since it was a common Macedonian name and very common in Ptolemaic Egypt among both the court elite and the rank-and-file. Nikanor's troops captured Laomedon, perhaps in the vicinity of Damascus, but according to Appian he bribed his way from captivity and escaped to the Perdiccan forces under Alcetas in Pamphylia. With Laomedon out of the way, Ptolemaic forces occupied several Syrian positions with garrisons. Most likely, Ptolemy and the naval forces worked their way up the coastal cities of Phoenicia, among whom Sidon and Tyre were the most important. Eusebius' Chronicle records that Ptolemy's conquest of Jerusalem and mass deportation to Egypt took place at this time, but most scholarship has dated those events later.[35] The occupying army was not large enough to occupy the whole province, as later events showed. While garrisons were left behind, the attack was also a raiding expedition. Ptolemy's forces brought numerous Phoenician ships to his fleet, which by 315 BC had grown to more than 200 ships.

While Nikanor was operating in Syria, it seems that Ptolemy sailed on with the fleet to Cyprus. He had already cultivated good relationships with several Cypriot kings even before Perdiccas invaded Egypt, especially Nikokreon of Salamis, and the cities of Soli, Paphos and Amathos (Arrian *Succ.* 10.6), but in 319 BC he must have used his fleet to visit the island and either reinforce friendly city-states or attempt to sway others to his side. A strong position on Cyprus made it possible for Ptolemy to project power toward Asia Minor, which Ptolemy first attempted to do in 318 BC, and it would threaten the flank of any Successor who might seize Syria and try to move against Egypt. Furthermore, the petty kingdoms of Cyprus all maintained navies, and could contribute large numbers of ships and crews to whomever they supported or served. This campaign would have been the likeliest time for Ptolemy to leave the 3,000 soldiers who were still augmenting the troops of the allied kings in 315 BC (Diod. 19.62.3). Ptolemy completed two efficient campaigns and returned to Egypt for the winter.

In 318 BC Phoe Ptolemy sailed to Cilicia to try to dissuade the famous Silver Shields, Alexander's former hypaspists, from serving Eumenes. Circumstances had changed dramatically while Ptolemy's forces were conducting their forays. Antipater died in the second half of 319 BC, and the venerable taxiarch Polyperchon replaced him as guardian of the kings. Meanwhile, Antigonus won a series of clear victories, and by the autumn faced no serious opposition in Asia Minor and led by far the largest army, which Diodorus claims numbered 60,000 infantry, 10,000 cavalry and war elephants (Diod. 18.50.3). Antigonus began planning to secure power for himself, and was encouraged in that direction when Cassander, Antipater's son, broke with Polyperchon and planned to seize power in Macedonia for himself. Antigonus entered into outright rebellion late in 319 BC when he invaded Lydia and expelled its satrap. This, in turn, led Polyperchon and the kings to legitimize the condemned Eumenes and seek his assistance in the war with Antigonus. Ptolemy had acted as a supporter of the kings at Triparadeisos, but from a position of practical independence in Egypt. In 318 BC he worked against Eumenes. He was in a reasonably good position to suborn the Silver Shields: he had exercised operational control of one or more hypaspist battalions on several occasions in Alexander's campaigns. The possible addition of 3,000 of the very best warriors then in the Mediterranean world would have been a great advantage for Ptolemy. His bid to gain their loyalty was one of Ptolemy's best moments to acquire a large group of Macedonians to build his army around. Instead, it seems he came on too strong, too transparently disloyal, and the Macedonians professed loyalty to the Argead family and Polyperchon. Ptolemy had landed at Zephyrium on the south-west coast of Cilicia, but his forces were insufficient to march inland against Eumenes. Ptolemy's failure to make a decisive move in this period of uncertainty limited his options in the future, just as his inability to acquire the Silver Shields forced him to continue relying on primarily non-Macedonian and even non-Greek recruits for his army.

Once Eumenes secured the support of the Silver Shields, he actually moved from Cilicia into Phoenicia, directly in the face of the Ptolemaic troops occupying parts of Syria and Phoenicia. Ptolemy and his army come off as very weak in Diodorus' account: Eumenes' agents recruited mercenaries in Cyprus and Phoenicia in 318 BC and Ptolemy could not stop them, and when Eumenes and his army of about 17,000 marched into northern Phoenicia, Ptolemy did not interfere. His troops continued to hold what they already held, but were firmly on the defensive. Eumenes intended to throw them all out until word came of Antigonus' pursuit. It may be that Ptolemy was unsure what strategy to pursue in 318 BC, especially after his failure to recruit the Silver Shields or at least keep them from joining Eumenes. At that point, perhaps he recognized that Eumenes might emerge victorious and that Antigonus represented a more significant danger to his plans than Eumenes or the kings did. Indecision – rather than simple weakness – probably inspired Ptolemy to sit out the remainder of the war.

At the end of the Second Diadoch War, Antigonus emerged victorious, in resounding fashion, with control of most of Asia. In response to Antigonus' growing power, Ptolemy and Cassander, former allies of Antigonus in their shared quests for self-rule, banded together with whoever else would aid them to keep Antigonus from uniting the empire under his own personal rule. Thus, as the second war ended the third war was already on the horizon. Ptolemy took in Seleucus, former satrap of Babylon and before that the ranking officer in Perdiccas' army. Seleucus, fearful for his life, had fled from Babylon and Antigonus. Several others who had been among Alexander's officers, who had not fled, died at the hands of the ambitious and talented general. He ruled nearly all of Asia Minor, Mesopotamia and the Iranian plateau, and the army with which he defeated the Royalist faction in Iran had numbered more than 40,000 men. Moreover, he possessed other land and sea forces, and incorporated some of the best troops from Eumenes' defeated army into his own. However much Ptolemy had expanded his army since Perdiccas' invasion, he was ill-equipped to face Antigonus and, with part of Syria wedged between Asia Minor and Mesopotamia, was particularly more exposed than the other members of his coalition.

As we conclude part one, let us take stock of Ptolemy's army at the end of 316 BC. He kept 3,000 of his soldiers on Cyprus and probably at least as many in Cyrenaica, which had also proven a fertile recruiting ground. Even more of his soldiers garrisoned numerous cities in Syria and Phoenicia, but they were clearly insufficient to hold the satrapy against invasion or even prevent other forces from operating in parts of the satrapy. These troops deployed abroad probably numbered within the range of 10,000–15,000. Ptolemy also possessed a significant fleet of at least 100 warships, some of them inherited from Alexander's force left in Egypt, with many gathered from Phoenicia and Cyprus during his most recent operations. Within Egypt, Ptolemy could call up thousands more troops, among whom many were mercenaries drawn to Egypt by Ptolemy's good pay and Cyreneans relocated to Egypt. Some thousands of them were Macedonians and other veterans from the Royal Army. Of these, some had garrisoned Egypt under Alexander, others had accompanied Ptolemy to Egypt, a few more had come to Egypt with Alexander's body and still more deserted to his side during Perdiccas' invasion. Many other troops were Egyptians, but probably not the *machimoi*, with whom readers may be familiar from later Ptolemaic history or the accounts of Herodotus and Diodorus. Ptolemy brought Egyptian elites over to his side, and the corps of Hellenizing Egyptians – raised from the Page programme and called 'Persians' – may well have been one of the largest contingents in his entire army. In his first years as Satrap, he avoided committing his army to a pitched battle, conquered three regions outside of Egypt and steadily grew the size and quality of his army. If Ptolemy longed for universal dominion, he had the prudence and temperance to see he had no short road there, and his best chances lay in Egypt first. The rise of Antigonus made Ptolemy's comparatively quiet growth impossible to maintain, and the next years were considerably more violent.

Chapter 3

The Antigonid Wars, 315–285 BC

Forging an Army and a Kingdom

When the Third Diadoch War (315–311 BC) began, Ptolemy and his allies (Cassander and Lysimachus chief among them) were stockpiling materials for the clash, and sent Antigonus an ultimatum demanding he split the spoils of his war with Eumenes. This ultimatum urged Antigonus to treat the victory as one achieved in his capacity as commander (and in a sense, steward) of the Royal Army, not as his own personal exploit with his own personal army. But Antigonus was already acting much like a monarch by late 316 BC, and had too much power and money at his disposal to consider sharing his gains. Ptolemy's holdings in Syria were the first target of the campaign. Ptolemy had garrisons in several cities, including at least Joppa and Gaza in southern Syria and in Tyre on the Phoenician coast. Furthermore, he was holding the civic fleets of the Phoenician cities (and their crews) in Egypt (Diod. 19.58.2), but he lacked the sort of army that could possibly withstand a determined invasion by Antigonus.

Antigonus invaded Syria himself in 315 BC. He took Joppa and Gaza by assault and enrolled Ptolemy's mercenaries, captured in the attacks, into his own army. Tyre, on the other hand, stood a long siege. After fifteen months camped around the city, he granted safe passage under arms to Ptolemy's garrison, and once they had departed for Egypt the city capitulated to Antigonus. Diodorus' narrative denigrates Ptolemy's response. This is to be expected when the account derives from sources friendly to Antigonus. We hear only, first, that Ptolemy sent Seleucus with the 100 finest ships in his navy, and he cruised past the siege at Tyre (Diod. 19.58.5). Between Seleucus' brazen brush past the Antigonid camp at Tyre and his withdrawal from an attack on Erythrai at the first sign Antigonid reinforcements were approaching (Diod. 19.60.4), Diodorus says nothing. In fact, he says

Seleucus withdrew with 'nothing accomplished'. But Erythrai is more than 2,000km from Tyre; even if Seleucus accomplished nothing of significance at Erythrai, he and the Ptolemaic navy must have carried out an extensive series of raids along the coasts, targeting places that supported Antigonus but were not actually protected by him. Ptolemy's strategy was not to meet force with force in Syria, but to favour the indirect approach. The problem for him was that Antigonus had enough resources to conduct campaigns on more than three fronts simultaneously.

Ptolemy's indirect approach, executed through Seleucus and his fleet, bore fruit in an alliance with Asander, the Macedonian dynast of Caria (Diod. 19.62.2). Asander controlled many Carian cities and had fairly strong armies of his own. Ptolemy sent his brother Menelaus with another fleet of 100 warships under an admiral named Polykleitos to reinforce his allies on Cyprus, and put 10,000 soldiers aboard under an Athenian commander named Myrmidon (Diod. 19.62.4). This should have raised the number of Ptolemaic soldiers on Cyprus to about 13,000, and when their fleet made a juncture with Seleucus, there should have been in the neighbourhood of 200 Ptolemaic ships active together. After a council of war, Myrmidon took some portion of the troops to Caria to give aid to Asander, while Polykleitos took fifty of the ships to the Peloponnese, and Seleucus and Menelaus with the remainder of the forces fought to secure the rest of Cyprus, which by negotiation and military action they very nearly did.

Polykleitos did not stay in the Peloponnese long, but returned to Asia Minor. While he was operating in Pamphylia and Rough Cilicia (the mountainous south-western part of the region), he discovered an Antigonid squadron had left Patara in Lycia and was headed east toward his position (Diod. 19.64). The naval squadron was under Theodotos, and according to Diodorus was wholly or mainly composed of Rhodian ships. They were matched on land by a small army under the command of Perilaos, one of the Macedonian friends of Antigonus. Polykleitos placed his men in ambush along the treacherous coast of Rough Cilicia and gained a total victory over Theodotos and Perilaos. Their entire force was slain or captured, then taken back to Egypt. Ptolemy lavishly rewarded Polykleitos, then returned Perilaos and other distinguished captives to Antigonus. Ptolemy and Antigonus actually held a short conference at a place called Ekregma, the 'Outbreak', on the coast a little east of Pelusium, but failed to negotiate an end to hostilities (Diod. 19.64.8). The war continued the next spring.

Troublesome Cyrenaica

Amid the escalating war with Antigonus, Cyrene again became a source of concern for the son of Lagos. It had been about eight years since Ptolemy annexed Cyrenaica and installed Ophellas as governor. In about 313 BC the people of Cyrene rebelled and besieged the Ptolemaic garrison in the citadel. Alexandrians sent to negotiate were slaughtered. Ptolemy did not go west himself, but sent two of his friends to restore control to the region; Agis – perhaps a Spartan soldier of fortune – with an army and Epainetos as *nauarchos* of a fleet. Agis stormed the city and settled affairs with considerable personal agency: he sent numerous captive ringleaders back to Alexandria, disarmed parts of the citizen population who had participated in or supported the rebellion, and reorganized the affairs of the city as seemed best to him (Diod. 19.79.1–3). At some point between 321 and 305 BC Ptolemy gave a new constitution to Cyrene (we know this from an inscription that records parts of the new constitution), and it is quite possible Agis oversaw the implementation of the new constitution at this point.[1]

The fragmentary text of Ptolemy's constitution reveals several interesting things about Ptolemaic military activities and military institutions. The text confirms that Ptolemaic mercenaries would remain stationed in the citadel at Cyrene, but that was to be expected. It also details the composition of Cyrene's new two-layered citizen body. Membership in the more restrictive body, the Ten Thousand, was determined by property qualifications more than ancestry. Ptolemy added the offspring of intermarriages with non-Cyreneans to the citizen rolls, plus the settlers in Cyrenean colonies, the Cyrenean exiles who had fled to Ptolemy and Cyreneans who were living in Ptolemy's military settlements. The mention of οἰκίας πτολεμαϊκὰς, 'Ptolemaic foundations', seems to confirm that by 312 BC at the latest Ptolemy was already establishing military settlements for his soldiers. Indeed, Cyreneans were one of the most numerous ethnics in the Ptolemaic settlements in Egypt. The soldiers settled in Egypt and elsewhere were confirmed in Cyrenean citizenship, and with the property qualification almost certainly qualified for membership in the Ten Thousand. Nonetheless, they were prohibited from performing any of the magistrate functions of the city, not only by practical distance, but also by law. Doctors, teachers and instructors in horsemanship or archery were similarly restricted, alongside a number of other trades. The appearance of these trainers in military arts, including *hoplomachia*, is actually the only evidence for their existence in the Ptolemaic empire, but it would not be surprising if such trainers were present in Alexandria and Egypt as well as at Cyrene.

Finally, it is noteworthy that the constitution appointed a body of *strategoi*, generals, to manage the affairs of Cyrene, and named Ptolemy as a permanent member of that body. The Cyreneans were authorized to raise their own military forces for local conflicts, probably for defending Cyrenaica against nomadic raids. A curious and fragmentary clause indicates the Cyreneans could also be mobilized for a conflict beyond their borders, and in those cases of serious conflict could elect new generals to lead the army. Did Ptolemy's constitution give Cyrene authority to wage warfare internationally on its own terms? This would be more than a little surprising. What may actually be involved in the constitution is Cyrene's commitment to provide a force for the Ptolemaic army in times of major war. At the Battle of Raphia, 3,000 'Libyans' were posted in a place of honour between the Macedonians and the Ptolemaic Agema. Their distinguished position at Raphia and this clause from the Cyrenean constitution might square best if these troops, armed in Macedonian style, were citizen troops from Cyrene and the other cities of Cyrenaica. Perhaps Cyrene and the other cities were required, if needed, to send 3,000 infantry and 300 cavalry. The Ptolemaic cavalry on the left wing numbered 2,300; perhaps 2,000 were from Egypt itself and the other 300 from the citizens of the Cyrenaica.

This episode was not the end of unrest in Cyrene. Ophellas, the former *trierarch* of Alexander and prominent friend of Ptolemy, was still in command over the rest of Cyrenaica. Four years later, he was convinced by Agathocles of Syracuse to raise an army to join him in the conquest of the Carthaginians (Diod. 20.40–43). Ophellas managed to raise more than 10,000 men for his march to the west. In Diodorus' narrative it seems the larger part of them were disenfranchised Athenians and freebooter Greeks, but Cyreneans must have played a significant role as well. Agathocles betrayed and killed Ophellas, and his expedition ended in failure.

The Third Diadoch War and The Battle of Gaza, 313–311 BC

As Agis settled affairs in Cyrene, Ptolemy turned his efforts to other arenas in the Third Diadoch War. Seleucus and other officers were still involved in supporting Asander in Caria, but in 313 and 312 BC the campaigns there took a turn for the worse. In 312 BC he launched another campaign into

Cyprus, extending his control of the island, leaped from there to raid several cities in northern Syria and then moved west into Cilicia.² In southern Cilicia he took Mallus, sold his captives and raided the countryside to reward his troops with extra pay. Antigonus' son Demetrius was around Tyre with about 20,000 men, but Ptolemy kept to the indirect approach at the start of the campaign in 312. That changed after these successes. A decisive campaign into Syria could swing the fortunes of the entire war.

Ptolemy set forth from Egypt with an army Diodorus gives as 22,000 men, 18,000 of them infantry and 4,000 cavalry. It was autumn 312 BC, and his rapid march from Egypt, to which he had recently returned, caught Demetrius off guard. Demetrius had to gather his troops from winter quarters to confront the Ptolemaic advance. The army of Demetrius is broken down in Diodorus (19.82) with excellent detail, but the only detail he provides for the Ptolemaic army is that 'some were Macedonians, some were mercenaries, but the largest contingent were Egyptians, of whom some were missile troops and porters, but others were armed and serviceable for battle' (Diod. 19.80.4).³ It is also a reflection of Ptolemy's increasing commitments of troops overseas. There were several thousand in Cyrene, of course. At least 13,000 had been committed to Cyprus and Caria, but Ptolemy likely recalled some portion of them for the campaign in Syria. Nearly all of these latter contingents would have been mercenary infantry. From these figures we may surmise that the maximum total size of the Ptolemaic army at this point was in the neighbourhood of 40,000 soldiers.

As for the army at Gaza, the large cavalry force is striking. The 4,000 cavalry were comparable to the number Alexander took with him to Asia, and just 1,000 fewer than Ptolemy's great-grandson commanded at Raphia a full century later. The ratio of infantry to cavalry is unusually low, less than five-to-one, which may be an indication of Ptolemy's rapid acquisition and immediate dispersion of wealth. That is, his access to wealth and power enabled him to raise more and more of his followers to the ranks of his cavalry, and by his largesse he attracted new followers. It seems likely that the cavalry would have included many of Ptolemy's Friends, Alexandrian citizens and perhaps some other Macedonians, mercenaries and even Egyptian nobles. Because Seleucus had taken refuge with Ptolemy, a small band of his followers, about fifty in all, might also have been at Gaza (Diod. 19.55.6). From examining the evidence, we may infer that the cavalry were the chief branch of Ptolemy's army, and Diodorus confirms as much, reporting that Ptolemy and Seleucus placed their greatest hopes in them. Indeed, the cavalry played the pivotal role in the engagement.

The infantry included, according to Diodorus, Macedonians, mercenaries and Egyptians. It seems likely he or his source elided some contingents, like Alexandrians and Cyreneans, into the Macedonian ranks, using Macedonian to signify professional troops armed in the Macedonian style with the sarissa. How many Macedonians might there have been? To this point it has been difficult to identify really large contingents of Macedonians in Ptolemaic service, and even after the desertions from Perdiccas' army, which included only a few real Macedonians itself, it seems difficult to imagine much beyond 4,000 in Ptolemy's army. Many of those would have been with Ptolemy's cavalry at Gaza. Perhaps Ptolemy conferred Macedonian status on some non-Macedonian deserters from the Royal Army, among whom auxiliaries trained in Macedonian arms might be most likely. Mercenaries – foreign troops serving for pay, the leftovers of Alexander's garrison and Cyrenean or other subjects serving for pay – almost certainly surpassed the number of Macedonians. The Macedonians would have fought as phalangites; whether the mercenaries did so is not clear. The kit of most Successor War mercenaries is not clear from any source. We know that they were, in many cases, heavy enough to fight in a phalanx, but that could include phalangites, multi-role peltasts and fairly traditional hoplites.

The Egyptian contingents merit further consideration, for two reasons. The traditional reading of Diodorus adds the Egyptian contingent to the 22,000 Greek soldiers in the Ptolemaic army, but the grammatical structure suggests the Egyptians were part of the 22,000.[4] The word I have translated as 'largest contingent' is *plēthos*, which could be construed generically as 'many' or, more specifically – and given the comparative quality relative to the Macedonians and mercenaries I prefer this – as 'the largest contingent' or possibly even 'the majority'. The smallest the Egyptian contingent could have been is 8,000, leaving 14,000 for roughly equal-sized contingents of Macedonians and mercenaries at about 7,000 apiece. This is only possible for the 'Macedonians' if by that word Diodorus, or his source, really meant the regular troops of Ptolemy's army. The Egyptian contingent could also be estimated as large as 11,000, half or the slight majority of the whole body. The only thing that can be said with confidence is that Diodorus' words require that the Egyptian contingent was the largest of the three components at Gaza, with a range between 8,000 and 11,000.

The Egyptian contingent was divided between porters, missile troops and line infantry. Diodorus describes the line infantry Egyptians with the word καθωπλισμένον, a term he repeatedly used for non-Macedonian troops armed in the Macedonian kit, as at 19.14, 19.27, 19.29 and 19.40, and this passage aside, never used for any other kit in Books 17–20. It cannot be said for certain, but we should recognize a distinct possibility that the Egyptian line infantry at Gaza were phalangites. After all, the missile troops were by definition also 'armed', so when Diodorus described them as *kathoplismenoi* he must have meant something more than just 'bearing weapons'. And of course, I have earlier argued that one of the sources of Ptolemy's troops in this early era were Egyptian graduates of Alexander's or his own Royal Page programme. Carrying pikes or not, these sorts of Egyptian troops, perhaps called 'Persians' but Egyptian nonetheless, were Ptolemy's best and likeliest source of Egyptian line infantry. It is at least conceivable that several thousand Hellenized and trained Egyptian soldiers were on hand for the campaign.

When they encountered the army of Demetrius, Antigonus' bold son, they faced a force not starkly stronger or weaker than their own. Demetrius had more cavalry, but not by much. There were 200 *epilektoi*, picked horsemen who formed Demetrius' guard; 800 Macedonian Companions, true Macedonian cavalry whom Antigonus received from Antipater when the latter returned to Macedonia; and 300 more heavy horse (Diod. 19.82). Then there were 100 Tarantines, shield-bearing light cavalry adept at skirmish tactics. There were 1,500 multi-national cavalry from Asia, who were either some of Antigonus' mercenaries from Asia Minor or absorbed soldiers from the ranks of the Epigonoi or other auxiliary contingents from late in Alexander's reign. And there were 1,500 mercenary cavalry. Demetrius' army had an even smaller ratio of infantry to cavalry, only a little more than three-to-one.

The accounts of Diodorus about Demetrius' army leave some doubts about his infantry force. There are two accounts of Demetrius' army, and between the two versions several numbers go up and others go down. Either way, the two accounts suggest the infantry in Demetrius' army were less numerous than in Ptolemy's, numbering 13,000–14,000. Some 2,000 Macedonians formed the heart of the phalanx, supplemented by between 500 and 1,000 Lycian and Pamphylian veterans, auxiliaries from Alexander's day. For the Gaza narrative there are 1,000 of the former and 8,000 mercenaries, but when the campaign began (Diod.19.69.1) there were 500 of the former and 10,000 of the latter. Perhaps a combination of small reinforcements, wastage and garrisons explains the discrepancy. We cannot know with certainty whether the Anatolians and the mercenaries were armed in the Macedonian manner or in panoply more like hoplites, but the latter is more likely. Forty-three Indian elephants and something like 2,000 light infantry screened the force. The 2,000 light infantry at Gaza represented a significant accession from the start of the campaign, when Diodorus identified just 400 Persian archers and slingers. Perhaps the easiest answer here is that some of the 10,000 mercenaries were best suited for skirmishing warfare rather than taking a stand in the line.

When the two armies arrived outside Gaza, a strange deployment unfolded prior to the battle. Diodorus tells us that both Ptolemy and Demetrius planned to place their best cavalry – their decisive arm – on their left wings (Diod. 19.83). Traditionally, both should have placed their cavalry on the right. It is possible that both were attempting to outwit the other, bringing strength against strength unexpectedly. Ptolemy at least wished to do so, for when he learned how Demetrius had deployed he rapidly shifted his cavalry contingents over to the right wing. This is a tremendous movement to undertake on the battlefield. Diodorus commented that they made this movement rapidly; the manoeuvre carried great risk since they were near contact with the enemy. Demetrius was drawn up in front of Old Gaza, and seems to have waited for the Ptolemaic force to reposition and lead the attack. Had he been more aggressive during the Ptolemaic redeployment, he may well have won the battle. Demetrius' battle plan was designed for a counter-punch, so he waited. He had refused his right flank, and planned to use the more open terrain on his left for cavalry manoeuvres. Squadrons of lighter cavalry screened in advance and off the left flank of his guard cavalry, while more than 2,000 further cavalry filled the space toward the phalanx. In essence, Demetrius committed several squadrons of cavalry to preventing a flanking manoeuvre against his left, so that his best cavalry could win a head-on engagement pivoting off his infantry or elephants closer to the centre.

Ptolemy saw Demetrius' elephants as an essential part of the battle plan. He devised a stratagem against them: some of the Egyptian porters with the army carried curious spiked contraptions, described as iron stakes linked with chains (Diod. 19.83.2); perhaps we are to imagine the iron stakes planted in boards chained together, or the iron spikes chained together like flails, or even a large fence comparable to modern barbed wire. They had prepared many of these anti-elephant devices, and Ptolemy and Seleucus deployed them to the front of their 3,000 cavalry. This would keep the elephants (and quite possibly the cavalry as well) from launching a direct attack, permitting Ptolemy's mounted force to manoeuvre onto the outside flank or charge into an exposed enemy flank if they attacked toward the centre.

When Ptolemy's army advanced, the combat began on the extreme eastern flank of the battlefield. The fight on the Ptolemaic right and Antigonid left was stalled while the smaller forces fought further out; perhaps the elephant deterrent had its intended effect. Diodorus (19.84.1) records the failed elephant charge after the main cavalry melee, but this may be an artefact of the narrative. In the midst of the skirmishing, Ptolemy and Seleucus were able to take their best cavalry around their far right wing, and charged into the skirmishing melee with fresh cavalry in good order and depth (19.83.3). This must have taken some time and considerable distraction amid the fighting if they were able to lead their best troops around and redeploy them for the key charge. The cavalry fight built from there and involved many conspicuous acts of valour as lances broke and the men resorted to swords. The charge of Ptolemy and Seleucus pushed past the extreme wing into combat with Demetrius' best troops. That deadly struggle continued until the elephant attack failed and the infantry phalanx began to flee. Demetrius was unable to rally his troops or to hold Gaza, and was forced to flee to distant Azotus before he could contact Ptolemy admitting defeat and requesting permission to bury his dead.

The ancient sources offer some different perspectives on the outcome of the fight. Diodorus (19.85.3) reports 500 killed, mainly from the leading cavalry units in Demetrius' army, while Plutarch (*Dem* 5.3) gives 5,000 killed. Both agree that Ptolemy captured 8,000 of Demetrius' soldiers. We should probably follow Diodorus on the casualty figures. This also means Demetrius may have been able to gather some 8,000 men to his camp within a day or two of the battle. This force was probably smaller, since Andronicus, who commanded the left wing at the battle, fled separately to Tyre and may have had several thousand men with him. In the aftermath of the victory, Ptolemy returned Demetrius' captured baggage and the court figures among the captives, all without ransom, as a token of goodwill and performative declaration of his sense that he and Seleucus were waging a just war against the Antigonids.

Following his grand victory, Ptolemy saw an opportunity to reward the excellent work of Seleucus in his service, as well as continue his indirect strategy against Antigonus. He gave Seleucus a force of infantry and cavalry, a thousand or so in all, to regain his satrapy (App. *Syr*. 54; Diod. 19.90.1). Seleucus' small army returned to Babylonia, and he successfully raised additional aid and gathered many loyalists to his side. Seleucus' campaign was so successful that he became far more than just a thorn in the side of Antigonus. He eventually established the largest of the Successor kingdoms and his descendants became the chief antagonists of Ptolemy's progeny. Out of their strong working relationship and shared victory at Gaza came, in time, the many and violent Syrian Wars. But in the short term, Ptolemy's strategy succeeded: when Antigonus lost Mesopotamia, he was forced to negotiate peace in the Third Successor War according to many of Ptolemy's terms.

In the aftermath of the victory at Gaza, Ptolemy campaigned throughout lower Syria and Phoenicia. He sent a column of his army, led by Killes the Macedonian, to pursue Demetrius and his shrunken force. Demetrius outmanoeuvred Killes; he captured Killes and the camp in a dawn raid (Diod. 19.93.1–2, Plut. *Dem.* 6.2–5, Paus. 1.6.5). Diodorus claims he captured the entire army, but unlike comparable moments there is no mention of what he did with the captured soldiers. Plutarch mentions only Killes and the camp, suggesting most of the Ptolemaic soldiers fled successfully. Pausanias says Demetrius managed only to kill a few Egyptians. Demetrius graciously returned Killes and the other notables he captured in the camp to Ptolemy (Diod. 19.93.2), just as Ptolemy had done for Demetrius after the Battle of Gaza.

Ptolemy and the rest of the army campaigned throughout Phoenicia, where some cities capitulated eagerly and others were taken by storm. At heavily garrisoned Tyre he brought the whole garrison over to his side, a windfall of several thousand more soldiers. They even included Andronikos, who was handed over by his turncoat soldiers and spewed vitriol at Ptolemy (Diod. 19.86.2), but Ptolemy handled him with grace and he became one of the leading friends at Ptolemy's court. This campaign is the likeliest time for Ptolemy to have taken, according to the *Letter of Aristeas*, 30,000 Jewish captives and soldiers back to Egypt, where some became slaves, while others became military settlers. The stark disparity between the outcomes for some of the Jews during this campaign probably represents the divisions within Phoenicia generally; some probably joined Ptolemy willingly, and others were conquered in the fighting. When Ptolemy withdrew from Syria in the spring of 311 BC, his allies probably joined him in the withdrawal.

As for the 8,000 prisoners from the battle, Ptolemy dispatched them to Egypt, where he divided them among the kingdom's provinces.[5] If later Ptolemaic practice can give any indication of what awaited them there, they were probably given plots of land with prisoner rather than soldier status, and then eventually rehabilitated into military settler status, with all its benefits. Here again we see early evidence for settlement activity under Ptolemy I. Whether all of these became military settlers is impossible to know, of course; but it is interesting that, in an age when many of the Successors simply enrolled captured troops into their own army and added them to the payroll, Ptolemy was limiting the expenses of his standing army and building military institutions for the long term.

The spring of 311 BC is an interesting time. Ptolemy won at Gaza and conquered much of lower Syria and Phoenicia, at least as far as Tyre. But when Antigonus and his full field army marched across the Taurus and into Syria, Ptolemy withdrew, burning several cities and carrying back as much plunder as possible to Egypt. Antigonus waited in Syria in the spring, while Demetrius launched forays against the Nabataeans east of Sinai (a prelude to invading Egypt?) and into Mesopotamia, neither of which achieved a signal success. Demetrius' campaign in the East captured an abandoned Babylon but only one of its citadels, and faltered at that point without dealing any significant blow to Seleucus, whose successes in the East continued mounting. At that point, Antigonus chose to negotiate an end to the war. Diodorus, who relied on Antigonus' friend Hieronymus as his chief source, says almost nothing about the treaty. It is known better from Antigonus' account of the negotiations in a letter that was inscribed at Skepsis in the Troad, near the Hellespont (*RC* 1, *OGIS* 6, Bagnall 6). The letter makes it clear that all the major Successor parties agreed to the idea of Greek freedom, that the agreement isolated Polyperchon – against whom Antigonus' nephew Polemaios was campaigning at the time – and that Antigonus made numerous concessions to Ptolemy. He may have recognized Ptolemy's conquests on Cyprus, and perhaps some of his lieutenants' actions in southern Anatolia. We may at least be confident that Ptolemy felt emboldened to launch further campaigns in the Eastern Mediterranean after the treaty.

Ptolemy into the Aegean

After the Successors made peace, Antigonus focused his efforts on a war against Seleucus in Mesopotamia. In the midst of this effort, Antigonus' nephew Polemaios, who was carrying on the war against Polyperchon in Greece, revolted, taking with him both the Hellespont region and many of the cities he controlled in south-western Anatolia. Ptolemy saw an opportunity in this division, and accused Antigonus of breaking the peace treaty by garrisoning Greek cities. Using this as a pretext for war, he dispatched an army under a commander named Leonides, who attacked Antigonid possessions in Rough Cilicia (Diod. 20.19.3–5). The cities of

Rough Cilicia were all fairly small and well-defended, and their value lay almost entirely in their significance for naval action across the coast of southern Anatolia. Some cities in the region belonged to Lysimachus and Cassander, and others assuredly belonged to Ptolemy, and were probably already garrisoned by Ptolemaic soldiers. But several cities belonged to the Antigonids, and Leonides captured most or all of these.

Leonides' campaign would have severely hampered Antigonid efforts to send reinforcements by sea between east and west, and thus provoked a heavy counter-offensive from Demetrius. Demetrius' attack was successful, and in Diodorus a passage suggests he may have not only sought to recover the cities he lost, but also to take the cities that had belonged to Ptolemy at the start of the campaign (Diod. 20.27.1). The raids of Leonides stoked the campaign of Demetrius, and it in turn provoked a large campaign that Ptolemy led personally.

Ptolemy's campaign into Asia Minor in 309 BC had the potential to be a major move in the Successor conflict. He probably launched the campaign from Cyprus. With the loss of cities in Cilicia, he seems to have struck further west, around Lycia. In eastern Lycia he captured Phaselis, a city with several natural harbours surrounded by practically impassable mountains. Diodorus' narrative of the campaign is brief (20.27.1–2), but mentions that Ptolemaic forces captured Xanthos in central Lycia, then Kaunos on the border of Karia and Lycia, before moving on the island of Kos, just off the coast of Asia Minor near Halikarnassos. These particular cities may have been the target of the campaign, or may have simply represented the most significant military actions or population centres seized.

The campaign yielded even more fruit through diplomacy, when Ptolemy arranged a deal with Polemaios (Diod. 20.27.3). Polemaios controlled numerous cities in Asia Minor, and it seems that when he joined Ptolemy the cities became Ptolemaic allies. Diodorus wrote nothing on this development, but an inscription from Iasos offers some insight into what happened (*I.Iasos* 83). Under Polemaios there had been three different mercenary detachments installed at Iasos or in its territory. Under the deal with Ptolemy he would guarantee the Iasians freedom and autonomy, and keep them ungarrisoned. Ptolemy made sure the mercenaries were given pay and then permitted to leave the city to whatever destination they wished or to reside in the cities as aliens.[6] Ptolemy guaranteed liberties to Polemaios' former cities and showed clemency (and probably offered future employment) to Polemaios' garrison troops. It is conceivable that Kos and Myndos, where Ptolemy was active at the start of 308 BC, fell into Ptolemaic hands through the deal with Polemaios. Poor Polemaios ended up poisoned by Ptolemy early in 308 BC, but many of his soldiers ended up in the Ptolemaic army. Polemaios had commanded more than 8,300 foot and 600 horse in the region of Caria a few years earlier (Diod. 19.68.5), so it is conceivable Ptolemy added thousands of good troops to his armies in 309–308 BC. Furthermore, the allied cities of southern Ionia, Caria and Lycia provided thousands more soldiers for the Ptolemaic army in years to come.

Ptolemy wintered at Kos and Myndos, and in springtime sailed west across the Aegean toward Greece. He liberated Andros, an island that looks toward Attica to the west. Andros became a significant Ptolemaic military base in time, so one must wonder whether Andros' liberation was more like its capture. From Andros he hopped to the Peloponnese and took Sicyon and Corinth, cities of great wealth and antiquity. Ptolemy liberated these cities and created an alliance with some of the Peloponnesians (Diod. 37.1–2). With his army and navy at the isthmus and two significant mainland cities in his alliance, Ptolemy was poised to become a major player in Greek affairs at a time when Antigonus was campaigning in Mesopotamia. But within a couple of months Ptolemy withdrew from Greece, frustrated, Diodorus claims, by the state of affairs in Greece and particularly by the lackadaisical Peloponnesian participation in their alliance. The Successors had committed themselves to Greek liberation, and many Greeks shrewdly became fickle allies. Ptolemy did not so much hold Corinth and the isthmus as find himself camped beside it and reliant on the Greeks for provisions. Here Ptolemy's famed munificence seems to have failed. Perhaps he balked at the high risk, high reward opportunity he faced in the Greek campaign, for he sailed away rather than push for more solid gains.

The Fourth Successor War and the Fall of Cyprus

The aborted Greek campaign looms ever more important when, in the next three years' campaign seasons, all Ptolemy had built so carefully nearly feel to pieces. Where Ptolemy pulled back after testing the waters in Greece, Demetrius sailed boldly to Athens the next spring, in 307 BC, and liberated that city and several others. He restored the democracy (there is no mention that Ptolemy intervened in the domestic affairs of Sicyon or Corinth, as he had at Cyrene), and that may have helped make the Athenians more engaged allies. They built or refurbished numerous warships to augment Demetrius' fleet, and ventured forth with him later that same year for a campaign into the eastern Aegean. Demetrius was aiming at Cyprus, but targeted the Ptolemaic conquests across the southern Anatolian littoral to prepare for the invasion to come. Many of Ptolemy's gains from 309 BC were thus of a fleeting nature.

Demetrius crossed from Cilicia to Cyprus in 306 BC with formidable naval and land forces. His army comprised 15,000 infantry and 400 cavalry, and his navy included 110 triremes and quadriremes plus fifty-three polyremes: massive, slower-moving ships with five, six and seven banks of rowers, plus large detachments of marines and complements of deck artillery (Diod. 20.47.1). The Ptolemaic forces on Cyprus were under the command of Menelaus, Ptolemy's brother, and with reinforcements had grown to more than 15,000 soldiers and some sixty ships, mainly triremes.[7] Menelaus was unable to contest Demetrius' landing, and opted to gather his garrisons and stick near Salamis while Ptolemy raised forces to bring against Cyprus. Demetrius landed near Karpasia in the north-east of Cyprus, on a peninsula that projects north-east toward Cilicia and Syria. Salamis was also on the eastern part of the island, but at the middle point of the eastern face. The two camps were probably about 30 miles apart.

The first major engagement of the Cyprus campaign was a pitched battle where Menelaus met Demetrius in the field about 4½ miles from Salamis. Diodorus says little on the engagement; only that Menelaus' army was overwhelmed and pursued all the way to the gates of Salamis (Diod. 20.47.3). Demetrius' forces killed 1,000 and took 3,000 prisoners. Demetrius tried, as had been conventional practice in the Successor Wars, to incorporate the captured mercenaries into his own units and expand his army, but the men escaped back to the Ptolemaic lines because their 'baggage' was back in Egypt (Diod. 20.47.4). This detail, discussed elsewhere in more depth, is likely to provide some evidence that Ptolemy was already establishing settler grants and other methods to distribute property to his soldiers and invest them in his kingdom. His Egypt was resource-rich and Greek-poor; naturally, Ptolemy was already seeking to use the former quality to alleviate the latter. Demetrius eventually gave up on adding them to his own forces and sent the remainder to his father in Syria.

The main engagement of the war followed some time later, after Demetrius laid siege to Salamis with impressive new artillery weapons (he would, after all, bear the cognomen 'Poliorketes', the Besieger) and was frustrated by the dogged persistence of Menelaus and his men. Ptolemy arrived in Cypriot waters with a large force on land and sea. His fleet had 140–150 warships, all reportedly fours and fives, and transport ships bringing 10,000 additional soldiers. He prepared for a naval battle against Demetrius, whose fleet had 163 ships at the start of the campaign, but Plutarch gives Demetrius 180 and Diodorus 108, often taken as a mistake in transmission from 180.

The fleets in the naval Battle of Salamis were not terribly dissimilar in number or quality, but there was one significant difference at play. Ptolemy's fleet was a little smaller, and of more uniform size. Demetrius' fleet included numerous triremes, but also at least seventeen sixes and sevens, all larger than any of Ptolemy's ships. Prior to the battle, Ptolemy had his transport ships and his soldiers in array behind his battle fleet. Demetrius, on the other hand, embarked most of his infantry and siege artillery aboard his ships, adding to their marine detachments and artillery capacity. That Ptolemy kept his infantry on transports, neither adding them to his marine detachments nor landing them before the engagement, was a terrible mistake.

In the engagement, each commander led from his left wing, as each had intended at Gaza. Each wing and centre in Demetrius' fleet probably had near sixty ships (there were fifty-seven ships in the left wing, where he fought, including twenty-seven of his fifty-three polyremes), confronting about fifty of Ptolemy's ships. Ptolemy had the largest ships and his best troops as marines in his left wing (Diod. 20.52.3), facing about sixty Antigonid ships, including 26 polyremes, all fives or larger. Nonetheless, Ptolemy defeated Demetrius' right wing quickly and captured or sank numerous ships (Diod. 20.52.3). He committed a second mistake at this time, it seems, securing the captured ships before turning his fleet toward the centre. Demetrius had his ship boarded, but fought off his attackers and routed the Ptolemaic right wing and began subduing the Ptolemaic centre. By the time Ptolemy had finished capturing much of the Antigonid right, his own right had been defeated and his centre was beginning to retreat. Admitting defeat, he rounded the cape and sailed west to Kition. According to Diodorus, more than half his transports and some 8,000 of his soldiers were captured, along with forty warships, and eighty more of Ptolemy's warships were crippled and towed back to Salamis (Diod. 20.52.6).

Demetrius' conquest of Salamis was a devastating defeat for the Ptolemaic army and navy. Between the garrison of Salamis and the troops captured from Ptolemy's fleet, at least 12,800 and possibly more than 20,000 Ptolemaic soldiers ended up as captives of Demetrius.[8] Thousands of sailors and hundreds of marines are likely to have perished too. Plutarch's description of the naval Battle of Salamis suggests an even more terrible outcome: Ptolemy was defeated at the first onset, escaped with only eight ships, seventy of his ships were captured and the other eighty crippled, and his entire transport fleet was captured with all the soldiers (*Dem.* 16.2–3). Diodorus' narrative is more detailed and, drawn from Hieronymus, likely to be more reliable. We should reject Plutarch's all-encompassing victory and opt for a careful reading of what we find in Diodorus, remembering that he, too, was writing with a pro-Antigonid slant. It seems likely that Ptolemy escaped with something like forty of his own ships and may have towed away some of Demetrius' ships while escorting dozens of his transports back to Kition. But the defeat was still devastating. Our earlier calculation suggested a Ptolemaic army in the range of 40,000 men prior to the Battle of Gaza. By the time of the Battle of Salamis, with troops added from the prisoners at Gaza, others from Ptolemy's operations in Syria and some from his operations in Anatolia and the Aegean, perhaps Ptolemy could have mobilized more than 60,000 soldiers and sailors. He lost at least one-third, and perhaps closer to half, of his military manpower in the defeat. Ptolemy and his army were on the precipice of total defeat.

'Extreme Peril': The Antigonid Invasion of Egypt

Demetrius had been Ptolemy's chief antagonist for eight years, but in late 306 BC King Antigonus himself took to the field for a grand campaign against his strongest adversary. Antigonus and Demetrius were both crowned after the victory at Salamis. The Antigonid campaign against Egypt was the largest mobilization of manpower and resources by any of the Successor powers in the entire Hellenistic age. Antigonus' field army had 88,000 soldiers, one of the largest in all antiquity. Demetrius commanded the navy and its 150 warships and 100 transports, with tens of thousands of sailors and marines. Antigonus spared no expense for this kingly campaign, and that is what saved Ptolemy.

Antigonus embarked on the campaign in the autumn of 306. On about 22 October he was at Gaza, and gave the order to march to Kasios and for the fleet to move alongside. After some difficulties at sea and on land (including the loss of three warships and more transports), he established his camp at Kasios, 6 miles from Pelousion. He had to secure supply lines there for 88,000 men, whatever camp followers were present and the eighty-three war elephants he brought with his army. The supply lines for such a massive force would be critical, whether he pushed up the Pelousiac branch of the Nile or across and into the Delta region. His strategy clearly was to use Demetrius' fleet to turn the position at Pelusium, allowing him to avoid the same difficult logistical trek up the Pelousiac branch that ended things for Perdiccas.

Antigonus pushed his camp up to the edge of the Nile, not far from Ptolemy's fortifications at Pelusium, where much of his army was encamped (Paus. 1.6.6), and that is when Ptolemy's strategy became evident. Egypt possessed natural defences and Ptolemy possessed great wealth. He had to suspect that Antigonus' men were in a precarious supply situation with such a large force and difficulty in sailing. Antigonus ordered the men to carry their own rations for ten days, and brought along a camel train with enough grain (130,000 *medimnoi*, or over 7 million litres) to feed his army and navy for at least forty more days, or his army alone for more than sixty (Diod. 20.73.3). The difficult passage along the coast probably meant that the camel train was straggling into camp throughout the days when Antigonus was building his camp and gathering his ships, which had been scattered back toward Raphia by storms. During this period Ptolemy sent heralds on small ships to announce his intent to grant liberal bounties to anyone who defected from Antigonus. The bounties were large: the two minas (200 drachmas) for regular soldiers represented nearly a year's bounty, and the talent (6,000 drachmas) for officers an incredible sum (Diod. 20.75.1). Ptolemy could count on the threat of defections unnerving Antigonus, especially as supply difficulties began to take hold. Eventually, a 'large number of men' deserted to him (Diod. 20.76.7), making good some of Ptolemy's losses on Cyprus.

The other aspect of Ptolemy's strategy was to use defensive positions and reserves on interior lines to thwart Demetrius' attempt to flank Pelusium. Demetrius made several attempts to land west of Pelusium, the most important at the Phatnitic branch, which emptied into the sea near modern Damietta. Ptolemy had taken a position somewhere toward the interior of the Delta, and could reach any of Demetrius' planned landing spots relatively quickly with his main field army. At the Phatnitic mouth he arrayed his army on the beach to resist any landing. In general the principle of interior lines would not have always granted him this advantage, but Demetrius and his fleet had become separated and delayed their landing by several crucial hours. Instead, Ptolemy counted on hardened defensive positions and his riverine fleet to deter and delay landings until Ptolemy could arrive. The riverine fleet comprised large numbers of small boats, many of them equipped with artillery (76.3). In that regard perhaps Ptolemy learned one of the lessons of the Battle of Salamis.

After several attempts to turn the Pelusium line all failed, Demetrius returned to Antigonus' camp between Pelusium and Kasios. Antigonid provisions were running dangerously low, and – in spite of Antigonus' threats of torture and use of artillery and other missiles against would-be defectors – mercenaries were switching sides in droves. Antigonus' camel train should have been sufficient to get the army into January 305 BC, by which point they should have been able to live off the land in Egypt. But in January whatever was left of the 90,000-strong army was still camped outside of Pelusium, against which their siege works had been ineffective. No description of the siege survives, but Diodorus references attempts to cross the river at Pelusium, which must have been combat actions, and Pausanias attests a siege (1.6.6). At that point, Antigonus held a council with his leading officers, and they strongly recommended abandoning the campaign. By February, Ptolemy was again the victor in a defensive campaign.

Ptolemy's victory against Antigonus' grand army, although it lacked any decisive engagement, probably provided the pretext for his acclamation as king. Ptolemy claimed Egypt once again as 'spear-won land', at least providing the basis for an acclamation by his troops. Appian's *Syrian Wars* (54) describe Ptolemy being acclaimed by 'his household troops' in response to the pronouncement of the Antigonid coronations. The words there are the *oikeios stratos,* a bit of an odd phrase that probably refers to his many court Friends and leading officers, his hypaspists or *somatophylakes,* and perhaps his company of Pages. Justin (15.2.11) agrees, but ascribes the acclamation to the full army. Plutarch's *Demetrius* gives Egyptians the agency for the acclamation (18.2), but Plutarch was clearly writing with the army in mind, because he added that they wished 'to show they were not dispirited by their recent defeat' on Cyprus. An acclamation in the aftermath of defeat would do little for Ptolemy's legitimacy, although there may have been a desire – in Egypt and abroad – to balance the Antigonid ascendancy. It may be possible he was acclaimed then, or at least was encouraged to do so. But the victory against the Antigonid kings and Ptolemy's claim of Egypt as spear-won land, less than a year after the defeat at Salamis, provide a stronger context for the acclamation.

The ancient source traditions otherwise suggest the date was no earlier than the Antigonid retreat from Egypt, and there is reason to believe Ptolemy was king by the start of the next major event in the Hellenistic world:

Demetrius' siege of Rhodes, which began in summer 305 BC. Diodorus (20.53.3–4) assigns Ptolemy's assumption of kingship chronologically after Antigonus but before Cassander, Seleucus and Lysimachus, and his narrative of the siege of Rhodes (20.100.3) identifies Lysimachus and Cassander as kings by the end of that siege in the spring of 304 BC. In the immediate aftermath of Ptolemy's defence of Egypt, he wrote to his allies, and in Diodorus there is no indication there that any of them were yet styled kings around February 305 BC (Diod. 20.76.7). And yet at 20.81.4 Diodorus describes Egypt as a kingdom in a statement that belongs to summer 305 BC, just prior to Demetrius' siege of Rhodes. This evidence is inconclusive, but it at least suggests that the Ptolemaic army's victory over the Antigonid invasion provided the basis for the army's acclamation of Ptolemy as king in the spring of that year.

It is also possible that Ptolemy's acclamation – or his official coronation – only took place the next year. It has been popular among historians and classicists to associate his coronation with the Ptolemaic army's role in the defence of Rhodes in 305/304 BC. That is because two (of four) important chronological sources date Ptolemy's coronation to that year. The Parian Marble dates Ptolemy's assumption of the crown to the year between July 305 and 304 BC, the same year as the siege of Rhodes, and the Astronomical Canon of Claudius Ptolemy gives his accession as between November 305 and 304 BC. Scholars have often preferred the bracketed date between these two sources: November 305 to July 304 BC.[9] However, a third chronological source, Eusebius' *Chronicon*, provides a date in 306/305 BC. The problem with a date after the successful defence of Rhodes is that according to Diodorus' narrative the siege did not end until after the start of the year 304/303 BC. Thus if Ptolemy claimed the crown because of the defence of Rhodes, the chronologies are all still wrong. Furthermore, the Lindos Chronicle identifies a Rhodian embassy to 'King Ptolemy' that was dispatched to request aid during the siege.[10] Whatever the date, from the end of 306 into 304 BC Ptolemy's military forces could do little wrong, and whether at Pelusium or Rhodes their performance and Ptolemy's leadership helped provide the basis for him to become king in Egypt.

Soter: Ptolemy and the Siege of Rhodes, 305–304 BC

Demetrius the Besieger's grand assault on Rhodes is famous in Hellenistic military history. The largest of his *helepoleis* ('city-takers') is the most famous element: a moving siege tower 100ft tall and bristling with siege engines (Diod. 20.91). The siege lasted a full year, and showcased the ways the money and violence unleashed by Alexander's conquests and early death had fuelled innovation in warfare. Amid it all, the Ptolemaic army played a crucial role in the defence of Rhodes. The key thing to bear in mind in a siege situation is that a fairly small number of well-trained, well-equipped soldiers could be disproportionately valuable. The expertise of Ptolemaic officers who served at Rhodes led to their appointment over many of the most important operations, especially after the start of the land phase of the siege in 304 BC.

When the siege began, after several months of preparations, there may already have been a small Ptolemaic detachment aiding the Rhodians. Polyaenus' description of the start of the siege (4.6.16) asserts that there were Ptolemaic allied forces adding to the defence of the city. Diodorus (20.84.1) says that the Rhodians sent messages to Ptolemy and the others to request aid prior to the start of the conflict, but makes no mention of these allies. Amid all the discussion of each side's technical preparations, it is possible this was simply left out. Any reinforcements would have needed to arrive prior to the onset of rough weather late in the autumn. After that point, the Rhodians had to face Demetrius and his army throughout the winter.

Diodorus' account mentions a total of three Ptolemaic reinforcements, to which may be added the early reinforcement mentioned by Polyaenus and a fifth that never materialized because Demetrius withdrew from the siege. The first in Diodorus' account arrived in the spring of 304 BC, 500 Ptolemaic soldiers and 150 Knossian Cretans, who were probably either allied troops or mercenaries in Ptolemaic employ (Diod. 20.88.9). The commander of this Ptolemaic force seems to have been Athenagoras of Miletos, whom Diodorus says Ptolemy had sent as commander for the mercenaries (20.94.3). It is also possible that, given his role as a commander of mercenary troops, he and the mercenaries were the Ptolemaic 'allies' referenced by Polyaenus as present at the start of the siege. Athenagoras ended up in command of the counter-mining operations, and captured one of Demetrius' leading Friends during the operations (Diod. 20.94.5).

Ptolemy's second reinforcement during the siege was primarily of materiel: among other items there were at least 300,000 artabas (about 10 million litres) of foodstuffs (Diod. 20.96.1). The fleet carrying these was pursued by Demetrius but came into the harbour safely. Did they bring soldiers as well? The relief fleets Ptolemy sent raise another question:

how did they sail to Rhodes without harbours between there and Egypt? The earlier reinforcement(s) may well have come from Sikyon, Andros or another Ptolemaic possession in the Aegean, but such a large convoy must have sailed from Egypt. It is often supposed that Ptolemy lost all his possessions in Asia Minor before or assuredly after his defeat on Cyprus.[11] But given the many harbour cities that dot the coastlines, and the difficulty of besieging them, it seems plausible that the Ptolemaic army managed to keep garrisons in several scattered cities. Perhaps the best evidence for a Ptolemaic reinforcement alongside the foodstuffs is the next piece of combat. Demetrius launched a heavy assault against the Rhodian walls with his siege engines, made breaches in two stretches of curtain wall and instigated 'desperate fighting' around the tower between the two fallen walls (Diod. 20.97.7). Amid this heavy fighting, the *strategos*, or general, over the defending troops was slain. His name was Ananias. Do we have in Ananias a Jewish Ptolemaic officer? The name is very rare in the Greek world before the Christian era, but common in the Jewish world, including in Ptolemaic military service.[12] It is virtually inescapable that we conclude this Ananias was Jewish; and how else should we imagine a Jewish soldier possessing such a high rank among the defenders of Rhodes, if not as commander of a Ptolemaic contingent? We should at least entertain the possibility that the general Ananias was a Ptolemaic officer sent to aid in the defence of Rhodes, and recognize as well the heights to which non-Greek soldiers could rise in Ptolemaic service even at an early date.

Not much later, the third Ptolemaic reinforcement arrived, bringing again 300,000 measures of food as well as 1,500 more soldiers, this time under a Macedonian officer, Antigonos (Diod. 20.98.1). Diodorus adds that these men were from Alexandria specifically (20.98.7), which probably means that they were part of Ptolemy's regular or even household troops, and not mercenaries. Shortly after their arrival, Demetrius sent some of his best troops on a daring night-time raid, during which they seized the theatre inside the city, on the acropolis in the south-western corner of Rhodes. The Rhodians sent the new Ptolemaic troops and their own picked contingent to drive the Antigonid forces from the city. The fighting was fierce, with many dead on both sides, and according to Diodorus (20.98.9), nearly the entire 1,500 elite Antigonid soldiers were slain or captured. After this success, Ptolemy planned to send 3,000 additional soldiers, but encouraged all parties to make a treaty and end the conflict (Diod. 20.99.2). With Ptolemy's support, the siege came to an end and Demetrius retreated. Ptolemy was hailed as a god by the Rhodians, and given the cognomen

Soter, 'Saviour'. In conclusion, at least 2,000 Ptolemaic soldiers served with distinction at the lengthy defence of Rhodes, and repeatedly played instrumental roles in saving the city from conquest. The fight at the theatre was also the third time some of the Ptolemy's best had gone head-to-head against some of the best Antigonid troops. In the cavalry fight at Gaza, on the Ptolemaic left at Salamis and at the theatre of Rhodes, the best of Ptolemy's soldiers outperformed those of Demetrius.

Following the fighting at Rhodes, there is little indication that Ptolemy took an aggressive stance against the Antigonids. He still held Sicyon with a garrison under the command of an 'illustrious general' named Philippos (Diod. 20.102.2). This general, so famous in the mind of Diodorus or his sources, is completely unknown to us apart from this narrative.[13] In 303 BC, Demetrius attacked Sicyon, and while laying siege to Philippos and the Ptolemaic garrison convinced them to surrender the city and depart with their arms back to Egypt. Until the winter of 302/301 BC, there is no indication of significant Ptolemaic military activity anywhere. Ptolemy's army was presumably still rebuilding after the devastating defeat on Cyprus.

In the midst of the campaigning that led to the Battle of Ipsos in 301 BC, Ptolemy led a winter campaign into Syria. Antigonus had taken his army across the Taurus, and the main forces of both sides of the Successor conflicts were concentrating in Asia Minor. Ptolemy's army was 'remarkable' (Diod. 20.113.1 – ἀξιόλογος), although what that should mean in this context is far from clear. Diodorus' word choice could speak to the quality of the troops more than their quantity. The army should at least have been on the order of magnitude of Seleucus' 'large' army (Diod. 20.113.4 – πολύς), which had 32,000 soldiers. Nonetheless when rumours came that Antigonus had defeated Cassander and Lysimachus, crossing the Taurus into Syria, Ptolemy garrisoned the cities of southern Syria and withdrew into Egypt. His strategy clearly emphasized stability and security rather than risk and reward. In this case, it cost him disastrously: the road was open north clear to the new Antigonid capital at Antigoneia, but Ptolemy stopped at the gates of Sidon. His hesitancy cost him the opportunity to fight at the Armageddon of the Successor era, and gave his subsequent conquest of middle (or Koile) Syria after Ipsos the look of a land grab rather than military conquest. For, after the other three allies had won their victory at Ipsos, and met to discuss the division of the spoils, Seleucus could at least claim he had been granted all of Syria.[14] When Ptolemy occupied middle Syria and Phoenicia (campaigning in the region for the fifth time), Seleucus declined to contest the matter with the man who had given him shelter and helped raise him to power, but his descendants were not so inclined. They always claimed Syria, as far south as Gaza, as theirs rightfully: a prize of war for the victors at Ipsos.

Conclusion: Planning for Posterity

From the dire straits of the years after the catastrophe at Salamis, Ptolemy I seems to have recovered his manpower and handed down to his son an army of formidable size and strength. The beginning of the shift was the windfall of deserters who came over to Ptolemy during Antigonus' miserable invasion of Egypt.[15] Ptolemy's best troops had never really suffered a defeat themselves, and Ptolemy could build around them – and through the attractions of wealth as settlers in Egypt – the core of a larger force. He reigned as sole king for twenty years, then shared in rule with his son for two years until his death. The last fifteen years of his sole rule are addressed in this conclusion, and while they were generally more peaceful than the years before, there were yet several significant campaigns.

The real key for the army Ptolemy would leave to his son, Ptolemy II, lay in replacing the mercenary army with a settler army of sufficient quality. The wealth of Egypt would always make it possible to levy mercenaries, but without a strong core force, Ptolemaic strength would always be contingent on the availability of mercenary soldiers, most of whom lived across the sea. Ptolemy must have rebuilt his army from 306–301 BC mainly through mercenary forces, which were expensive, fickle and market-dependent. After that time he surely sought to expand the activities in which he had already been engaging: enticing soldiers to settle in Egypt by giving them lands, Alexandrian citizenship or both. He may well have begun by hiring them as mercenaries. It may have been in this period that Ptolemy founded another *polis* in Egypt, Ptolemais in the Thebaid. It was the second Greek city in all Egypt, after Alexandria, and had similar institutions to Alexandria. Although it was a good bit smaller, by the first century BC it had grown to approximately the size of Memphis (Strabo 17.1.42). The settlers in Upper Egypt, or the Thebaid, seem to have come from all parts of the Greek world. At Elephantine, at least, three papyri attest a Greek community under Ptolemy I that included settlers from all across the Greek world. Among twenty-nine Greeks with identified origins we find a large population from the small city-state of Temnos in Aeolia, numerous Cyreneans (as we might expect), three Arkadians from the Peloponnese – among the most famed Greeks as mercenary adventurers – a Magnesian from south-east Thessaly, an Aeginatan from the Saronic Gulf, a Sidonian from Phoenicia, a Gelan from Sicily, a Maronitan from the north Aegean, a Cretan and five Koans. These texts also reveal several women, wives and mothers, confirming that some of Ptolemy's settlers were indeed choosing to leave their homes behind but take their families with them to establish new lives in Egypt.

Ptolemy returned to action in 295 BC. From Pausanias (1.6.8) it seems that Cyrene rebelled yet again around 300 BC, and Ptolemy dispatched his stepson Magas to command against the rebels, whom he conquered in the fifth year of the revolt. Magas then ruled Cyrenaica loyally so long as Ptolemy I lived. By 295 BC the Cyrenean revolt was over. At the same time, Cyprus, Tyre and Sidon all still belonged to Demetrius, and with them he also still had many of the Greeks as allies. Athens, however, had fallen under the tyrant Lachares' rule, while Demetrius and Seleucus had suffered a falling out of their own. Demetrius swept into Attica, hoping to seize Athens in another bold manoeuvre. He ended up encamped in the region, laying a desultory siege and launching raids against the Athenians. Amid this action, Ptolemy sent a fleet of 150 ships to break the siege (Plut. *Dem.* 33.5–7). They might have succeeded, but the remainder of Demetrius' fleet arrived and brought his forces to nearly 300 ships. The Ptolemaic fleet withdrew, and soon thereafter Athens and many other Greek cities came back under Demetrius' leadership.

While Demetrius was busy in Greece, and had concentrated his entire fleet in the waters near Attica, Ptolemy recognized the opportunity in the eastern Mediterranean. In late 295 or early 294 BC, Ptolemy's army invaded Cyprus. The whole island fell rapidly, except Salamis, which the Ptolemaic forces besieged for several months before it capitulated (Plut. *Dem.* 35.5). Salamis, significantly, had served as a royal residence for Demetrius for several years. Ptolemy's descendants maintained a firm grip on Cyprus, with a few lapses, for nearly 200 years. He may well have captured as many soldiers in this campaign as he lost a decade earlier, although Demetrius' military position probably dictated a smaller garrison on Cyprus than the sort of force Ptolemy had maintained in former times.

From Cyprus, Ptolemy could again project power into Asia Minor, and it is probable that his army launched additional campaigns into that region. It is conceivable that a handful of strongholds in Rough Cilicia or Lycia, perhaps even in Caria, maintained Ptolemaic garrisons and facilitated Ptolemaic fleet movement ever since Ptolemy's campaign in 309 BC. Most of the region was under the nominal control of Pleistarchos, brother of the recently deceased Cassander and ally of Lysimachus, but Demetrius had seized whole stretches of the coast and all of Cilicia. There was no clear power in the region, which presented an opportunity for Ptolemaic commanders.

A text from Aspendos in Pamphylia may belong to about 294 BC and provide some insight into Ptolemaic military forces operating in the region. In the text (*SEG* 17:639), the citizens of Aspendos granted honours to two important Ptolemaic officers and their soldiers. The officers, Leonides and Philokles, are surely the Leonides who campaigned for Ptolemy in the same region in 310 and 309 BC, and likely Philokles, the King of Sidon and naval commander over the Aegean on behalf of Ptolemy II in the 280s and 270s BC. There are numerous problems with dating the text, but the twenty years between the two officers' mentioning in other sources is foremost. The text does not identify Philokles as King of Sidon; it could be a different Philokles, or more likely the text could predate the Ptolemaic conquest of Sidon in 288/287 BC. Either way, it provides some insight into the makeup and activities of Ptolemaic forces in southern Asia Minor late in the reign of Ptolemy I.

Philokles and Leonides brought their troops to give succour to the Aspendians. The scenario may have involved conflict with Demetrius or another major actor, or it may have been a local conflict. The Aspendians declared the Ptolemaic expeditionary force to have shown themselves both useful and to be good men, granted Aspendian citizenship to all and offered them full citizenship (membership in one of the tribes of the citizens) for a price. The inscription describes the Ptolemaic force by nationality: Pamphylians, Lycians, Cretans, Greeks and Pisidians. Three of the five were local peoples. The Pamphylians, Lycians and Pisidians could have been new recruits, mercenaries raised to service in short notice for a local campaign. They could also have been parts of the garrison of Cyprus, which for most of Ptolemaic history organized units around their ethnic identity and drew heavily from the Anatolian coastline to the north. The Greeks and Cretans were presumably either long-serving mercenaries or even members of the Ptolemaic settler population in Egypt. The troops' organization by nationality could reflect different units and officers, and perhaps even different panoplies. Because they are listed first, the Pamphylians and Lycians may have been the largest contingents. It is also worth noting that Pamphylians and Lycians played enormously important roles in the Ptolemaic aristocracy during the third century BC. Even if the troops at Aspendos with Philokles and Leonides were new mercenaries, they or their countrymen quickly established themselves in Egypt as significant soldiers and officers.

The next major Ptolemaic campaign was not until the winter of 288/287 BC. Demetrius was gathering forces across Greece for a grand campaign into Asia, and all his enemies struck prior to spring to prevent him from concentrating his armies or fleets. Demetrius would field 110,000 soldiers and 500 ships for the campaign, but was marshalling them at five different embarkation points. Ptolemy's navy targeted Demetrius' concentration points in mainland Greece – Athens, Chalcis and Corinth – and Demetrius rushed north to Macedonia to contend with Lysimachus and Pyrrhus. Ptolemaic forces probably faced Antigonus II in the Greek world, or several of Demetrius' lieutenants. The Ptolemaic fleet had included 150 ships in 295 BC; the evidence is unclear for 288/287 BC, but the fleet's freedom of operation suggests a larger and stronger force. The outcome of the Ptolemaic campaign is not detailed in any surviving source, but the armies of Demetrius were broken up and his great enterprise fell to pieces. The Ptolemaic army expanded its foothold in the region. At the very least, the fleet established a large operating base at Andros, not far from either Attica or Delos. At the same time as the Ptolemaic action in Greece, another Ptolemaic force attacked in Phoenicia and conquered Tyre and Sidon.[16] With those key cities finally secured, Ptolemy I controlled a coherent Phoenicia and southern Syria, the entirety of Cyprus, scattered holdings in Asia Minor, Cyrenaica and even a small foothold in Greece.

In 287 and into 286 BC, when the Athenians revolted against Demetrius, an Athenian officer who held one of the command positions at Andros leading Ptolemaic troops to provide assistance. Until an inscription honouring the role of Kallias, son of Thymochares of Sphettos, was discovered at Athens, the only sources on the Athenian revolt made no mention of a Ptolemaic role in the fighting (*SEG* 28.60). Kallias observed that the Athenian revolt was threatened by the impending arrival of Demetrius and his army from the Peloponnese, and picked out 1,000 soldiers from the mercenaries stationed on Andros to take to Attica. If 1,000 could be selected out from the garrison on Andros, it must have been a large garrison. Kallias and his troops helped provide security while gathering the harvest, fought against Demetrius' troops stationed in Piraeus, launched sallies against Demetrius' camp during the siege and provided additional security while Ptolemy's diplomat, the famous Sostratos of Knidos, architect of the Pharos lighthouse, negotiated a peace. Thus, late in Ptolemy's reign his soldiers were once again committed to sharp fighting with Demetrius' troops.

The Athenians honoured another Ptolemaic commander after their revolt, Zenon (*SIG*³ 367). Zenon commanded a squadron of *aphraktoi* in Ptolemaic service. The aphracts were undecked ships, triremes and lighter vessels designed for speed rather than the artillery pieces and marine contingents standard on the polyremes of the day. Zenon's squadron was perfectly suited to patrol and interdiction missions in the waters of Attica, and he was honoured for his good works and fine comportment in guarding sea lanes and assuring the safe delivery of grain to Athens. He was also honoured at Ios about the same time in an inscription (*OGIS* 773) that reveals the rapid expansion of Ptolemaic power in the Aegean. The Ptolemaic army and navy had much to gain through safe shipping in the Aegean, since Egyptian grain made up so much of the trade. The Ptolemaic role in the Aegean only continued to expand in the 280s and 270s BC, and it became one of the main theatres of operations for the Ptolemaic army under the great king Philadelphus.

Chapter 4

Origins of Soldiers in the Ptolemaic Army

The Ptolemaic kings faced a challenging environment in staffing a Greco-Macedonian army in Egypt. They were across the sea from the Macedonian homeland, of course; neither were there substantial veteran settlements in Egypt from the Alexander era, nor large concentrations of Greek or Hellenizing populations, nor any identifiable single large influx of population. The Antigonid dynasty had access to a large Macedonian population once it settled in Macedonia, and the Seleucid dynasty controlled many veteran settlements in Asia. Despite these obstacles, the Greek population of Egypt grew large enough for Ptolemy IV to put more than 50,000 non-Egyptian troops in the field at the Battle of Raphia. The population of Alexandria in time made it, for a while, the largest city in the Mediterranean. Where did all these immigrants come from? How did they enter Ptolemaic service? This chapter seeks to establish some picture of how the Ptolemaic army came to be staffed, especially in the third century BC, and thus present some picture of the role of Greeks, Macedonians, Egyptians and Hellenizing non-Greeks in the Ptolemaic army. It also offers a nod toward the relationship between Ptolemaic empire and diplomacy and the personnel of the Ptolemaic army. The documentary tradition of the Ptolemaic bureaucracy is helpful in this regard. The papyrus *P.Hamb.* 2.168 records a law, passed no later than the early part of Ptolemy II's reign, that required soldiers identify themselves in all business by their name, their ethnic identifier (such as Macedonian, Athenian or Judean), their unit in the army and their military rank. Similarly, Alexandrians serving in the army provided their father's name and their Alexandrian demotic before giving their military unit and rank. While only a small fraction of Ptolemaic soldiers are recorded in the papyrological tradition, we actually know quite a lot about that minority. The following discussion addresses a range of categories of evidence in several sections: Alexandrians, Greek military settlers (and especially cavalry), soldiers in the Ptolemies' possessions outside Egypt, Judeans in the Ptolemaic army and the various and important roles of Egyptians, Libyans and Ethiopians.

Alexandria

Alexandria is a perilously tough nut to crack. Precious little is known, especially from the Ptolemaic era, about the size and obligations of its citizen body. The extent to which military service was normal among the Alexandrian citizens is not clear, but the proportion was probably far higher in the time of Ptolemy son of Lagos and steadily declined during the remainder of the dynasty. That it was a grand city in the early third century BC is clear enough in the works produced in Philadelphus' day, but whether such a city had 20,000 male citizens or 80,000 cannot be determined with any real confidence given the sources available today. Furthermore, it is very clear that a significant portion of the population was Egyptian, and so for at least the early Ptolemaic period had little or no military obligation. Thus, even if the city did become the first Mediterranean metropolis, the actual size of its citizenry could be far smaller. What follows is my best surmise, aimed more at showing what was not than asserting what was.

Ancient Tallies

By the close of the Ptolemaic era, Diodorus (17.52.5–6) could claim census returns pointed to 300,000 free individuals at Alexandria, and that it was the largest and finest city in the known world. The inclusion of slaves, and the question of whether Diodorus' figure included children, could push the population to 500,000 or more. Diodorus' figure has helped establish the baseline for most figures offered by modern scholars, at least for the Alexandrian population at the end of the Ptolemaic dynasty: about 500,000 in all.[1] The roundness of the figure strongly suggests simplification, probably exaggeration and possibly fabrication. A papyrus describing Alexandria at the time of Caligula (AD 37) but written closer to AD 200 identifies a body of 180,000, variously taken to refer to male citizens, adult citizens, Jewish citizens or all citizens of Alexandria.[2] The papyrus, being very fragmentary and of questionable historical value, is even less reliable than Diodorus. It has nonetheless been useful evidence for those who suggest that Alexandria and its environs were home to as many as a million people in the days of Cleopatra and Caesar Augustus.[3]

I am not sure either of these figures are much use. Apart from the difficulty in interpreting their meaning or authenticity – do they identify the number of adult male citizens of a particular ethnic group, all free inhabitants or something in between? – they relate to a time when the city had taken on a very different character, as had the military institutions of Egypt. Just to demonstrate the futility of these figures: if there were over 100,000 adult male citizens at Alexandria during Ptolemaic rule, the Ptolemies should never have had any trouble staffing their army, replacing casualties or fighting wars on multiple fronts. The story of Ptolemaic Egypt would have been one of mobilizing manpower aggressively and having the capacity to compete directly with the Roman Republic in the second century BC. This was far from the case, and assuredly the actual citizen population was significantly smaller.

Demographic Models

As an alternative, we might consider the comparative demographic approach used by Scheidel (2004: pp.1–31). Developing models from early modern capital cities (Edo – now Tokyo – and London) led Scheidel to suggest that the population of Alexandria probably topped out at no more than 300,000 in total, probably around 200 BC, and fluctuated at or below that figure until the very end of the Ptolemaic era.[4] Manning's recent overview of the Ptolemaic dynasty embraced similar figures for the population of Alexandria by the end of Philadelphus' reign just after 250 BC: upwards of 200,000.[5] However, the population of Alexandria and the Alexandrian citizens are different things, especially when determining military roles. Women, children, old men and slaves would have had no military obligation. The large Egyptian population in the city, to the extent they were mobilized for military service at all, certainly did so at a lower rate, or primarily in the navy. If in the Ptolemaic era there were ever 300,000 free residents of the city, only a minority were Alexandrians and other Greco-Macedonian or Hellenized male inhabitants eligible to serve in the ranks of the Ptolemaic army. The size of this minority surely shifted over time, but should easily have been less than 10 per cent of the total, for a rough maximum figure around 30,000.

The Royal Pages

Before turning to documentary evidence, there is one last piece of evidence that could help develop a better estimate of the actual Alexandrian citizen population, rather than the resident population. In about 272 BC, Ptolemy II Philadelphus held a grand procession through Alexandria. In that procession, 1,600 *paides* (boys) marched, clad in white tunics and wearing crowns of ivy and pine (Ath. 5.30). These were most likely the Pages of the Ptolemaic court at Alexandria. The Ptolemaic Pages were very likely drawn from Alexandrian citizens and foreign elites resident at Alexandria (whose sons could end up with Alexandrian citizenship). If these boys represented the Pages, then we might take a shot at estimating the adult citizen body. The first question, however, is the number of age classes represented in the 1,600. There is no clear-cut answer to this. They could represent the boys nearing adulthood, just two age classes or the four that came before. The narrative of the procession records four divisions of the boys, based on the items they carried, so perhaps there were four age classes, of about 400 on average. Another group of boys followed them, who were not clad in white tunics and crowned as the Pages were, and they numbered 370, which is on the same order of magnitude as 400; perhaps they were the next age class to join the Pages. According to male model life tables popular with historical studies of ancient Mediterranean populations, the five age classes in the later teens should represent about 22.2 per cent of the military age male population (ages 20–50) and 9.6 per cent of the male population as a whole.[6] So if the 1,970 Pages and boys represented five age classes of young Alexandrians, the military age male population might have been between 8,000 and 9,000, and the male citizen population, old and young, around 20,000. Because some of the Pages were probably not from the citizenry but were the sons of the kings' Friends, the totals may be a little high. The total population of Alexandrians would be between 30,000 and 40,000, not counting Egyptians, slaves or other non-citizen residents. Scheidel (2004: pp.15–16) estimated that between 270 and 200 BC the Alexandrian population might have doubled in size. If so, and if the citizen population increased at the same rate (which is unlikely), we might set as an upper figure that the Alexandrian citizen population peaked around 200 BC with about 15,000 military age males. A more conservative, and probably more reliable, figure is to stay a little below 10,000 military age citizens.

In the documentary sources, it is at least clear that Alexandrians often held high status roles in the Ptolemaic army and administrations. For example, many Alexandrians were represented among the honorific, eponymous priesthoods of Ptolemaic Egypt, like the priesthood of Alexander and the Ptolemies. In a study of the origins of these priests, Clarysse could demonstrate that Alexandrians became the main source of these priests early in the second century BC.[7] But that picture may be misleading: while we may know the foreign origins of some third-century BC priests, we also know many of them were permanent residents of Alexandria. In most cases where evidence exists, it is clear that their sons and daughters definitely held Alexandrian citizenship. That is, many second-century BC Alexandrian eponymous priests were descendants of third-century foreign eponymous priests. Did these men from Macedonia, Samos, Lycia and other places already possess a dual Alexandrian citizenship when they held their various military commands and priesthoods?

Of Alexandrian citizens attested in papyri under the second and third Ptolemies, I feel confident connecting twenty-three to military service and land allotments. Of these, at least seven to nine were officers, at least fourteen were cavalrymen, two to four were in the foot or horse *agema* and two were infantrymen.[8] Two of the officers were infantry officers. The general impression is that most Alexandrians who did military service were associated with the cavalry and the officer corps. Many more Alexandrians are attested in inscriptions as officers, diplomats and administrators abroad, like the Alexandrians who oversaw the garrison and government on the island of Thera in the north Aegean.[9] All of the attested military settlers had land in the Fayum region, where they comprised a tiny minority among the other settler populations. The Fayum only became a major centre for military settlement in the third century BC, but in the fourth century it seems likely that land grants were given in the neighbourhood of Alexandria, where an entire nome along the Canopic branch of the Delta was renamed the Menelaite nome after Ptolemy's brother (Strabo 17.1.18), but also across the Delta toward Pelusium in the east and then further south along the Nile, in the vicinity of Memphis, and yet further upstream to places like Hermopolis, near the entrance to the Thebaid.

The aforementioned Hermopolis was the site where a band of cavalry soldiers received land allotments at some point very early in the Ptolemaic regime, and we only know of them because their unit was transferred to land in the Fayum in the reign of Philadelphus. Fully half of the (admittedly few) attested soldiers were Alexandrians, representing approximately one-in-five of the attested Alexandrian military settlers.[10] The cavalry unit was known as the 'troop of Menelaos, the Firsts from the Hermopolites'. Their title, 'the Firsts' (*Prōtoi*), could signify two things, either their antiquity in landed service at Hermopolis or their status as a military unit in Ptolemaic service. Few other groups of settlers in the Fayum had similar claims to antiquity in Ptolemaic service. They also had much smaller ratios of Alexandrians. The prevelance of Alexandrians in the Hermopolite *Prōtoi* suggests that Alexandrians may have held military positions more frequently in other parts of Egypt where settlements had taken place earlier, but where papyrological evidence has seldom survived.

An archive from the early Roman era (mostly 15 and 14 BC) offers some ways to flesh out the picture of Alexandrian military service and holdings.

From these texts, in *BGU IV*, we learn that the territory of the Alexandrians (the *chōra Alexadreōn*) included large stretches of land in the neighbouring provinces, especially the Menelaite nome (BGU 4.1123, 1132) but also the Bousirite nome (BGU 4.1129). A prominent Alexandrian held a military allotment in the Bousirite nome, located in the Delta region (BGU 4.1129), with more than 200 arouras, which fits with the picture of Alexandrians as officers, since no regular soldier is ever attested with more than 120 arouras. The military land bordered on a stretch of Alexandrian territory, which suggests the Alexandrian territory did not have the nature of military allotments. An interesting example in this collection is the 'Macedonian' Alexandros son of Nikodemos (BGU 4.1132), who was a Jewish resident of Alexandria. His brother Theodoros had passed away and Alexandros was handling some of his affairs, amid which we learn that his brother possessed land in the *chōra Alexadreōn*. From this we learn that the city territory was divided into *gyoi*, or tracts, probably within grid patterns of dikes and embankments, and then further into *episēmai*, or plots. The latter were named after persons, and may relate the names of citizens who held the land centuries earlier. Undoubtedly Alexandrians could hold a piece of the *chōra* but also gain an allotment elsewhere, whether near Alexandria (BGU 4.1129) or further south, along the Nile above Memphis (BGU 4.1060, 1104, 1130, 1167).

Alexandros and Theodoros were Jewish residents of Alexandria, but Macedonians rather than Alexandrians or Jews in the eyes of the bureaucracy. The first-century AD Jewish historian Josephus claimed exactly this: that under the Ptolemies the Jewish population at Alexandria was recognized as equal to Macedonians.[11] Josephus' claims long met with scepticism, but at least for the sons of Nikodemos it was true: they were not equal to Macedonians; they were Macedonians. Under Alexander, Josephus claims the Jewish population was settled at Alexandria and affiliated as allied troops (this was probably Cleomenes of Naukratis' doing, who had only 4,000 troops to garrison all Egypt), and given rights equal to the Greek citizens; under Julius Caesar, the Jewish population was given full Alexandrian citizenship (Jos. *Ant.* 14.10.1). The Jewish population at Alexandria was not small: at least by the Roman era they were the dominant population of the 'Delta' neighbourhood in Alexandria, with over 50,000 total residents (Jos. *BJ* 2.18.8). Josephus quoted two different Hellenistic sources that asserted 'thousands' or as many as 'thirty thousand' Jewish immigrants to Egypt were enrolled in the Ptolemaic army.[12] The figure 30,000 is surely an exaggeration, but there was clearly a large Jewish population both at Alexandria and in the Egyptian countryside, where Jewish synagogues and civic associations abounded.[13] As Macedonians, the Alexandrian Jewish population in particular should have been subject to military obligations, especially in the phalanx, but they may have owned Alexandrian territory rather than being granted allotments as military settlers. It is also possible that Alexandrian citizens who served in the phalanx were accorded Macedonian status too, but there is only a single text to begin to forge such an interpretation. *P.Enteux*. 88 (221 BC) provides our only example of a man recorded as both Alexandrian and Macedonian. It nonetheless holds out the possibility that Alexandrian military service was not wholly in the cavalry or officer corps; by re-categorizing some Alexandrian citizens or residents as Macedonians, they served in the units of the phalanx.

Many other non-Alexandrian Greeks resided in the city, and military service may not have been unusual for them. A third-century BC papyrus (*P.Lond.* 7.1986, 252 BC) indicates that many Greeks from Cyrenaica lived at Alexandria and served in military units. Of the eight military men in that document, we know the citizen status of five, of whom three came from Ptolemais-near-Barke in Cyrenaica, one was Roman and the other a Persian. These military men probably comprised parts of the city's mercenary garrison (two held the rank *taktomisthos*, a fairly low mercenary rank) or served in elite units stationed at the court. The Persian served in the elite palace guard, the *peri Aulēn*, and one man – an Alexandrian because his father's name is listed rather than his ethnic – was a member of the *agema*. A much later text (*SB* 3.7169, later second century BC) probably contains more information on Alexandrians affiliated with the military sphere, and includes men from Lacedaemon, Elis, Thessalonica, Carthage and several from Rome and Messalia (modern Marseilles). Among them were officers, men from the Mediterranean fleet, mercenaries and several soldiers from 'the king's *deuteroi epilektoi*', perhaps the second echelon of picked men. Describing his visit to Alexandria in the second century BC, after a series of disturbances had negatively impacted the citizen population, Polybius (34.14) described the mercenaries as a large and dangerous subset of the population. Elsewhere in Polybius we learn that in about 222 BC there were some 4,000 Peloponnesians and Cretans among the garrison, while 'Syrians' (perhaps Jews?) and 'Carians' (presumably Lycians, Pamphylians and Pisidians should be included as well) comprised large sub-groups among the other mercenaries (Poly. 5.36.4–5). The papyri suggest that our picture from Polybius should be augmented with a strong body of troops hailing from the central and western Mediterranean, lured to Alexandria by the generosity and wealth of the Ptolemies. The attractiveness of Alexandria provided the Ptolemies with one of their greatest recruiting tools, and even near the twilight of Ptolemaic power could bring military men from distant shores to enter Ptolemaic service.

The Greek Settlers

The second city of Ptolemaic Egypt was Memphis, just south of the apex of the Delta. Memphis had military settlers from the Aegean region before Alexander's conquest, was where the small Persian garrison left in Egypt had surrendered to Alexander (Curtius 4.7.4), and he left small Macedonian garrisons in it and Pelousion. It may also have been the home base for the small field army he left in Egypt, since one of its commanders, Peukestas, left a written notice to his soldiers at the entrance to a shrine in the sacred complex at Saqqara, outside Memphis.[14] The notice, written in big letters in epigraphic rather than common papyrographic style, reads: '[By order] of Peukestas: no one is to enter without permission. This is a holy place.' We might imagine curious – or perhaps greedy – Greek mercenaries poking around the many holy places and tombs at Saqqara. Pelusium, the gateway to Egypt from Syria, had been a garrison site for centuries before Alexander installed the other of his Macedonian garrisons there. Pharaohs had long ago granted lands near Pelusium to foreign soldiers, including some Greeks (Hdt. 2.154, Diod. 1.67.1–2), thus it would be surprising if the Ptolemies were an exception. Herakleopolis was later the core area for the land grants given to men from some of the most prestigious units in the Ptolemaic army, which suggests it may have been one of the first regions where Ptolemy, as satrap, gave land grants to his Friends, officers and leading soldiers. A whole region of the Herakleopolite province came to be known as 'Agema' after the elite soldiers whose land allotments were located there. Even further south, the second Greek *polis* of Egypt was established at Ptolemais Hermiou during the reign of Ptolemy I, and a substantial Greek population – military and civilian – grew up around Syene and Elephantine in remote Upper Egypt, near the frontier with Meroe. A text from the early Roman era confirms that there were once infantry and cavalry allotments, and thus military settlers, alongside citizen holdings in the vicinity of Ptolemais (*P.Lond.* 3.604B, AD 47). More settlers were at Diospolis Mikra, halfway between Ptolemais and Thebes (*P.Ashm.Dem.* 81); they included cavalry settlers, infantry settlers and some citizen settlers who were probably from Ptolemais.[15]

There are several general studies of the ethnic composition or places of origin of Ptolemaic soldiers.[16] Most of these treat the Ptolemaic record as a whole, or make divisions between the earlier and later Ptolemaic era. These naturally find that diversity declines over time, because 'Macedonian' and 'Persian' became popular pseudo-ethnics (indicators of official categorization in the military or state) rather than indicators of actual origin. I argue that 'Persian' was always a pseudo-ethnic, but of lesser importance and slightly different impact in the third century BC, and that 'Macedonian' also attained a primarily pseudo-ethnic value no later than 230 BC. What has not generally been done is to study particular sub-regions or particular units for their own composition. In the pages that follow, I present several small studies, all from the third century BC, to reveal some of the intriguing variances within the composition of the Ptolemaic army. For example, while studies like those of Uebel and Fischer-Bovet have shown that Macedonians comprised nearly 20 per cent of military personnel in the third century BC, those comprehensive studies obscure that in two neighbouring provinces of Egypt, there was one hipparchy that was nearly half Macedonian and another with not a single attested Macedonian. The studies that follow favour cavalry units, both because they are better attested and because there was no pronounced pseudo-ethnic value attached to cavalry service until well into the second century BC.

The Elephantine Community under Ptolemy I

By far the earliest Ptolemaic settler community for which we have any evidence at all on their makeup is that at Elephantine. One text from 310 BC and four from the 280s BC provide the names of at least twenty-six individual adults males from the community (two possible duplicates are excluded). Unlike all the studies that follow, this community was uniformly Greek. The simplified table entries used for the others, chosen for ease of use, would have left twenty, or 77 per cent, of the Elephantine individuals as simply hailing from the 'Greek world'. For that reason, this one table is broken down, with the same number of entries, into the various sub-regions from whence the men hailed. The men are all presented without patronymic (the name of their father) and with an ethnic, but no marker of military service. The detailed identification procedures that became routine under Ptolemy II were not yet in effect. Therefore, the precise military role of the population is unclear.

The presence of the Cyreneans may be related to Ptolemy's operations in Cyrenaica and his recruitment of Cyreneans into military settlements

Table 1: Elephantine Community

Alexandria	1	4%
Cyrenaica (Cyrene)	4	15%
Peloponnese (Arkadia)	4	15%
Central Greece	4	15%
North Aegean (Maroneia)	1	4%
East Aegean	9	35%
Crete	1	4%
Phoenicia (Sidon)	1	4%
Sicily & Italy (Gela)	1	4%

in Egypt. The Alexandrian in remote Egypt, even in the reign of Ptolemy I, is an interesting case. His presence in Elephantine suggests a role in service to Ptolemy, military or civic, since as a settler one would expect him to be in Alexandria at so early a date. It is tempting to tie the men from Arkadia, Chalkis and Phokis to the mercenary forces of Alexander's army and massive hiring drives of the early Successor Wars, given that all three (and Arkadia in particular) were prominent sources of mercenary troops. Crete fits in the same category, but also came into the Ptolemaic periphery early on. The largest population group hailed from the Eastern Aegean world: Rhodes, Kos, Magnesia and Temnai. The numerous families that came from Temnai, in Aeolia, do not fit into Ptolemaic recruitment from the south-western seaboard populations, where his own forces were operating in the late fourth century BC. It has been suggested before that perhaps the Temnitans were some of the pro-Persian Greeks exiled to Egypt under Alexander. It is certainly conceivable that most of the Elephantine settlers – aside from the Cyreneans and Alexandrians – reflect a community that took shape in the time of Alexander.

The Arsinoite Cavalry Registers

Thousands of Ptolemaic papyri come from the Fayum, and many provide information on the military settlers of that region. The Ptolemies settled cavalrymen there in large numbers. Several of the studies that follow treat archives from the Fayum, and they relate mainly to the origin places of cavalrymen. First, this study takes the three third-century BC texts from the Arsinoite that provide the largest number of origin-places. Two of these texts, *P.Petr.* 2.35 and 3.112, only contain military personnel. The first is a record of cavalry horses, the second a tax record for military settlers, all but two of them cavalry. The third text, *P.Tebt.* 3.1.815, contains abstracts of contracts, and includes many cavalry, many civilians, and several infantry. The results from these three texts are divided into two tables, the first with only the cavalrymen, the second with civilians and infantry also included.

The cavalry personnel are not dramatically different from the combined population group, but there are enough distinctions to merit their separate presentation. There are no Syrian military settlers in the texts, for example, and the Persians (3 per cent), Macedonians (12 per cent) and Cyreneans (10 per cent) comprised a smaller percentage of the cavalry than they did of the population overall. For the latter two, the difference is small enough to

Table 2: Arsinoite Registers – Cavalry Only

Alexandria	1	2%
'Persian'	2	3%
Macedonia	7	12%
Cyrenaica	6	10%
Greek World	28	48%
Thrace & Balkans	12	21%
Anatolia	1	2%
Cyprus	1	2%
Syria (incl. Judea)	0	0%

Table 3: Arsinoite Registers – All Personnel

Alexandria	2	2%
'Persian'	9	9%
Macedonia	14	14%
Cyrenaica	11	11%
Greek World	40	39%
Thrace & Balkans	18	17%
Anatolia	2	2%
Cyprus	2	2%
Syria (incl. Judea)	5	5%

be of little consequence. Conversely, half of the cavalry settlers were from cities and regions of the Greek world (48 per cent). The number of men from the Balkans (21 per cent) also increases among the cavalry. A few of the more unusual ethnics present among the group are a man from Seleucid Antioch (presumably the one in Syria), a Galatian and Iapygian, the latter from an ancient Italian people who by the Hellenistic period were fairly Hellenized, and for most of the third century BC were ruled by the Roman Republic. There are limits to what can be confidently concluded from these figures. As an example, ethnics do not survive for more than thirty cavalrymen from the list in *P.Petr.* 3.112. Instead, aside from observing the general proportions – Greeks and Thracians predominate – it may be more useful to examine some of the particular origin places among the Greek population.

The origins of the Greeks in Ptolemaic service in the Fayum offer some interesting insights into Ptolemaic recruitment. One important question about the sources of soldiers for the Ptolemaic army is the correlation between Ptolemaic empire and the origins of Ptolemaic soldiers.[17] That is, did most soldiers come from within the Ptolemaic footprint? And if they did not, how did they come into Ptolemaic service? Certainly a good many future soldiers emigrated to Egypt for opportunity at the court of the reputedly open-handed kings, and recruiters convinced others to enrol and travel across the sea. The results from the Fayum cavalry, half of whom may have come from the cities of the Greek world, sheds a good bit of light on this question.

Between nine and fifteen of the Greeks came from cities or regions that were under Ptolemaic control at some point. This includes Sicyon, garrisoned by Ptolemaic soldiers briefly under Ptolemy I, several cities in Ionia, several Cretans and a couple of men from Ainos, a small city in the Thracian Aegean that came under Ptolemaic control in the Third Syrian War. The larger tally also includes men from Heraklea, Magnesia and Pharos, all origins that potentially lay within the Ptolemaic sphere at times. But there were at least five Herakleas and three Magnesias in the third century BC, and Pharos could refer either to Paros in the Aegean or Pharos (a Parian colony) in the Adriatic. Of these, Heraklea merits further discussion: more than thirty Herakleotai are attested in Ptolemaic service in inscriptions and papyri, more than all but a handful of Greek places of origin: Cyrene, Thessaly, Athens and thus one of the largest minorities in Ptolemaic service. Heraklea Pontika on the Black Sea was large enough to have seen large numbers seek service in Egypt, but it was far from the borders of the Ptolemaic empire.

Heraklea in Ionia was much smaller, but came under Ptolemaic control at several points; perhaps Ptolemy I lured many Ionian Herakleotai into his service and they travelled to Egypt as a prominent community. But this seems at least a little unlikely: the number of Herakleans far exceeds the number of Milesians or any other Ionians. Most likely their numbers reflect immigration from multiple historical Herakleas, from as far off as Italy and the Black Sea.

Twenty-five of the Greeks came from cities and regions that clearly were not under Ptolemaic control. Three were from city-states of Greater Macedonia: Olynthos, Apollonia and Amphipolis. Could these men have portrayed themselves simply as Macedonians? Did it work to their benefit to assert Greek citizenship instead of Macedonian identity? Olynthos is also remarkable because that city was destroyed in 318 BC to make way for Kassandreia. We may surmise, then, that Aristokles the Olynthian was descended from some soldier who came to the army in Egypt very early, as part of Alexander's garrison, or one of Ptolemy's early mercenaries or a deserter from the Perdiccan campaign. Of the rest, Pergamon and Kyzikos represent regions of north-west Anatolia beyond Ptolemaic power. Including a Larissan there were four from Thessaly, to go alongside men from Athens, Boeotia, Chalkis, Phokis and more remote Dolopia in central Greece. The cities and regions of the Peloponnese included Lakonia, Argos, Achaia and Arkadia. There were even men from Italy and Sicily: Taras, Iapygia and Syracuse. There is no evidence that suggests any sort of concentration of soldiers from particular regions or cities that might lead us to consider whether the Ptolemies developed recruitment agreements or networks to privilege some areas. In fact, it even raises questions about the importance of Ptolemaic mercenary recruiters: the overwhelming diversity of origin, and the preponderance of soldiers from outside areas under the influence of the Ptolemaic empire, should suggest a high volume of individual or small-group immigration to Egypt, rather than systematic Ptolemaic recruitment.

The Petrie Wills

The *Petrie Wills* are a collection of wills drawn up in the Fayum region in the reign of Ptolemy III. Many of the wills belonged to soldiers, many of them cavalry, some from elite guard units and some infantry, and the men who registered as witnesses for the wills were often soldiers themselves. The majority of these soldiers were high-ranking officers. With the exception of several civilian wills, the *Petrie Wills* provide a window into the milieu of the Ptolemaic military elite in a way none of our other sources do. The concentration of officers from many different units should reflect either the prioritization of officers in assigning allotments, so that numerous officers are attested from eponymous commands never attested for a rank-and-file soldier, or the concentration of an elite, networked officer class in nome capitals, like Krokodilon Polis (also known as Arsinoe) in the Fayum. The following table presents the ethnic affiliations of more than fifty military men from the wills.

The *Petrie Wills* have the largest collection of Alexandrians of any of the source bodies studied for this chapter. Nearly twenty other Alexandrians are attested in the *Wills*, but many were civilians and the military or civilian status of others is lacking. The number of Alexandrians seems to correlate to the frequency of officers and frequency of membership in elite units. There are nearly as many Alexandrians in the *Petrie Wills* as all the Greeks from the Aegean world combined, and more Alexandrians than Macedonians or any other single ethnicity (if including civilians in the tally). And again, the large number of Macedonians also seems to reflect the elite status of many of the men in the collection. Yet again Herakleans comprised a significant constituency among the Greeks, outnumbering Thessalians. One man from Kardia and another from Lysimachia may provide evidence for earlier and later emigration to Egypt, since the Kardians were transplanted to populate Lysimachia. Among the Greeks, the six from various parts of the Peloponnese comprise a significant minority. A Campanian and a Syracusan from the west demonstrate the far-reaching allure of service with the Ptolemies. Finally, the ten Balkan 'barbarians' comprise a large minority within the group, and at least two

Table 4: Petrie Wills Military

Alexandria	6	11%
'Persian'	0	0%
Macedonia	15	27%
Cyrenaica	5	9%
Greek World	16	29%
Thrace & Balkans	10	18%
Anatolia	3	5%
Cyprus	0	0%
Syria (incl. Judea)	1	2%

were officers and another served in the *agema*. For the officer-heavy *Wills*, that is actually a low ratio of officers to soldiers. Does it reveal some of the limits of Hellenization? And while dozens of civilians are attested in the wills, none were from the Balkan regions; that is, their presence in Egypt was more essentially military than other groups.

The CPR XVIII Contracts

The papyri in *CPR XVIII* are a valuable archive, mainly of contracts, from the town of Theogonis in the southern Arsinoite nome, called the precinct of Polemon. Theogonis and several nearby towns appear frequently in the texts. Compared to the *Petrie Wills*, the *CPR* texts relate to the lives and activities of relatively lower-status soldiers and civilians. The precinct of Polemon controlled the southern approaches to the Fayum and had a much lower proportion of the Fayum's cavalry settlers compared to the other two precincts at the time of the *P.Count* 1 survey, late in the reign of Philadelphus. That had begun to change by the time of this archive of contracts, which attests quite a few cavalry settlers – mainly from the class of 70-aroura horsemen that did not exist at the time of the *P.Count* 1 survey – and a good many infantry settlers as well. The settlers' community, including the civilian *epigonoi*, was diverse. As the table below shows, the largest ethnic contingent were the Macedonians, due in part to the pseudo-ethnic status of 'Macedonians' among the infantrymen, but even so the Macedonians represent just one-fifth of the attested male population.

The strong Judean presence is largely due to the town of Samaria, located near Theogonis. While Heraklea again proves ubiquitous, like Arkadia and Achaia in the Peloponnese, there is a strong eastern Aegean and Anatolian

Table 5: CPR VIII Population

Alexandria	8	11%
'Persian'	7	9%
Macedonia	15	20%
Cyrenaica	2	3%
Greek World	15	20%
Thrace & Balkans	13	18%
Anatolia	5	7%
Cyprus	0	0%
Syria (incl. Judea)	9	12%

presence. Even beyond the Pisidians, Pamphylian and Mysian, the presence of a Kappadokian is striking, and the Galatian, although counted here among the Balkan troops, may also have come to Egypt from Anatolia. The Anatolian contingent is still not particularly large, but in comparison to some of the other, presumably older, settler populations, we might see in this body the first strong evidence for Ptolemaic recruitment in areas that came into the Ptolemaic empire or near its borders in the wars of the middle third century. At the same time, while most of the Anatolian Greeks and Hellenized peoples who appear in the Ptolemaic army were from cities and regions that were at some point under Ptolemaic control, imperial recruitment is not an explanation for the Kappadokian or the Mysians.

The Herakleopolite Hipparchy

The Herakleopolite nome was an administrative region south of Memphis, along the Nile immediately east of the Fayum basin and Arsinoite nome. The region hosted settlements of soldiers from the Ptolemaic army's elite units, but also a good number of regular infantry and cavalry. The elite units gave their names to parts of the Herakleopolite, like the substantial island called 'Agema' or the locales that came to be known as 'Around the Palace', 'Around the City' or 'The Veterans'. The many elite soldiers attested in the *Petrie Wills* archive lack good comparators among the settlers evidence from the Arsinoite nome; quite a few may have actually been residents of the Herakleopolite nome (when they were not at Alexandria). These elites notwithstanding, there was also at least one hipparchy of regular horse active in the province, and papyri from the early third to the early second centuries provide the names of the main unit's eponymous

Table 6: Herakleopolite Hipparchy

Alexandria	2	4%
'Persian'	2	4%
Macedonia	24	45%
Cyrenaica	0	0%
Greek World	15	28%
Thrace & Balkans	10	19%
Anatolia	0	0%
Cyprus	0	0%
Syria (incl. Judea)	0	0%

commanders and dozens of its personnel. The hipparchs in the early third century were Alexandros, Antiochos and Antigonos, all good Macedonian names, while Automedon and then Neoptolemos commanded in the first half of the second century.

The Herakleopolite cavalry are remarkable for two features. First, they have by far the largest concentration of Macedonians of any cavalry unit attested in the first half of the Ptolemaic era. The prominence of Macedonians as an ethnic in Egypt is attributable primarily to the phalanx, where it was more an indicator of martial culture than of actual origin. Among the cavalry, however, there was no such practice until the middle of the second century: these were true Macedonians, and so, most likely, among the earliest Ptolemaic settlers. By contrast with the Oxyrhynchites cavalry, discussed below, there are no attested Cyreneans. Second, the Herakleopolite cavalry developed a heavily Thracian character quite suddenly in the early second century. No Thracian trooper is attested in the third century, but nearly one-in-three from the second century. This sudden shift could be due to the chance nature of papyrus survival, but the significance of the shift suggests an influx of Thracian cavalry around 200 BC. There could be a connection to the Raphia campaign, for which 2,000 mercenaries from Thrace and Gaul came to Egypt. Although they came as infantry, it is conceivable that Ptolemy IV rewarded their performance with large, cavalry-sized allotments in the Herakleopolites. They may also have come to Egypt even later, perhaps in the context of the Fifth Syrian War.

The Oxyrhynchite Hipparchy

The Oxyrhynchites was a region further south from the Herakleopolites. The two shared a border, and it also had easy access to the Fayum via the canal that fed the basin. Cavalry settlers were present in that region from as early as there are Greek papyri there (271 BC). The region was not nearly so densely settled as the Fayum, and there are no indications of the sorts of elite troops who gained allotments in the Herakleopolites. More than sixty soldiers can be identified in the papyri under a series of eponymous commanders – Telestes, Sadalas, Zoilos and Philon – down to the end of the third century.

The most striking thing about the Oxyrhynchite hipparchy is the enormous representation of troopers from Cyrenaica. Most of these were Cyreneans, but Barkans, Hesperitans and Libyans are also represented. The Cyrenean character of the Oxyrhynchite settlers is evident from

Table 7: Oxyrhynchite Hipparchy

Alexandria	1	2%
'Persian'	6	10%
Macedonia	0	0%
Cyrenaica	24	38%
Greek World	15	24%
Thrace & Balkans	11	17%
Anatolia	4	6%
Cyprus	0	0%
Syria (incl. Judea)	2	3%

the earliest texts. This, combined with the independence (and occasional hostility) of Cyrenaica under Magas' rule for nearly all of Philadelphus' reign, means these Cyreneans (or their ancestors) almost certainly came to Egypt under Ptolemy I. While Cyreneans appear in nearly every settler context as far south as Elephantine, this region had an unparalleled concentration. After Cyreneans, Thracians are the next largest contingent. They too were present in the region's cavalry settlers from very early. If they, like the Cyreneans, also belonged to the army of Ptolemy I, should we see in them acquisitions from the royal army under Perdiccas, or mercenaries hired by Ptolemy the Satrap? Despite their numbers, very few of the attested Cyreneans and none of the attested Thracians were officers, save for the hipparch Sadalas himself, whose name is unquestionably Thracian.

Just as striking as the Cyreneans and Thracians is the total absence of any Macedonians. No other soldier pool is entirely without Macedonians. Even with the Oxyrhynchite cavalry data, Macedonians comprised almost 20 per cent of the total pool of manpower. But in the Oxyrhynchites there are not even Macedonian *epigonoi* reported until the late third century. What makes this even more interesting is the sudden appearance of numerous Macedonians, all infantrymen, in the Oxyrhynchites in the years immediately after the battle at Raphia. It is possible the Ptolemies settled Macedonian soldiers there after the campaign. More likely, *epigonoi* of Cyrenean, Thracian or other ancestry became Macedonians by the wave of a bureaucratic wand, like Straton son of Stratios, a Thracian of the *epigonē* who became a Macedonian infantryman by fiat during the Fourth Syrian War (*BGU* 10.1958). The sudden addition of many Macedonians in that region fits with the expansion of the phalanx for the Fourth Syrian War and the larger pattern of increased military settlement in the late third century. Similarly, the 70-arouras cavalry who appeared in the Arsinoites with their ethnic hipparchies also appeared in the Oxyrhynchites late in the third century. Instead of an ethnic hipparchy, however, they had an eponymous commander, one Nikomedes. The two attested 70-arouras cavalry were a Persian and a Bithynian.

The Paneion d'el Kanais Dedications

The last source base for soldier populations is the archive of inscriptions from the Paneion shrine in the desert wastes of Upper Egypt, where soldiers involved in the Red Sea trade, border defence and elephant hunts left numerous inscriptions. Many are fragmentary, but we nonetheless are able to collect 24 ethnics, all for military personnel, from the list.

This particular body has by far the largest percentage of Anatolian soldiers. The Ptolemies had been drawing on Anatolians for the army since the time of Ptolemy I, but the recruitment relationship probably accelerated under Ptolemy II, who conquered extensive stretches of the southern coast. Certainly numerous noble Lycians and Pamphylians held some of the highest positions at the Ptolemaic court in the second half of the third century BC. All eight of the Anatolians from the Paneion inscriptions were from Lycia and Pamphylia. Ptolemy II also initiated elephant hunts; it may be that new officers and mercenaries from Anatolia became peculiarly prominent in the elephant hunts. Some may have been mercenaries who returned home, but we know Lycians and Pamphylians settled in some significant numbers in Middle Egypt: one of the quarters of Oxyrhynchos was named the 'Lycian camp' (*P.Oxy.* 2.250), a dedication in

Table 8: Paneion Soldiers

Alexandria	0	0%
'Persian'	0	0%
Macedonia	2	8%
Cyrenaica	5	21%
Greek World	7	29%
Thrace & Balkans	0	0%
Anatolia	8	33%
Cyprus	0	0%
Syria (incl. Judea)	2	8%

the Fayum was made to Artemis of Perga by the Pamphylians settled there (*I.Fay.* 3.199) and a Lycian is attested serving in a unit of Pamphylians, perhaps the same one (*P.Ryl* 4.583, 170 BC).

Among the Greeks, the Cretans make up the largest minority. This may be chance, but it could reflect two things: first, the prominence of foreign mercenaries in the garrisons of the region; and second, the value of missile troops in the wild places of north-east Africa. Both are plausible explanations for the number of Cretans, and the latter is especially strong when we consider the renown of the Ethiopian tribes for archery. Otherwise, the places of origin seem fairly representative of other source bases. The Cyrenean contingent is strong, but there are Macedonians, an Argive, a Thessalian, two Judeans and men from Aegina and Naupaktus. The complete absence of both Thracians and Persians, on the other hand, is fairly striking. If the troops were mainly mercenaries, the lack of Persians would make sense. As for the Thracians, it might be the case that their service as mercenaries then military settlers came in bursts, as Thracian lords and their retainers found service abroad. In that case, the Paneion inscriptions might simply miss the Thracian waves. Alternatively, the Ptolemies preferred to deploy their Thracian troops closer to their borders rather than in Upper Egypt.

Conclusions

In conclusion, this study of Ptolemaic military settler populations shows considerable diversity within and between Ptolemaic units. Units could take on the character of Ptolemaic recruitment at the time the unit came into being, thus the heavily Macedonian Herakleopolite cavalry belongs to the earliest Ptolemaic era, while the heavily Cyrenean–Thracian Oxyrhynchite cavalry reflects recruitment in an era when Macedonians and most Greeks were bound up in the operations of the powerful Successors like Antigonus the One-Eyed and Demetrius the Besieger. Additionally, the footprint of the Ptolemaic empire has been shown to have very little correlation to the personnel of the Ptolemaic army. A strong correlation between the two has often been presupposed, but at least among the cavalry the evidence is very weak. Finally, Thracians comprised 15 per cent of Ptolemaic military personnel in the units studied here; a broader study would show basically the same thing. The significance of Thracian soldiers in the Ptolemaic army has been consistently understated. The Thracians were pulled between a reputation as fierce barbarian fighters and a propensity for Hellenization;

taking service in Ptolemaic Egypt seems to have been a particularly attractive path for gaining wealth and status, whether or not the Ptolemies controlled a foothold on the Thracian coast.

Before moving on, a brief word about the infantry seems merited. If a study of the documentary evidence for the line infantry were done, approximately nine-out-of-ten of all the infantry with an attested origin would be Macedonians. But while many Macedonians seem to have actually found roles in Ptolemaic service, both as cavalry and infantry, common sense demands and documentary evidence gives us confidence to declare that the infantrymen of actual Macedonian origin were only a subset, and likely a minority, of the supposed Macedonian infantry. For the most part, the origins of these men – a huge part of the Ptolemaic army – are simply lost. But the population study, while it focused on cavalry units, may provide an opportunity to make some comparison. At the proportions from the previous studies, a similar breakdown of origins for the 30,000 Ptolemaic line infantry (the phalanx and the *agema*) would look something like this:

Although this table surely misses the mark by a fairly wide margin, it must be much closer than the monolithic Macedonian class that appears in the papyri. And there is some reason for defending these numbers. After all, many infantry recruits in the Ptolemaic army were *epigonoi*, the sons of military settlers. Thus many would have been sons of cavalry troopers, who tended to have larger families, and at least part of the Ptolemaic infantry would thereby tend to mirror the makeup of the cavalry. On the other hand, a section later in this chapter will explore the case of the Judeans and the evidence that suggests that group, especially common among the Syrians and Asians in the population study, sometimes served in the Macedonian infantry. So 5 per cent from Syrians, or even from Judeans alone, may

Table 9: Ptolemaic Phalanx and *Agema* at Population Study Proportions

Alexandria	2,400	8%
'Persian'	2,100	7%
Macedonia	5,400	18%
Cyrenaica	3,600	12%
Greek World	8,700	29%
Thrace & Balkans	4,500	15%
Anatolia	1,800	6%
Cyprus	300	1%
Syria (incl. Judea)	1,500	5%

Origins of Soldiers in the Ptolemaic Army   95

be too low. The 'Persian' contribution is almost certainly too low, if I am right that thousands of Hellenized Egyptians held the status of Persians and eventually became Macedonians in the eyes of the Ptolemaic military bureaucracy. Given that Aspendians from Pamphylia commanded the phalanx at Raphia, one might also suspect a larger Anatolian presence in the infantry than appeared in the cavalry study. The Macedonians might also be larger than 18 per cent, although perhaps not by very much. All of these contingents, if larger, could only really take away from the infantrymen whose origin lay in the Greek world. Identifying a Greek given Macedonian bureaucratic status because of infantry service falls to unwieldy conjecture: in Tholthis of the Oxyrhynchites, when the Macedonian infantry suddenly appeared, one was named Hermias (*P.Frankf.* 4 and elsewhere); in the same town there was Agathinos son of Hermias, a Mytilenean of the *epigonē*. The community at Tholthis was not large, and no other Hermias is attested for the town, so it is possible Hermias the Macedonian infantryman was father or brother of the Mytilenean Agathinos. Even if very few Greeks served as Macedonians in the phalanx, the core conclusion should remain: actual Macedonians represented a minority in the phalanx units, alongside large numbers of Thracians and other peoples.

Soldiers' Associations

Associations for soldiers, which existed by the later third century BC and flourished in the second century, are another way to examine the sources of manpower in the Ptolemaic army. These were often called either *koina* or *politeumata*, less and more formal civic associations, respectively. They were associated with a city or region of Egypt, often had strong ties to the local military units and were generally named for a – or the – prominent national origin among the founding members. Launey described *politeumata* as offering 'in some degree the impression of a *polis*, without a territory, without an acropolis, without real autonomy; despite these limitations, it assured its members forms of a political and national life. It was, in the kingdoms and apart from the few *poleis*, the institution that best represents the Hellenic city.'[18] The most famous *politeumata* are those of the Judeans, at Herakleopolis, at Berenikis in Cyrenaica and at Alexandria.[19] The Judean *politeumata*, while famous, are hardly the only ones attested, and were not explicitly military. Some of the known associations belonged to regions that are already fairly well known, thanks to papyri or other sources. Associations of Cilicians (*I.Fayoum* 1.15, late first century BC) and Cretans

(*P.Tebt.* 1.32, 145 BC) were established at some date in the Fayum in Middle Egypt, and one of the Idumaeans was at Memphis (*OGIS* 737, 112/111 BC). All three had heavily military memberships. The Cilicians and Cretans in the Fayum are somewhat surprising, since neither ethnic appears very frequently in documentary papyri, but suggests there may be a gap in what we learn from the papyrological record. The Cretan association had 500 men, and the papyrus identifying it records a Macedonian military settler being added to its ranks.

The associations can also help us learn about regions where the papyrological record is weaker. For example, a *politeuma* of Boeotians was located at Xois (also known as Khaset) in the central Delta.[20] We know little about Ptolemaic settlement in the Delta, and have few examples in Middle Egypt of Boeotian settlers. That this central location, surrounded by water and Egyptians, had a large, militarized Greek population is helpful for conceptualizing the Ptolemaic colonization of the region. The head of the association was also the governor of the nome, and himself a Boeotian. There is only one Macedonian *politeuma* attested, and it comes from a dedication for a gymnasiarch at Sebennytos in the Nile Delta, not that far from Xois.[21] An association, or *koinon*, of Lycians existed at Alexandria and probably existed early in Ptolemaic history (*OGIS* 99, 186–181 BC), and by the Roman era (and probably earlier) it was replaced with or transformed into a *politeuma* of the Lycians. A military unit or political association (probably both) of Bithynians was active at or near Alexandria in the Ptolemaic era as well (*SEG* 8.357). Early in the Roman era, there is evidence for a *politeuma* of Phrygians (*OGIS* 658, 3 BC) whose roots must lie in the Ptolemaic era; it was also active in or near Alexandria.

It seems probable that some of the associations were formed out of brigading for military service rather than settlement in the same locale. A late second-century BC text identifies a *politeuma* for all the soldiers serving in the garrison of Alexandria (*SEG* 20.499, 112/111 BC). It must have had some sort of revolving membership, and was apparently too diverse to be identified by any national marker. In 146 BC, a detachment of (or called) Mysians was dispatched from the Herakleopolite nome down to Ptolemais-in-Pelousion along with forty-one picked men (*P.Gen.* 3.131) for military service. This brigaded unit furnishes one example of the basis for the creation of a soldiers' association. An even stronger example can be found in a late third-century BC inscription from Alexandria. It identifies a *koinon* (a less defined association) of Tralleis from Thrace, Massyles from Libya, Persians and Cyreneans.[22] Were these serving in the city garrison together, or soldiers brigaded together for a campaign abroad? The inscription identifies the *koinon* as having been, originally, a Trallian institution. The Massyles had been attached to them, probably in a military sense at first, but then were also added to the association (the vicissitudes of the contemporaneous Second Punic War might help explain the presence of Massylians in the Ptolemaic army). The verb tense is perfect, suggesting it had taken place prior to the inscription. The Persians and Cyreneans, however, had joined the brigaded force at about the time of the dedication, because in the present tense it reads that they 'are campaigning together'. Trallians and Massyles are likely to have been mercenary light troops, infantry and cavalry respectively. The Persians and Cyreneans represent a different sort of body altogether. There were large numbers of Persians and Cyreneans in Ptolemaic Egypt as cleruchs, but it seems contingents of each were deployed alongside the Trallians and Massylians for campaign. Whether service in the garrison might qualify is unclear; perhaps the brigade was formed for service in Syria or Cyprus, or against rebels in Egypt.

In some cases the actual core identity of the association practically disappears between the diverse groups involved. One such example is the association at Hermopolis in Middle Egypt (*I.Herm.* 5 and 6, 78 BC). There, the two groups forming a *politeuma* are foreign mercenaries from Apollonia in Idumaea and their *sympoliteumoi* the descendants of the founders of the military settlement at Hermopolis, who apparently lacked a common ethnic origin to characterize their association. The members' names appear in the inscription organized by military unit, which only reiterates the close association between the military formations and the associations.

The evidence for soldiers' associations is also strong from the island of Cyprus, where numerous associations are attested from epigraphic evidence. Groups of soldiers from the garrisons on that island would make dedications to or on behalf of their commanding officers, the island governors or the Ptolemies themselves. Many of these were commissioned by the officers and give no indication of the origins of the soldiers, but others were commissioned by soldiers' associations. From both old and new Paphos, on the south-west of Cyprus, there is evidence for five associations: the Lycians, Cilicians, Ionians, Thracians and local Cypriots.[23] On the other side of the island, at Salamis, there are inscriptions in the volume *Salamine XIII* attesting Thracians, Cretans and Hellenes (Greeks), and in *Salamine XIII* 91 (146 BC) a joint dedication, prior to the formation of a *koinon*, by the citizen soldiers of Salamis and the foreign soldiers stationed in the city. Their dedication, while a collective action, was not organized around an association at that time but may reflect the sorts of joint action that eventually gave rise to an association. It can at least be inferred from these texts that the Ptolemaic garrison on Cyprus, while drawn from across the Mediterranean world, contained large numbers of local Cypriots and settlers on the island, the latter dominated (in the second century BC at least) by Thracians, Lycians, Cretans, Cilicians and Ionians.

It is interesting that Anatolian soldiers, while present in the papyri, are far more prominently attested in the names of the associations. In fact, nearly every region of the Anatolian coast from Bithynia round to Cilicia, and even inland Phrygia, have attested associations in the Ptolemaic army. Is this an accident of survival in the sources? Or is it a function of recruitment and change over time? The evidence on associations is largely from the second and first centuries BC, while the best evidence on the origins of military settlers comes from the third century. Perhaps we should conclude that the Ptolemaic army became more and more reliant on Anatolian soldiers, due either to the Ptolemies' weakening reach or Roman expansion into Greece.

Soldiers in the Empire

Aside from Cyprus, evidence for the personnel serving in the Ptolemaic army outside Egypt is fairly scanty. Inscriptions from Crete and Thera never provide the ethnics for regular soldiers serving in those garrisons.[24] Nevertheless, in several cases we do learn their officers were Alexandrians, and a minority of the regular soldiers, who were listed with their patronymics, may also have been citizens of Alexandria. Perhaps more importantly, several of these texts affirm that large numbers of Egyptians were stationed on Crete and Thera as part of the Ptolemaic navy, both as sailors and marines. The military roles of Egyptians in the Ptolemaic army are addressed in the following section.

There are two rosters from Ptolemaic soldiers stationed abroad. One is from Ras ibn Hani, just north of Seleucid Laodikeia in modern Syria. It dates to the third century BC, prior to the Seleucid reconquest of that part of the coast.[25] The roster includes twenty-six ethnics, presented in Table 10 below.

The interesting question with this set of soldiers is whether they represent mercenaries or regular troops from the Ptolemaic army, or perhaps even military settlers. The prevalence of men from Cyrene, the couple of Macedonians and the citizen of Alexandria or Ptolemais all throw some

Table 10: Roster from Ras ibn Hani in Syria

Alexandria/Ptolemais	1	4%
Macedonia	1	4%
Cyrenaica	5	19%
Mainland Greece	6	23%
North Aegean	1	4%
East Aegean	2	8%
Thrace & Balkans	2	8%
Anatolia	4	15%
Cyprus	4	15%

weight toward the Ras ibn Hani troops being regular Ptolemaic soldiers, not mercenaries. Similarly, the four men from Salamis on Cyprus suggest that most of these troops came from within the Ptolemaic empire and were part of the Ptolemaic army, not mercenaries. They also suggest that the Ras ibn Hani troops were deployed from the garrison of Cyprus. Except for one Pisidian, all the Anatolians came from cities or regions that were under Ptolemaic control for much of the third century BC: Miletos, Aspendos and Etenna. The ten or eleven from the rest of the Greek world could have been mercenaries recruited from abroad or venturing to the Ptolemaic world to find employment, but they could just as easily represent military settlers in Ptolemaic service. All are well represented among the cleruch population, including Macedonians, Thessalians, Thracians, Boiotians and an Athenian.

An inscription from Samos, *IG XII^6*, 1:217 (third century BC), lists fifteen Ptolemaic military personnel from that important military base. Most of their origins are fairly straightforward (Akarnanians, for example), but two were from Egypt. One's ethnic, Pharbaithites, identifies the bearer (Ammonios) as a native Egyptian with a Hellenized name, while the other's, Hestiaieus, probably identifies him as a citizen of Alexandria or Ptolemais, or perhaps as a Samian citizen, depending on where Hestiaieus was a demotic. It was a demotic at Athens, and much later at Antinoopolis in Egypt. In the following table I assume the bearer (Eurydamos) was Alexandrian. Ammonios Pharbaithites came from the eastern Nile Delta. More than almost any other body of soldiers, the rest of the personnel at Samos were overwhelmingly Greek. There are no Anatolians, no Macedonians and no Thracians. But there was also no organizing principle among the Greeks,

Table 11: Roster from Samos in the Aegean

Alexandria	1	7%
Egypt	1	7%
Central Greece	4	27%
Western Greece	4	27%
Peloponnese	2	13%
Crete	2	13%
Ionia	1	7%

who hailed from all around Greece. This body, aside from the two hailing from Egypt, may depict a pure Greek mercenary force better than any other set of sources in this chapter. Even so, the diversity of origin places for the Greeks is striking, and exhibits no link between states with better or worse relationships with the Ptolemies.

Nearly all of the evidence, both in the Ptolemaic empire and in the settlements in Egypt, points toward diverse units in both the settler army and the mercenary forces. While place of origin was important, for most of the Ptolemaic army this did not matter. Nor did the footprint of the Ptolemaic empire, since so many of the attested troops hailed from regions and states outside of Ptolemaic control.

EGYPTIANS IN THE ARMY

Coverage of the personnel of the Ptolemaic army is terribly incomplete without a discussion of Egyptian troops. The Egyptians in the Ptolemaic army were not a uniform component of the service. There were elite Egyptian units who served at the court and held distinguished ranks and titles. Other Egyptians held positions of lower status in police forces, the navy and army. I have already mentioned my position that the 'Persians' of the Ptolemaic settler army were Egyptians or other non-Greeks who were officially Hellenized by Ptolemaic military institutions. I offer a defence for that position below, following discussions of regular and elite Egyptian recruitment.

Many Egyptian soldiers were known as *machimoi*, or fighters, in the Ptolemaic era, at least to the Ptolemaic state. The word *machimoi* was reported in Herodotus (2.164–68) as the name of the Egyptian warrior caste. Herodotus' *machimoi* were divided into the *kalasiries* and the *hermotybies*

(Herod. 9.32), two classes separated more by geography than by role or status. The last mention of the *machimoi* warriors in pre-Ptolemaic Egypt is in Diodorus' narrative of the campaigns of Nektanebo II in 343/342 BC (Diod. 16.47), where they numbered 60,000. How these *machimoi* corresponded to Herodotus' or to those in the Ptolemaic era is unknown. The Ptolemies used the term as well, but it is unclear whether it was inherited from before the Macedonian conquest or applied by the Ptolemaic bureaucracy as a suitable moniker for a status and function mainly filled by Egyptians.[26] Most *machimoi* were culturally Egyptian, although there are several examples of *machimoi* with Greek names beginning in the later third century BC (*P.Princ.* 2.18), and by the first century there were 'Greek *machimoi*' in Egypt (*P.Tebt.* 1.120). More significantly, the overwhelming majority of evidence for the role of *machimoi* prior to the Fourth Syrian War and the Battle of Raphia depicts them in non- or para-military functions.

In earlier Ptolemaic Egypt, *machimoi* were used as adjuncts to local officials involved in economic or legal affairs, were dispatched (often just up to three at a time) to escort money or officials on business, and augmented police in making seizures of property or persons.[27] These were useful roles in enforcing Ptolemaic authority in the countryside, but they were not really military duties, and probably did not add up to full-time employment. Census returns confirm that the *machimoi* were filling occupations, not military roles (*P.Count* 14, 15). The *machimoi* of Lykophron in *P.Zen.Pestm.* 49 are part of an official's retinue or staff, rather than soldiers under an officer's command. *Machimoi* may have received land grants from the start of Ptolemaic rule, or held lands that carried over from previous rulers, but the first evidence of *machimoi* allotments comes from late in the reign of Ptolemy III (*SB VIII* 6285, 229/228 BC), after which point evidence for their use as police and escorts declines. The possession of allotments (5 arouras) probably corresponds to an increasing military or paramilitary obligation, and definitely corresponds to an increase in Greek names among attested *machimoi* (*P.Petr.* 3.100). There was at least the potential to mobilize *machimoi* in greater numbers and in a paramilitary or military capacity, as exhibited in one of the earliest texts on *machimoi* (*P.Yale* 1.33, 253 BC), in which *machimoi* were levied and dispatched, under the command of an officer. The ongoing Second Syrian War, which was winding down but did not end until 252 BC, raises the possibility they were to depart on some sort of military mission.

The *kalasiries* are attested only a handful of times in Greek papyri (e.g., *P.Tebt.* 3.1.701, *P.Petr.* 3.99), but are well-represented in demotic

Egyptian documents, where *gl-šr* = *kalasiris*. In many cases, especially in Middle and Lower Egypt, men identified as *gl-šr.w* in demotic papyri seem to be filling police roles, and in at least some examples were equivalent or nearly so to Greek *phylakitai*. In Upper Egypt, the evidence suggests a more militarized role, especially as guards at the key garrison sites at the southern border, Elephantine and Syene. But the institutions of Upper Egypt were mostly holdovers from the pre-Hellenistic era until the late third century BC. There is no piece of evidence to suggest that, for the Ptolemaic era, the *kalasiries* were actually a subset of the *machimoi*; instead, it seems to have been a parallel institution. Perhaps the *machimoi* grew out of what formerly had been the class of *hermotybies*.

The Ptolemies certainly used Egyptians in military roles, in spite of the mainly non-military duties of the Egyptians attested in third-century BC papyri. The porters and light infantry at the Battle of Gaza most likely came from the *kalasiries* or *machimoi* of Egypt. Many Egyptians served in the Ptolemaic navy, including rowers, who were often pressed into service, and higher-status marines, who seem to have been *machimoi*.[28] Some 20,000 Egyptians fought at the Battle of Raphia, equipped in the Macedonian manner as phalangites. Polybius' account of the battle does not use the word *machimoi*, but in the eyes of the Ptolemaic state that is probably who they were. Compared to the roles of *machimoi* prior to that war, their sudden appearance on the battlefield in large numbers and as heavy infantry indicates a major militarization reform. I suggest we can see some evidence for this in the papyri. The Ptolemies began giving some *machimoi* 10-aroura allotments around the time of the Fourth Syrian War. Allotments of doubled size resonate with the increased militarization and line infantry role required by Polybius' narrative. The first possible case is attested in 220 BC (*P.Sorb.* 1.43), before the war, and four 10-aroura allotments (*P.Hib.* 2.265, 204/203 BC) are attested after. We know from later sources that a class of *dekarouroi machimoi* existed (*P.Tebt.* 1.5, 1.81); whether these sources identify early members of that class is unclear. Of the five men with the allotments, three had Greek names. From 210 BC, a roster of fourteen *machimoi*, including their leader Ptolemaios, has three Greek names to eleven Egyptian (*P.Tebt.* 3.2.884). We might suppose that increased privileges and militarization made membership in the *machimoi* appealing for some Greek (or at least Hellenized) men in Egypt. Finally, a text from 219 or 202 BC is particularly crucial here (*P.Köln.* 11.452). It confirms the existence of a centralized military office for the *machimoi*, the existence of sub-units at least as large as the pentakosiarchy

(500-men), the possession of such a high-ranking command by an Egyptian, Nechthambes, and the deployment of Nechthambes (and, presumably, his unit) to Syria. We may confidently conclude that, at precisely the time of the Fourth Syrian War, the role and status of at least part of the *machimoi* class (or up to 20,000 *machimoi*) was fully militarized. The experiment with *machimoi* heavy infantry was short-lived, however. Beginning in the early second century BC, police (*kalasiries*) received 10-aroura allotments in large numbers (e.g., *BGU* 10.1957, 177 BC). They are much better attested in documentary papyri than the *dekarouroi machimoi*, and we may speculate that the Egyptian rebellion, led as it was by *machimoi*, precipitated the shift.

The *machimoi* and *kalasiries* are not the full population of Egyptians connected to Ptolemaic military service. Elite Egyptians were also associated with the army. The best piece of evidence on the early Ptolemies' success in courting the Egyptian elite is a stele from Mendes in the Nile Delta. The interpretation of the Mendes stele is debated, but one passage concerns a moment around 270 BC when Ptolemy II Philadelphus raised a cohort of Egyptian youths to serve as an elite unit in his army. Derchain suggested that the passage describes Philadelphus raising army units from the children born to Greeks and Macedonians who had settled in Egypt over the preceding decades.[29] His interpretation rests upon translating *tp.w≠sn m ms.w [t3]-mry* as 'the first generation of sons born to his army in Egypt', which Klotz and others have shown cannot be the correct reading.[30] The *tp.w≠sn* must be, as elsewhere, leaders or officers. Klotz's own translation, the most recent offered, suggests that the passage refers to Egyptian youths raised for military and government careers in Egypt. Klotz's translation rests upon using generalized readings for five or six words that often carried specifically military connotations, like *mnfy.t* as 'elites' of society rather than 'soldiers', or *mh.w-ib.w* as 'trusted agents' rather than 'guards'. In such close confines with one another, the words really should all be read with a military meaning.[31] Thus, I read the text as follows: 'Moreover, his Majesty raised new troops of picked youths from among the sons of the soldiers of Egypt, their officers from the sons of Egypt, to serve as guards.'

By my reading of the Mendes stele, it describes two existing classes of Egyptians in the Ptolemaic army in the time of Philadelphus and his creation of a third. The first class is the *mnfy.t* of Egypt, which probably describes the military elites of the Egyptian army, men like Somtutefnakht (see Chapter 2) who possessed social standing, religious connections and a strong martial tradition. The context of the stele suggests that the priests of Ram at Mendes were partly among that warrior elite, their sons among those enrolled in the third class, a new unit, and their temple may have helped fund or garrison the new unit. The second class is those 'sons of Egypt' from whom Philadelphus appointed officers for the new unit. The difficulty with this second class is that it seems broader than the military class, yet its sons produced the officers.[32] Klotz pondered (p.302, n.152) whether the text could be read as a reference to the class of men described as 'Greek, born in Egypt', but rejected it mainly because the text seems to be celebrating specifically Egyptian contributions to the Ptolemaic army and 'Greeks' is certainly lacking from the text. However, the Egyptian demotic marker 'Greek born in Egypt' was equivalent to the Greek marker 'Persian' and, as I intend to show below, referred to the class of Hellenized Egyptians first raised by Alexander's subordinates and also by the first Ptolemies. The text does not make a firm conclusion possible, but I suggest that adult officers among the 'Persians' – Hellenized Egyptians – of the Ptolemaic army trained and commanded the youths from the Egyptian nobility. The third class is of course the unit of elite guards raised through Philadelphus' programme. As a system for training high-status youths into military service, it hearkens back to Alexander's recruitment of the 'Persian' auxiliaries. These may have been used as guards at the palace at Alexandria. It all suggests that, prior to Philadelphus, during the reign of his father, Egyptian contributions to the land army of Egypt came in two forms: service from the *mnfy.t* military aristocracy and service from the Egyptian products of a Hellenistic page or ephebic programme. Thus, it seems likely that Ptolemy the Satrap raised numerous troops from the population of Egypt, some Hellenized, others from the Egyptian aristocracy.

Philadelphus' regiment of aristocratic Egyptian guards may actually be attested in two third-century BC sources. First, in *P.Lond.* 7.1986, one of the soldiers attested in the document is a 'Persian' member of an elite unit *peri aulēn*, at the palace. The general service of Persians in Ptolemaic regular units was established in the above study of military settlers, so this particular soldier could have been in either the elite Egyptian guard unit or any of the several elite Greek guard units. The fact that he could have been a member of either is remarkable, and has not been appreciated in studies of the early Ptolemaic army. Second, around the turn of the third century BC, two Egyptian brothers made a dedication at Alexandria in honour of Ptolemy V (*OGIS* 731). They were both officers in the *epilektoi machimoi peri aulēn*, the 'elite Egyptian troops at the court', which almost certainly was, *circa* 200 BC, the current version of the unit founded under Philadelphus.

Two later texts confirm that the *epilektoi machimoi* continued to exist and to serve at Alexandria (*UPZ* 1.110, 164 BC; *P.Tebt.* 1.5, 118 BC).

On the subject of the so-called Persians, a little more needs to be said because it has been a source of considerable confusion in works on Ptolemaic Egypt and the Ptolemaic army,[33] and I am going to push a different interpretation than what has been previously suggested. Alexander's agents established a training programme in Egypt, as elsewhere, for local youths to be trained in Macedonian warfare and schooled in Greek customs, and the graduates were called Persians at first, then often *pantodapoi* in Diodorus' account – and thus presumably in Hieronymus' contemporary account – of the Successor Wars. This programme ceased operating across most of the Macedonian empire amid war and perhaps the wishes of each respective satrap, but I contend that Ptolemy kept the programme running in some form and used it to train and Hellenize Egyptians (and presumably other locals too) to enroll in his army. Further, I suggest that the classes of 'Persians' attested in documentary sources from the third century BC were the descendants of Ptolemy's programme from the days when he was satrap and then king. Thus, the Persians in the documentary sources were overwhelmingly Egyptian in origin yet largely Hellenized in custom and martial tradition.

We know that large numbers of Egyptians (and Nubians and Libyans residing in Egypt) gained status as Persians in the second century BC, mainly in Upper Egypt.[34] It is now firmly established that they did so through paid military service in the Ptolemaic army and their sons were called 'Persian of the *epigonē*', which identified them as civilians rather than soldiers, but also as potential recruits in Persian or even Greek units. If they became soldiers in the Ptolemaic army they became 'Persian' in their own right. These Persians often had dual Greek and Egyptian names, but were in such a heavily Egyptian context they did most of their business using their Egyptian identities, and most of them did not go a long way toward Hellenizing. Although they were overwhelmingly Egyptian (or Libyan or Nubian), they possessed a more flexible and sometimes higher status than most of those who served in the Ptolemaic army as *machimoi* or did not serve in the army at all.

The connection of the late Ptolemaic Persians to the early Ptolemaic Persians or Alexandrian Persians is not established, and generally rejected. Fischer-Bovet rejected a third-century BC connection to the army and called it an 'origin marker', but noted that there is no evidence that any Ptolemaic Persian was of Iranian descent. Something as nonsensical as an origin marker unrelated to the marked origin almost must come from the military world. She and many others have suggested the third-century BC Persians were actually descendants of the Greek settlers of Egypt from before the Macedonian conquest, or some other form of second-class Greek, or descendants of Persian garrison troops from before Alexander's conquest.[35] Yet one of the main things we have learned recently is that in the third century BC, a tax class of 'Persians' were ranked inferior to Greeks and generally possessed Egyptian names for tax purposes. It seems likely that many of the third-century BC Persians had dual names, but unlike the second-century Persians relied heavily on their Greek identities. Identifying them as native Greeks seems unlikely if they used Egyptian names. It also seems unlikely based on the prosopography of third-century BC Persians. More than one-third of the attested names were shared with senior officers from Alexander's army, like Perdikkas, Parmenion and Neoptolemos.[36] Another, Leontiskos, is likely a reference to Ptolemy I's son. They are more likely to reflect names adopted in the Macedonian context than family names from the Greeks who settled in Egypt centuries earlier.

To close the argument, it is best to look at the Persians from the early documentary period, which begins around 270 BC down to Philadelphus' death in 247 BC. In that period there are twelve documented Persians in military service and two Persian *epigonoi*. In the subsequent period, from 246–200 BC, there are fewer attested in military service and dramatically more Persian *epigonoi*.

The early group of soldiers also includes three to five infantrymen and one infantry officer, a taxiarch.[37] All of the soldiers in the later era were definitely cavalrymen. The scarcity of Persian *epigonoi* in the early era (both are attested at the end of that era, as well, in 250 BC) and their increasing numbers later suggests that there were not yet, in the early era, compounding generations of Persians. The absence of infantry Persians, all the way from Theophilos the Persian taxiarch in 251 BC down to about 185 BC,[38] might also suggest that the infantry Persians were recategorized in the reign of Ptolemy III as Macedonian infantry. In conclusion, it seems

Table 12: Persians in Third-Century Papyri

	270–247 BC	246–200 BC
Persian, soldier	12	10
Persian by descent	2	33

likely that the Ptolemaic Persians were much like Alexander's Persians, went by Greco-Macedonian names and were raised mainly under the first Ptolemy, and possibly Ptolemy II. Their descendants were classed among the *epigonoi* like other Greeks, but with the Persian ethnic. Many infantry Persians may have simply become Macedonians in the second half of the third century BC, thus disappearing as an identifiable group, and leaving mainly Persians of the cavalry and Persian *epigonoi* until the military reforms of the second century that saw Egyptians again recruited into the army as 'Persians'. This conclusion squares three difficult pieces of evidence: the battle-line Egyptians at Gaza in 312 BC, the prevalence in Greek units of 'Persians' with Macedonian names in the third century BC, and the inferior status and role of most culturally Egyptian soldiers in the third century. When 20,000 *machimoi* took the field as phalangites at the Battle of Raphia, they were not the first Egyptians to fight in the main line since Gaza. They were instead the first to do so specifically as Egyptians. That means they were also not the only Egyptians in the battle line at Raphia: several hundred 'Persian' cavalry and perhaps thousands of formerly 'Persian' infantry were scattered throughout the force.

Chapter 5

The Age of Midas, Part I

The Wars of Ptolemy II Philadelphus, 282–246 BC

With the second of the Ptolemies we are faced with a bit of an interpretive problem: later Ptolemaic writers, some observers outside Egypt and many modern historians have all tended to describe the reign of Philadelphus as a golden age: the *floruit* of Hellenistic culture in Egypt and perhaps even across the Mediterranean generally, the apogee of Ptolemaic political, military and cultural power. His was an age defined by wealth but not yet corrupted by it. 'Lord and master of all is proud Ptolemy,' wrote Theocritus (*Idyll* 17), and his 'wealth exceeds that of all the princes of the earth put together'. Thus, Ptolemy II is our Midas, and we should therefore ask how much of Philadelphus' legendary power and prosperity are really myth.

Philadelphus was an excellent propagandist, or at least recognized the value of excellent propagandists at his court. He was a builder, and many permanent structures of the Ptolemaic army took shape under his rule, but they were not complete and were often developed piecemeal rather than as part of a grand strategy or blueprint for the army. The same held true for his architectural, literary, fiscal and cultural endeavours; in fact, they may have leaped ahead of military developments in some respects. The initial incongruence between the piecemeal, partial construction of military institutions and the golden age of Philadelphus may help illustrate the tension between the two genres of army operative in the Hellenistic age: the warband, bound by patronage to a powerful leader, and the institutional force, bound by law and custom to a state. Most Hellenistic armies, since the days of Philip and Alexander, mixed elements of both. The qualitative and quantitative distinctions between these two genres can be explored at greater depth in this and subsequent chapters. Philadelphus, during his reign, was sliding the scales of his army toward the institutional force, but that was a lengthy process, and throughout his reign, as we shall see, the imprint of the warband is often visible, even as the elements of the institutional army take shape and multiply.

The Context

In thinking about the politico-military developments of the Hellenistic Age, three phenomena occurred in Philadelphus' reign with far-reaching strategic implications. All occurred in nearly-simultaneous fashion, all-told fitting within a single decade: the last true Successor War, the Galatian invasion and Pyrrhus' wars with Rome.

First, in 281 BC, the last major upheaval among the Successor kingdoms took place until more than a century later. The war between Seleucus and Lysimachus ended in the latter's death and the disintegration of his kingdom. Just as Seleucus was poised to seize Macedonia – the homeland he had not revisited in fifty years – he was assassinated by one of Ptolemy II's half-brothers, Ptolemy Keraunos ('the Thunderbolt'). While Seleucus' son Antiochus held affairs together in Asia, Ptolemy marched on the Macedonian capital, sent those of Lysimachus' family he could not kill fleeing and made himself the new king of Macedonia. The conquest of Lysimachus' kingdom was the last overthrow of one Hellenistic kingdom by another, and coming twenty years after Ipsos reflected the first major disruption of the old coalition against the Antigonids.

Second, Ptolemy Keraunos had barely begun to settle affairs when an army of Galatians invaded his kingdom. The Galatian invasions, which spanned the 270s BC, mark a really significant moment in Hellenistic history: they were the first foreign people to break the apparent hegemony of Macedonian armies. Under a leader called Brennos, they marched into Macedonian territory, killed Keraunos and plundered the heartland of the Macedonian world with terrible savagery. For several years Macedonia was lost. A year or so after Keraunos' death, part of the Galatian army advanced into mainland Greece and was defeated while plundering Delphi. This signal event was immediately comprehended through an apocalyptic lens: an epiphany of the Olympic deities saved Greece where Macedonian armies failed, lending supernatural aid to regular Greeks. For the next decade, Macedonians sought to relegitimize their authority by demonstrating their own ability to contribute to the salvation of the Greek world from the Galatian menace. Even as they succeeded, the Galatian attack shattered the Macedonians' aura of invincibility. While the Macedonian dynasts held to power, the eventual triumph of one or another Macedonian power in the

Greek world could no longer be assumed. It would be a generation before the Macedonian homeland had the economy or population to power imperial ambitions.

Third, Pyrrhus of Epirus, the only blood relative of Alexander among the Successors, waged years of warfare against the Roman Republic, marking the first time the Macedonians and Romans met in battle. Pyrrhus failed to either subjugate or negotiate peace with the Romans, and returned to Greece in 275 BC. Ptolemy had good relations with Pyrrhus, who stayed at the court of Ptolemy I years earlier, and according to Justin, Philadelphus even sent him several thousand of his own soldiers and fifty elephants (Just. 17.2.14). These may have garrisoned Epirote holdings while Pyrrhus took his own army to Italy; at least, no references to Ptolemaic troops appear in the narrative sources, and the number of elephants Ptolemy is supposed to have sent is more than double that which Pyrrhus possessed in Italy. In the account of Justin, the troops were made available for two years; if so, Ptolemy wished to limit the length of Pyrrhus' absence from Greece and cap his own contributions to the western adventure. The two-year limit has also been read into the subsequent erosion of Ptolemaic support. Two years into Pyrrhus' campaign, he had failed to defeat the Roman hydra and had turned his armies against the Carthaginian Republic, with whom the Ptolemies had a treaty. In either case, two or three years into the campaign, Pyrrhus had lost Ptolemaic support. He may have gotten it back when he returned to Epirus in about 274 BC, then resumed his war against Antigonus for control of Macedonia. He certainly was able to hire mercenaries for the campaign, including Galatians (*Pyrr.* 26.2–6), and yet had been in dire straits financially when he crossed; Tarn (1913, pp.444–45) reckoned that this was possible only with Ptolemaic support. Within a couple of years, around 273/272 BC, Ptolemy II and the Roman Republic had established some sort of relationship of their own; while later sources claim Ptolemy sought out the Romans, it may be more likely the Romans hoped to prevent another attack on Italy by Pyrrhus.[1] The friendly disposition of the Ptolemies and the Republic, which began when the Ptolemies were the more powerful state, seems never to have wavered, even as the Republic became the leading state in the Mediterranean by defeating the other leading Macedonian powers.

In Ptolemy II's reign his military engaged in five major military actions in the Mediterranean world, and at least three major actions and likely many more in Africa. A basic timeline follows. He became co-ruler with his father in 284 BC, and sole ruler after the death of his father in 282. He then ruled another thirty-five years until his own death at the start of 246 BC. In the Mediterranean, he was involved in what is sometimes called the Carian War after the death of Lysimachus and then Seleucus I Nikator in 281 BC. That war, which may not have featured much fighting, ended by about 279 BC. Ptolemy then engaged in a campaign against Ethiopians, probably in the far Upper Nile region above Philae and Elephantine, likely around 276 BC. The First Syrian War, fought between the Ptolemies and Seleucids, began around 274 BC and lasted until about 272. Fighting probably took place in southern Asia Minor and definitely in Syria and Phoenicia. Fighting also occurred in Africa, where Magas of Cyrene, adopted son of Ptolemy I by his first wife, allied with the Seleucids and attempted to invade Egypt. Around 269 BC, Ptolemy started launching a series of major elephant-hunting expeditions, some from the Thebaid, others through the Red Sea. These continued on a fairly regular basis throughout the third century BC. In late 268 BC the Chremonidean War began, in which Ptolemaic forces lent support to a Greek coalition fighting against Antigonus. That war officially lasted until 262 BC, but naval confrontations between Ptolemaic and Antigonid forces continued for at least another year, and intermittently thereafter for nearly twenty years. The Second Syrian War began in 260 BC, and lasted until 253/252, with fighting in the Aegean, Asia Minor and Syria.

The Army of Philadelphus

There are only a handful of scattered reports on the size of the Ptolemaic army in Hellenistic literary sources from the reign of Philadelphus, and even fewer clear sources on their military operations. Theocritus' *Idylls* refer several times to Ptolemy's army, though he does not give specific numbers. He remarked on the pervasive Macedonian dress worn by the heterogeneous mass of soldiers in Alexandria ('all boots and military cloaks'), the general desirability of mercenary service for Ptolemy ('of paymasters a free man could have, the best') and Ptolemy's successful conquest and recruitment from southern Asia Minor ('all the Pamphylians and spear-wielding Cilicians, all the Lycians and war-loving Carians'). As for the size and quality of the army, he wrote that 'many the horsemen, many the foot with flashing bronze shields marshalled thickly about him'.[2] The first and last quotations refer to Macedonian-style troops, for whom the flashing bronze aspis, boots and military cloak nearly complete the full Macedonian costume (only a reference to the *kausia* cap or *sarissa* pike are lacking), while the middle two emphasize the importance of mercenaries and adventurers (see plate 7 fig. 11).

Two other sources provide numbers, though both have dubious credibility. In Callixenus' description of the Grand Procession at the Ptolemaia, he reports that the army totalled 57,600 infantry and 23,200 cavalry, 80,800 in all.[3] The cavalry are obviously too many, since the Ptolemies were only ever otherwise reported to have had 4,000–5,000 cavalry at Gaza (312 BC) and Raphia (217 BC) respectively, which in both cases included recently contracted mercenaries.[4] The infantry numbers are somewhat more reasonable, although still perhaps a little large. If 57,600 infantry marched, somewhere above 20,000 Egyptians must have been included and a similar number of mercenaries. If the numbers are to be taken as giving any indication of Ptolemaic manpower, one should at least elide δισμύριοι (20,000) from the text in describing the number of cavalry, for an army totalling a little more than 60,000 men, including 3,200 horse. If this adjusted number is of any reliability, it probably marks out an approximate maximum size for the Ptolemaic army under Philadelphus: about 61,000 soldiers. If it includes the marines from the Ptolemaic fleet, 61,000 may be fairly close. The last statement of manpower from the reign of Philadelphus is even less credible. Porphyry (*FGrH* 280.42) claimed to have learned from court histories that the Ptolemaic army had 'two hundred thousand infantry, twenty thousand cavalry, two thousand war chariots, and four hundred elephants'. These figures make those of Callixenus appear more attractive, but in general one must look with scepticism upon most sources for Ptolemaic manpower in the first half of the third century BC, precisely because of the tendency in later Ptolemaic sources to look at the reign of Philadelphus as a golden age.

The last measure from literary sources is the aforementioned account, in Justin, of Ptolemy's reinforcements for Pyrrhus. In 280 BC, Pyrrhus lobbied for support from the other Hellenistic monarchs as he prepared to embark on his campaign in Italy. From Ptolemy, he asked for 'some troops of Macedonians'. Ptolemy sent him '5,000 infantry, 4,000 cavalry, and 50 elephants' for two years' service (Just. 17.2.13–14). Is this testimony of any value in establishing the size of the Ptolemaic army? Justin had added beforehand that Ptolemy 'could not claim a lack of soldiers as an excuse'.[5] Pyrrhus asked for Macedonian troops in particular; these were probably some of the only troops truly in short supply in Ptolemaic Egypt. Therefore, the troops Ptolemy gave were probably mercenaries instead, and the number of cavalry is undoubtedly exaggerated. It would have been a massive undertaking to dispatch 4,000 horse from Egypt to Epirus, and Pyrrhus' expeditionary force only had 3,000 cavalry all told, and twenty elephants (Plut. *Pyrr.* 15.1). Around 5,000 infantry and 400 cavalry might be closer to the truth. The dispatch of those troops must also have left Ptolemy II with an army still more than sufficient for all his needs. Plutarch's *Pyrrhus* might provide some useful comparative evidence on what a sufficient army might be. Three times Plutarch recorded a size for Pyrrhus' army in Italy: 25,500 infantry and 3,000 cavalry (Plut. 15.1); 30,000 infantry and 2,500 cavalry (Plut. 22.4); and 20,000 infantry and 3,000 cavalry (Plut. 24.4); and then again for his campaign against Sparta, with 25,000 infantry and 2,000 cavalry (Plut. 26.9). It should follow, then, that Ptolemy II could comfortably field at least 30,000 foot and 3,000 horse for major campaigns.

As for the major military operations of Ptolemy II's reign, the First and Second Syrian Wars and the Ethiopian campaign, no narrative exists and no information on the size or makeup of the Ptolemaic army. Of course that is true for nearly every Hellenistic campaign after Ipsos in 301 BC and before the start of Polybius' narrative in the 220s. Documentary evidence assumes a critical role in discussing the army. Most of the documentary evidence relates to the military settlements rather than to the army in the field. But by addressing the settlements we will be in better shape to make sense of the scattered evidence for the field army and its operations. As a simple exemplar: from documentary evidence we know that Ptolemy II engaged in a major mobilization of *epigonoi* (civilian sons of military settlers) during the Second Syrian War for service as infantry. That he did so strongly suggests the manpower available among his military settlers and standing forces was insufficient for his wartime needs. This is the very opposite of what we might have guessed if we gave too much weight to Justin's claim about Philadelphus' abundant manpower. The idea of the Philadelphan Golden Age would lead us to imagine that the army at Raphia was only a shadow of what Philadelphus could have fielded. However, the documentary evidence suggests the opposite: under Philadelphus, the army was stretched thin, was too small to meet one of its most serious challenges and had to be expanded under both him and his son Ptolemy III and again under Ptolemy IV to field the 75,000 men at Raphia. Our good fortune is that a great deal of the process is evident in the documentary evidence.

Ptolemy the Founder, or Ptolemy Soter, fought and commanded under Alexander and claimed victories over great captains of his era and all time. His was a tough act to follow. Even in his advanced age, as the settling Hellenistic world saw fewer big wars, he and his forces figured prominently in the defence of Athens and the scuttling of Demetrius' plans to conquer the empire of Alexander. Seleucus captured Demetrius in autumn 285 BC, and that event may have convinced Ptolemy I to hand over the kingdom to his youngest son in spring 284. The two reigned together until the first Ptolemy's death in 282 BC. According to a tradition in Justin, Ptolemy I published to the people his wish to share the throne with his son while still living, and furthermore, Ptolemy I spent the last two years of his life as one of the bodyguards (*somatophylakes*, or in Latin *satellites*) of Ptolemy II (Just. 16.2.9). The reprise of his role under Alexander in service to his own son is a poetic conclusion. It has often been doubted, but may not be as far-fetched as sometimes imagined. Justin's text does not mean that Ptolemy I, at old age, joined the ranks of the hypaspists, but that he was one of the few senior staff officers to the new king. It may not be true, but it is not laughably implausible. Theocritus' idyll for Ptolemy has a fitting characterization of Ptolemy I, whom he imagines sharing raucous table in the afterlife with Heracles and Alexander in the halls of Zeus and carrying Heracles' club.

Ptolemy II was praised as a warrior, but there is no definitive evidence he was ever in battle, and in many cases may not have even been on campaign, although it seems likely he personally commanded three campaigns in the 270s BC. His strategic sense was impressive, however, as we may see in his actions amid the war between Lysimachus and Seleucus (282–281 BC). Lysimachus died in the Battle of Kyroupedion, fought in winter, early 281 BC. Well before the battle, Philadelphus was already increasing his own position in the contested Mediterranean littoral in Asia Minor. Memnon of Herakleia asserted that Seleucus was emboldened against Lysimachus when the latter lost legitimacy in the eyes of the people by ordering the murder of his son and heir and several other leading courtiers (*FGrH* 434.6); perhaps Ptolemy sensed the same weakness. Ptolemy's conquests in 282 and 281 BC seem to have been mostly or wholly bloodless. There was probably already a Ptolemaic presence in a few key coastal towns, but in this period Ptolemaic control extended over much of Lycia and Pamphylia.[6] Then Lysimachus was slain in battle, and seven months later Seleucus was assassinated by Ptolemy II's half-brother, Ptolemy Keraunos (Just. 17.2.4). So by late 281 BC, the last two of Alexander's officers were dead and the division of their empires was no easy task: while Lysimachus had no heir, both Keraunos and Antiochus I, son of Seleucus, could lay claim to parts of the combined empires as spear-won (Livy 33.40). Whether they could assert control over lands they claimed was another matter altogether. In the period of confusion that followed, Ptolemaic forces advanced even farther: Samos, Miletos, Halikarnassos and various other cities and regions of Ionia and Caria came under Ptolemaic control. A decree from Samos depicts the Ptolemaic admiral Philokles, king of Sidon, as an authoritative figure over cities across the Aegean coast (*IG XII*^{6} 1.95, *SEG* 1.363). Samos became a very important Ptolemaic naval base and numerous Samians entered Ptolemaic service.

The nature of the Ptolemaic conquests after Kyroupedion is ultimately unknown. It has often been assumed that there was a brief war between Ptolemy II and Antiochus, called the 'Carian War' or the 'War of the Syrian Succession'.[7] It is even possible that Keraunos' peace overtures to his brother included the gift of cities in south-west Asia Minor (Just. 17.2.9). He did not control them to gift, but in such a fluid situation following the death of two great kings, it is conceivable. Antiochus faced trouble in all corners: Keraunos was in Macedonia with some important portion of his father's royal army; Antigonus was lending aid to a coalition of north Anatolian states that refused to acknowledge Antiochus; the Seleukis – the core of Seleucid military settlement and city foundation in Syria – revolted; and a foreign power attacked the kingdom. The foreign attacker, mentioned mysteriously in an inscription from Ilion in Asia Minor (*OGIS* 219), should refer to either Antigonus or Ptolemy, and if to Ptolemy, then this 'War of the Syrian Succession' has feet. The eponymous officials of Miletos highlight some of the instability of these years (*Milet I* 3.123). In 282/281 BC, the year of Kyroupedion, the god Apollos was listed as the eponym, which functionally meant the seat was vacant. Then for 280/279 BC, King Antiochus was named, which means the city at least temporarily recognized his rule, not that he was physically present in Miletos. But the very next year the list records that Philadelphus made a gift of land to the city. The land given to the city was presumably royal land, and thus for Philadelphus to gift it to the city he must have been able to claim rights to the royal land in the region. So did Philadelphus' forces, very likely the fleet under Philokles of Sidon, capture Miletos from Seleucid forces or appeal successfully to the city to grant them entry instead of Antiochus' forces? Some historians have suggested Antiochus signed a treaty with Philadelphus that granted the cities, but that complicates subsequent Seleucid claims to the cities in a way that no later diplomacy acknowledges. For many cities, Philadelphus' assurances of protection must have been considerably more appealing than the desires of combatant forces, and Ptolemaic naval forces could probably act more quickly than Seleucid forces who were facing multiple threats simultaneously and attempting to occupy the whole of Lysimachus' former empire. Whether taken by violence or not, the Ptolemaic conquest of lands Antiochus claimed by his father's victory provided an important flashpoint for subsequent conflicts.

The early 270s BC are a particularly murky period, not because none of our ancient sources speak of the time, but because the era was marked by instability and violence. Keraunos claimed a large portion of Seleucus' field army and Lysimachus' navy, defeated Antigonus II and claimed Macedonia. As rapidly and violently as he rose, so was he tossed down, slain in battle against the Galatians. When the Galatians advanced into Greece, both Antiochus and Antigonus are recorded to have sent small detachments to help the Athenian-led defence at Thermopylae (279 BC), but there is no evidence Ptolemy sent aid. This is surprising, since Athens and Ptolemy were close allies. The Galatians were defeated at Delphi, and immediately a tradition broke out that the Olympian gods and various heroes' shades had contributed to the salvation of the Greeks. Kos, an island in the Ptolemaic sphere, offered thanks to the gods for the Greeks' common salvation (*Syll.3* 398), but made no mention of Ptolemaic assistance. Relations between Athens and Ptolemy were very good at that time, so the nature of Ptolemaic assistance may have been chiefly monetary. It may also be the case that all Ptolemaic forces in the Aegean were committed to the occupation of new territories in Asia Minor in 279 BC. For example, Amyzon in Caria – well inland, east of Miletos – was under Ptolemaic control, and honouring a Ptolemaic military governor of Caria, in 276 BC (*Amyzon* 7). At Erythrai in Ionia, it seems Ptolemaic troops helped secure that city against a possible attack by Galatians (*Syll.* 410), but did not actually secure it as a Ptolemaic possession. As the legend of the epiphany of the gods at Delphi grew, and as kings, cities and leagues gained credibility and honour for contributing to the defence of Greece, Ptolemy must have regretted the distraction or caution of his own commanders, who failed to secure him some signal credit in the salvation of Greece.

The Ethiopian War

In the early 270s BC, the Greek world was ravaged by Galatians, Antiochus and Antigonus fought a war against one another, and the throne of Macedonia was a revolving door of men who could not secure power; and yet Ptolemaic forces were content mainly to assert authority over a series of coastal cities in the Aegean. Instead, Ptolemy II's attention was in Egypt, and south of Egypt. Sometime before 275/274 BC, when the First Syrian War began, there was a war in Ethiopia. The historian Agatharchides wrote an account of the war, but little of it survives. However, Diodorus, who used

Agatharchides as a source, relates that whereas before Ptolemy Philadelphus hardly any Greek had ever visited Ethiopia or knew anything about it, that the king 'invaded Ethiopia with a Greek army' and subsequently the facts about Ethiopia were more accurate (Diod. 1.37.5).

A papyrus often connected to this war reports on the siege of one of the Ptolemaic forts around Elephantine by Ethiopians.[8] The fragmentary text is a draft of a letter to 'King Ptolemy' from Pertaios son of Arnouphis, usually identified as a garrison commander. Arnouphis is a common enough name in Egypt for us to conclude that Pertaios was an Egyptian in Ptolemaic service. He reported that Ethiopians had come down the Nile and laid siege to somewhere, perhaps Elephantine. He says that he and 'two brothers' (we might interpret these as officers) have instead surrounded the attacking force, and he requested further aid, promising to keep the attackers hemmed in. Pertaios might be viewed as a field commander rather than fort commander, who alongside the 'two brothers' mobilized local troops, broke up the siege and instead trapped the attackers somewhere. If Pertaios was from the Egyptian priestly-military aristocracy, the other two officers might literally have been his brothers.

From the fragments of Agatharchides we possess only the story about 500 mercenary cavalrymen from Greece whom Ptolemy recruited for the war. The 100 horsemen who operated in the vanguard of the army received special equipment for themselves and their mounts, with 'felt robes, which the people there call *kasai*, and cover the whole body except for the eyes' (F20). Their armour, made of felt, was probably a type of quilted garment; thick layers of wool were pressed together and sewn. The *kasai* are known even from early modern times. Ptolemy probably had them distributed to defend the riders against missile weapons, and especially the poisonous javelins and arrows used by Ethiopian warriors (Theophrastus *Hist.Plant.* 9.15.2, Agatharchides F10). The addition of 500 mercenary horsemen suggests the campaign was conducted on a fairly large scale, while the provision of local armour to protect against local weapons suggests planning and preparation for a major operation.

The limited evidence suggests that Ptolemy II himself went on the campaign. It may have begun with the Ethiopian attack from the Pertaios letter, although it is easy enough to imagine that the ill-defined southern border invited fairly regular raids. But the raids may have escalated to the point that Ptolemy himself took an army up the Nile beyond Elephantine. A Roman campaign in the reign of Augustus culminated in the sack of Napata near the fourth cataract (*Res Gestae* 26); it is conceivable Ptolemy's campaign drove as far or further. He definitely secured Ptolemaic claims to the 'Dodekaschoinos', a region stretching from the first cataract at Syene, Elephantine and Philae upriver (south) to Pselkis and Takompsos, modern Al-Maharraqa. Ptolemy II gave the revenues of the region to the temple of Isis at Philae, so at the least his campaign secured that region. However, studies of temple inscriptions at Philae have indicated that Ptolemy claimed the subjugation of the Nile even beyond Meroë, essentially as far as modern Khartoum.[9] A reference in Pliny the Elder (6.180) attributed to Bion, a Cypriot in service to Philadelphus, contains an itinerary of the Upper Nile and a remark that elephants are not spotted until near Meroë, while two others of Pliny's sources were Ptolemaic naval commanders from Philadelphus' reign, one of whom, Timosthenes, reported that it took sixty days to sail from Syene to Meroë (Pliny 6.183). Together, these testimonies suggest the Ptolemaic campaign extended that far, about 1,000 miles beyond Syene and Elephantine.

Because Agatharchides' book concerned the Red Sea, we might also conjecture that Ptolemy's forces struck into that region as well. Eventually the Ptolemies built permanent settlements on the western side of the Red Sea, but in the early 270s BC Ptolemaic forces may have campaigned there too. The Pithom stele (*CM* 22183) may even make reference to the campaign when it describes how Ptolemy II ordered the delivery of horses from or the marshalling of his cavalry in the land of Punt, and how the people of Punt recognized his kingship and sent him tribute (line 9). It is difficult to be sure, but 'Punt' should be a reference to the Ethiopian regions closer to the Red Sea, which in modern terms included the south-east of Egypt through Eritrea. The Pithom stele entry describes the king's activities between those of his sixth year (most likely 280/279 BC[10]) and the First Syrian War, which fits the chronology for the Ethiopian campaign. It may then be appropriate to speak of multiple campaigns rather than one, one down the Red Sea and the other down the Nile. The Ptolemies eventually devoted enormous resources to their activities in Ethiopia, only in part to secure elephants for their armies; I suspect Philadelphus' war was profitable and encouraged further campaigns. It did not, however, end in the real conquest of the Meroitic kingdom, but instead its tributary status.

The First Syrian War

The war in Ethiopia ended and the First Syrian War, between Ptolemy II and Antiochus I, began soon after. This war has no real narrative source. Theocritus' celebration of Philadelphus' conquests in *Idyll 17* 77–94 is a helpful starting point, penned at the end of the war. In it, he notes Ptolemaic control of parts of Phoenicia, Arabia, Syria, Libya and Ethiopia. This last country surely captures a reference by the poet to the Ethiopian war. The next part of the list refers to his control over Pamphylia, Cilicia, Lycia, Caria and the Cyclades islands. His control of the entire south Anatolian coast, after Ptolemy I controlled nothing more than a few ports in the region, often led to the view that the war was mainly conducted in Asia Minor. However, it is clear now that Ptolemy II gained his foothold in Lycia, Caria and Pamphylia well before the war began. Only Cilicia lacks any firm evidence, and so it alone might mark a conquest of war. Even so, Rough Cilicia, east of Pamphylia, is probably meant, not the Cilician plain. The Ptolemaic conquests of Anemurion, Nagis, Meydancik Kale and perhaps as far as Aphrodisias may belong to this conflict. The territorial references are often militarized: 'the Cilician spearmen' and 'war-loving Lycians and Carians'. The conquests are situated within the actions of the Ptolemaic military, 'the finest fleet sailing the sea' and the many troops of his field army, 'cavalry and *aspidiotai* in flashing bronze', the latter a clear reference to Macedonian-style phalangites.

A little more useful than Theocritus in setting up a narrative of the war is the account in Pausanias (1.7), written centuries later. Pausanias relates that after Ptolemy II married his full sister Arsinoe, in response his maternal half-brother Magas, the governor of Cyrene, led the Cyreneans in a revolt and was proclaimed king. This touched off a short war between Ptolemy II and Magas in which Ptolemy contracted numerous mercenaries and prepared the defences of Egypt. Magas' campaign fizzled out because of a revolt in Libya, but he also convinced Antiochus I to join him in an attack on Ptolemy. Because the threat from Magas ended abruptly and Ptolemy was already prepared for war, Ptolemy's forces were able to act more quickly than those of Antiochus, and according to Pausanias, 'Ptolemy dispatched forces against the whole realm of Antiochus, against the weaker raiders to ravage the country, against the stronger an army to shut them off. The result was Antiochus was never able to attack Egypt.' This suggests a far-ranging war, with naval power and regional forces used to harry less dangerous foes, and here Cilicia or parts of Caria and Ionia that were not in Ptolemaic hands come to mind. But the field army must have been active in the Levant, where Pausanias' wording could imply a campaign into Seleucid territory to prevent a Seleucid invasion, or a strong defensive arrangement in Ptolemaic territory in Syria to deter an attack.

In chronological terms, the Pausanias evidence suggests that Magas' attack only shortly preceded the outbreak of the larger war, and that it followed fairly soon after Ptolemy's marriage to Arsinoe II. Pausanias also adds that, among the mercenaries Ptolemy hired when he learned of Magas' revolt, there were 4,000 Galatians. These Galatians then became seditious themselves and sought to find a way to plunder Egypt. Ptolemy feigned ignorance of the plot and led them to land in the Delta that could be flooded to make an island. Trapped, they were starved to death, or according to other sources, were burned in an attack by Ptolemy, who may have employed artillery to set fire to the island. Ptolemy capitalized on the Galatian mutiny – rumoured or real – to gain his own reputation-building Galatian victory. The court poet Callimachus incorporated the Galatian invasions in his *Hymn to Delos*, and equated the victory at Delphi with Ptolemy's rescue of Alexandria – from his own mercenaries. Some scepticism about the number of Galatians is warranted, and also whether Ptolemy actually killed them all: after all, Galatians were present in large numbers in Egypt, especially in Alexandria. But we can take from the account how heavily Ptolemy relied on newly recruited mercenaries at this juncture, since the 4,000 Galatians were only one contingent among the troops he hired.

Ptolemaic and Seleucid documents suggest that much of the war was fought in Syria, where Pausanias described the Ptolemaic army holding off the Seleucid army. The Pithom stele is a monumental inscription set up by Egyptian priests and the king at Pithom, east of the Nile. It provides a very rough outline from the Ptolemaic side, and an astronomical diary from Babylon provides a few choice details from the Seleucid side. The Pithom stele records two events from the war. First, an undated entry, fitted chronologically between the Ethiopian war and November 274 BC, reports that Ptolemy personally invaded Asia, and depending on the interpretation of the stele, claimed a victory there, either in Palestine or in Persia.[11] An exaggerated reference to 'Persia' may be more likely indicative of the tenor of court propaganda than the range of the campaign. He acquired plunder, and in the priestly Pithom stele the most significant finds were Egyptian gods who could be returned to Egypt. In Egypt, he celebrated his victory, and sections 14–15 of the Pithom stele celebrate 'Ptolemy, to whom foreign lands are in subjection, abiding on the throne, lord of all lands.' From this we might interpret that Ptolemy launched an initial attack or raid that was successful enough to claim victory.

Second, in the next lines (15–16), dated to the start of Ptolemy II's year 12 (November 274 BC), the stele records that Ptolemy and his wife,

Arsinoe II, returned to Pithom (Heroonpolis) to discuss the defence of Egypt against enemies. In 274 BC at a city near Sinai and the eastern desert, the enemies must by the Seleucids, not Magas and the Cyreneans. From 'discuss' we might infer the management of an ongoing campaign in the Levant as well as preparations for any possible Seleucid offensive into Egypt itself. There is no reference to Arsinoe II in the Pithom account until this entry. Their marriage is not firmly dated, but a Phoenician inscription from Cyprus refers to Ptolemy II's first wife, Arsinoe I, in year 11, or 275/274 BC. If the Pithom stele entry refers to November 274 BC, the marriage must have taken place at some point between, approximately, November 275 and October 274.[12] This poses a difficulty for reconciling the evidence from Pithom and from Pausanias, since Pausanias casts the marriage to Arsinoe as the event that ignited the wars, first with Magas, then through Magas with Antiochus. If correct, this compresses an awful lot of activity into a year or less: the marriage, Magas' revolt, his and Ptolemy's subsequent campaigns in Libya and Ptolemy's invasion of Syria and triumphant return. Especially given the need to hire mercenaries abroad, the timeline does not work. We might weigh the possibilities, first, that Ptolemy actually instigated the war in Syria, not Magas and Antiochus, or second, that Magas revolted before the official wedding to Arsinoe II, setting off a series of campaigns that could have stretched back into 275 or even 276 BC.

The Babylonian astronomical diary provides details on the war that are firmly dated to March and April 273 BC.[13] King Antiochus I was marching to Syria from Sardis in Asia Minor to fight against the Egyptians, whose army was operating in Seleucid Syria. The Egyptian attack and Antiochus' march had both begun sometime prior to March. Meanwhile, on 26 March the satrap of Babylonia dispatched twenty elephants sent from Baktria and enormous stores gathered from Babylonia to support the war effort in Syria. Then, in April, after levying troops across the length and breadth of Babylonia, a Seleucid general marched with an army to join the king and his other forces in Syria. When Antiochus and his marshalled army moved to confront the Ptolemaic army, it withdrew to friendly territory. The diary also adds that throughout the year bronze coinage was used in Babylon instead of silver, which almost certainly relates to the concentration of silver bullion in royal coffers to pay soldiers. Nothing in the text suggests that particularly heavy fighting took place. Unless the Pithom stele dates should be adjusted to Ptolemy II's sole rule, we can identify the Ptolemaic force in Syria as an army dispatched around November 274 BC, when Ptolemy and

Arsinoe were at Heroonpolis, and driven back to Ptolemaic territory in April or May 273. This shades the discussion at Heroonpolis, recorded in the Pithom stele, in a more offensive tenor: while defensive issues may have been discussed, they may also have been overseeing the marshalling of troops for a winter campaign.

The diary also demonstrates that, whatever the nature of Ptolemy's initial campaign into Seleucid territory, Antiochus did not march to meet him then. Instead, the diary makes it clear that Antiochus had been at or around Sardis in Asia Minor since at least 276/275 BC. Inscriptions support the same view.[14] Antiochus was facing the Galatian invasion in Asia Minor, and if he was preparing a campaign against Ptolemy, he was probably planning to attack Ptolemaic positions in Asia Minor first. It seems he did not count Ptolemy's first invasion, which we should probably characterize as a large raid, as meriting his withdrawal from the theatre of operations against the Galatians and against Ptolemy's possessions in Asia Minor. Perhaps Ptolemy was already withdrawing by the time Antiochus knew of the campaign. It is also possible that Antiochus was not able to react effectively at that time: he had recently completed a war against rebels in the Seleukis of Syria, may not have been confident in their loyalty, and the forces around him in Asia Minor were short on the heavy infantry he would need to face Ptolemy's phalanx head-to-head: 'a small force, mostly peltasts and ranged troops'.[15] Bar-Kochva has suggested that Ptolemy's raid reached the city of Apamea-on-the-Orontes, where he captured most of the Seleucid elephant herd still living out of the hundreds of elephants Seleucus I received from India.[16] That would explain two things: first, the importance of just twenty elephants from Baktria to the Seleucid war effort; and second, the presence of at least twenty-five and as many as 100 trained elephants in Ptolemy's Grand Procession, before the creation of elephant hunting grounds in Africa. At the Procession, elephants drew twenty-five chariots, singly or in pairs or fours. Thus, when Antiochus did eventually defeat the Galatians in battle, in a battle known as the Elephant Victory, he only had sixteen elephants (Lucian, *Zeuxis* 9), which represented either a rump force that were not seized in Ptolemy's campaign, or most of the elephant reinforcement sent from Baktria in 273 BC.

The Grand Procession of Ptolemy II fell within or soon after the First Syrian War, in late winter of either 274 or 270 BC. It is described in Athenaeus (*Deip.* 5.196a–203b). The Procession was part of the Ptolemaia festival, an event of Olympic scale designed to honour Ptolemy I, Berenike I, Alexander and, by extension, Ptolemy II too. Shields taken from the defeated Galatians decorated the grand pavilion where Ptolemy II hosted foreign guests. Indian elephants drew chariots in the procession, and a huge portion of the parade was dedicated to wild animals, ivory and ebony from Ethiopia. All three of these elements in the parade push the date of the Procession past their occurrence: the Ethiopian campaign was probably between 278 and 275 BC, while the victory over the Galatian mercenaries and the attack on Syria may have occurred in 275 or even later. As previously mentioned, Athenaeus' account, drawn from the second-century BC Ptolemaic official and historian Callixenus, recorded 57,600 infantry and 23,200 cavalry marching in the Procession. The display did not centralize Ptolemy's military victories, but rather situated them within a narrative of filial piety and shared divinity: Ptolemy's campaigns into distant lands associated him with Dionysus, while his piety toward his father associated Ptolemy I with Dionysus' father Zeus, reinforced by the abundant wealth Ptolemy put on display.

The outcome of the First Syrian War is unclear. If either side gained truly significant territory or inflicted a significant defeat on the other side, the evidence for it is lost. Ptolemy certainly claimed victory (perhaps multiple times, after his personal invasion of Syria and then at the end of the war), but the measure of the victory is difficult to measure, and Antiochus likely also counted himself the victor. There probably was, for example, a victory in this period for Seleucid allies in Asia Minor, where a combined force of Pontic troops allied with Antiochus, and their Galatian allies, now fighting on their side, defeated a Ptolemaic expeditionary force and plundered their ships (Apollonius (*FGrH* 740) 14). In all, the war appears to have been something of a draw. It merits recollection, however, that this was the first conflict between the Seleucid and Ptolemaic families, that Seleucus I had fought at Ptolemy I's side at Gaza, and Ptolemy helped Seleucus regain Babylonia. Tensions had risen over the Ptolemaic role in the last war against Antigonus, and presumably over Ptolemaic expansion at Seleucid cost after Lysimachus' death, but in the 270s BC there was a longer record of accrued friendship than of enmity or antagonism. That would, of course, change.

The Chremonidean War and Ptolemaic Sea Power in the Aegean

In the 260s BC, the Ptolemaic military operated extensively in the Aegean in support of mainland Greeks in the Chremonidean War, and also in the Red Sea as the Ptolemies opened elephant hunting grounds. The Chremonidean War is probably best characterized as a disaster.[17] It was an attempt to re-establish the Greek League on Athenian and Spartan leadership, backed by Ptolemaic support from abroad, and opposed to Antigonid activity in Greece. There is no reason to doubt Ptolemy II instigated the war, which began in the autumn of 268 BC. He was the king who 'ruled the waves' (Theocritus 17.85), and the Chremonidean War was a test in power projection.

Ptolemaic naval power was preliminary to Ptolemaic power in the Aegean world. The Ptolemaic navy attained world-class status under Ptolemy II. Incredible investment in the navy yielded a massive fleet with many of the largest vessels of the day. The most complete listing of the ships in the fleet comes from Athenaeus. We might suspect that his account, compiled from earlier sources centuries later and selected for impact rather than necessarily accuracy, contains invention or exaggeration. However, an inscription from Philadelphus' reign confirms one of the most incredible elements, and suggests that much of Athenaeus' account is reliable. Athenaeus recorded that the largest ships in Philadelphus' fleet were two 'thirties' and a 'twenty'. Polyremes were named for the number of personnel in each rank on each bank at the oars. These three largest ships were almost certainly catamaran-style galleys that combined two 'tens' or two 'fifteens', ships of enormous scale in their own right.[18] A designer named Pyrgoteles built at least two of these ships for Philadelphus, at least one of the 'thirties' and the 'twenty', and Ptolemy honoured him with a statue at a sanctuary at Paphos in Cyprus (*OGIS* 39). The fleet had at least 109 other polyremes, twenty rated higher than 'tens', sixty-seven rated as 'nines' or 'sevens' and twenty-two rated as 'sixes' and 'fives'. There were another 200 lighter warships rated as 'trihemiolias', 'trieres' and 'tetreres'. These figures probably did not even include the Nile navy and its hundreds of smaller craft. A papyrus from 257 BC refers to a 'ten', unmentioned in Athenaeus, which might mean that his source was providing figures on the Ptolemaic fleet at some point earlier than 257 BC, or could simply reflect inaccuracies in his record (*P.Col.Zen.* 63). The polyremes in the fleet, even those of lesser size, were very expensive to build and operate. The crew of large polyremes numbered in the upper hundreds. Maintaining the Ptolemaic naval presence in the Aegean, called the Ptolemaic 'thalassocracy' (rule of the sea), incurred tremendous expense, that was only intensified in a time of war.

Antigonus II Gonatas was the premier power in mainland Greece when the Chremonidean War broke out. After the death of Lysimachus, the Galatian invasion and Pyrrhus' death at Argos, Antigonus gained preeminence in Greece practically by default. Yet he also bore the reputation of an able, prudent monarch. Athens had, with Ptolemaic assistance, liberated many of the strongpoints in Attica from Macedonian control in the 280s BC, but there were still Macedonian garrisons near the city, including in the port at Piraeus. Furthermore, Antigonus controlled the 'fetters of Greece': Corinth, Chalkis on Euboea and Demetrias in Magnesia. The aim of the Chremonidean War was, under the shared leadership of the conventionally royal Areus of Sparta and the anti-Macedonian faction at Athens, to break the fetters and contain the Antigonid kingdom. In such a conflict, Athens and Attica became a natural flashpoint, the easiest of the anti-Macedonian partners to knock out of the conflict. Thus Athens' allies – chiefly Sparta and the Ptolemaic forces in the Aegean – had to be able to either operate in Attica to shore up Athenian defences or prevent the concentration of Macedonian forces by operating and threatening everywhere else. Antigonus attacked Athens soon after the war began, and laid siege to the city before the Ptolemaic fleet could send aid (Paus. 3.6.4).

The leader of the Ptolemaic effort in the Chremonidean War, at least in its early stages, was a general named Patroklos, the son of Patron, a Macedonian in Ptolemaic service. He was a prominent courtier at Alexandria, and perhaps a favourite of Queen Arsinoe II. The Ptolemaic admiral, Kallikrates, the son of Boiskos, a Samian, was certainly a favourite of Arsinoe and major supporter of court propaganda.[19] He managed to establish several bases of operations in Attica, but according to the meagre ancient testimonies to the war was never able to intervene at the sort of scale that could actually challenge Antigonus. The chief Ptolemaic base in Attica was on an island at the peninsula's southern tip, which is sometimes called 'Island of Patroklos' even to this day. From there, and with the permanent naval bases at Methana (Arsinoe) and Andros nearby, the Ptolemaic navy should have been able to effectively blockade the Macedonians at Piraeus. If Arsinoe-Methana had not been founded prior to the Chremonidean War, it certainly was founded in the course of the war.[20] Then Patroklos should have been able to establish a series of fortified beachheads in Attica and used those to take an indirect approach against the Macedonians. With naval dominance, he could use his freedom of movement to concentrate his forces selectively against weak Macedonian defences and steadily push them toward the western borders of Attica. Indeed, Patroklos and his forces established several fortified positions in Attica, chiefly at Koronoi in the north-east and around Hieropolis in the south-west, while linking up with Athenian forces at Rhamnous in the north and perhaps with Spartan forces further west.

From a promising start, Patroklos' operations never materialized as a significant threat to Macedonian operations in Attica. As for why, the traditional answer is that the Ptolemaic military was already ineffective, lacking the military will to attack, and was mainly there to subsidize the Greek forces fighting Antigonus. Instead, it seems that pirate raiders were a real problem in Attica (*SEG* 24.154), and their impact should be considered more seriously than anyone has. The pirates should be recognized as the eager agents of an Antigonid stratagem to circumvent the Ptolemaic forces' dominance in conventional naval warfare. Antigonus had a famous pirate, Ameinias, as one of his foremost Friends (Polyaenus 4.6.18 and Plut. *Pyrr.* 29), and when Antigonus' nephew Alexandros rebelled at Corinth around 250 BC, he sent pirates to raid Antigonid positions around Attica (*IG II²* 1225). Continual raiding by light craft would damage and distract Ptolemaic operations, and thus effectively hamper the Ptolemaic military advantages that would have existed under a purely conventional conflict. Thus, when Patroklos should have been orientated toward effective attacks on Macedonian land operations in Attica, he was instead distracted by building a series of additional supporting bases around the Aegean, at multiple sites on Crete, Thera, Keos and perhaps elsewhere.[21] There are two possible explanations for building bases in the middle of the war that were further removed from the theatre of conflict than those that existed when the war began. The first is that the naval domain was contested – by raiding craft using irregular tactics – and the development of additional bases was meant to facilitate resupply, communication and deterrent patrols. The second is that the concentration of Ptolemaic capital to support the war effort in the Aegean encouraged Patroklos and his naval commander, Kallikrates, to build what they could while they could. Either way, the construction of bases in the outer Aegean necessarily distracted from operations in Attica.

The crisis of the war was a series of engagements around 266–264 BC. Pausanias (3.6.5) records that Patroklos and King Areus were trying to coordinate their movements to allow them to attack the Macedonians from front and rear when the Macedonians moved to attack Areus. In Pausanias, it seems Patroklos criticized the military qualities of his Egyptian forces, 'it being implausible for Egyptian sailors to confront Macedonians on land'. The text certainly carries some prejudicial sentiment, but also reflects a more straightforward military condition: the Macedonian army included well-trained and well-equipped heavy infantry and cavalry in fortified camps, while Patroklos' forces, even if they too were Macedonians rather than Egyptians, were sailors and marines attacking a prepared enemy. This realization on the part of Patroklos accords well with his fortification strategy. It points toward a desire to conduct a less regular engagement with the Macedonians, or at least one outside their fortifications. In Pausanias' account (3.6.6), the campaign season ended without a battle after Areus' troops ran low on supplies. Between Justin and the Prologue of Trogus, it is possible to expand the plan of Patroklos and Areus to force a battle. From the Prologue (26) and Justin (26.2), we know Antigonus was drawn out of the siege of Athens to deal with a revolt by a band of Galatian mercenaries posted in Megara, west of Athens. Perhaps Patroklos or Areus convinced them to mutiny. The Galatians came out against Antigonus' force, and both the Spartan and Ptolemaic armies were nearby and beheld the engagement. Their presence at the battle between Antigonus and his own Galatians suggests they were attempting to catch Antigonus in the open and defeat him. But the Galatians were wiped out, and according to Justin, at the moment the Macedonians were most vulnerable to follow-up attack, the Spartan and Ptolemaic armies marvelled at them and withdrew from the field of battle. These events probably took place in 266 or 265 BC. Then in spring 264 BC, Areus, the Spartans and their Peloponnesian allies set out for Attica again, and were met at the Isthmus near Corinth by the Macedonian army. A general engagement took place, without any Ptolemaic forces on hand, and Areus was slain.

The closing years of the war involved mainly the siege of Athens and its eventual capitulation, and at some point a grand naval battle at Kos. The Battle of Kos may have taken place at the end of the war, or quite plausibly several years later, but even so it serves as the ending point for the Ptolemaic campaign in the Aegean against Antigonus. At some point in the war, Patroklos sent Antigonus a gift of fish and figs: the Ptolemaic navy controlled the sea, so Antigonus could eat figs (Ath. 8.433a–b). Perhaps Patroklos sent the taunt early in the war, but it might also belong to the period after the capitulation of Athens. While the Greek League failed to break the fetters of Greece, Ptolemaic control in the Aegean had only increased over the course of the war. Kos is on the opposite side of the Aegean from Attica, so how the battle came to take place there needs explanation. It seems most likely that, with the Peloponnesians out of the picture, Antigonus was able to push Patroklos and his forces steadily out of Attica, and then undertake a more conventional naval campaign to challenge Ptolemaic dominance in the Aegean. That campaign may well have taken years, and melded with the Second Syrian War as a challenge to Ptolemaic power by both Antiochus II and Antigonus from the middle 260s into the 250s BC. Thus Miletos, in the Ptolemaic sphere, faced unrest and attacks in the late 260s BC, which led to activity there by Ptolemy II's heir Ptolemaios the Son (most likely the son of Lysimachus and Arsinoe II), the admiral Kallikrates and a host of Ptolemy's friends and military forces (*I.Milet.* 1.3.139). A dedication in honour of Pelops son of Alexandros at Samos, present there as a campaign commander (*IG* XII[6] 1:119), but eponymous priest of Alexander in 264/263 BC, may also date to this period in the late 260s. Whenever the battle occurred, Antigonus met the Ptolemaic navy with his own fleet, and though they were outclassed and outnumbered, they gained the victory.[22] We know that Antigonus chided his admirals for their fearfulness of the Ptolemaic armament (Plut. *Mor.* 545.b–c), and that Antigonus fought from a 'sacred trireme' of exceptional size and quality, which he dedicated after the battle.[23] Unfortunately, that is all we know about the battle.

Ptolemaic power in the Aegean ebbed after the Chremonidean War, and we might ponder briefly whether Ptolemy's containment outcome might have been accomplished more successfully if he had been willing to commit more land troops to the struggle. The effort was undoubtedly an enormous inefficiency: the cost of a naval armament like Ptolemy's must have been huge, and the economic return on the investment quite limited. Why refuse to risk ground troops in the campaign but expend a fortune on a grand but under-utilized navy? In contemplating this question, Ptolemaic strategy may become more familiar, but perhaps not any clearer.

The Elephant Expeditions

The elephant hunt operations in the 260s BC set a trajectory for Ptolemaic military endeavours that lasted the rest of the third century. The Pithom stele helps date the key developments to the period between 269 and early 264 BC. According to the stele, Ptolemy II himself was present for the construction of some of the key stations, ports and especially the lock on the canal between the Nile and Red Sea through Heroonpolis (lines 20–21, see also Diod. 1.33.11). After securing access to the Red Sea with a foundation called Arsinoe-in-Egypt, he commissioned a grand expedition under his 'first general' far down the coast (lines 22–25). This general led forces far down the Red Sea and established a city there named for Ptolemy, which must therefore be Ptolemais Theron (Ptolemais 'of the hunts'). The founder of that city, according to Strabo (16.4.7), was a courtier named Eumedes. Neither the Pithom stele nor Strabo provide extensive detail, but what they provide is complementary. Eumedes built defences, avoided major conflict with local powers and occupied the city and other posts with soldiers. He hunted large numbers of elephants and gathered an array

1. Gold issues of the first four Ptolemies:
a. Stater of Ptolemy I. MET DP.16199.004. (*Public domain*)
b. Trichryson (*pentadrachm*) of Ptolemy II. ANS 1944.100.64172. (*Public domain*)
c. Mnaieon (*oktodrachm*) of Ptolemy II. ANS 1967.152.620.obv. (*Public domain*)
d. Mnaieon of Ptolemy IV. MET inv. 30.115.21. (*Public domain*)

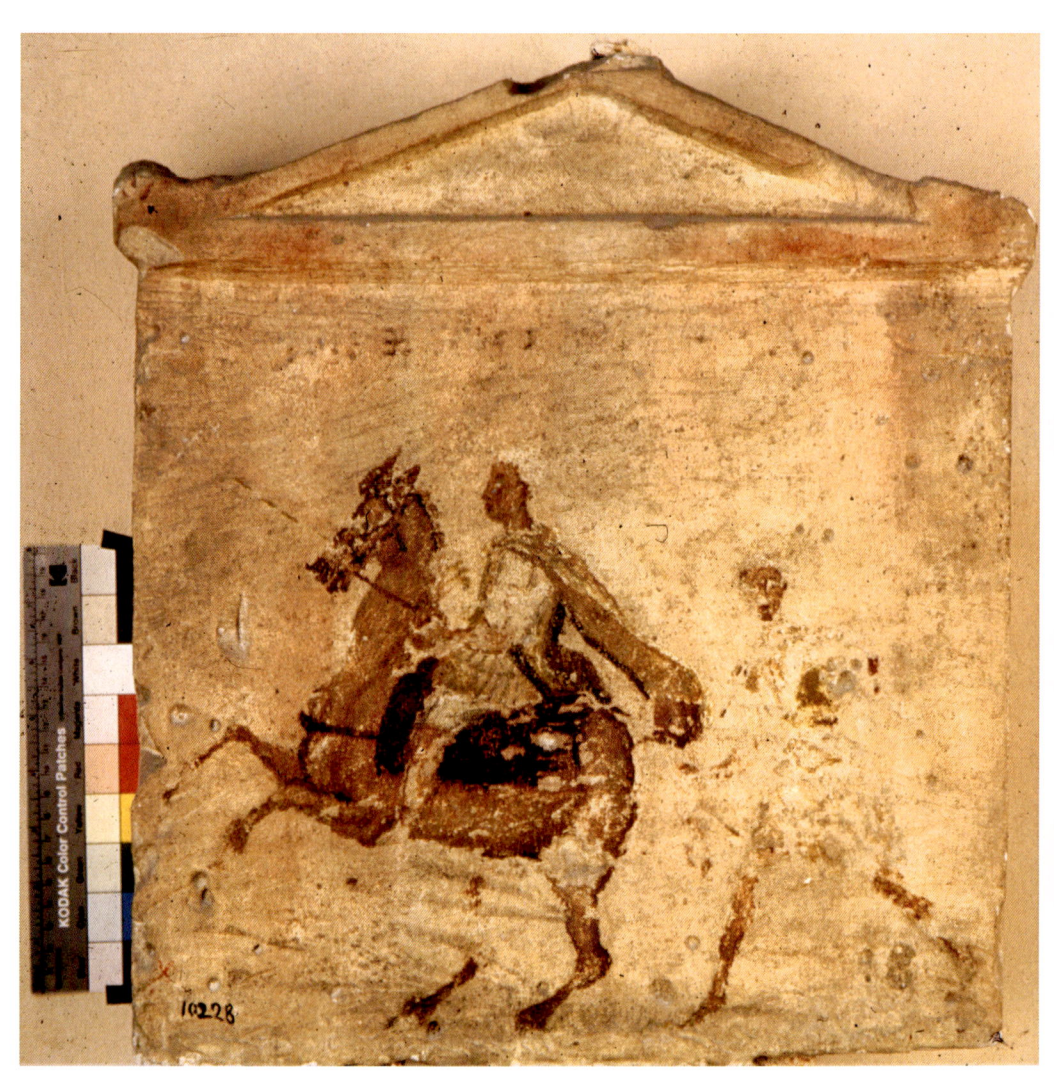

2. Stele of a Macedonian cavalryman, Alexandria Museum inv. 10228. The deceased, mounted on a rearing horse, rides to the left. The horse furniture is all in dark leather, with a deep scarlet-brown riding blanket. Reins in his left, a *xyston* in his right, the rider is helmetless, with a fine chlamys in saffron yellow and purple stripe flowing behind him, like the Companions in Alexander's army. (*Photograph A. Lecler, © CEAlex archives, with thanks for this and others to Marie-Dominique Nenna*)

3. Stele of an *Agema* officer, Alexandria Museum inv. 10689. The deceased stands with a long spear gripped above eye level in his left arm. His red helmet is in the Phrygian style, with a silvered Atticizing visor, a horsetail crest and two feathers. His chiton is also red, a chlamys over his arm white. He wears greaves and a bronze muscled cuirass with bronze pteryges. A rimless shield was bronze with traces of red paint. (*Photograph A. Pelle, © CEAlex archives*)

4. Stele of the Thessalian Polyoktos, Alexandria Museum inv. 10233. Two men in armour grasp hands, with a boy attending the man on the left. The left figure wears a muscled cuirass in bronze over a long white chiton, and a conical helmet. The man on the right wears a white corselet, presumably of linen, with two or three rows of long ptergyes, over a deep scarlet chiton, and a chlamys in a dark ochre yellow. (*Photograph A. Lecler, © CEAlex archives*)

5. Stele of the Thessalian Lykinos, Alexandria Museum inv. 18824. The deceased extends his hand to a son or boy attendant. Lykinos wears a tanned corselet with two rows of pteryges and a reddish stripe on his belly. He wears a saffron yellow chlamys, a violet chiton and tanned boots. The boy stands behind a nearly rimless and very convex reddish-bronze shield. (*Photograph A. Lecler, © CEAlex archives*)

6. Stele of a Ptolemaic soldier, Musée Archaeologique Nationale inv. 31232. The deceased stands leaning on a spear in his right hand, gripped at shoulder height. He wears a bronze muscled cuirass and a long yellow chiton, with an even longer chlamys draped over his left shoulder, brown, with a light blue-green stripe at the end. Behind his right leg are the traces of a sizeable shield. (*© MAN (France)/Loïc Hamon, with thanks to Françoise Aujogue*)

7. Stele of a Ptolemaic soldier, Alexandria Museum inv. 19110. The deceased stands between two attending boys. He wears a white corselet with deep red shoulder harness and a deep red stripe across his belly. A chlamys is over his shoulder, and a sword hangs in its scabbard on a baldric by his left. He grasps a spear low in his left hand, cradling it along his left forearm as it extends over his shoulder. Barely visible by his left leg is a small round shield. (*Photograph A. Lecler, © CEAlex archives*)

8. Stele of the Bithynian Dionysios, Alexandria Museum inv. 20919. The oval shield was borrowed from the Galatians over the course of the third century BC. Dionysios' attendant wears his conical hat or helmet and carries the shield and two javelins. Dionysios carries a heavier spear himself and wears a brown chiton with a thick vertical stripe in white or cream, and a wreath upon his head. (*Photograph A. Lecler, © CEAlex archives*)

9. Stele of the Galatian Bitos, Metropolitan Museum inv. 04175. We see the nearly body-length *thureos* with a round bronze thimble boss. The red-bearded Galatian warrior wears the typical woad blue cloak. The pommel of a sword, belted high on his right waist, is barely visible, and his right hand holds a spear. Like many Galatians, he presents ready for military service, nude under the woad-dyed cloak. (*Public domain*)

10. Stele of the Galatian –atos, Metropolitan Museum inv. 04176. The soldier is again nude save for a long woad blue cloak. He has a dark moustache, but many other details are lost. A sword with typically La Tene trilobate pommel seems visible at his right waist, suiting Celtic fashion. An attendant holds a long, narrow *thureos*, lavishly decorated with triplet red crescents on each end, blue and yellow fields, and a white boss and spine. (*Public domain*)

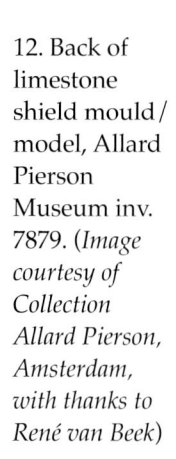

11. Limestone mould/model for Ptolemaic bronze shields, Allard Pierson Museum inv. 7879. (*Image courtesy of Collection Allard Pierson, Amsterdam, with thanks to René van Beek*)

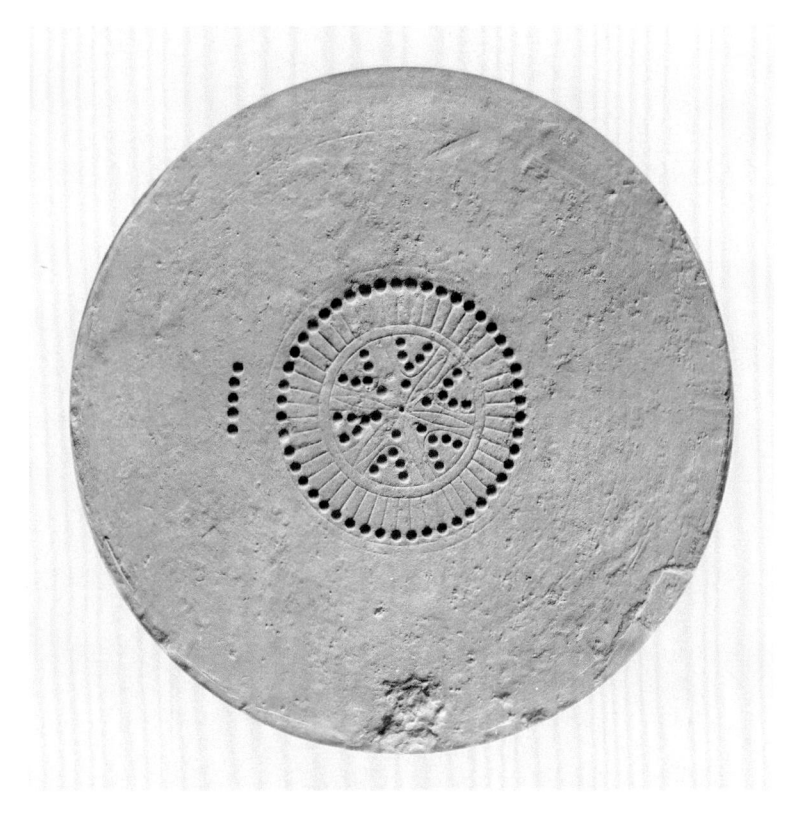

12. Back of limestone shield mould/model, Allard Pierson Museum inv. 7879. (*Image courtesy of Collection Allard Pierson, Amsterdam, with thanks to René van Beek*)

13. Ptolemaic shield medallion, Museum für Byzantinische Kunst inv. 4377. This small medallion was made in imitation of a Ptolemaic pikeman's shield. (© *Staatliche Museen zu Berlin, Skulpturensammlung und Museum für Byzantinische Kunst, Photo: Antje Voigt, with thanks to Cäcilia Fluck*)

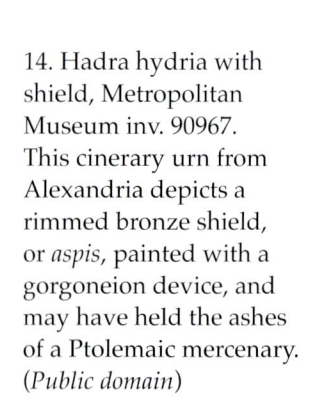

14. Hadra hydria with shield, Metropolitan Museum inv. 90967. This cinerary urn from Alexandria depicts a rimmed bronze shield, or *aspis*, painted with a gorgoneion device, and may have held the ashes of a Ptolemaic mercenary. (*Public domain*)

15. Terracotta Bes as warrior, Paul Perdizet, *Les terres cuites grecques d'Égypte de la collections Fouquet*, 1921. Pl. XLI. These examples depict Bes in elements of Hellenistic military costume. Neither Bes wears body armour, but each wields a sword and carries a Macedonian shield. (*Public domain*)

16. Bes as a shielded cavalryman, SzM inv T 505. This Bes appears in heavy armour, on rearing horse, with a large round shield, reminiscent of the appearance of Macedonian cavalry on monuments from the late third and early second centuries. (© *László Mátyus, Museum of Fine Arts, Budapest, with thanks to Csaba Bodnár*)

17. Stele of Somtutefnakht, National Naples Archaeological Museum inv 1035.
(*Photograph Berthold Werner, Wikimedia Commons, CC BY-3*)

18. The Perdiccas pediment from the Alexander sarcophagus, Istanbul Archaeological Museum. (*Courtesy of Egisto Mannini*)

19. Macedonian cavalryman from the Alexander sarcophagus, Istanbul Archaeological Museum. (*Courtesy of Stephen Zucker, used with permission*)

20. Statue base for Honours to Ptolemy I (I.Milet. 7.244). (*Author's photograph*)

21. Bronze bust of Ptolemy III, Museo archeologico di Firenze. This depicts Euergetes as Herakles, with lion skin tied around his neck, a depiction that was also employed on silver coins during the Third Syrian War. (*Photograph Francesco Bini, CC BY-SA-3.0*)

22. Ptolemy III as Pharaoh, Neues Museum Berlin. (*Photograph Miguel Cuesta, CC BY-SA-4.0*)

23. Coins of Euergetes and the Third Syrian War:
a. Year 2 Soter-series Tetradrachm from Joppa. ANS 1944.76348. (*Public domain*)
b. Ptolemy III Tetradrachm from Ephesus. ANS 1992.35.1. (*Public domain*)
c. Year 4 Mnaieon of Arsinoe II from Joppa. ANS 1944.100.76346. (*Public domain*)
d. Year 5 Soter Tetradrachm from Sidon. ANS 1944.100.76361. (*Public domain*)
e. Berenice II Mnaieon-and-a-half. ANS 1967.152.562. (*Public domain*)

24. Alexandria, French Imperial sketching. From *Recueil des observations et des recherches qui ont été faites en Égypte pendant l'expédition de l'armée française*, 1809, Carte générale des côtes, rades, ports, ville et environs d'Alexandrie. NYPL b14212718-1268199. (Public domain)

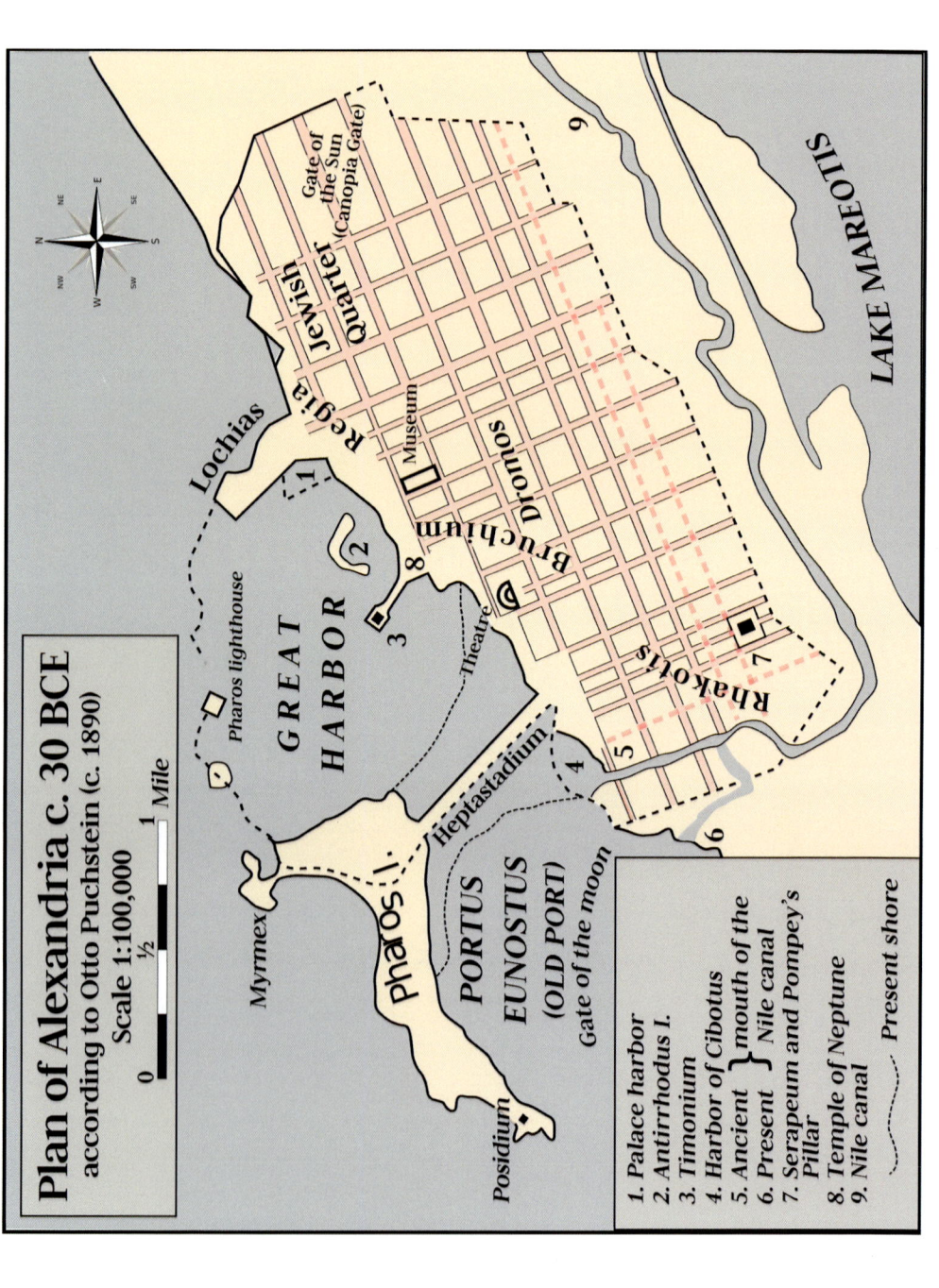

25. Alexandria in the Late Ptolemaic era. Drawn from the plan of Otto Puchstein c.1890. (Wikimedia Commons)

of tributes and treasures to take to the king. The expedition of Eumedes may have followed an earlier excursion by an explorer named Satyros, who marched from Koptos in the Thebaid toward Qosseir on the coast, where he established a station called Philoteras, in honour of Ptolemy II's daughter. Unlike Eumedes, he did not hunt elephants. Satyros left a dedication to Arsinoe Thea Philadelphus at the Paneion on the desert road, which suggests the queen had already passed away. So perhaps Satyros set out in the autumn of 268 BC (*OGIS* 30). Like Satyros, at least some part of Eumedes' expedition took the Koptos to Qosseir road, where an engineer with the expedition left a dedication at the Paneion, right beside that by Satyros, on the desert road on the return trip from hunting elephants (*Paneion d'el Kanaïs* 9 bis).

After Eumedes' successful campaign, more followed. Elephant hunting was apparently lucrative business, as well as a way to provide a corps of elephants for the Ptolemaic army.[24] The hunting expeditions were military campaigns. Leading men from the Ptolemaic army and court led the expeditions, and hundreds of military men participated in each one. Several of the expeditions are partially recorded in documentary papyri, and Strabo's account of the Red Sea lists place-names left by more than a dozen generals over the hunt. Four of the five most southern names can all be tied to the last quarter of the third century BC – Pythangelos, Lichas, Pytholaos and Charimortos – which suggests the expeditions steadily moved further south along the coast. Eumenes, who appears in the middle of the list, was an eponymous commander under Ptolemy III, and his son and grandson were prominent military commanders, governors and hunters in the second century BC. This suggests that the place-names north of 'The Grove of Eumenes' date from the reign of Ptolemy II and the elephant expeditions during his reign. They include – after Eumedes – Tosouchos, Strato, Demetrios, Konon, Korax, Koraos and Antiphilos. Few of these can be identified with confidence. The best case is Demetrios, who was titled 'over the supply of elephants to the Thebaid' in a papyrus from the 250s BC (*P.Hib.* 2.110.v). The same text mentions an official 'from the elephant country', but his name is missing. Many of the later elephant hunters were featured in the annual priesthoods of the Ptolemaic regime. Looking for these men there produces little fruit. It is tempting, however, to connect Antiphilos son of Lykinos, priest of Alexander in 258 BC, with the elephant hunter (*BGU* 6.1228). Additionally, one of the officers in the company of Patroklos in the Chremonidean War was a Cyrenean named Antiphilos, the son of Mnastikles. Either the officer or the eponymous priest might be a candidate for leading an elephant hunt. The number of place-names suggests at least seven expeditions took place in the last twenty years of Ptolemy II's reign. It would not be surprising if the Second Syrian War interrupted the dispatch of elephant hunters for several years in the mid-250s BC, so for the rest of the period there was probably at least one hunting campaign every other year. Each one traversed a minimum of 1,500 miles from Egypt to the hunting grounds and back. While they were not full-scale military campaigns with thousands of men, the distance, rigour and danger involved were assuredly excellent additions to Ptolemaic military readiness.

The Second Syrian War

The Second Syrian War began in about 260/259 BC, following soon after the death of Antiochus I in June 261. Initiated by Antiochus II, the war lasted about seven years, and was fought in the Aegean, Asia Minor and Syria.[25] It ended in 253 BC and was not a particularly successful foray for Ptolemy II. Porphyry described it as 'troublesome', and Ptolemy's concession of his daughter Berenike as a new wife for Antiochus II came with an enormous treasure (indemnity?), such that Berenike was nicknamed *Phernophoros*, or 'dowry-bearer' (*FGrH* 260 43). Though the war began more than sixty years after the first Ptolemy gained control in Egypt, documentary evidence indicates that Ptolemy lacked a sufficient number of military settlers to handle the pressures of a lengthy war. Mercenaries had also been an important part of previous wars (and we may surmise the mercenaries hired for the Chremonidean War were mainly in the army of Areus). In the Second Syrian War, the Ptolemaic army also relied heavily on the *epigonoi* for new soldiers, probably for the first time. This indicates both that the Hellenized population of Egypt was growing well by the 250s BC, and that the pairing of the existing military settlement system and mercenary recruitment was an insufficient source of military manpower.

The war began in Ionia, where there had been disturbances since the late 260s BC. In about 262 BC, Ptolemy's admiral Kallikrates and his heir, Ptolemy the Son, were in Miletos, which had been assaulted by a fleet, presumably a Macedonian one under Antigonus. When stability was restored, Ptolemy and the Milesians exchanged honours, promises from Egypt to help provide for the defences of Miletos, and promises from the Milesians to be diligent in training their *ephebes* (the young citizens) and swearing them to loyalty to the treaty with Ptolemy (*I.Milet*. 1.3.139). This last element is interesting, because it reveals the way the Ptolemaic state happily devolved military responsibility on its allies abroad. Some Milesians did end up in Ptolemaic service (six are recorded in Greek documentary papyri), but Ptolemy II valued the strength of his allies as a way to strengthen his position at lower cost to himself. However, Miletos fell under the control of a tyrant, Timarchos, in 260/259 BC. Timarchos was an Aetolian and a mercenary captain; he may have been the Ptolemaic garrison commander at the city before he seized power for himself.

Timarchos and Ptolemy the Son rebelled against Ptolemy II later in 259 BC, and their rebellion somehow instigated the larger war. They may have attacked both Ptolemaic and Seleucid possessions near Miletos. They (or at least Timarchos) probably conquered Samos, off the coast a little north of Miletos. In Frontinus' *Stratagems*, one entry tells how Timarchos murdered the Ptolemaic garrison commander Charmades, took his Macedonian cloak and his conspicuous helmet, then impersonated him to gain access to the harbour 'Saniorum', most plausibly a mistake for *Samiorum*, the harbour 'of the Samians'.[26] They may also have attacked Seleucid Ephesos, on the coast just north and east of Samos. At least, according to Polyaenus, Timarchos landed an army in Asia Minor, burned the ships to inspire his men and achieved his conquest (*Strat.* 5.25.1). I identify this conquest as Ephesos, because previously it seems to have been Seleucid, but subsequently Ptolemaic forces were active there, forcing Antiochus II to recapture the city (see below).[27] At some point in 258 BC, the forces of Antiochus launched their own counter-attack and killed Timarchos at Miletos, after which Antiochus (or his local general) restored the democracy and the Milesians awarded Antiochus the title 'Theos' (App. *Syr.* 65, *OGIS* 226).

The Ptolemaic and Seleucid responses to a common foe culminated in a war of their own. Perhaps Ptolemy the Son sought to return to the Ptolemaic side after the Seleucids slew Timarchos. If so, he may have granted Ptolemaic forces entry both to formerly Ptolemaic Samos and formerly Seleucid Ephesos. That he repented of his rebellion is strongly suggested by his subsequent life: as the dynast Ptolemy son of Lysimachus at Telmessos in Lycia and a friend of the Ptolemies.[28] He is first attested there in 257 or 256 BC, when the Telmessians – still loyal to Ptolemy II – awarded honours to one of his Macedonian Friends (*Clara Rhodos 9*: 183), so his repentance, reconciliation and demotion must have transpired quite rapidly. This turn of events would mean that Miletos and Ephesos had both changed hands, providing a pretext for further conflict.

There is no evidence for a Ptolemaic attempt to regain Miletos, but the Seleucid attacks on Ephesos are relatively well known for a war otherwise shrouded in mystery. The Ptolemies had troops in the city and a naval squadron in the port. The naval forces were under the command of the Athenian Chremonides, namesake of the Chremonidean War, who with his brother Glaukon had entered Ptolemaic service after Athens' defeat. Chremonides' forces were defeated outside the harbour of Ephesos by the Rhodian navy, whose commander Agathostratos used a stratagem to deceive Chremonides and catch the Ptolemaic ships out of formation (Polyaenus 5.18.1). The Rhodians, formerly allies of Ptolemy I, may have turned against the Ptolemies after the defeat at Kos. Their war is referenced in the Lindos Chronicle (item 37), when the Rhodians dedicated a shield to Athena Lindia in accordance with an oracle's guidance for how to end an ongoing war against Philadelphus.[29] Nonetheless, in 255 BC Glaukon became the eponymous priest at Alexandria and subsequently restored the friendship between Rhodes and the Ptolemies.[30] His selection for the priesthood may have signalled Philadelphus' continued support for and confidence in his family and other patriotic Greeks who had found their way to the Alexandrian court and the Ptolemaic army. After the naval victory, the Rhodians by sea and Seleucids by land continued to lay siege to Ephesos, until sequential assaults – the first by the Rhodians on the port, the second, successful, on the land walls by Antiochus – brought the city back into Seleucid hands (Front. *Strat.* 3.9.10). Between Miletos and Ephesos, the mainland territory of Samos, called the Anaitis, also came under Seleucid control. A Samian embassy sought out the king at Ephesos, then followed him to Sardis to ask for the lands to be given back to the citizens of Samos, since after he conquered the land Antiochus had given it out among his Friends (*SEG* I 366).

Two other pieces of evidence may relate to the Second Syrian War in Asia Minor. A papyrus from Egypt relates how in early 257 BC, repairs were ordered for a Ptolemaic *ennere* (a very large warship) based at Halikarnassos (*P.Cair.Zen.* 1.59036). The repairs cost nearly one talent, and did not come out of normal accounts or through normal channels, which suggests the ship may have been involved in combat fairly recently. A date in later 258 BC for Chremonides' defeat at Ephesos might be fairly close. Additionally, the trierarch of the Ptolemaic *polyreme* was a man named Xanthippos, a high-ranking Friend in the court of Ptolemy II. Xanthippos is also mentioned in a papyrus from the time of the war (*P.Petr.* 2.42.C), a letter from a son in Alexandria to his father in the Fayum, informing him of the latest politics of the court. He appears in that text, which is too fragmentary to be much use, alongside Tlepolemos, a well-known courtier and officer in the military high command no later than 251 BC (*PSI* 5.513). Tlepolemos of Xanthos in Lycia was victor in the Olympic horse race in 252 BC (Paus. 5.8.11, Eus. *Chr.* p.205), was eponymous priest of the royal cult at Alexandria from 247/246–246/245 BC and was an important Ptolemaic general in Asia Minor during the Third Syrian War.[31] There is mention as well of a prisoner, of ambitions, hostility, the king and several other personages who must have been part of the young elite at court. Xanthippos and Tlepolemos, the former in particular, played more significant roles in the Third Syrian War.

The other piece is a Lycian epigram in honour of a Ptolemaic commander, Neoptolemos, who defeated a coalition of Pisidians, Agrianians from Paeonia and Galatians near Tlos in the Xanthos valley. The text is from Stephenus of Byzantium, s.v. *Agriai*, and records that Neoptolemos 'confronted and routed them' on behalf of the citizens of Tlos.[32] The text lacks a date, but the same Neoptolemos was eponymous priest in 252/251 BC, and so the text has generally been interpreted as reflective of a Seleucid attack in the Second Syrian War, which might have made Neoptolemos either an expeditionary commander or the *strategos* over Lycia at the time of the war. A fragmentary inscription from Tlos related to the same event may secure the dedication to 254/253 BC (*SEG* 54.1442), and the battle not much earlier. The forces he defeated recall the mixture of Pamphylians, Cilicians, Lycians and Pisidians who accompanied Philokles and Leonides when they relieved Aspendos decades earlier. For both the Seleucids and the Ptolemies, there was considerable advantage in leveraging bellicose local populations to augment their smaller expeditionary forces in the theatre of war. Because local populations on short campaigns could augment expeditionary forces with thousands of additional, short-term warriors, it was possible for the Ptolemies and Seleucids to conduct serious campaigns against one another across their lengthy shared borders.

Another Ptolemaic general, Aetos son of Apollonios, from Aspendos in Pamphylia, founded a colony on behalf of Ptolemy II, perhaps during the war itself.[33] It was called Arsinoe and was near Nagidos, in the eastern part of Rough Cilicia. There was also a Ptolemaic fort near the two cities, and an inscription praised Aetos for defeating barbarians in their vicinity (*SEG* 39.1426). Aetos was eponymous priest in Alexandria the year before Neoptolemos, two years after Glaukon. At this point it is safe to make the observation that in wartime the eponymous priesthood of the royal cult attained a military character. The man before Glaukon was the son of the Ptolemaic commander Leonides, and before him the Thessalian Antiochos son of Kebbas, presumably one of the two Antiochos's who were senior military commanders other than Antiochos son of Kratidas. This latter was later eponymous priest himself, had served on the staff of Patroklos in the Chremonidean War and was called 'Antiochos the Cretan' to distinguish him from the other two contemporary high-ranking officers of the same name (*P.Hib.* 1.110). Between Glaukon and Aetos, *SEG* 54.1442 from Tlos suggests the eponymous priest for 254/253 was named Thraseas, which suggests a connection to the family of Aetos, whose most famous son was likewise named Thraseas. As for the war in Asia Minor, it seems quite likely that Ptolemy II lost all or most of his mainland possessions in Ionia and Pamphylia, and retained or strengthened his positions in Caria and Lycia, with probably fairly small changes along the coast of Rough Cilicia. Given the impact of the defeat at Kos as well, Ptolemaic power in the Aegean and Asia Minor suffered a fairly heavy blow.

The theatre of war where the respective kingdoms' own armies were involved in the heaviest fighting seems to have been Syria. As early as November 258 BC, there is papyrological evidence for Ptolemaic forces operating in northern Phoenicia (*PSI* 5.495). A hipparch named Spinther was in command of troops around Tripolis, and more senior military officials based at Ptolemais-Akko were dispatching men and horses to reinforce Spinther's troops. This suggests an early zone of conflict was on the Phoenician coast north of Tripolis, south of Laodicea, so perhaps in the coastal plain between Orthosia and Arados, along the modern-day border between Syria and Lebanon. We may surmise Spinther's own troops were mercenary cavalry by his son Ptolemaios' subsequent command of mercenary (actually semi-professional) cavalry in the 240s BC (*SB* 12.10858). We know from *SB* 5.8008 (260 BC) that Ptolemaic forces in Syria and Phoenicia included 'those on active duty and the settlers', and the ordering, with the active-duty soldiers first, might indicate that more of the soldiers in such an important border region were mercenary or regular troops, like Spinther's, rather than military settlers. Early in the war, Ptolemaic operations may have depended heavily on the troops stationed locally.

Ptolemaic troops seem to have also operated much further north, at the very gates of Antioch. A large hoard of Ptolemaic gold coins was uncovered south-west of Antioch, about halfway between Antioch and Seleukeia-by-the-Sea. The coins were all minted by 261 BC, and the initial publication felt comfortable dating the hoard very precisely to 259 or 258

BC.³⁴ We might imagine a group of mercenaries hid the coins in hopes of retrieving them later. Aperghis assigned the hoard to the Third Syrian War because the evidence for the war very clearly places Ptolemaic forces near and in Antioch. However, those forces were victorious, with no reason to hide their wages, and as Grainger has pointed out the dates of minting point toward a deposit closed around 258 BC. If Antiochus was operating in Ionia in 258 and probably until about 255 BC, Ptolemaic forces may have attempted their own raid deep into Syria while he and many of his chief generals and best troops were away. The deposited coin hoard suggests the campaign still met determined resistance and retreated toward the coast. An expedition of that sort may have been naval from the outset: reaching Antioch overland would require either capturing Laodicea to push up the coast or campaigning east of the Libanon up the Orontes valley past Apameia, either of which would surely have required tremendous effort and considerable time. Ptolemaic naval power enabled them to bypass the physical defences and disembark troops in the Syrian heartland. Many of the coins in the hoard were minted in Phoenicia or Cyprus, which may also identify the point of origin for the expedition. Perhaps the expedition was launched under Philinos son of Philotimos, who left a dedication to the kings early in the reign of Ptolemy III at Salamis on Cyprus (*Salamine* XIII 56), and is probably to be identified with the eponymous officer Philinos, three of whose senior officers were granted large allotments in the Fayum at the end of the war (*PSI* 5.513).

The regular Ptolemaic army marched out to Syria in the spring of 257 BC. Papyri indicate large numbers of troops were passing through the Delta around Athribis, convenient for troops travelling from Alexandria to Pelusium (*P.Lond.* 7.1938). Ptolemy II was himself in the Delta in spring 257 BC, celebrating Egyptian festivals at Mendes and other cities, as well as his accession at Memphis.³⁵ The king and a large entourage were in the Delta, and from the aforementioned text we know that the banker in Athribis could not make a loan to Zenon of the amount requested because his reserves had been cleaned out to provide money for rations for the soldiers. Perhaps Ptolemy II oversaw the marshalling of troops in the Delta before participating in the festivals. At least the Mendes text (lines 25–26) refers to the presence with the king at Mendes of 'the captains of the *Nefami* warriors' in their full equipment. The reference there is obscure, but perhaps it signifies the mobilization of the elite Egyptian contingent he founded after the death of Arsinoe II (line 14). Then in late 257 BC there is a reference in a papyrus to a body of troops gathered in Alexandria under the command of 'the boy' (τοῦ παιδός) (*SB* 16.12818). This should be a reference toward the future Ptolemy III, who after the revolt of Ptolemy the Son became heir to Ptolemy II. He may have still been in his late teens in 257 BC, which would explain 'the boy', but it seems a body of troops had been placed under his command for that year's campaign. On their return to Egypt they made a joint dedication at the Serapeion in Alexandria.[36]

Again large bodies of troops passed through Egypt, presumably toward Syria, in the spring of 255 BC (*P.Mich.* 1.32, *P.Cair.Zen.* 2.59175). Precisely where these troops went, or what they did on campaign, is unknown. It was nonetheless a major mobilization of manpower. The sieges, small actions, raids or battles they may have fought are lost to history. However, the whole border in Syria and Phoenicia was extensively fortified by the time of the Fourth Syrian War, and it is possible that the fortification of that borderland dates to these campaigns. If so, the campaigns would have been terrifically expensive, with little opportunity for plunder. The war ended in 253 BC, and the marriage of Ptolemy's daughter Berenike to Antiochus II sealed the peace, along with a large dowry. A letter to Zenon from a friend, Artemidoros, informed him of Apollonios' party's arrival in Sidon after escorting the princess to the frontier to meet Antiochus (*P.Cair.Zen.* 1.59251).

In the context of the mobilizations of the Second Syrian War, the Ptolemaic army added to its ranks in a novel way. Whereas mercenaries or other troops from abroad provided the primary infusions of new Greek manpower, in the 250s BC the Ptolemies added thousands of soldiers from the Greek population in Egypt. Many of these were subsequently settled in the Fayum, which was renamed the Arsinoite nome while the war was raging. What is significant in this is that, previously, the Ptolemaic army had been unable to expand its core Greco-Macedonian manpower domestically in any significant way. A growing colonial population, sufficient in itself not only to replenish its military ranks but also to expand them, signalled an important point in Ptolemaic development. The Ptolemaic army from then on could be less reliant on mercenaries, and as the Greek population continued to grow the core of its army could grow too. It reflected a level of prosperity and resilience that could help the Ptolemies prosper even if overseas recruitment faltered.

With the exception of one text, all we know of these new recruits comes from their settlements in the Fayum from 255–251 BC. The exception is *PSI* 6.588, which probably belongs to the Second Syrian War. It describes the mobilization of *epigonoi*, with weapons, for a military mission.

Mobilization of *epigonoi* may have taken place in the Third Syrian War, which could also provide the backdrop for the papyrus, but it is otherwise unattested for that war. For the Second Syrian War, however, men from the *epigonoi* served in large numbers, in two categories. Their settlements were, first, the *neaniskoi* 'youths' among the cavalry settlers, who were sons of men who were already and simultaneously military settlers elsewhere, and who comprised a large proportion of the 100-arouras cavalry settled in the Arsinoite nome on the model of Apollonios. The second category was the *eikosipentarouroi epigonoi*, an entire military class levied from the non-military Greek population of Egypt for service together. Their moniker related to their 25-arouras allotments, and they were part of the Ptolemaic infantry. That the *epigonoi* designation stayed with them even after they received *kleroi* suggests it was a military title used during the war, and stuck even when their institutional classification changed, from members of the *epigonoi* to members of the *klerouchoi*. These groups comprised large parts of two of the three settler populations who were allotted land in the Fayum as the Second Syrian War wound down, and especially in the years after it ended.

Chapter 6

The Age of Midas, Part II

The Settlements

The Ptolemies lacked a large Greco-Macedonian population already settled in cities, and so took an entirely different approach to military recruitment. Aside from hiring mercenaries, whose availability was subject to what we might call market conditions, the main way the Ptolemies built up their army was through military settlers, the cleruchs. The settler system wedded military service and agricultural productivity, while minimizing the importance of cities or citizenship. The individual *cleruch*, so-called for the land allotment (*klēros*) that he received from the king, owed military service to the king as the condition of his tenancy on the land. The army was the total of men granted allotments in return for oaths of loyalty and commitments to military service, rather than a theoretical levy of citizens from scattered cities. The management of such a direct system advanced the development of the Ptolemaic bureaucracy in Egypt. A complex system of land management developed in the third century BC to accommodate the steady expansion of the Ptolemies' settler army. The following study demonstrates that the construction of the settler army followed inconsistent patterns and lasted for decades, trending slowly toward greater uniformity, consistency, control and size.

There is only limited evidence for Ptolemaic military settlements down to about the 260s BC, but from scattered sources it is possible to trace the patterns of early settlement. In the literary sources there are only two, maybe three pieces of evidence. Following the Battle of Gaza in 312 BC, Ptolemy I settled some 8,000 prisoners of war in Egypt (Diod. 19.85.3–4). At about the same time he also took several thousand Judeans and settled them as soldiers in Egypt (Ps-Aristeus 13; Josephus *Antiquities* 12.1.7–8). The final piece of evidence is less direct. In the Antigonid conquest of Cyprus in 306 BC, Demetrius tried to incorporate several thousand war captives in his army, a common practice in the early Successor period.

The men immediately began deserting, because, Diodorus says, all their possessions were in Egypt.[1] This may refer to men who had been settled on estates back in Egypt. Documentary evidence from the reign of Ptolemy I is rare: the only Greek settlements well-attested in Egypt down to his passing are at Elephantine in extreme Upper Egypt (*P.Eleph.* 1–4). In short, this community of soldiers on the southern frontier of Egypt, more than 600 miles inland from the Mediterranean coast, included men from all corners of the Greek world.[2] A few texts survive from the Oxyrhynchite nome in Middle Egypt in the 280s BC, and also reflect a diverse settling population.[3] Whether at Elephantine or in the Oxyrhynchites, the Greek settlers are simply present in the papyri by their name and ethnic, with no mention in any of our earliest texts of their patronymic, military or civilian status. It is difficult to learn much from these texts because they provided so little information.

All of that changed around the start of Ptolemy II's reign, when he promulgated a law (mentioned in the previous chapter) that required soldiers to give better identifying information in contracts. We know the text of the law from two later documents (*P.Hamb.* 2.168 and *BGU* 14.2367): 'each of the soldiers shall have written down his name, his *patris* [place of origin], the name of the *tagma* [unit] to which he belongs, and the rank he happens to hold.'[4] This change is evident already in a text that must date between 282 and 274 BC (*P.Hib.* 1.30).[5] Suddenly, compared to texts from just a few years earlier, details abound. That earliest text concerns personnel from the *tagma* of Alexandros. Although it is fragmentary and much is missing, the text still reveals three Macedonian soldiers (ranks lost), a man from Kos with the rank of private and two officers, one a *dekanikos* (sergeant) and the other a *chiliarchos*.

The officer ranks and the title of the *tagma* merit a little digression, as a way to introduce the particularities of Ptolemaic military organization. *Dekanikos* is straightforward enough: a commander of ten (or perhaps a file-leader, whatever its size), attested very well (about twenty times in all) in cavalry contexts and perhaps among infantry as well. Regular soldiers were identified in most cases as either *idiōtēs*, literally 'private', or as *klērouchos*, 'allotment-holder'. But the rank of *chiliarchos* is particularly striking. The name indicates the 'commander of a thousand', and thus we might expect the chiliarch to be the unit's commander; that is, its titular Alexandros. And in this particular case, because the name is missing, perhaps it was Alexandros himself. Or perhaps the command of Alexandros had more than 1,000 total men. However, it is likely that Alexandros' *tagma* was a cavalry, none of which ever had as many as 10,000 men. However, it is also apparent that in Ptolemaic Egypt, cavalry units nonetheless accorded the rank chiliarch not for 'commander of 1,000' but as an honorific, perhaps for a staff officer to the hipparch, who was clearly of higher rank than the hipparch. For example, Nikasiboulos of Ainos was the chiliarch in the mercenary hipparchy of Eteoneus (*P.Petr.* 3.21), Diodorus was the chiliarch in the hipparchy of Demeas (*P.Petr.* 3.54) and Alkaios of Corinth was chiliarch in the hipparchy of Zoilos (*BGU* 10.1978). This might also explain why so many chiliarchs are attested: fifteen or sixteen, depending on how a couple of papyri are reconstructed, and thus nearly as many as the lowly file-leading sergeants. If the cavalry chiliarchs were staff officers, their apparent over-representation in documentary papyri is fairly easily explained: their duties tended to involve them in the sorts of business – contracts, grievances, fiscal reports, testaments – most often found in the papyri.

As for the title of the unit, 'of Alexandros', it represents the standard way of naming units under Philadelphus, which with some modifications remained fairly standard for most of Ptolemaic military history. Classicists and historians call these 'eponymous commands' – that is, units named after a commander. The nature of these commands is not a settled issue in Ptolemaic history.[6] Here is what we do know, restricted to the third century BC. First, many of the eponymous commanders can be tied to elite figures at the Ptolemaic court, the latter identified mainly through the annual priesthoods at the court, which selected a man as the year's 'Priest of Alexander' and eventually priestesses of Arsinoe II and Berenike II. So, for example, Eteoneus, son of Eteoneus the eponymous cavalry commander and brother of another eponymous cavalry commander, was priest of Alexander. Daughters of the eponymous commanders of the Oxyrhynchite nome cavalry, Zoilos and Philon, were priestesses of Arsinoe in 224/223 and 217/216 BC, respectively. Many others are identifiable, and thus it seems fairly safe to conclude that most eponymous commanders were Friends of the kings. Second, at the same time it is also clear that at least some of the eponymous commanders really did command their units. The aforementioned Zoilos and Philon provide two of several examples where documentary evidence survives to prove this (*BGU* 10.1905, 10.2003). Third, there are many other cases where men who were not eponymous commanders, or at least are never attested as such, held unit command ranks, most notably hipparch (*P.Lille* 1.32–34, *P.Hib.* 2.198). Fourth, the eponymous commands were *tagmata*, units, which should mean they were coordinated and structured commands that could be deployed on campaign.

Fifth, dozens of eponymous commanders were attested just in the Fayum and its vicinity under Philadelphus and Euergetes before contracting dramatically late in Euergetes' reign.

P.Hib. 2.198, a famous collection of royal ordinances, demonstrates the complexity of eponymous command and the apparent flexibility of its usage. The first ordinance regards promotions or gifts decreed by Ptolemy III in 244 BC. The list of recipients is organized first by nome, then by eponymous command. At least eleven eponymous commands were listed (only most of the right half of the list survives, so there were almost certainly several more), although only six names survive. Two of those are for the same eponymous commander, Petalos, whose command must have spanned two nomes. Three from both the eponymous commanders and officers are probably otherwise documented. The eponymous commander Nautas was undoubtedly the father of Ptolemaios son of Nautas, an eponymous commander of cavalry later in the reign of Ptolemy III (*P.Petr.* 2.16, 236/235 BC, and frequently thereafter). The eponymous commander Andronikos may have commanded 231 soldiers embarking on an elephant hunt in 223 BC (*Chr.Wilck.* 451). And at the end of the list are at least three men called *epistatai* (administrators), who were probably given both lands and authority in the vicinity of Memphis to assist with enrolling regular soldiers in the cleruchy. One of these men, Aineas, whose title of *epistatēs* is inferred in the fragmentary text, could be connected to the eponymous commander Aineas, whose cavalry settlers were likewise posted in the Memphite nome (*P.Lond.* 7.2015, 242 BC). For Petalos we find both a hipparch and chiliarch; for one lost eponymous command *two* hipparchs and a chiliarch. That a *tagma* could have a hipparch who was not the commander is bewildering. That it could have two is confounding. In this case, my guess is that the ranks tell us more about the size of the allotments men were receiving than their actual rank, and bore little relation to the actual size of the military units involved.

This guess leads to a general point about military settlement and army rank structure in Ptolemaic Egypt, especially in the earlier era, and particularly among the cavalry: the Ptolemies had an overabundance of land, but a shortage of warriors. Ptolemy II Philadelphus, probably following the pattern of his father, gave land and title outsized to a man's actual battlefield role as a way to lure him into permanent settlement in Egypt. Philip II of Macedon had done precisely the same thing, granting huge tracts to his cavalry companions, recruiting numerous Greeks to enjoy his largesse, such that 800 of these cavalrymen held as much properties' wealth as the 10,000 wealthiest men in mainland Greece (Theopompus *FGrH* 115, 225 B). This could help explain why, in spite of the on-face simplicity of the eponymous command system, there were nonetheless numerous hipparchs and chiliarchs who were not eponymous commanders, far too many eponymous commands for the military population of the region and a dramatic over-representation of high-ranking officers in the documentary evidence. Several examples, related to the mercenary cavalry, the earliest settlers in the Arsinoites, will highlight the appeal of this interpretation.

1. *The Mercenary Cavalry of Eteoneus.* The command of Eteoneus is fairly well-attested for an eponymous command. It does not come on the scene until the end of the Third Syrian War, when it appears in the Arsinoites. While comparatively later, it preserves the structures of the Philadelphus era as regards unit composition, and was probably founded under an earlier commander in the reign of Philadelphus. The eponymous commander, Eteoneus, was in the Fayum in 243 BC, perhaps to visit some new settlers (*P.Tebt.* 3.2.937). Ten soldiers from the command are attested with their rank information. They are presented in the table below.

    The first really striking thing about this group is the preponderance of officers. Eight of the ten were officers. Of the officers, those of high rank are surprisingly common. Above the file-leading *dekanikos* was the *lochagos*, who led a couple of files, then the *ilarchēs*, who commanded one of the *ilai*, a unit of sixty-four (or at times fifty). One of each

Table 13: Solders from Eteoneus' Mercenary Cavalry

Name	Rank	Date	Documents
Kephalon	*Epilarches*	243/2–236/5	*P.Petr.* 3.82, *P.Petr.*2 16
Theodoros	*Epilarches*	238	*P.Sorb.* 3.89
Ammonios	*Epilarches*	236/5	*P.Petr.* 2 16
Nikasiboulos	*Chiliarchos*	234	*P.Petr.* 3.21
Epikrates	*Dekanikos*	223/2	*P.Petr.* 3.114
Aristomachos	Cleruch	221	*P.Enteux.* 8
Ergodates	*Epilarches*	221/0	*P.Petr.* 3.112
Unnamed	Cleruch	221/0	*P.Petr.* 3.112
Unnamed	*Ilarches*	221/0	*P.Petr.* 3.112
Unnamed	*Lochagos*	Undated	P.Heid. 6.377

of these ranks appears. An *epilarchēs* commanded two *ilai*, 100–128 troopers, or half of the hipparchy of 200–256 men. There should have been either one or two in a hipparchy at most, and most Ptolemaic hipparchies did not use that rank at all. Surprisingly, out of the ten men, we have two contemporary epilarchs in the unit: Kephalon and Ammonios in 236/235 BC. Yet another epilarch, Theodoros, was contemporary with Kephalon at least, but he passed away in 238 BC, so in theory Ammonios could have replaced him. However, Ammonios and Kephalon were both 70 in the text two to three years later (*P.Petr.* 2.16), so it is unlikely Ammonios was promoted to the rank after the passing of Theodoros. Instead, all three had presumably started their military careers decades earlier, around the time Philadelphus became king. Thus it seems quite possible there were three contemporary epilarchs in the cavalry of Eteoneus, and all well past their prime. Aside from the hipparch, the epilarchs and staff chiliarch should be the handful of top officers in a unit. Is it mere chance that four epilarchs and the chiliarch comprise 50 per cent of the attested personnel, when, if the command was fully staffed and organized, they comprised about 2 per cent of the command? When we consider as well that the attested personnel include at least 50 per cent more contemporary epilarchs than there should have been, two conclusions seem increasingly likely: many of the hipparchies were probably understaffed with soldiers, but over-staffed with officers.

2. *The mercenary cavalry of Eupolemos*. A roster of mercenary cavalry horses from 242 BC (*P.Petr.* 2.35), thus contemporary with the command of Eteoneus, once contained at least thirty personnel entries, and presumably many more. For only eighteen of the entries can we determine rank status. Half of those eighteen were officers. The officers are scattered among the regular troops, except for one fragment with two ilarchs, an officer whose title is difficult to decipher and the hipparch grouped together. The hipparch, Eupolemos, is not connected to a known eponymous command, but perhaps he was the eponymous commander. But with the hipparch, two *dekanikoi*, two *lochagoi*, two ilarchs, an epilarch and another officer, a large proportion of a hipparchy's officer corps are listed, while something like 200 regular troopers may be presumed missing. If Philadelphus were seeking to convince wealthy and powerful men to serve him in Egypt, would such men have been more effectively lured through the offer of their own hipparchy? And if such a man were sanctioned to create

a hipparchy, he would naturally fill out his officer corps first, and then hope to fill out the ranks of the command over time, would he not?

3. *The mercenary cavalry of Demeas.* This unit is also attested only through a roster, and the hipparch Demeas is never attested elsewhere as an eponymous commander. What is left of the roster contains fifteen names (*P.Petr.* 3.54, 248 BC). Here the officers account for one-third of the troops, and four of the five officers were senior commanders: Demeas the hipparch, a chiliarch, an ilarch and an *epilochagos*. As with Eupolemos, the regular troopers and officers were intermingled in what survives of the list, which makes it doubtful the randomness of papyrus survival just happened to leave us with most of the officer corps for the unit. Once again, it seems likely units were over-officered and under-staffed. Even among the officers, it is remarkable that there are not multiple *dekanikoi* (just one); after all, about the same number of hipparchs and chiliarchs are attested in the papyri as *dekanikoi*, who should have outnumbered them by about sixteen to one.

4. *The mercenary cavalry, eponymous commanders and manpower.* We happen to possess a document, *P.Count.* 1, which dates between 254 and 231 BC, that provides incredible insight into the military and civilian populations of the Arsinoite nome. For now, we care only for what it tells us about the population of mercenary cavalry. There were 1,426 adult males in the families of the mercenary cavalry, including various family members and servants beside the soldier himself. The editors of the papyrus, judging from household samples, guessed this represented not much over 400 soldiers (Clarysse and Thompson, 2006: p.152). That should correlate to at most two hipparchies. And yet the Petrie Wills papyri, dating to 238–235 BC, attest the existence of a minimum of six contemporary eponymous commanders of mercenary cavalry in the Fayum: Eteoneus, Pythangelos, Damon, Sosipolis, Eumenes and Lichas.[7] Was there an average of seventy men in each of these hipparchies?

In conclusion, these short studies seem to indicate that the early Ptolemaic cavalry rewarded commanders of smaller units with higher rank, perhaps as an incentive to permanent settlement, and the unit commanders or administrators overseeing the units awarded high ranks at a rate far outstripping the actual size of the units, and perhaps even officer corps of a fully staffed unit.

A study of officer allotments demonstrates that awarding rank was an excellent way to reward a soldier or veteran, and thus was probably an effective strategy for building up the Ptolemaic army under the first Ptolemies. Regular cavalry might already receive large tracts of land, but officers got even more. Five papyri in the Lille collection concern management of allotments for cavalry officers: an ilarch had 145 arouras (*P.Lille* 1.31), while three hipparchs (none ever attested as an eponymous commander) had 315, 342 and 312 arouras (*P.Lille* 1.32–34). Another officer, whose rank is missing, had somewhere around 200 arouras (*P.Lille* 1.37), while one Seleukos, presumably an officer and probably a hipparch, had almost 400 (*P.Lille* 1.38). *Chomatikon* (dyke tax) rates, which normally charged 1 obol (one-sixth of a drachma) per aroura, allow for rough calculations of taxable land within an allotment even when we lack a statement on its size. A bank record from the Arsinoite nome (*P.Sorb.inv.* 371, 233/232 BC) lists the dyke tax paid by groups of mercenary cavalry and *hekatontarouroi hippeis*, the '100-arouras' regular cavalry force of Ptolemaic Egypt. The twenty-eight 100-aroura cavalrymen, true to their name, paid dyke taxes for 100 arouras of land: 16 drachmas and 4 obols.[8] Several of the mercenary cavalry, on the other hand, paid amounts reflecting allotments as large as 381, 334.5 and 325 arouras. Aside from those, there were two just shy of 200 arouras and two more just over 150. The three allotments over 300 arouras seem to be in the range of a hipparch's allotment, yet were all located in close proximity to one another. The number of officers declined after the cavalry reforms under Euergetes, but the remaining officers still often had allotments well above the normal size. So Herakleitos of the 3rd hipparchy had 250 arouras, Seuthes and Nikias of the 4th hipparchy had 400 and 150, respectively (*SB* 26.16634), and Philoxenos of the 5th hipparchy paid property dyke taxes indicating a kleros of 255 arouras (*Petr.* 3.112, 221/220 BC).

Under Euergetes, the Ptolemaic army was more established, and the system of massively rewarding men who were probably only officers on paper would naturally have been less attractive. Several pieces of evidence suggest the Ptolemaic administration sought to undo the preponderance of officers and officer-sized allotments. *P.Hib.* 1.81 contains repossession orders for allotments of cavalrymen who had passed away in late 239 into early 238 BC. The deceased included troopers from the eponymous commands of Eumenes, Lakon, Sosipolis, Damon and Lichas. Six of the deceased are legible in the papyrus, and all six were officers: three *lochagoi*, two *dekanikoi* and the sixth was probably also a *dekanikos*. With deceased men from five different commands, all of them officers, combat mortality seems unlikely. A key to the text is the repossession order: the state took control of all the allotments and could redistribute or divide them as administrators saw fit. The inflated numbers of officers reflected a distribution of *klēroi* that favoured officers not only over rank-and-file but also over the state. So perhaps it is not that only officers died in those five commands in that year, but that the state permitted sons to inherit from their rank-and-file fathers, but capitalized on the death of officers to restructure the sizes of allotments. In a tax record from 221 BC (*P.Petr.* 3.112), almost twenty years later, property-based dyke taxes prove that subaltern officers, called *hyperetai* (probably roughly equivalent to *dekanikoi* or *lochagoi*), had allotments of the same size as the rank-and-file troopers. The mercenary cavalry were increasingly standardized around an 80-arouras allotment. In 222 BC, an *epilarchēs* from a unit of mercenary cavalry possessed an allotment with just 82.5 arouras (*P.Enteux.* 55). He kept his officer's title, but not an officer's allotment. By such a mechanism the state could assure the cultivation of grand estates and the recruitment of vital personnel in the early period, then redistribute property to an enlarged army a few decades later as men died or retired.

As this section ends, it makes sense to consider where things stand. Philadelphus did pass laws that made it easier for the administration to keep track of soldiers, and for us to study the organization of the army and the military settlements. However, it should be fairly clear that the early Ptolemaic army, or at least its cavalry forces, were not very sensibly organized. Perhaps the multitude of hipparchies and officers might help explain the outlandish account of Callixenus that more than 23,000 cavalry marched in Philadelphus' Grand Procession in the 270s BC: while there may only have been 3,000 cavalry, they were quite possibly organized in fifty or more separate hipparchies, adding to an illusion of far greater manpower. Perhaps the idea had been, beyond incentivizing mercenaries to settle in Egypt permanently, to build out each of the units with new recruits, so that in a mobilization scenario the skeletons of hipparchies would be fleshed out to nearer full size. If so, it reflected a rosy optimism about the ability to levy large numbers of troops and find large numbers of war-horses. Finally, we might also consider whether the dozens of understaffed and over-officered hipparchies among the military settlements of Egypt had any negative bearing on the operations of the Ptolemaic army. Perhaps multiple units were brigaded together in a deployment scenario. For example, in the Second Syrian War the hipparch Spinther was commanding near Tripolis (modern Tripoli, Lebanon), and other commanders in Ptolemais Akko (north of Haifa) enquired about the number of soldiers in his command (*PSI* 5.495). The Greek word used for the inquiry, συνίστημι, carries considerable contingency: the soldiers were not the men of his hipparchy, but those who were combined or organized – stood up together – under his leadership. At a later date, we know that his son was eponymous commander of mercenary cavalry in the Arsinoite (*SB* 12.10858), so there probably was a core of Spinther's troops under his command, but there were clearly also other troops, either new recruits or men from other commands, brigaded together for operational purposes. If cavalry units were unable to train together, and formed unit discipline and cohesion *ad hoc* on campaign, we might surmise they were limited to simpler tactics and perhaps encountered frequent command difficulties.

Military Settlement Prior to the Second Syrian War

As far as the settlements of Philadelphus' reign are concerned, we can approach them in two groups: the settlements evident before the prosecution of the Second Syrian War and those that took place during and after that war. The Second Syrian War marked a decisive shift in settlement. The documentary papyri from 282–260 BC, though hardly large, provides an early glimpse of Ptolemaic military institutions and settlements prior to the Second Syrian War. Though the sources are limited, it seems that settlement was focused upon the Nile Valley in the region known as Middle Egypt, and of course in the Alexandrian *chōra*. The Fayum, so important to settlements later in Philadelphus' reign, is mostly shrouded in mystery for the early period. Many of our earliest texts regarding the Fayum come from the archive of Zenon, son of Agreophon, a Kaunian man who was secretary to the *dioiketes* Apollonios, Philadelphus' chief economic official. Apollonios possessed a *dōrea* – a large gift estate he received from the king – in the Fayum from 258–246 BC, and Zenon managed it for most of that period. The gift estate narrowly preceded several major waves of military settlement in the Fayum, but before that time military settlement in the Fayum seems to have been fairly limited and non-systematic. Many of the mercenary cavalry, discussed above, were probably settled in this early period, while others likely were not settled until after the Third Syrian War under Ptolemy III.

Middle Egypt stretches along the Nile Valley, from Memphis near the apex of the Delta and south to Hermopolis, about 200 miles north to south. The best way to get a picture of how settlement worked in the earlier part of Ptolemy II's reign is through a pair of archives belonging to officers or officials in Middle Egypt, Hippodamos and Apollonides. Hippodamos and a couple of other key military and administrative officials, Lykomedes and Lykiskos, managed the affairs of military settlers in Middle Egypt, especially in the Oxyrhynchite nome. Hippodamos' son was secretary for a cavalry hipparchy (*P.Sorb.* 1.17, 257 BC); that may have been Hippodamos' role as well. Apollonides was their near contemporary, and also an important administrative official, called a *nomarch*, in the Oxyrhynchites. Among these papers we learn about the distribution of allotments and quarters among the population, the process of succession for soldiers on the land, confiscation and redistribution of allotments and the military organization of settlers in the region.

When a soldier in the service of Ptolemy I or Ptolemy II settled in the countryside of Egypt, he received a *stathmos*, or quarters, and if he was a cleruch (and most were) an allotment. The quarters were often half of a civilian residence. Quartering the army upon the civilian population, even with compensation, was a source of constant friction. Hippodamos' papers, and other documentary papyri, suggest that there were really two types of friction (*SB* 6.9454). Ptolemy II issued laws in 275 and 274 BC, excerpts of which were found in Hippodamos' archive, to curb abuses of quarters by soldiers, which could include harassing or ejecting the civilian residents, but the laws actually emphasized the soldiers' habit of leasing out their quarters (*SB* 6.9454.3–4, 6). The *stathmos* was officially royal property, so soldiers could not sub-let, sell or bequeath them. Several times in the laws and decrees in Hippodamos' collection we see this point reiterated: 'the quarters are royal property'. Leasing out quarters incurred stiff fines. That Ptolemy II issued a new series of laws in 275 BC and thereafter, and attempted to apply parts of them retroactively, suggests that Ptolemy I had taken a more relaxed approach to the settlers' use of the quarters. In about 271–270 BC, sometime after the end of the First Syrian War, Ptolemy II seems to have called a halt on distributing quarters in order to carry out an inspection of the system and curtail fraud (*SB* 6.9454.1–2). Civilians may have sometimes claimed their residences were used as quarters when they were not, some military quarters may have been possessed by non-military and some soldiers may have had multiple quarters. From 260 BC, a complaint survives that three cavalrymen had claimed an entire house as their quarters and ejected the owner (*P.Sorb.* 1.13). In 259 BC, complaints were filed about soldiers seizing the houses of townspeople in the Thebaid as their *stathmoi* rather than following the process of filing for them with local officials, and boarding up their quarters whenever they departed on military duties (*P.Hal.* 1). The system required constant maintenance, and no later than under Ptolemy III the administration had grown more lax in its regulation of quarters, increasingly recognizing them as semi-private property.

When soldiers received allotments, these, like the quarters, were still royal property (*P.Rev.* 2nd ed. 36.13–14). Soldiers were generally expected to either be on military duty or farming their own allotment; leasing their allotments to land managers forsook some tax breaks (*P.Rev.* 2nd ed. 24.5–7). If a soldier passed away, the allotment reverted to the Crown until administrators (including Hippodamos and his colleagues) could reassign it. Eventually, sons were the default leading candidates to replace their fathers (*P.Lille* 4, 217 BC), and in time the allotment was directly heritable. In the days of Ptolemy II, it seems to have been possible to designate an adult son as military heir, or *synkleros*, to assure and speed that process (*P.Cair.Zen.* 1.59001, 274 BC). But it is only attested in one document, which suggests it was not a common practice. The text is early enough, and it may have been something Ptolemy I invented but Ptolemy II scrapped to increase administrative authority over the military settlements. The allotments could also revert to the Crown for other reasons. Under Ptolemy II, it seems likely that allotments were considered *basilikoi*, royal, when soldiers were on campaign. This was probably an artifice to facilitate cultivation, and the allotments reverted when the soldier returned. Hippodamos' archive includes a complaint from a military settler who argues – the text is fragmentary so it is hard to be certain on the nuances here – that an administrator made an error apportioning royal revenues from the soldier's allotment (*P.Sorb.* 1.11).

Military allotments could also revert to the Crown as part of restructuring of the settlements. Around 262 BC a number of allotments reverted to the Crown, and Lykomedes, colleague of Hippodamos, received a letter from the king ordering him to make sure their quarters were also recovered by the state. The letter added that the king (or more likely, a very senior official on behalf of the king) might write another letter with a list of soldiers who could be given quarters (*SB* 6.9454.5). It is clear from the text that the cavalrymen were still living and their allotments were confiscated, so the move was permanent (that is, the men were not simply on campaign). Instead, numerous soldiers, or perhaps entire commands, were relocated. Perhaps the settlers were simply moved to a nearby area, part of a scheme to bring more land into cultivation by moving settlers into land needing improvement and handing out the improved land to someone else. Or perhaps the relocation served a military purpose. We know, for example, that an eponymous commander named Antiochos had his command transferred to the Thebaid around 259 BC (*P.Hib.* 1.110.v, *P.Hal.* 1), probably to facilitate elephant hunts, but at that time his men may have been serving soldiers rather than military settlers.

Many men already held allotments before the archives of Hippodamos or Apollonides began. One of Hippodamos' documents refers to multiple hipparchies in the area (*SB* 12.11056), and between the two archives many eponymous commands are attested. In Hippodamos' case we know a number of men lost allotments around 262 BC; in Apollonides' case we can infer that quite a few men gained allotments around 259/258 BC.

As a final point, the Apollonides material points to the significant role in facilitating military settlement played by 'the *dioikesis* formerly of Simaristos'. A *dioikesis* seems to have been a name for an administrative estate. It must have been enormous, because Apollonides was the new administrator of it, and his title, *nomarch*, was accorded to administrators of large precincts within the nomes of Egypt. Simaristos' *dioikesis* is a fairly important piece of property. From one text we know that it was one of numerous similar estates (*P.Petr.* 3.40). From Apollonides' texts we know that the estate was distributed among military settlers once it had entered 'formerly of Simaristos' status in or before 259 BC. And from the famous Revenue Laws papyrus we know that the estate's vineyards were both granted a special tax status in 259 BC, and that other estates that shared some now-lost quality with the estate formerly of Simaristos also gained this tax status for their vineyards. The only others to receive that special tax status on vineyards were cleruchs, specifically those who were either on campaign or farming the vineyards themselves. My guess is that Simaristos' *dioikesis* was a large estate given in gift by the king to Simaristos, to be developed and cultivated for a period of time, for the ultimate, specific purpose of distributing the developed lands to cleruchs, which is exactly what was taking place in the estate in and after 259 BC. I conclude, then, that the king gave privileged tax status to encourage entrepreneurs to develop land on a temporary basis in preparation for military settlement.

The last striking thing about the two archives of texts is the number of military units attested, and their apparent diffusion across multiple provinces of Middle Egypt. While both officials seem to have mainly been active in the Oxyrhynchite nome, their business and the military units with whom they interacted carried over north into the Herakleopolite nome, possibly even further to Memphis, and south into the Cynopolite and

Hermopolite nomes. So the command of Philagros had men active in the Hermopolite nome, but is especially well-attested in the Oxyrhynchites, from 268–244 BC. Judging by 30-aroura allotments for two of Philagros' men, he may have commanded phalanx infantry (*BGU* 6.1229–30). Most of the eponymous commands in these archives were cavalry commands. Aside from Philagros, Lysanias' command may have also been infantry: all the attested members were 'Persians' or Libyans, and they are also not confirmed as military settlers. Otherwise, all were cavalry commands, listed here with the years for which the command is attested in papyri: Sadalas (270–266 BC), Zoilos (268–228), Antiochos (268–243), Telestes (270–261), Spartakos (260), Nikokles (260) and Nikadas (257). Antiochos was a common-enough name that there may have been two or three near-contemporary eponymous commanders; for the latter half of the range above, it is attested only in the Herakleopolite or Arsinoite nomes, not the Oxyrhynchite. An Antiochos was also an eponymous commander of active-duty soldiers in Apollonopolis Megale in the Thebaid, where they were probably stationed to support elephant hunts and the security of the southern frontier (*P.Hal.* 1 Fr. 8, 259 BC). The number of units is striking, but it is also possible that several of them succeeded one another. So those of Spartakos, Nikokles and Nikadas have no attested overlap with those of Sadalas or Telestes. Even so, after 257 BC, Zoilos is very nearly the sole attested eponymous commander of cavalry in the Oxyrhynchites. Part of this could be a story of unit reorganization, as laid out above; part may also relate to the intensive settlement of cavalry in the Arsinoite nome in the 250s BC.

Further north, in Memphis, we know there were more cavalry and infantry settled because of a few documentary references. Most intriguing is the evidence for Thracians in the area, and in the 270s BC even an ethnically Thracian unit: the command of Lykophron (*P.Cair.Zen.* 1.59001). Lykophron's unit is a unique example in the papyri for a warband transitioning toward an institutional unit. In most cases, men in the same command tended to have allotments of similar size, like 100 arouras for heavy cavalry or 30 for phalangites. But in Lykophron's unit of Thracians there are men with 110 arouras, 70 arouras, 60 arouras and 40. There were also soldiers called *synkleroi* ('heirs of an allotment'), who listed their fathers' names and so were comparable to *epigonoi*, but must have already been listed on the unit's rolls. There is no clear case beside that of Lykophron's command where we can see such variation of allotment size within a single unit. Is it possible Lykophron's men, with such a range of allotment sizes, included both infantry and light to heavy cavalry? Were those with larger allotments chieftains and those with less land their former retainers? We may surmise they arrived in Egypt as a group of Thracian mercenaries, with varying equipment and status, and the settlements they subsequently received reflected the distinctions within their number.

Thracians, as previously argued, comprised a very important population within the Ptolemaic army, and Memphis was a significant location for military settlement, especially early on. Just a few years later, when King Ptolemy visited Memphis (267 BC), where Lykophron's unit was settled, there were games held in the king's honour, and the father of several of the victors set up a monument for all the victors (*SEG* 27.1114). The dedicator was a Thracian, Amadokos, and his sons Ptolemaios, Chrysermos and Bastakilas were three of the victors (he may have also been Amadokos son of Satokos, winner of Pankration in the 'Ptolemaikous' class). Perhaps their family possessed lands around Memphis near the other Thracians, although in time they attained Alexandrian citizenship. Chrysermos became an eponymous commander himself (attested 251–221 BC), and his son and grandson were eponymous priests. Many of the victors were local soldiers and officers, like Mnesimachos son of Ameinokles, whose distant descendant Aminokles son of Mnesimachos was a cavalry settler in the Herakleopolite nome in 60 BC (*BGU* 8.1814). Similarly, the victor Lykomedes may well have been the aforementioned military official, and it is a little tempting to see a connection between the Tarantine Hephaestion son of Demeas and the mercenary cavalry of Demeas attested a couple of decades later, given the Tarantine reputation for horsemanship and mercenary service. On the other hand, one of the victors was Kineas son of Alketas, a Thessalian of very high standing at the court of Pyrrhus and then of Ptolemy. He had negotiated with the Romans on behalf of Pyrrhus and was eponymous priest of Alexander in 263 BC. A connection is possible between the evidently elite Thracian Amadokos son of Satokos and three elite cavalrymen whose name or surname were Satokos (*SB* 16.12221), and it is even conceivable that Amadokos was a member of the Odrysian royal family, among whom Amadokos was a popular name.

Before proceeding to the period of the Second Syrian War, it is worth briefly revisiting the *dioikesis* of Simaristos. That estate and its management reflect one of several ways Ptolemy II was encouraging the expansion of cultivable land or the quality of the cultivation thereon. Far more is known, actually, of two other types of administrative area: gift estates, or *doreai*, and *myriarouriai*, tracts of 10,000 arouras. All three probably shared numerous features, and if we add *epistateia* it is conceivable the Ptolemaic state used several redundant organizing principles for large tracts of land. These latter three are all attested in the Fayum. The Fayum basin was transformed dramatically during Philadelphus' reign, reflected in its renaming from 'Limnē', the Marsh, to the Arsinoite nome, in honour of Ptolemy II's sister-wife. Centralized administrative estates, of all their kinds, helped advance the recovery of land and construction of infrastructure in preparation for intensive settlement, especially military settlement. The gift estates were given to prominent officials; the most famous is Apollonios the *dioiketes*, whose gift estate in the Fayum was managed for a number of years by the aforementioned Zenon.[9] Apollonios had at least one other gift estate near Memphis. Numerous other gift estates existed in Egypt. For example, Chrysermos son of Amadokos possessed a gift estate in the southern part of the Fayum (*P.Enteux.* 60). Apollonios' estate was divided into four basins, irrigated by a network of canals and dykes (*P.Lille* 1) around the town of Philadelpheia in the northern Fayum. They were not simply privileged properties given in reward for service: there was an expectation of investment and development, especially related to irrigation works.[10] The gift estates in time could return to the Crown and be redistributed, like the estates of Simaristos, for military settlements.[11] Apollonios' gift estate was eventually known as the lands 'formerly of Apollonios' and administered by an *epistates* on behalf of the state, perhaps for military settlement (*P.Cair.Zen.* 3.59366, 241 BC).

A more straightforward process was probably involved in the case of the *myriarouroi*, administrative officials – often Egyptians – who oversaw what was probably reckoned royal land, but could be divided up for soldiers' allotments. The *myriarouria* and *epistateia* ('administrative estate' is all I can offer in translation) were particularly important for the settlements that took place in the 250s BC. One early example is *P.Lille* 5 (260/259 BC), and it sheds helpful light on the process. It records seed distributions across a large estate under the management of a Greek named Nikostratos, and thus was probably the estate of Antisthenes (*P.Enteux.* 1, 259 BC). What type of estate it was is unclear, but does not particularly matter. The distributions of seed would nearly all correspond to standard sizes for military allotments: twenty to thirty for infantry, and many of 100, customary for Arsinoite cavalry. This suggests the estate was already internally organized to facilitate settlement. Moreover, two of the distributions fell in land that was characterized as part of the precinct of the *nomarch* Maimachos, a man well-attested in relation to the settlement of cavalry, and the two distributions provided seed for three men and 300 arouras. Perhaps those categorized as under the *nomarch*'s control were in the process of being distributed to military settlers. It is doubtful that all the land in these districts ultimately went to settlers, but it is useful for highlighting the administrative process of setting aside regions to prepare for military settlement.

Finally, the activity of Apollonios and others in the Fayum suggests that Ptolemy II intended to engage in a major military settlement there in the 250s BC even before the Second Syrian War began. Often we think of a model of Ptolemaic activity wherein war sparked settlement, and waves of settlers followed the conclusions of war. This interpretation, which is standard across the literature, makes the Ptolemies appear to be quite shortsighted, or to have approached military preparations as an afterthought. If they had not occasionally got into wars perhaps they would never have bothered much with military settlers. Instead, the grand Fayum military settlement of the late 250s BC was planned before the war ever started, and was interrupted by the war while yet in its early stages. The settlement was only partially carried out while the war was going on, and then steadily accelerated as the war – the last of Philadelphus' reign – wound down.

Military Settlement During and after the Second Syrian War

In November 253 BC, a young discharged soldier named Artemidoros found his way to Philadelpheia in the Fayum. He had with him a letter of introduction to hand over to Zenon, Apollonios' powerful secretary, written by a countryman who knew Zenon from a former important civil service position (*P.Zen.Pestm.* 67). The letter was Artemidoros' special ticket, because it set him apart from the mass of soldiers gaining allotments as the war ended. The letter relates how Artemidoros had been sent into the countryside 'with the rest of the soldiers to the farmsteads'. The farmsteads, or γῄδια, were small plots, and the implication in the letter is that a host of soldiers were discharged into the settler class as the war ended. The letter asked Zenon to show zeal on behalf of Artemidoros in overseeing the measurements on his behalf. Quite a few letters like this found their way to Zenon in the hands of young veterans. While the project to establish a major military settlement in the Fayum had begun before the Second Syrian War broke out, the scheme proceeded haltingly once war came, then spurred forward, perhaps in modified form, as the conflict slowly came to an end. At least three bodies of troops gained allotments in the Fayum in those years: the aforementioned 100-arouras cavalry, among whom many were *neaniskoi* (young men); numerous infantry, among whom most were the 25-arouras *epigonoi*; and a fairly large number of *presbyteroi*, veterans, who apparently included both infantry and cavalry.

Zenon is our primary window into the settlements, which is intriguing because he was not officially responsible for the settler process. But as Apollonios' senior subordinate he exercised effective influence in the region around Philadelpheia. His links to the land being prepared for settlers was extensive enough that in at least one case he personally took charge of distributing allotments (*PSI* 5.513). That case involved just four allotments, all for officers, ordered from the top of the military hierarchy, and Zenon was perhaps deputized for the duty by the nomarch Maimachos. Mainly the letters of recommendation he received begged him for assistance in making sure the land measurements were favourable, or in helping the cleruch acquire a good *stathmos*. These were the sorts of influence-related tasks Zenon could normally undertake, and personal influence carried as much or more weight then as it often does in the present. The earliest such letter (*P.Mich.* 1.33) is from January 254 BC, before the official end of the war. It introduced Zenon to the father of one of the *epigonoi* who were receiving allotments; it is possible his son was still away with the army. Then the letter on behalf of Artemidoros in November 253 BC corresponded with a large influx of soldiers from the army. The last letter of recommendation was delivered in March 250 BC, over two years later, and shows that even then new soldiers were arriving in the Arsinoite to receive land in the settlement system (*P.Cair.Zen.* 2.59284). The writer, from Alexandria, asked Zenon to help make sure the new settler was treated well, and if his unit gained allotments somewhere far from Philadelpheia, asked Zenon to write the settler a letter of recommendation to the *epistates* in charge of distributing his allotment. The Fayum became a prosperous, Hellenized core of Greek settlement in Egypt, but for friends and family of young soldiers sent to settle the new province it must have appeared heavy laden with risk.

The settlements themselves seem to have been orchestrated mainly between 255 and 250 BC, from a lead-up that began around 260. The plan was coordinated through the efforts of two very senior officials. On the domestic side, the *dioiketes* Apollonios, whose gift estate in the Arsinoite nome served as a model for the other developments that provided space for the cavalry. On the military side, the cavalry secretary Phanias, senior staff officer to whomever commanded the full Ptolemaic cavalry, spent considerable time in the Fayum, often with Zenon at Philadelpheia near the *dioketes*' estate. Irrigation infrastructure was erected with the location of existing and future cavalry-sized allotments in mind; that is, in blocks of 100 arouras whenever possible. The earliest evidence for new settlers is a document from April 256 BC, which tells us that a cleruch named Symbotes was haggling with the local royal secretary over the measurement to be used for his 100 arouras, hoping to add an extra 10 (*P.Cair.Zen.* 1.59132).[12] It is doubtful Symbotes was successful, given that the planning prior to the settlements had already surveyed and divided the land. In December 256 BC, there was an urgent letter commanding preparation of housing for the *neaniskoi* (young cavalry troopers) who would be arriving around Philadelpheia soon (*P.Cair.Zen.* 2.59153). Then in early 255 BC, the *dioiketes* Apollonios, the *epistates* Phanias and the nomarch Maimachos were coordinating the implementation of taxes on the new allotments (*PSI* 4.344). The text comprises parts of four letters, in one of which Phanias ordered Maimachos not to collect two types of taxes from cleruchs for however many years the allotments (and their fruits) were reckoned to the Crown. This suggests three things: that in 255 BC there were some settlers on the ground, that the allotments had been reckoned as land for settlers (*klērouchikē gē* they called it) for one or more years *before* 255, and until recently – and to some degree even then – many of the settlers were not available to take possession of or farm their allotments. This was undoubtedly due to the war.

The evidence on hand suggests that, while settlement began before the war ended, most of the settlers came to the land from late 253 to early 252 BC. A Macedonian military settler, Antigenes, had land around Philadelpheia in 254 BC (*P.Mich.* 1.34). He was in the eponymous command of Nikanor, and probably an infantryman. Another Macedonian 'of the cleruchs from Philadelpheia' is attested in 253 BC, Neoptolemos son of Stratippos, who lobbied for Zenon to intervene on behalf of his father, who was a cavalry cleruch in the Aphroditopolite nome between the Fayum and Memphis (*P.Cair.Zen.* 2.59236). Neoptolemos must then have been one of the *epigonoi* recruited for the war and then allotted one of the new lines within the settler army.[13] In late 253 BC, there is textual evidence to confirm two instances of infantry settlement aside from the activity at Philadelpheia. In one case, about twenty-five veteran infantry were measured land in the Memphite nome in the lands of two *myriarouroi* (*P.Zen.Pestm.* 38, November 253 BC). Around the same time a group of infantry, either veterans or perhaps *epigonoi*, gained lands around the village of Ammonias, which is in the north-eastern Fayum (*P.Lond.* 7.1981). The papyrus is a complaint from the 150 farmers the infantry wanted to lease their land to, after the deal was disrupted in February 252 BC. Also in February 252 BC, all the Egyptian farmers of the newly allotted settler plots abandoned their works and took refuge in the temple of Isis in the Memphite nome (*P.Cair.Zen.* 2.59245). In this last case, the Egyptians were employing a form of strike behaviour, probably to address grievances about the nature of their work agreements under the new settlers. Texts from the spring and summer of 252 BC seem to confirm that most of the settlements, at least in the vicinity of Philadelpheia and other areas where Zenon was influential, had already been completed. Most importantly, in July 252 BC the cavalry secretary for Ptolemaic Egypt, Phanias, travelled to the Arsinoite to inspect the *neaniskoi* cavalrymen and administer their oaths (*P.Cair.Zen.* 2.59254).

Beyond the summer of 252 BC, most of the texts available refer to the management of the settlements themselves rather than the measurement of allotments for the settlements. The most helpful of these texts is a missive regarding the settler bureaucracy (*P.Freib.* 1.7). It contains two letters, both written in January 251 BC, regarding the management of the new cavalry settlements. The earlier letter was from the cavalry secretary Phanias to an *epistates*, Antipatros, attached to a cavalry unit. Antipatros was ordered 'to look after all the cavalrymen allotted land capable of being sown for the 35th year [251/250]', not only to ensure the agricultural project was carried out, but also to ensure the military men were 'ready to go down to the king mounted and furnished with every necessity'. The letter emphasized the need for diligence until the affairs of the massive military project were more settled, and dangled the prospect of a promotion before the young officer's eyes. Additionally, *P.Lille* 1.39–42 and 1.51 relate to seed loans for *epigonoi* infantry allotments in late 251 BC, all located in the precinct of Polemon in the southern Fayum, and *P.Lond.* 7.1996 relates to seed loans for veteran troops in late 250, located in several locales on the eastern edge of the Fayum, not far from Philadelpheia. Even so, the late letter of recommendation suggests more military men were arriving in the Fayum to gain allotments even in 250 BC. Perhaps many of the later arrivals were dispatched to the Polemon or Themistos districts in the south and west, respectively, while the activity in Philadelphia and throughout the Herakleides precinct proceeded quite quickly, in the space of perhaps six months and immediately after the end of the Second Syrian War.

The *epigonoi* infantry are an intriguing case. The nature of the *epigonoi* class and its relation to the designation τῆς ἐπιγονῆς in papyri has elicited numerous takes from scholars.[14] The *epigonoi* included the male family members of Greek military settlers, as well as Greeks who had no direct family link to the military. Their conscription in the Second Syrian War proves they were eligible for military service. What is unclear is whether military service practically guaranteed a settler's allotment after the campaign ended. It is clear the *eikosipentarouroi epigonoi* were an exceptional group, but were they exceptional because the Ptolemaic army normally did not have to draw from the well of *epigonoi* in Egypt, or because the Ptolemaic state did not normally reward *epigonoi* with land in return for service? A common interpretation is that the *epigonoi* comprised the regular army, compared to cleruch reservists; this interpretation should almost certainly be discarded. There is no evidence that widespread military service by *epigonoi* was normal, but there is evidence that some *epigonoi* did serve, in wartime, and often in return for new military settlements. There is one example of a man of the *epigonoi* with active military status (*P.Sorb.* 1.17, 257 BC, a cavalryman), and it belongs to the Second Syrian War period. It is conceivable that man was eventually reckoned one of the *neaniskoi* among the cavalry settlers. A single additional text provides another example of a member of the *epigonoi* who was also enrolled in the cleruchy (*BGU* 6.1278, 215/214 BC). The post-Raphia context for the papyrus suggests *epigonoi* may have been called up for that war as well. Most of the *eikosipentarouroi* seem to have been settled in the Polemon precinct, the southern Fayum, where they gave their name to the town of Ibion '*Eikosipentarourōn*'.[15] It is possible the infantry settlers mentioned in *P.Lond.* 7.1980, located in the north-east Fayum, were also *epigonoi*-turned-cleruchs. However, at some point numbers of other *pezoi* and *triakontarouroi* gained allotments in the Fayum, so in the absence of further information we must be content to summarize as follows: the Ptolemaic army raised numerous *epigonoi* as additional soldiers in the Second Syrian War, and rewarded many of them with land allotments after the war, especially in the Fayum.

The veteran settlers, or *presbyteroi*, must have been a somewhat smaller population and present a more puzzling case. Given their title, they must have been in Ptolemaic service for some significant time, perhaps long enough to be considered time-expired, which might mean they were in their 50s. Some veterans were settled in the Memphite nome, but others were transferred from the Memphite to the Arsinoite nome. A handful of Greek and demotic Egyptian texts identify a class of *presbyteroi* cavalry, concerning whom next to nothing is known. *P.Sorb.* 1.18, from about 250 BC, suggests there were settlements of them in three nearby locales under different overseers, and that in one of those locales a distribution, probably for seed, was 258 artabas. If we knew the number of men in the plot we might estimate the size of their allotment, but compared to 100-aroura cavalry the men were presumably either very few or their allotments were much smaller. In a census document (*P.Count.* 2), there are four men who are reckoned *presbyteroi hippeis*, among whom one man seems to have had a fairly large family and holdings (although still smaller than most 100-aroura cavalrymen), while the other three had families and holdings indistinguishable from records for infantrymen and *epigonoi*. Several texts that specify the sizes of *presbyteroi* holdings list them between 18 and 25 arouras (*P.Zen.Pestm.* 38, November 253 BC), while the *chomatikon* taxes of seven *presbyteroi stratiotai* in another text suggests their average holdings were about 20 arouras (*P.Lond.* 7.1996, 250 BC), and three more also suggest averages of 20 arouras each (*P.Petr.* 2.39, 246/245 BC). Another text lists a seed distribution (*PSI* 6.627) of 574 artabas for at least twelve *presbyteroi*, which could support a range of about 50 arouras for just twelve men, or closer to thirty men at 20 arouras apiece. It seems likely that either the cavalry veterans were a minority of the veterans or their appellation as cavalry was functionally honorific, and their allotments consistently in range with those given to infantrymen in spite of their name. *Presbyteroi* are not attested as military men after 229 BC, but their common 20 arouras suggests their successors on the allotments were often known as *eikosiarouroi*, the 20-arouras cleruchs. Papyri give evidence that groups of them – at least several hundred, perhaps 1,000 or more in all – were settled around Memphis, or in the north-eastern precinct of the Fayum, where they have been attested at Ephyr, Tanis, Kerkesoucha and Sebennytos, and in lesser density in other parts of the Fayum.

Of the three groups of settlers, the best-attested and most important were the 100-arouras cavalry, or *hekatontarouroi hippeis*. The settlement of these cavalry in the Arsinoite nome reflects, unlike most of those before and after it, a planned development on a truly massive scale. Five basically complete hipparchies, approximately 1,300 cavalrymen, gained settlements in the region in one major endeavour, the shared project of Phanias and Apollonios. Many were the *neaniskoi*, but evidence in the form of unit titles confirms that several existing hipparchies also transferred to the Fayum, like the Firsts of Menelaos from the Hermopolite nome, and perhaps Antiochos' men from the Oxyrhynchites. Compared to the mercenary settler cavalry, among whom large allotments and hyperbolic rank were practically standard, the *hekatontarouroi* were ordered and structured according to institutional function, the product of internal Ptolemaic growth, power and authority, rather than an expression of Ptolemaic concessions in recruiting permanent settlers. These *hekatontarouroi* constituted the dominant Greek class in the Arsinoite nome after 250 BC, and one of the most significant concentrations of Greek wealth and cultural capital in the whole of Egypt after Alexandria.

The settlers in the Fayum are attested in the most detail of any part of Egypt in the generations after the settlements of the 250s BC. At the same time we should not overstate the extent to which the Fayum contingents were representative of the settler army as a whole. In the Fayum there were the mercenary cavalry, the 100-arouras cavalry, the veteran settlers, the 25-arouras *epigonoi* and a smattering of other troops. For comparison, P.Petr. 2.31 includes a list of the military settler contingents 'below Memphis', or north of Memphis toward and into the apex of the Delta. Perhaps the settlements concerned were those around Heliopolis, Leontopolis and Athribis. The contingents are 'the mercenary cavalry, the [text missing] infantry, the Macedonian [infantry], and the other contingents [of infantry]'. This list leads to several observations. First, that in Ptolemaic Egypt many mercenary cavalry (and perhaps mercenary infantry were the incomplete second category) were in fact settlers, identified as mercenaries because they served for a pay some substantial portion of the year, longer than the liturgic month of service other cleruchs owed. Second, there are no 100-arouras cavalry in this list, affirming that these were overwhelmingly settled in a triangle from Memphis to the Fayum and the Oxyrhynchites. Third, the absence of the 100-arouras cavalry also points toward the general significance in the Ptolemaic military of the mercenary or serving cavalry. Fourth, if the missing infantry contingent were mercenary or serving infantry, they represent a force that is not reliably attested in the Fayum until the end of the third century BC, but must have been a significant contingent if they were listed ahead of the Macedonians. Fifth, it signals that Macedonian infantry settlement was common in those regions, whereas it is comparatively less well-attested in the Fayum. Finally, it points, in its 'other contingents' of infantry, toward national bodies of troops, among whom Cretans, Galatians and Thracians are most famous. Other than this text, there is practically no other evidence for the military settlements in the apex of the Delta below Memphis, so we must exercise prudence in not taking the Fayum model as a sufficient picture of Ptolemaic settlement.

As the years of Ptolemy II's rule drew to a close, the institutions of the Ptolemaic army had developed in size and organization. The addition of several thousand new military settlers in the Fayum can figure as a capstone of Ptolemy's reform projects, although greater reforms lay in store under Ptolemy III. The settler army, as opposed to mercenaries or a small core of standing, royal troops, fought in several wars, and units gained experience of long-distance campaigning through elephant hunting. That experience proved useful in the reign of Ptolemy III. Ptolemy II was an infrastructure king: the development of improved and expanded irrigation systems made the expansion of the settler system possible, while particular developments to enhance viticulture made it more attractive for the settlers themselves. Ptolemy II cultivated court propaganda that made his reign into a golden age, but his actual rule actively built the institutions and infrastructure that made the reign of Ptolemy III the true Golden Age for the Ptolemaic army.

Chapter 7

Ptolemy III and the Third Syrian War

'At that season when the king, blest in his new marriage, had gone to waste the Assyrian borders'

—Catullus, *Coma Berenice* 11–12

In the summer of 244 BC, the merchant Theodoros, son of Kallikrates, transported a shipment of wine from the Arsinoite nome to Alexandria. Of the pay that he received, he deposited 20 drachmas into an account at the royal bank. The account was called 'the distribution for the soldiers'.[1] While much in Egypt may have gone on with seeming normalcy, Theodoros' donation provides a window into a chief concern among the people of Egypt and Asia: the Ptolemaic army was near the end of its second full year of war against the Seleucid Empire, a war that had ranged from the Aegean and Hellespont as far as Mesopotamia. The concern was also evident in the palace, where Ptolemy III had been forced to leave behind his new wife Berenike, the daughter of Magas, practically on their honeymoon to rush to the aid of his sister, likewise named Berenike. The newlywed Berenike's devotion of a lock of her golden hair to vouchsafe the return of her husband captured the imagination of the Greeks of Egypt. It became the subject of a court poem by Callimachus, and is known today most famously through the Latin translation by Catullus, the *Coma Berenice*. Ptolemy's sister had been taken to Syria in 252 BC to marry Antiochus II, but the king's ousted first wife Laodike, and her eldest son Seleucus, organized his assassination and then sought to kill the newly widowed queen and her infant son. Ptolemy's intervention was too late to save the life of his sister, which turned his action from a rescue operation to an avenging mission and campaign of conquest, the greatest military exploit of the Ptolemaic army: the Third Syrian War.

The Third Syrian War, begun in late summer 246 BC, was the first significant test of the Ptolemaic settler systems following their construction over the first half of the third century. The preceding chapter described the piece-by-piece development of the settler system, which was fairly

Ptolemy III and the Third Syrian War   163

complete after the Arsinoite nome settlements following the Second Syrian War. Study of this war poses considerable historiographical difficulties, like the first two Syrian Wars, and as Heinen has pointed out, the result has been a wide range of scholarly reconstructions.[2] By careful comparison of the narrative and documentary sources pertaining to the war, this chapter seeks to construct a coherent narrative and analysis of the performance of the settler system during the conflict. Even the most recent examinations of the Third Syrian War have failed to examine all the sources. I shall argue that the war lasted longer than often thought and highlights both the positives and negatives of the Ptolemaic military system. Ptolemaic forces won a handful of early victories and thereafter managed a largely defensive struggle, without paying a heavy price in men or materiel. The Ptolemaic army reached its pinnacle in this war, successfully campaigning on two fronts, and the main field army successfully campaigned for lengthy periods deep in Asia. At the same time, internal unrest cast in sharp relief the importance of the military settler class as an occupation force, and not simply a military reserve.

The Narrative from Historical Sources

Polybius' *Histories* becomes increasingly relevant the later this narrative moves into the third century BC, yet the work – what survives at least – contains only a passing reference to the Third Syrian War: Seleukeia-by-the-Sea held a Ptolemaic garrison at the onset of the Fourth Syrian War, having been seized by Ptolemy Euergetes, 'when that prince, owing to his indignation at the murder of Berenike, invaded Syria and seized that town' (Plb. 5.58.11). Ptolemaic forces probably bypassed or blockaded Seleukeia in their raid on Antioch in the Second Syrian War, but its conquest was one of the principal lasting territorial conquests of the Third Syrian War. Instead of Polybius, we find a short summary of the war in *The Book of Daniel*'s account of the kings of the north (Syria) and the south (Egypt). The sixth verse describes Berenike's marriage to Antiochus at the end of the Second Syrian War: 'the daughter of the king of the south shall come to the king of the north to make peace; but she shall not retain the strength of her arm, and he and his offspring shall not endure; but she shall be given up, and her attendants, her child, and he who got possession of her.' The seventh and eighth verses record Ptolemy's response: 'he shall come against the army and enter the fortress of the king of the north, and he shall deal with them and shall prevail. He shall also carry off to Egypt their gods with their molten images and with their precious vessels of silver and of gold.' The recovery of Egyptian sacred materials plundered generations earlier figured there and elsewhere as a major feature of the war, especially from the Egyptian perspective. The account concludes, saying of Ptolemy that 'for some years he shall refrain from attacking the king of the north. Then the latter shall come into the realm of the king of the south but shall return into his own land.' The number of years between the first and second phases of the war is a curious feature, and the account of the war's resumption suggests it was an inconsequential campaign or series of campaigns.

The murder of Berenike is the starting point for the war in practically every source. Versions of the assassination appear in Justin's *Epitome* of Pompeius Trogus' *Histories*, Book 27, in Polyaenus' *Stratagems* (8.50, under Laodike), in Appian's *Syrian Wars* (65), in Porphyry's discussion of *Daniel* in Jerome's commentaries (*FGrH* 260 F43) and in *The Book of Daniel* itself. The spurned queen Laodike, from a powerful cadet branch of the Seleucid family based in Asia Minor, and her eldest son Seleucus were both responsible for planning the removal of the new queen. Berenike and her infant son Antiochos were at Antioch, and an initial assassination attempt by city officials left Antiochos dead, but Berenike was able to escape to the suburb of Daphne, where her handmaids and a bodyguard of Galatians protected her. From Daphne she was able to send word to her brother in Egypt, and he hastened to Syria 'with all his forces' (Just. 27.1.6). A second assassination attempt left her dead, but according to Polyaenus the assassins were driven off or slain and the handmaids were able to convince the people Berenike had survived the attempt by using one of the wounded girls as a stand-in for her. They were able to sustain this ruse long enough for Ptolemy III to profit from it. The outrage against a Seleucid queen and Ptolemaic princess is purported in several of the accounts to have basically resulted in the surrender of whole stretches of the Seleucid Empire into Ptolemy III's hands. What is important for our study is to establish the extent of the real mobilization Justin described as 'all his forces', and to establish the veracity and effectiveness of the Ptolemaic ruse. Did Ptolemy value swiftness or strength in deciding how quickly to leave Egypt? Did he take the forces at hand and speed by ship, or take the time to call up his full army to march with him?

Ptolemy III, by responding rapidly to his sister's misfortune, very nearly became king of the whole Seleucid Empire. Polyaenus said the whole of Asia 'from Taurus to India' submitted to him without any fighting. Justin and Appian used similar language, although Appian specified Babylon as the furthest limit of Ptolemy's actual military campaign. Porphyry suggests it was a rapid conquest, but not without fighting, and included Cilicia, Syria, the countries beyond the Euphrates (and so we might read here the satrapies of Mesopotamia) and nearly all of Asia. At the very brink of becoming master of both Egypt and Asia, Ptolemy was compelled to return to Egypt by an outbreak of rebellion at home (Just 27.1.9: *domestica seditione*, also in Porphyry). According to Porphyry, he did not entirely abandon the conquests, but left a general (*dux*) named Xanthippos to continue the campaign in Mesopotamia and handed over Cilicia to a Friend (*amicus*) named Antiochos. Both of these men may number among the aristocracy encountered in the previous chapters: Xanthippos is more likely that high-ranking member of the aristocracy from the Second Syrian War than the Spartan mercenary general who served in the First Punic War, and Antiochos is more likely to be one of the several famous Antiochi in Ptolemaic service in the later reign of Philadelphus than the younger brother of Seleucus II. Before returning to Egypt, Ptolemy plundered the temples of the East, and went home with a train of treasures and 40,000 talents of silver (Porphyry). Our study should concern what sort of army was left with Xanthippos and for how long, and the extent of the Ptolemaic military activity beyond Ptolemy's own campaign: clearly there were operations in Cilicia, but where else in this earliest phase?

Ptolemy's return to Egypt did not end the war then, but permitted Seleucus II to launch counter-attacks. Justin records that Trogus wrote a narrative of a naval counter-attack, in which Seleucus took a grand fleet to recover his lost territories. He embarked 'after Ptolemy had departed', but a storm wrecked most of the fleet and he barely escaped with his life. His tragic turn worked to his benefit, however, when out of pity some of the cities returned to him. The story does not appear in any other source, and the tragic reversals should arouse some suspicion on our part. If it did happen, Seleucus must have set sail from Ephesos, where his father had passed away, and the recovered cities might be those of the Seleukis in Syria, certainly Antioch and perhaps Apameia, Laodikeia and others. This expedition could have departed in late autumn, but Justin situates it after Ptolemy returned to Egypt in spring 245 BC. Then Seleucus counter-attacked in Syria, but was defeated by a Ptolemaic army in an unnamed pitched battle, and fled back to Antioch with just a handful of men (Just. 27.2.5). Bereft of his field army, Seleucus struck a deal with his younger brother Antiochus and his uncles (Laodike's brothers), who were Antiochus' guardians back in Anatolia, to share power in return for aid to resume the war with Ptolemy

(Just. 27.2.8). It does not appear in any ancient source, but Seleucus may have won a battle that earned him his epithet *Kallinikos*, 'a beautiful victory', after acquiring this aid. According to Justin (27.2.9), Ptolemy and Seleucus signed a ten-year peace soon after Seleucus' arrangement with his brother. A Seleucid victory might help explain the truce. Antiochus was aged 14 the year of the accord with his brother, and the peace was not much later. Antiochus must have been born before the repudiation of Laodike by Antiochus II in 253 BC, so the latest year for the war-ending truce would be 240. This does fit fairly well with Eutropius' testimony (3.1.1) that a Roman embassy to Ptolemy III after the conclusion of the First Punic War offered assistance in Egypt's war with Syria, but Ptolemy III turned down the offer because the war was over. Eutropius placed the embassy between the end of the war (241 BC) and the consulships of Lentulus and Flaccus (237 BC), so the war should have ended somewhere in or shortly before that range of dates.

The next phase of fighting was actually a Seleucid civil war, when Antiochus Hierax and one of his uncles, Alexander, rebelled against Seleucus II. The sources for this civil war, called The War of the Brothers, include Justin's *Epitome* and *Prologi* of Trogus Book 27, as well as Eusebius (*Chron*. 251) and a pair of stratagems from Polyaenus.[3] They had been left in power in Anatolia after Seleucus left, and were probably in a stronger position in Anatolia than Seleucus was across the Taurus in Syria. Antiochus hired the Galatians as allies and fought Seleucus when he invaded Asia Minor. Seleucus won a battle in Lydia, but could not recover either of the chief Seleucid cities: Alexander held Sardeis secure and Ptolemaic forces held Ephesos. Antiochus II had died at Ephesos in 246 BC, so Ptolemy III must have acquired Ephesos during the war, sometime after Seleucus' fleet departed. Seleucus and Antiochus fought a second battle near Ankyra in Galatia, where Antiochus had the Galatians and Mithridates of Pontus as his allies. According to Eusebius, Seleucus suffered a terrible defeat and lost 20,000 men (Eusebius reports, in error, that Seleucus was killed). This defeat was one of the worst military disasters of the Hellenistic period. Seleucus' army was destroyed, his men killed, captured or scattered, his camp and court captured, and Seleucus himself was for a while presumed dead. Instead he escaped, disguised as the personal servant of Amaktion, commander of the royal guard cavalry, with just a handful of followers.[4]

The Seleucid king's defeat inspired rebellions in the Upper Satrapies, and in Eusebius' telling may also have encouraged Ptolemy to resume the war. The next item Eusebius reported after Seleucus' defeat was that he raised a new army – if we trust these sources, it is his *fourth* army after losing the first three to shipwreck, defeat in Syria and defeat at Ankyra – and broke up Ptolemaic sieges at Orthosia and Damascus, after the fighting in Anatolia encouraged Ptolemy to again invade Syria. Seleucus' ability to keep raising troops surely means some of the defeats were not as bad as the sources state, but is also indicative of the resilience of the Seleucid military population. Eusebius dated that action to the third year of the 134th Olympiad, between summer 242 and summer 241 BC. This raises potential chronological problems, for while the war may well have ended in 242/241 BC, compressing the War of the Brothers up to the Battle of Ankyra before that date can cause some difficulties. It may nonetheless be the case, but we might also consider whether a Ptolemaic attack on Damascus and Orthosia may have occurred, separate from the main events of the Third Syrian War, in the early 230s BC. That is, Eusubius correctly dates the end of the war to 242/241 BC, followed by the outbreak of the War of the Brothers. After the catastrophe at Ankyra, a Ptolemaic campaign in Syria and Phoenicia sought to regain a couple of border towns sacrificed in the truce of 242/241 BC (for both Damascus and Orthosia had at an earlier time been Ptolemaic), and Eusebius mistakenly assigned that campaign to 242/241. Orthosia was a city on the Phoenician coast between Tripolis and Laodikeia, while Damascus of course was the chief city of Koile Syria, 75 miles south-south-east from Orthosia, but along one of the other lines of advance from Ptolemaic territory into Seleucid Syria. Violence, but perhaps not involving the Ptolemies, spread into Asia in the early 230s BC: Babylonian tablets record heavy fighting, with 'two or three dead in every household' between 'the king's guard troops' and 'the citadel garrison' in late spring 237 (*BDIA* 3283) and again between 'the rebels in the citadel' and 'many troops of the chief' in autumn 234 (*BDIA* 3282 '-234), indicating unrest in the Seleucid Empire was widespread for several years after the defeat at Ankyra. The unrest from 237–234 BC is probably related to Antiochus' invasion of Mesopotamia (Polyaenus 4.17.1) or the Parthian revolt (Just. 41.4.6–7). While Eusebius' wording is more likely to mean that Ptolemy's forces failed to capture the two cities, the narrative of the Fourth Syrian War suggests Seleucid territory began north of Arados, well to the north of Orthosia (Plb. 5.68.7). Damascus may well also have been Ptolemaic at the time: Antiochus went to great efforts to break Ptolemaic lines between the Lebanon and Anti-Lebanon ranges and in Phoenicia, when, if he controlled Damascus, he would have been able to get well around the Ptolemaic flank. He did precisely that in the Fifth Syrian War, which led Grainger to suggest Polyaenus' stratagem about an 'Antiochus son of Seleucus' capturing Damascus belonged to the opening of the Fifth Syrian War.[5] For these reasons, it seems likely either that Eusebius was wrong, or that, after the sieges failed, the subsequent treaty negotiations resulted in the return of Damascus and Orthosia to the Ptolemaic fold.

The War of the Brothers continued with more fighting in Asia Minor and the reappearance of Ptolemaic forces. Antiochus Hierax was betrayed by his allies and fled to Magnesia (either that 'on-the-Meander' near Miletos and Ephesos, or that 'by-Mount-Sipylus' nearer Smyrna and Sardis). He gathered allies there, including 'soldiers sent by Ptolemy' and other forces, offered battle and won (Eus. *Chron.* 251). The other forces may have included troops sent by King Ziaelas of Bithynia, because after the victory he married Ziaelas' daughter. Epigraphic evidence shows that Ptolemy and Ziaelas were allies in about 242 BC (*IG XII*^{4} 1.209), and seemingly were still allies when they came to Antiochus' aid at Magnesia. Was Antiochus Hierax then a Ptolemaic ally as well, supported by Ptolemaic forces as a way to foster instability in the Seleucid realm? It is not even clear who Antiochus' enemy at Magnesia was. Justin (27.3.1) reported that Eumenes of Pergamon attacked Antiochus after Ankyra, but Eumenes died in 241 BC (Strabo 13.4.2), before most dates for the Battle of Ankyra; his successor Attalus did fight and win several battles over Hierax, but not until 229 BC (Eus. *Chron.* 253). His enemy then could have been the Galatian allies and his own seditious army, or troops commanded by men loyal to Seleucus II, like his uncles Andromachos and Achaios, against whom Antiochus fought when he invaded Syria and Mesopotamia. It is entirely possible that his uncles were in fact the commanders of his own seditious army, and had shifted their loyalty to Seleucus. The battle is difficult to date, but Ptolemaic participation suggests yet again the war did not entirely end with the ten-year peace. This Battle of Magnesia may have been fought at about the same time as the actions at Damascus and Orthosia.

The remaining pieces of the war are a pair of events in the Aegean, mentioned ever so briefly in the *Prologi*: 'Ptolemy captured Adaios for the second time and put him to death, and Antigonus defeated Opron [or Sophron] at the battle of Andros.' Adaios was a dynast of Thrace ruling on behalf of the Seleucids, a former lieutenant of Lysimachus or that man's son, and presumably also father of the Adaios addressed in a letter of Philip V concerning the city Ainos (*Mac.Inst. II* 9). Adaios ruled – the term should be taken very loosely – much of south-eastern Thrace, mainly along the Aegean coastline between Lysimacheia and the borders of Macedon, but also much further north and inland, as far as Kabyle and Messembria. Perhaps Adaios had surrendered to Ptolemaic forces or flipped to the Ptolemaic side early in the war, attributable even to the Berenike ruse, but returned to his Seleucid loyalty later. Ptolemy's forces captured and executed him, and Ptolemaic control extended over his *dynasteia* in Thrace. It is difficult to say when this happened, except the *Prologi* implies it was before the Battle of Andros.

The Battle of Andros was the final major engagement between the Ptolemaic and Antigonid navies. It had such an effect that, even though the Third Syrian War ended with the Ptolemaic naval position in Asia Minor and the eastern Aegean strengthened, the Ptolemaic competition for control of the Aegean Sea basically ended after the defeat. Andros must have been fought before 239 BC, when Antigonus Gonatas died, since Antigonus was present for the battle (Plut. *Pel.* 2.2.). The Battle of Andros is linked in several sources to the Ptolemaic acquisition of Ephesos. If Sophron is rightly identified as the Ptolemaic commander at Andros, then he is also presumably the former Seleucid governor of Ephesos, whom Laodike attempted to execute when he came to Sardis (Athenaeus 13.593B–C). He learned of the plot and escaped back to Ephesos. If Ephesos and Sophron were both aligned with Ptolemy III soon after, it is plausible that Sophron handed the city over, which explains its Ptolemaic conquest. After the plot against his life by Laodike there was no basis for continuing his loyalty to the Seleucids, and Seleucus, who had been in Ephesos, must have already left with the Seleucid fleet at Ephesos to sail to Syria. The adjacent story in *Deipnosophistae* tells how Ptolemaios 'the son of Ptolemy Philadelphus the king' was commander of the garrison at Ephesos and was killed in an uprising by Thracian mercenaries (Ath. 13.593A–B). He may have sailed to Ephesos to occupy the city when Sophron handed it over. Ptolemaic evidence helps clear up this part of the war. Another possible link here is the story in Appian, and only in Appian, that Ptolemy avenged his sister by capturing and killing Laodike (*Syr.* 65). Laodike is not attested alive again after the plot against Sophron,[6] and her absence from the conflict between the brothers is quite striking, especially considering the roles played by her brothers. If Laodike really was killed in the early stages of the war, it was probably in fighting around Sardis and Ephesos and plausibly involved Sophron.

As for the Battle of Andros, Eusebius, Porphyry and Justin provide no evidence beyond the words of Trogus' chapter summaries. Andros is on the opposite side of the Aegean from Ephesos, about 130 miles to its west. It controls approaches from the northern Aegean toward the Saronic Gulf and Athens, and just a few miles separate it from the island of Euboea. Ptolemaic forces may have garrisoned Andros continually since 308 BC, and in the years before 246 they would have been very near the action as Antigonus waged war against his nephew Alexandros, son of Krateros, who had seceded from Antigonus and taken both Corinth and Chalkis on Euboea with him. Alexandros died and his rebellion ended within a year or two, about 246 or 245 BC, so the Battle of Andros may reflect increased Antigonid aggression after the end of its internal conflict. It is difficult to narrow the date for the battle much more. A date in late spring 245 BC just barely squares all the available evidence: time for the Ptolemaic conflict with Adaios in Thrace, avoidance of seagoing in the winter months of 246/245, Seleucus' departure from Ephesos in early spring and Sophron's betrayal of the city to the Ptolemies, and an engagement before Antigonus founded two festivals on Delos, one for the Saviour Gods and the other for Pan, in June 245.[7] At the same time, it is not necessary to link the battle to the Delian festivals, so it could have taken place a year or two later, although probably before Aratus captured Corinth in 243 BC (Plb. 2.43.4). Ptolemaic forces abandoned Andros after the defeat; there was a Macedonian garrison on Andros in 201 BC (Livy 31.15), so the change of hands is as likely to have happened then as at any later point.

In sum, the Third Syrian War was really several related conflicts. First was Ptolemy's rapid campaign to rescue then avenge Berenike in Syria and into Mesopotamia, which began in late summer 246 BC, and ended abruptly due to a revolt in Egypt, perhaps in spring 245. At about the same time, there was a general Ptolemaic offensive against Seleucid possessions in the Aegean and Asia Minor, helped by divided loyalties on the Seleucid side. The Antigonid victory at Andros probably fits within this period. Various Seleucid and Ptolemaic campaigns across the theatre of war then lasted until 242/241 BC, in which Seleucus II was defeated in pitched battle in Syria but later defeated a Ptolemaic army, perhaps that of Xanthippos, in Mesopotamia. To some degree that marks the end of the Third Syrian War, except the ensuing war between the Seleucid brothers encouraged further Ptolemaic hostilities in about 239/238 BC. Apart from this basic outline there are many questions, chiefly the nature of the Ptolemaic military effort, its scale, duration, combat role and accomplishments. Additional source material, from Ptolemaic, Seleucid and intermediate perspectives, can actually help answer many of these questions.

Ptolemaic Accounts

Five Ptolemaic documents lie in a murky area between documentary evidence and history. Together, these corroborate and extend many of the details from the literary sources. The documents are: Callimachus' court poem 'Berenike's Lock', as known from its Latin translation by Catullus; a collection of short biographies of members of the Ptolemaic dynasty, *Papyri Haunienses* 1.6; a Ptolemaic account of the war's early operations, *Chr.Wilck.* 1, which might even be the first-person account of Ptolemy III himself, or was styled as such; a monumental inscription erected by Ptolemy's agents on the coast of the Arabian Sea, *OGIS* 54, the so-called Adoulis inscription; and the trilingual 'Alexandrian' decree of 243 BC, composed by a synod of Egyptian priests for Ptolemy III. Callimachus' poem and the last three sources dated from the reign of Ptolemy III, while *P.Haun.* 6 probably dates to the second century AD, based on histories from the Ptolemaic era.

Catullus 66, the *Coma Berenices*, is, as mentioned, a translation of the poem by Callimachus (*Aetia* Fr.110). The story goes that Berenike, wife of Ptolemy III, devoted a lock of her hair to the gods in the hope that her husband would return safely from the war. Callimachus himself was contemporary with the war, and the song followed the war by just a handful of years. It makes sense, then, to treat its evidence as Ptolemaic source material. As literature it is not necessarily concerned with precision or veracity above all else, but it nonetheless provides several useful and consistent pieces of evidence. It describes (66.12) King Ptolemy as having departed to 'lay waste the territories of Assyria', implying much of the fighting took place beyond the Euphrates in Mesopotamia. He further mentions that by 'fierce battle' (*proelia torva*, 66.20) and in a short campaign (66.33–34), Ptolemy added Asia to the realm of Egypt.

P.Haun. 6 provides brief biographies of members of the royal family, all tied to events in the Third Syrian War and the rule of Ptolemy III, whose own biography appears second in the surviving text.[8] The first section (numbered as the fifth entry) concerns the life of Ptolemaios, 'so-called (ἐπικλησιν) "of Andromachos"'. The description of his career mentions military activities in Thrace, participation in the naval battle at Andros and his death in a revolt at Ephesos (ἐν ἐφεσωι κατεσφαγη). Thus his career bears immediate connections to most of the Ptolemaic activities in the Aegean Sea during the Third Syrian War. The meaning of his cognomen has elicited too much debate from those unwilling to accept the obvious answer: that he was called the son of Andromachos, but was not truly.⁹ There is no reason but a patronymic (father's name) to render Andromachos in the genitive case. It is a striking coincidence that Ptolemaios Andromachou fought at the Battle of Andros, but because it appears in the genitive, there is little basis for assigning the cognomen to his participation at the battle. Instead, his father was a man named Andromachos, but his sire would have been Ptolemy II Philadelphus, which is what the Athenaeus text said of the Ptolemaios slain by Thracian mercenaries at Ephesos. He is of course, then, the eponymous priest of the royal cult at Alexandria in 251/250 BC, alongside Philadelphus' courtesan Bilistiche, plausibly also his mother. The entry for Ptolemaios Andromachou helps tie parts of the narrative together: he captured Ainos and many other cities on the Thracian coast, which connects him to the conflict with Adaios. Then he participated in a sea battle (ναυμαχησας) at Andros, which connects him to Sophron/Opron. Finally, he was at Ephesos, which connects him again to Sophron and the story in Athenaeus, where he was betrayed and murdered.¹⁰ The text does not mention Thracian soldiers, but he had campaigned in Thrace previously, and furthermore an inscription from Ephesos contains a list of soldiers, many of them with recognizably Thracian names, and their ranks listed too (*SE* 593*2). There are several *idiōtai* (private soldiers), several *diakonoi* (servants or batmen) and a handful of officers, including two of high rank, a *syntagmatarchēs* and *pentakosiarchos*. Their ranks are familiar in comparison to those common in Ptolemaic Egypt. Most importantly, there are two men identified as hypaspists. Hypaspists were, in Ptolemaic tradition, an elite component of the *agema* stationed at the court or in the company of royals. Their presence at Ephesos in a list of Thracian soldiers seals the identity of Ptolemaios Andromachou.

The second section, from which fragments of nine lines survive, concerns the reign of Ptolemy III Euergetes. It begins with events from the Third Syrian War.¹¹ Following 'of the Euphrates', which might help situate the geographical position of Ptolemy III, the next line's surviving letters plausibly spell out 'were there not at that time a revolt of the Egyptians' (και ει μη τοτε αιγυπτιων απος[ταςιν). Thus the Ptolemaic text affirms the rumoured Egyptian revolt. In this text, too, it forced him to return 'to Egypt again'. The next line reads, 'and after securing the country with garrisons, he returned to Alexandria' (φρουραις καταλαβων επανηλθεν εις αλεξα[νδρειαν). This last line affirms that Ptolemy's return, whenever that may have been, did not end his army's activity in Asia and thus corroborates the tradition in Porphyry of the continued activity of the Ptolemaic army under Xanthippos. A significant part of his army may have continued on, perhaps even across the Euphrates, for months or years after the end of the king's campaign. However, to what degree were they split into garrison detachments, rather than a unified campaign army? The last parts of his entry regard his alliance with the Aetolians in a war against the Macedonians, a subject broached in the next chapter.

The next papyrus, *Chr.Wilck.* 1, contains fragments from four columns (I–IV) of narrative concerning the early stages of the war, from the dramatic palace intrigues after Antiochus' death to Ptolemy's triumphal entry into Antioch.[12] Some of the earliest surviving lines set the context: queen Berenike's loyalists manned the walls at her refuge (Daphne?), and she dispatched letters to the cities and rulers of the Seleucid realm and to her brother 'relating what things had transpired', which must mean the attempt(s) on the lives of her and her son Antiochus. In response, someone led out their army (I.6: τοὺ]ς στρατιώτας προσαγόντων) as an immediate response to the letter. Grainger (2010: p.156) viewed the soldiers as Seleucid troops loyal to Berenike, but it may more likely be a reference to Ptolemy III himself setting forth with his army. The narrative uses a first-person plural repeatedly (first at I.18) and refers to 'the sister' (I.24 and IV.21), so parts of it are definitely from the king's perspective, employ the royal 'we' and are consistent then with the participle for 'leading out' in line 6. The king is not firmly identified with the text until column II line 16, and by then was already at a harbour, with his fleet, less than two day's sail south of Seleukeia. That of course means that part of the preceding text concerned the progress of Ptolemy's campaign. We may be confident that Ptolemy travelled to Syria by sea. It was by far the quicker way, but also necessarily limited the number of soldiers who could travel with him.

Lines 7–21 of column 1 describe the peaceful acquisition of two or three Seleucid cities, all presumably on the Syrian coast leading toward Seleukeia. The hopelessly fragmented description mentions two officers, Eumachos and Aristeas, who were entrusted with the garrison and citadel of one city, then an officer – perhaps a Seleucid officer – named Andriskos involved in the handover of a city, and finally an officer named Epigenes, who received charge of a city (the text's use of *polis* suggests an organized Greek settlement, either Seleukeia or Laodikeia). At lines 14–15 there is a military reference to 'as many [soldiers] as were in the ready units' (ἅπαντας ἐν τοῖς ἐπιτη[δείοις). It does not fall at a point in the text where one may easily conclude it describes the army units that accompanied Ptolemy on his campaign, but it could describe a triage of the hastily gathered force to keep only the most-fit soldiers with the fleet as it sped toward Berenike. The rest could stay at the newly acquired cities and catch up later. The description of garrisons surrendered to the siblings reinforces the picture of a generally peaceful conquest waged by a brother championing the just treatment of his sister. My guess is that the city handed over to Eumachos and Aristeas was Laodikeia. We know from lines 18–19 of column II that Ptolemy disembarked from one harbour taking only as many ships as he could fit into the harbour at Seleukeia (this would tie, then, to the triaging of the most-ready soldiers), and stopped off at the fortress of Posideion for the night before finishing the journey the next day. Ruins at Ras al-Bassit are often identified with Posideion, and are almost exactly halfway between Laodikeia and Seleukeia. It marks a reasonable staging point for the Ptolemaic fleet: about 30 miles for the first and 23 for the second, both very reasonable distances for daytime sea travel. So Ptolemy left part of his fleet and some of his soldiers at Laodikeia, as well as two garrison commanders at the city, before finishing the naval component of his journey two days later. By posting garrisons he took steps to secure the cities long term; in leaving soldiers and ships behind, in part because they could not all fit into the harbour at Seleukeia, he must have had a fairly large fleet.

At the same time as Ptolemy's fleet was advancing toward Berenike in Syria, some of Berenike's own officers seem to have carried out raids in Cilicia. Two commanders, Pythagoras and Aristokles, sailed to Soloi in Cilicia with a small squadron. The satrap of Cilicia, Aribazos, had gathered 1,500 talents, which he planned to send to Ephesos, to the court of Laodike (II.5–7). At this early point in the war Ephesos was definitely still Seleucid, and may have still been the location for the court. The people of Soloi, soldiers present at the city and the men in the crews of Pythagoras and Aristokles seized the treasury from Aribazos and shipped it to Seleukeia (II.4–5). The city ended up in Ptolemaic hands (II.11–13) and stayed Ptolemaic until about 200 BC. Aribazos tried to cross the Taurus to reach Laodike, but the tribesmen in the highlands ambushed his party, cut off his head and took it to Antioch (II.13–16). That must have taken place later in the autumn, but signals that news of Ptolemy's control in Syria had advanced far enough for the mountain tribesmen to know where to go seeking reward.

Ptolemy and his fleet reached Seleukeia and an enthusiastic welcome before finding a similar reception in Antioch. The Ptolemaic royal narrative emphasizes the presence of the Seleucid officers and soldiers in the welcoming crowd alongside the citizens. In the third fragment, Ptolemy departed Seleukeia for Antioch, accompanied by the high-ranking military officers and administrative officials who had met him there, plus those soldiers not assigned to garrison the city. After an even more splendid welcome in Antioch, in the fourth fragment, Ptolemy mentions seeing his sister during the evening. The wording at the end of the surviving text reads: 'we went straightaway to our sister, and afterward managed some important affairs, holding audience with the officers and soldiers and others in that country, taking counsel regarding the whole situation.'[13] The account very clearly depicts Berenike as yet living, which suggests that a tradition of her survival was part of the official Ptolemaic discourse concerning the conflict, and corroborates Polyaenus' stratagem. If Berenike somehow had survived until her brother arrived, it must have been in a weakened state and she soon died. The document does not actually specify that she was still living; only that Ptolemy went to see her. The welcome and salutes from the satraps, generals, officers and soldiers come across in the text as something approaching acclamation as king, but the text also avoids claiming an actual acclamation occurred. Nonetheless, Ptolemy held court and issued rulings as if he were king. What could Ptolemy have done at that juncture to secure his position? What mistakes did he make that led to Seleucus' return to power in Antioch? Seleucus II certainly held Antioch at the time of his defeat in battle against a Ptolemaic army (Just. 27.2.5), but that battle could have been fought at any point between summer 245 BC and the end of the war, meaning the window for Ptolemaic rule at Antioch might have been anywhere from a few months to a few years.

The Adoulis inscription (*OGIS* 54, Bagnall and Derow 2004: no. 26) was recorded for posterity by the monk Cosmas Indicopleustes in the sixth century AD. It is lost today. Adoulis was a Ptolemaic base in the Red Sea. The inscription offered another official Ptolemaic account of the war. Because it does not refer to Ptolemy III as 'Euergetes', it is usually dated before he received that title between May and September 243 BC; if so, it is among the earliest sources on the war, composed before the war was concluded.[14] After describing Ptolemy III's heritage, even including his paternal link to Herakles and his maternal link to Dionysos – fitting for a conquering hero in the tradition of Alexander – the text went on to list the lands Ptolemy ruled by inheritance: Egypt, Libya, Syria and Phoenicia, Cyprus, Lycia, Caria and the Cyclades. The absence of Pamphylia, Cilicia and Ionia suggests Antiochus II conquered them from Ptolemy II in the Second Syrian War, while the listing of the Cyclades provides some further merit to the idea a Ptolemaic fleet defeated the Antigonid fleet around

250 BC. Then the text says Ptolemy 'campaigned into Asia with infantry and cavalry and a fleet and Troglodytic and Ethiopian elephants, which he and his father were the first to hunt from these lands and, bringing them back into Egypt, to fit out for military service'. The material in the synod decree discussed below generally shares some features with the Adoulis version, but the Adoulis text, coming from the Red Sea, put particular emphasis on the Ptolemaic elephant corps. If the inscription is correct, Ptolemy must have ordered a second army to travel by land through Syria, including the cavalry and African elephants. Ptolemy VI did the same thing when he invaded Syria almost exactly a century later (Jos. *Ant.* 13.103).

The Adoulis text then described Ptolemy's campaign. Grammatically, the description divides the campaign into three phases. The first phase consists entirely of participles, minimizing the personal agency of Ptolemy III even while ascribing to him mastery 'of all the land this side of the Euphrates and of Cilicia and Pamphylia and Ionia and the Hellespont and Thrace and of all the forces and Indian elephants in these lands'. Many of these lands may have been surrendered rather than subjugated, and the text's use of the verb κυριεύω, 'rule', celebrates Ptolemy's authority, not his conquest. The reference to the forces of the Seleucid army is interesting. The Seleucid elephants were kept at Apameia in Syria, and Ptolemy II may well have plundered the elephant park there at the start of the First Syrian War. Did the Ptolemies ransack the Seleucid elephant population twice in the first three Syrian Wars? Did the Ptolemaic army gain an accession of new troops in Egypt from the campaign? The reference to gaining control of the Seleucid army (or a large part of it) could have this meaning, but may also contain little more than a reference to the collaboration of Berenike's partisans and the warm welcome he received from the Syrian city-states. In the second phase of the campaign, however, Ptolemy 'crossed the Euphrates' to make subject to himself 'Mesopotamia and Babylonia and Sousiane and Persis and Media', and even the other satrapies as far as Bactriane. The text does not use the word for rule, which actually leaves open the possibility that the campaign did not ultimately succeed, and likewise opens the door for questioning whether the geographic list expresses intent more than providing a record of actual travel and conquest. While the second part of the campaign did not necessarily lead to rule, the text describes an active campaign of conquest: Ptolemy was making regions subject to himself. His title in the text, 'Great King', may be taken as a reference to his conquests in Mesopotamia. As we shall soon see, Ptolemy's campaign across the Euphrates contained quite a bit of combat, which is consistent with the Adoulis text. Finally, the campaign narrative concluded with a quintessentially Egyptian report that Ptolemy recovered Egyptian temple artifacts that the Persians had plundered, as the highlight of a story of plunder and return. The end of the narrative is missing, but the dispatch of Ptolemy's army, a great quantity of plunder and the temple plunder back to Egypt suggests the campaign of conquest had turned into a predatory expedition.

Finally, the Alexandrian Synod Decree of December 243 BC is a recently published award of honours to Ptolemy III by the Egyptian priesthoods.[15] The return of temple goods was a major component in the praise for Ptolemy. Four-and-a-half years later, the Canopus decree of March 238 BC also praised Ptolemy for the return of temple property plundered by the Persians (*OGIS* 56, Bagnall and Derow 2004: no. 136). The priests of Egypt praised Ptolemy for a range of benefactions in the Alexandrian decree, but gave particular attention to Ptolemy's recovery of sacred relics stolen from Egyptian temples by the Persians. The decree tells how Ptolemy embarked in the first year of his rule (by the Egyptian calendar, his first year ended 23 October 246 BC) on his campaign to Asia, won a victory and captured great numbers of infantry, cavalry, elephants and ships, many of which he sent off to Egypt. The satrapies where Ptolemy's army recovered temple goods were listed as 'Syria and Phoenicia and Cilicia and Babylonia and Persia and Susiane'. In December 243 BC, the war was almost certainly, in some degree, still going on, as indicated by the following lines, which praised the king 'who has kept the country in peace by making war far off on her behalf'. In determining the extent of Ptolemy's army's reach, the Alexandrian decree's 'Persia and Susiane' probably expresses the maximum plausible eastward reach, but could still carry some measure of propagandistic exaggeration, even while the war was still going on.

By comparison, the Canopus decree likewise praised Ptolemy for his campaign to Syria, in which he returned the sacred images to their Egyptian temples. But there are two distinctions in the text worthy of discussion. First, the clause that praised Ptolemy for waging war abroad to maintain peace at home was modified: Ptolemy had waged wars against 'many peoples and rulers'. This suggests that there had been additional fighting of some sort outside of Egypt since December 243 BC. It also praised Ptolemy and Berenike for providing for law and order domestically (τὴν εὐνομίαν), chiefly by providing reserves of grain in a year when a catastrophically low Nile flood imperilled the social cohesion of Egypt. The Egyptians were 'terrified' and were 'thinking upon the destruction that had taken place under some former kings' until the king and queen acted as benefactors of the whole nation by purchasing grain to meet the needs of the country (*OGIS* 54.12–19). While two of the points of praise relate to warfare, this last, which praises domestic law, order and euergetism, may well point to the revolt mentioned in several of the narrative sources. The praise for the royal couple's upholding of law and order, not only for their virtuous deeds, points in this direction. If there was a very low flood, the people of Egypt would have anticipated the famine well before its effects, which would have stoked unrest and lawlessness. The praise for the queen, and not the king alone, also points in this direction: if Ptolemy was still in Asia when the revolt broke out, the burden of the initial response would have fallen on her. The Canopus decree concludes with a statement that the gods had granted peaceful stability (εὐσταθοῦσαν) to the kingdom of Ptolemy and Berenike as reward for all their good acts, which suggests that Egypt was at peace by the spring of 238 BC.

Does the reference to the poor harvest, disarmed revolt and royal euergetism in the Canopus decree mean these things happened after 243 BC? Perhaps the Alexandrian decree made reference to the revolt in less specific terms. In it, the clause after Ptolemy's wars abroad, in the same place as the law and doing good deeds in Canopus, praised the king for 'reviving the life of the people'. That curious little line might reference many things, but it certainly could refer to the crisis. Near the start of the decree's list of benefactions, the priests praised Ptolemy for cancelling some burdensome taxes and relieving a number of debts; without context for those decisions we cannot say much, but by way of comparison, the Ptolemaic royal benefactions that endeavoured to ameliorate the causes of revolt in the second century BC often remitted taxes and wrote off debts (e.g., *P.Köln.* 7.313, 186 BC). So we should not conclude that the revolt was later than the Alexandrian decree, although some effects of unrest may have continued past 243 BC. As for the decrees and the war, Ptolemy's own campaign was certainly concluded before any of the three decrees, but full peace was not achieved until some point between December 243 and March 238 BC.

Babylonian Chronicles

Documentary evidence from the Seleucid Empire consists of several Near Eastern cuneiform tablets, mainly from Babylon. There are also several inscriptions from Asia Minor of import, but they are discussed in the following section. The Babylonian chronicles are extremely helpful for dating the beginning of the war, its pace and intensity, and its extent. The astronomical chronicle (BM 132276) for the first half of year 66 of the Seleucid Era (246–245 BC) mentioned a visit by the royal family to Babylon in the spring of 246, then recorded that news arrived in Babylon of the death of Antiochus II on 20 Abu, or 19 August. It added that 'fear was in the land'.[16] The fear in the land could mean that news of Ptolemy's invasion arrived not long after the news of Antiochus' death, or could refer to the conflict between Laodike and Berenike. Whatever succession struggle existed in the western Seleucid Empire, the astronomical diary records that Seleucus was regarded as the next king from the month of Abu. The astronomical diaries exist for many years or half-years in the third century BC, but no astronomical diary entry has survived between September 246 and February 242, leaving the record for the time of the war frustratingly empty.

The most important Babylonian text is *BM 34428*, *BCHP* 11, 'The Invasion of Ptolemy III Chronicle', which describes Ptolemaic military activities in Mesopotamia. Recent doubt about the value of this text is unjustified. *BCHP* 11 is preliminarily published online by van der Spek, Finkel and Pirngruber with comments and corrections from others.[17] It is the most extensive narrative of the war from an eyewitness source, apart from, arguably, Ptolemy's account of the war's opening scenes. The chronicle follows the latter part of Ptolemy's invasion of Asia, picks up in about December 246 BC and covers events into late February or late March 245. The entry for Kislimu, the ninth month of the Babylonian calendar – 26 November to 25 December 246 BC – locates Ptolemy and his army at Seleukeia-on-the-Euphrates-and-the-Royal-Canal, probably ancient Sippar.[18] The ruins of ancient Sippar are south-west of modern Baghdad, just 16 miles west of Seleukeia-on-the-Tigris, but about 40 miles north of Babylon. We do not know when Ptolemy began his campaign, but it was no earlier than late August and probably not much later. He went first to the Seleukis, and conducted affairs of state at Antioch, probably in early October. By December he was at Seleukeia-Sippar, well over 600 miles from Antioch. It seems that Ptolemaic forces besieged that city, and in anticipation of an attack on Babylon the Seleucid officers there fortified the gates and readied their troops.

The Ptolemaic siege of Babylon began on 9 January 245 BC, when troops and siege engines arrived from Seleukeia-Sippar. Whether that city had fallen is unclear, but a substantial part of the army was still there, including King Ptolemy. Nothing in the chronicle indicates that Ptolemy himself ever came to Babylon. The chronicler called the Ptolemaic troops

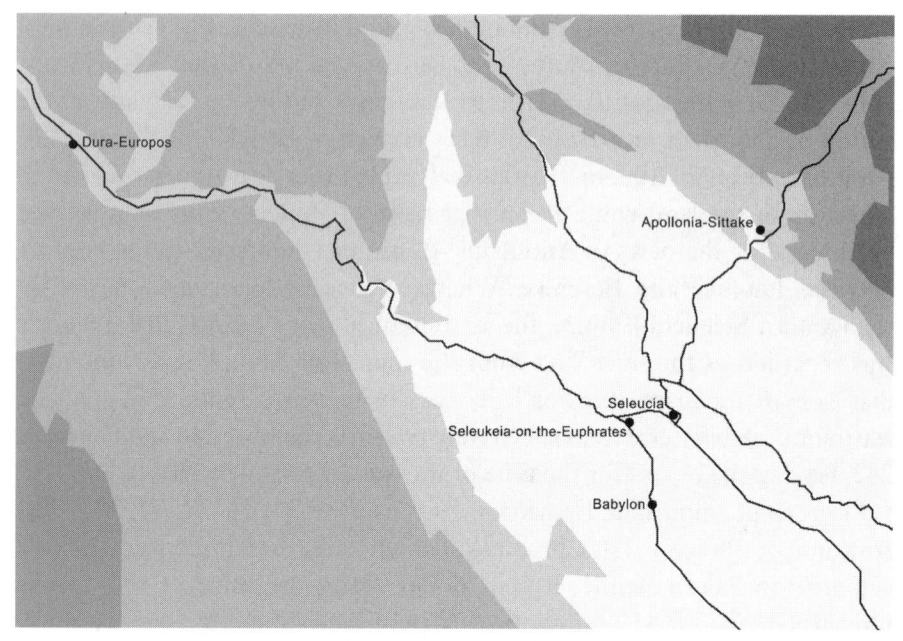

Mesopotamia in the Third Syrian War.

who arrived outside the city 'Hanaeans', and consistently used that term for the Ptolemaic army throughout the chronicle. The Hanaeans were despised invaders and nomads in ancient Babylonian tradition, but chroniclers used it for hostile Macedonians in the Hellenistic period (i.e., Alexander was 'King of the Hanaeans'). They did not respect the Babylonian gods and were 'armed and armored in iron'. The chronicle repeatedly refers to the iron-clad, iron-wielding Hanaeans of the Ptolemaic army. At a minimum, the chronicler sought to contrast well-equipped, professional troops on the attacking side with the less-prepared defenders. But it might also mean that in wealthy Ptolemaic Egypt, many soldiers were paying top dollar for heavy iron armour, whether iron plates to reinforce linen and leather armours, highly expensive muscled cuirasses of iron or perhaps even chainmail armour. On 19 Tebetu (12 January), the Ptolemaic army assaulted the Bêlet-Ninua citadel, which was probably the strongest of Babylon's fortifications on the west bank of the Euphrates. The chronicler reports that those in the citadel fled from it for the palace (on the east bank of the Euphrates) and 'the people were slaughtered by the Hanaeans'. If Bêlet-Ninua fell, then it seems the whole west of the city fell with it; the slaughter of the people may describe its sacking.

Five days later, 24 Tebetu (17 January), a large number of Ptolemaic reinforcements arrived under the command of an unnamed 'renowned prince, a representative of the king, who had come from the land of Egypt'. Finkel and van der Spek are probably correct in identifying him as the *dux* Xanthippos from Porphyry's account. Their arrival did not mean that there was not still an army at Seleukeia-Sippar, as later events show, but it is not clear whether the king was still there. Then on 26 Tebetu (19 January), the Ptolemaic army gained control of the Esagila, the great temple of Marduk. The record there is mainly lost, but the Esagila was on the east bank of the Euphrates, and near the river, so perhaps on this day a Ptolemaic attack successfully gained a significant foothold in the heart of Babylon. The narrative picks up on the other side of the tablet, and describes how the prince (presumably but not necessarily Xanthippos) and others performed Greek rituals in the Esagila, then fortified it for their assault on the last Seleucid part of Babylon: the royal citadel. The royal citadel was a large, well-fortified complex on the north side of the city. The Ptolemaic forces made an attack on the citadel and slaughtered huge numbers of the enemy, but failed to take the citadel or kill its commander. How could the Ptolemaic army, as the assaulting force, slaughter their foes yet fail to gain their objective? The Ptolemaic army was fighting bloody street battles, sieges within a siege, in those last weeks of January and beyond. Babylon was a large city, and it is conceivable that Ptolemaic attacks could claim formidable defended positions – the Etemenanki stepped pyramid, the temple of Ishtar, the theatre or blocks of the north-eastern quarter of the city – and slaughter Seleucid defenders, as the text says, but not yet enter the citadel itself.

The Seleucid counter-attack to relieve Babylon came on 15 Shabattu, about 7 February. The military governor of Seleukeia-on-the-Tigris (the text simply calls it 'Seleukeia', while Seleukeia-Sippar is always 'Seleukeia-on-the-Euphrates-and-the-Royal-Canal') led a relief force from the troops under his command the 40 miles to Babylon. The text says they entered the city but were slaughtered by the Ptolemaic general's forces. At the same time, Ptolemaic forces entered Seleukeia-on-the-Tigris and slaughtered more Seleucid defenders there. A few days later, the Ptolemaic troops at Babylon continued their attacks there and again inflicted heavy casualties on the Seleucid garrison. The tablet breaks off at that point, so the outcome of the Ptolemaic attacks is unclear. But in late February 245 BC, there was little hope of relief remaining for the beleaguered defenders. There are several striking conclusions we may reach from the narrative. First, a large Ptolemaic army did indeed operate in Seleucid territory, at least as far Babylon and Seleukeia. If Ptolemaic forces broke into both of those major cities and, moreover, won two victories over the military forces stationed at Seleukeia, there was little but distance to stop Ptolemaic armies from marching into Susiana or Persia as well. The Ptolemaic army that campaigned in Mesopotamia was large enough to keep a sizeable force at Seleukeia-Sippar, even after sending two 'divisions' to the attack at Babylon. The division remaining at Seleukeia-Sippar must have been responsible for the attack on Seleukeia-on-the-Tigris, and must have been quite large: presumably the elephants were in that division, and certainly the king was, at least until he returned to Egypt. Army divisions large enough for these sorts of operations must have been quite large. It is difficult to imagine the three independent corps numbering less than 5,000 apiece, and a total around 30,000 or more seems likely, given the scale of Ptolemaic operations. Finally, the description of Ptolemaic troops as iron-clad Hanaeans seems to suggest impressive troops, more than run-of-the-mill mercenaries: it suggests Macedonians in particular, and perhaps elite troops like the Ptolemaic *agema*. The operations described in the Invasion Chronicle practically necessitate the involvement of the Ptolemaic settler army as a field force.

Another chronicle, the so-called 'Seleucid Accessions Chronicle', *BCHP* 10, contains punctuated histories of the accessions of several Seleucid rulers.[19] There is much of interest in the text, but the most important detail is that Seleucus was enthroned as king at Sittake. The Babylonians recognized Seleucus as successor in August 246 BC, but Seleucus was in Ephesos then. Sittake was also known as Apollonia, and was a modest city in the Assyrian piedmont, namesake of the general region, which was called either the Apolloniatis or Sittakene. The main settlements of the Apolloniatis were on the road into Media from the confluence of the Diyala and Tigris rivers. Sittake, if correctly identified with Baradan Tepe, was about 100 miles north-nort-heast from Seleukeia.[20] The report means that Seleucus, after taking the crown at Ephesos, was not enthroned at a power base in the East until he reached Sittake. As a seat of power, it counts for little: Seleucus could try to draw on support from Media (and here the absence of Media from the list of raided provinces in the Alexandrian synod's decree has resonance) or retreat into Media if Ptolemy marched up the Diyala. The Apolloniatis had at least some military settlements, so he may have been able to draw some local support as well (Plb. 5.51).

Being enthroned at Apollonia-Sittake is a clear statement on the power of Ptolemaic arms in Syria and Mesopotamia.

Precisely when Seleucus was enthroned at Sittake is unclear. The interpretation of the other side of the tablet is fraught with difficulties, but a reference to events in the month of Ululu (approximately September) falls after entries about siege engines and fighting, presumably the Ptolemaic Mesopotamian campaign, but before Seleucus was enthroned. If all of the references really were to the Third Syrian War (likely, but not certain), then the Ululu is most likely that of 245 BC, meaning Seleucus was not enthroned at Sittake until at least a year after the war began.[21] His enthroning at a fairly weak position in Sittake must have preceded his 'Kallinikos' moment, his beautiful victory, probably in Mesopotamia against Xanthippos' forces. Seleucus refounded a city on the Euphrates (modern Raqqa) as Kallinikon, in honour of his own new surname, sometime in the second half of 244 or first half of 243 BC.[22] The refoundation of the city should have followed close upon the military victory, and perhaps it was even fought nearby. If so, the battle was probably fought well after he was enthroned at Sittake. The victory helped catapult him from his weak position at Sittake to the recovery of much of the core territory in the Seleucid Empire by the time the war ended in 242/241 BC.

Epigraphic Evidence

The clearest statement on the war from Asia Minor is the famous treaty of *sympoliteia* that merged the cities of Smyrna and Magnesia-ad-Sipylos at or near the end of the war (*OGIS* 229, Bagnall and Derow 2004: no. 29). The treaty incorporated the population at Magnesia, which seems to have mostly been a Seleucid military base, into the citizenry of Smyrna. The context for the move was the Third Syrian War. King Seleucus 'had crossed over to the Seleukis' in Syria, and in his absence there had been 'an attack of the enemy' (l.1–3). This confirms that Seleucus did leave the court at Ephesos (or Sardis) to return to Syria, although the Babylonian evidence suggests he was forced to make his base in the Apolloniatis rather than the Seleukis after arriving there. While Seleucus was fighting in the East, Ptolemaic or allied forces attacked the region around Smyrna. The text repeatedly hints that the military forces at Magnesia wavered in their loyalty to Seleucus. Those forces, some of which may have briefly sided with Ptolemaic units, included both active-duty troops encamped near the town and military settlers with lands around the town, as well as several contingents posted at the fortress of Old Magnesia: a detachment from the Seleucid phalanx, a body of Persians and a contingent of mercenaries. While these were not Ptolemaic forces, they nonetheless provide a useful example of the diversity of military bodies that could be present in a fairly small area given the complexities of recruitment and military role in the Hellenistic period. Their incorporation into the citizen body at Smyrna strengthened the local city-state's territory and expanded its population. The military units stayed on active duty after the merger. Thus Smyrna could assert both its loyalty to Seleucus even when professional units were wavering, and its contribution to the Seleucid army through the units of newly minted citizens that continued in service.

Numerous inscriptions from Asia Minor confirm and extend understanding of Ptolemaic operations in that region, largely corroborating Ptolemaic claims. A few examples will illustrate the point. Probably the earliest Ptolemaic inscription from the war is a letter of commendation to the people of Kildara in Caria from Tlepolemos, the Lycian aristocrat who had been prominent at the Ptolemaic court since the Second Syrian War.[23] Tlepolemos was eponymous priest at Alexandria when Ptolemy II died, and Ptolemy III kept him as eponymous priest in his second year, which included the start of the Third Syrian War. Tlepolemos may have campaigned in south-western Anatolia in the first months of the war, because the commendation thanks the Kildarans for their loyalty to Berenike and her son Antiochus. The letter affirms the literary historical accounts that Ptolemy extended his power through advocacy for his sister and nephew as if they were still alive. It is unclear how long Ptolemy could manage that strategy, but it is difficult to imagine it prevailing for more than a year after their deaths in about August–September 246 BC. Elsewhere in Caria, a text from Mylasa confirms Seleucid control in that region, but through a friendly dynast named Olympichos rather than direct control, and the interactions with the king emphasize his support of local autonomy for the cities of the region.[24] It is a pattern that appears elsewhere, but the result of Ptolemaic and Seleucid competition in Asia Minor generally seems to have been to offer local privileges in return for nominal rule.[25] It also proves that, when Ptolemaic victory texts claimed the conquest of Caria, they really meant the conquest of only parts of Caria. Texts from remote Gulnar (*SEG* 31.1321) and coastal Arsinoe-Nagidos in Rough Cilicia affirm Ptolemaic activity there, and suggest that Ptolemy III at minimum made good the Second Syrian War's losses in that region.

The epigraphic and numismatic evidence for major Ptolemaic gains in Ionia is large and growing.[26] The violence there may have been known locally as the 'Laodikeian War' (*I.Priene* 162), which might encourage the idea that the conflict between Sophron and Laodike, combined with the absence of Seleucus II, initiated a wider conflict when Sophron defected. The Ptolemaic conquests in Thrace and the Hellespont are affirmed through honours to a Ptolemaic official at Priapos in the Hellespont (*SEG* 34.1256), the Ptolemaic allegiance of the Ainians (*Asylia* 28) and two later dedications from Samothrace for two of Ptolemy III's generals.[27] The Samothracian dedications were for Epinikos, the governor of Maroneia, and Hippomedon, son of Agesilaos of Sparta, who was governor of the 'Hellespont and regions of Thrace' from around 240 until at least 219 BC. The dedications are undated, but related to Ptolemaic military interventions on behalf of the Samothracians, whose mainland possessions had come under attack. The attackers, probably Thracians or Galatians, met stiffer than expected resistance when the Ptolemaic commanders dispatched their own cavalry and infantry contingents plus batteries of catapults to aid the Samothracians.

The *Asylia* texts from Kos provide several reflections of Ptolemaic power.[28] They all date from 242 BC or soon after, when the Koans sent ambassadors around the Greek world seeking recognition for the sanctity of the temple of Asclepius on their island. The Koans were allies of the Ptolemaic kings, and of course one of the letters is from Ptolemy III (*Ayslia* 8). Another letter is from another king, presumably Seleucus II, who refers to a recent peace and a common hope that it would last (*Asylia* 9). That letter is undated, but probably belongs to late 242 or early 241 BC, corresponding to Eusebius' date for the end of the war. The letter from King Zielas of Bithynia refers to Ptolemy as Zielas' 'friend and ally'. The alliance between the two probably developed during the war, but what is interesting is that Zielas and Antiochus Hierax developed an active military alliance about this same time, or not much later, which could point toward cooperation between Antiochus and Ptolemy III. The one specific reference to Ptolemaic cooperation with Antiochus, in Eusebius' account of the battle near Magnesia, also ties in to Zielas, whose daughter Antiochus married after (and perhaps as a consequence of) the victory, and whose troops might have been the 'other forces' who joined with Antiochus in the battle. So while Ptolemy and Seleucus may have established a peace in about 242 BC, the expanded network of Ptolemaic allies (like Zielas and eventually Antiochus) made a resumption of conflict more likely.

Documentary Papyri and the Third Syrian War

The Revolt

The war's early course, as reconstructed thus far, saw Ptolemy III gain rapid victories in Syria and Cilicia as he was often welcomed at the gates of formidable cities, then expand his power into Mesopotamia, at least as far as Babylon, with a large army capable of operating in multiple divisions, before hastily withdrawing to Egypt to deal with a real or rumoured domestic sedition. Ptolemy's return to Egypt brought a cash windfall for Egypt, but also allowed Seleucus to strengthen his position and continue the war for several more years. Because only Porphyry and Justin mention the Egyptian rebellion, some commentators dismiss these accounts as a convenient fiction that excused Ptolemy III's hasty retreat from Asia after the inhabitants of Syria finally realized that Berenike was dead and began turning their support to Seleucus.[29] Some historians have suggested that the sedition was actually orchestrated by the *dioiketes* Apollonios, who disappeared from the papyrological record around 246/245 BC, or that it referred instead to a sedition in Cyrenaica among dissident Greeks.[30] Still other early commentators, like Mahaffy, considered the sedition an Egyptian uprising, perhaps related to the crisis referenced in the Canopus decree of 238 BC.[31] According to the decree, when the populace was terrified as a result of a severe drought, the king wisely released stored grain and purchased additional grain overseas, averting the crisis and assuring the stability of the realm. Although one might question the scant mention of revolt and interpret Porphyry and Justin in a variety of ways, *P.Haun.* 6 has changed that perspective, providing an account of a specifically Egyptian rebellion in a document from Ptolemaic Egypt.[32] So now it is generally accepted that some form of Egyptian uprising took place while Ptolemy was absent.

Documentary evidence for the revolt is scant to nonexistent. The best documentary evidence for a bad Nile flood around that time is actually for 247/246 BC (*P.Sorb.* 3.84, 86). Those texts suggest that, at least in the Fayum, leading administrative and engineering officials were deeply concerned with the flood, water supply and possible tampering. If so, unrest was probably brewing over the anticipated harvest well before Ptolemy left on his campaign, and perhaps even before the death of Ptolemy II in January 246 BC. Another Petrie papyrus, *P.Petr.* 2.23, may be helpful, but it cannot be dated more specifically than the 240s BC, thanks to several of the officials involved in the text. One of the texts on the papyrus records how the writer and some others, who were making regular patrols to monitor the irrigation infrastructure, caught at least one Egyptian tampering with a sluice gate, but not before significant damage had already been done. The language in the text corresponds closely to the order in *P.Sorb.* 3.84, but whether *P.Petr.* 2.23-1 relates to 247 BC's poor flood or to some other year is unclear. What these do show, however, is the potential for local agricultural-economic conditions to inspire subversive acts and even violence. If Mahaffy's conjecture that drought and near-famine lay at the root of the near-rebellion is correct, then vigilante vandalism of irrigation works would constitute early acts of rebellion on the part of concerned farmers. This may be further strengthened by a near-contemporary document, from late summer 246 BC, *P.Petr.* 2.37, a series of orders about the state of repair of the Fayum irrigation system and the management of water flows within it. It also includes orders to the nomarchs in the Fayum to meet certain quotas (fifty wagon loads per day), presumably of grain, to set aside for a state reserve. The works in the Fayum were so new – many projects were being bid out during the Third Syrian War – and the importance of the annual flood so great, there was practically always concern over the management of the flood. That was still the case in the first century AD (Pliny 5.10.58). Even so, stockpiling state supplies and privileging water release to meet administrative priorities might only have exacerbated tensions in Egypt the year after a poor inundation. What the writer in *P.Petr.* 2.37 called prudence may have contributed to a wider outbreak of violence after Ptolemy – and tens of thousands of soldiers – left Egypt and another poor flood ensued. If we may put any stock in *P.Edfou* 8, there were at least three poor inundations consecutively. The papyrus is usually reckoned to the middle of the third century BC, and in it a cleruch, Philotas, from Apollonopolis (Edfu) near Thebes requested a royal audience to share an invention to improve the inundation for the whole Thebaid. If *P.Edfou* 8 was written during the Third Syrian War, the three poor floods occurred in 247 BC, while Ptolemy II was still living, in 246 as the war began and again in 245, by which time Ptolemy III may already have returned from the war, even if much of his army had not.[33] Ultimately, however, more evidence is needed to resolve the nature of the Egyptian revolt.[34]

Military Mobilizations from Egypt

One of the most significant questions about the Third Syrian War for present purposes is the extent of the involvement of the Ptolemaic settler army. A soldier who left Philadelpheia, Zenon's hometown in the Fayum, and fought at Babylon would have travelled at least 1,200 miles by the time he fought in the street battles of that ancient city. Of course, the Adoulis inscription from the elephant hunting grounds would have been just as far from the Fayum, if not further. But how many left? Ptolemy's hasty departure may have emphasized mercenaries and the small permanent military forces at Alexandria or serving in the navy. Similarly, his scattered conquests in Asia Minor are likely to have relied heavily upon naval forces, mercenaries, Seleucids loyal to Berenike and cooperative local dynasts. What role, then, if any, did the settler army, the focus of so much recruitment and settlement during the reign of Philadelphus, play in the Third Syrian War? There is little direct evidence for large-scale mobilizations, which we might expect to be reflected in extended land leases or loans transacted by soldiers departing on campaign, or complaints filed after their return about events at home while the soldier was campaigning with the king.[35] The absence of that sort of evidence might lead us to wonder whether the domestic unrest might even have been caused by an under-utilized army left at home while the king and his mercenaries conquered abroad. Yet the scale and duration of Ptolemaic operations across the Euphrates practically demands the involvement of the settler army, and if the war continued to 242/241 BC, with some other operations into the next decade, then the settler army must have played some role.

In a search for the army's whereabouts during the war, we might start with its return: when did the campaigning army, or components of that army, return from the campaign? We know the king returned to deal with the revolt, but its outbreak cannot be firmly dated. A papyrus confirms a return, but not necessarily of Ptolemaic soldiers, no later than May 245 BC. *P.Petr.* 2.29.E is a small fragment of a letter, dated to 13 May (24 Peritios), and treats the handling of a detachment of prisoners of war who had arrived in the Fayum. The tenor of the note is generally positive, encouraging the subordinate to monitor the situation of these remaining prisoners, to provide for their needs and to encourage them toward their *synapokatastasis*, which might be read as meaning something like 'rehabilitation'. The note closes, however, with an admonition to ensure that none escape. Given the early Hellenistic practice of enrolling prisoners into the army of the captor, it should not be too surprising to find the same end in mind during the Third Syrian War. Aside from prisoners of war, *P.Col.* 4.87 describes 'Syrian slaves' working in the properties of Apollonios the *dioiketes*. *P.Lond.* 7.2052 (241 BC) describes several men, probably escaped slaves from the former entourage of Apollonios, including a man with dual Greek and Babylonian names, and two men from the household of 'Alexander the former hostage', a Babylonian masseur and a Median coachman. We cannot be certain, but Alexander may have been a Seleucid official of some rank taken back to Egypt, and the three men from Babylon and Media captives from the campaign. Some military detachment must have escorted the prisoners, slaves, temple goods and other booty back to Egypt, and given the scale of what was escorted it seems plausible to connect their return with that of the king, and thus his arrival in Egypt sometime before 13 May 245 BC.

Papyrological evidence for Ptolemaic cleruchs physically present in Egypt is completely lacking from late summer 246 BC until about the same time as the order regarding prisoners. With the nature of documentary papyri, an argument from silence is a very weak thing. What follows is more concerned with what can be said, not the many things that cannot. If Ptolemy III was on campaign from about August 246 until about April 245 BC, there is only one dated papyrus that mentions a cleruch in this period. A man from the hipparchy of Antiochos appears in a text from February 245 BC (*P.Hib.* 1.32), at the time of the fighting in Babylonia. The cleruch, Neoptolemos, had some of his property seized by an Alexandrian citizen as part of a court case in which Neoptolemos, the defendant, had not presented himself for a defence and so the Alexandrian won by default. The absence of Neoptolemos from both the trial and the seizure would make sense if he were with the army; but this would also require that the Ptolemaic legal system lacked protections for soldiers who were campaigning in the company of the king! It is perhaps more likely Neoptolemos had not deployed. A taxation report on taxes paid from military allotments for year 2 of Ptolemy III's reign (*P.Petr.* 3.110.E, 246/245 BC) identifies the men – or perhaps boys – concerned as 'orphans', which probably means they had inherited the allotment from their fathers but were not old enough to mobilize with the army. The first text with a physically present soldier is *P.Hib.* 1.33 (21 April–20 May 245 BC), which identifies a Thracian soldier in the eponymous command of Aetos, based in the Herakleopolite nome. This Aetos was one of the military elite at court: he had commanded in Cilicia in the Second Syrian War and had been eponymous priest at Alexandria. Another Thracian of Aetos' command is attested in 241/240 (*P.Frankf.* 5). Perhaps Aetos' command never left on campaign, but if the king and a part of the army returned in the spring, leading a host of war captives and a great train of plunder, Aetos is the sort of figure we should not be surprised to find in the king's company.

From the lack of evidence in the first months of the war, the evidence for cleruchs present in Egypt is fairly abundant for the summer and autumn of 245 BC. In the Arsinoite nome, *P.Mich.* 1.66 from summer 245 BC attests three cavalrymen and an infantry subaltern officer. *P.Cair. Zen.* 3.59350r (November 245 BC) tells of a complaint against some local cavalrymen, Neon the *epistates* of the cavalry settlers at Bakchias and some of the other troopers, who had reportedly stolen a pig to celebrate a festival. *P.Cair.Zen.* 3.59347 is a witness deposition from December 245 BC recording events that transpired in October that year. The witness is an Alexandrian citizen who was hipparch of the *archaion agema*. A sub-unit of the Guard cavalry almost certainly would have accompanied the king on campaign. Thus, even if the king had not returned by late April or the start of May, he and some of the elite units were back in Egypt no later than October. The accumulation of evidence from late spring through to summer 245 BC seems to suggest the king's return with part of the force in the spring.

Other commands lack evidence over a longer period. The evidence for the hipparchy of Zoilos, in the Oxyrhynchite nome, is a good example because it is comparatively well-documented from the 260s to the 220s BC. A cavalry settler from the unit appears in *P.Hib.* 1.102 from 249 BC, but none is attested again until numerous troopers appear in texts from July onwards in 244 (*P.Hib.* 1.91, *SB* 12.11059 – which also attests the command of Philagros). This demonstrates the difficulty of arguing from silence. Are we to imagine the hipparchy was away from late 249 to mid-244 BC, when the war only began late in the summer of 246? Rather, we may only be confident that, whether or whenever Zoilos' cavalry deployed to Asia, they were undoubtedly back in Egypt by the summer of 244 BC. Another text from the Oxyrhynchite nome refers to crown *hemikleroi*, allotments under partial, temporary state control in May 244 or 243 BC (*P.Tebt.* 3.1.746). Menedoros, an agent in the office of Phanias, the secretary of cavalry for all Egypt, distributed orders to the local military tax officials (*logeutai*) to organize tax collections from the local cavalry settlements. The missive concerned the category of crown *kleroi*, which means the cavalry allotments had been formerly under full state control, but earlier that year the allotments had been split between cavalrymen and the crown, and state officials would have to manage payments of fees, first from the crown's half of the allotments, then reconcile the revenues from the two halves.[36] Then, presumably, the *kleroi* could fully return to the cavalrymen. Another papyrus, dateable only to the 240s BC, mentions the oversight of *kleroi* in the Oxyrhynchites that were temporarily being administered by the state (*P.Hib.* 1.52). If I am correct in relating these documents, *P.Hib.* 1.52 probably dates between August 246 and May 244 BC. Menedoros advised caution and prudence, and added that he had written to Phanias to clarify proper procedure. Menedoros' uncertainty implies that the tax collection of the fourth year had become a significant event. This arrangement most likely reflects the return of soldiers from campaign and their reincorporation into life in Egypt. The text has usually been dated to May 243 BC, using the Egyptian calendar, but because it concerns taxes, it should probably be dated by the financial year, which would move the text to May 244. That would place Menedoros' letters a little earlier than the July papyrus naming several cavalrymen from Zoilos' command, and may provide proof, then, that Zoilos' unit did depart for the war and returned late in the spring of 244 BC, about a year after the king returned.

Additional documentary evidence points toward the return of the Ptolemaic army, perhaps in several detachments, over the course of 244 BC. The key evidence on the Oxyrhynchite cavalry was in the state's oversight of soldiers' allotments while they were gone. Similar evidence exists in the Arsinoite nome. There is also evidence for new settlements and the redistribution of allotments that had belonged to soldiers who perished during the war. Numerous papyri indicate that the burden of managing many cleruchic allotments fell on the state during the first years of the war, and can actually clarify the Oxyrynchite evidence while also pointing toward 244 BC as the year much of the army returned. Nine texts from the Lille papyri record a nomarch's management of soldiers' allotments over several years corresponding to the Third Syrian War (*P.Lille* 1.30–38). The nine texts contain fragments of records for more than a dozen allotments, some belonging to regular cavalrymen with 100 arouras, many to officers with hundreds of arouras, including several hipparchs. The nomarch's oversight began as early as August 246 BC (*P.Lille* 1.30), not later than February 245 (*P.Lille* 1.30–31, 33, 35), and in most cases seems to have been maintained through to about April 244 (*P.Lille* 1.31, 36, 38), or in two cases as late as December 244 (*P.Lille* 1.30, 36.1). The texts are all fragmentary, but they suggest a general correspondence with the date ranges from the previous discussion: mobilization in August 246 BC and large-scale return in spring 244, meaning some significant component of the Ptolemaic army left Egypt for almost two years.

There is not much evidence for new settlement, but there is a little, and most of it points toward a return of troops from the war in 244 or early

243 BC. The royal decree in *P.Hib.* 2.198.1, which awarded ranks (and presumably allotments) to a lengthy list of officers from many different eponymous commands and in many different provinces of Egypt, was dated to 26 October 244 BC. Most of the army must have been back in Egypt by that point in order to give awards to officers up and down the Nile. Then the mercenary cavalry of Eteoneus seem to have been settled in 243 BC, judging by Eteoneus' personal presence in the Fayum (*P.Tebt.* 3.2.937) and the appearance of men from his command only after that date (*P.Petr.* 3.82, 243/242 BC). Their settlement tells us nothing about the mobilization of the settler army for the war, but does suggest the mercenary cavalrymen were not demobilized until 244 or even 243 BC. Another text, a register of horses distributed to mercenary cavalry (*P.Petr.* 2.35), includes numerous dates from 243–240 BC, but the earliest date in the text is from the Macedonian month Gorpiaios, year 4 of Ptolemy III, approximately November 244. Their acquisition of horses may not have been related to settlement (there were mercenary cavalry settled in the Fayum before the war too), but it does identify their presence in Egypt by the end of 244 BC. Together, and with varying levels of certitude, these pieces of evidence point toward a significant return of troops – some of whom were apparently true mercenaries rather than military settlers – between summer 244 and the beginning of 243 BC, with awards, promotions, settlements and other business taking place over the ensuing months.

The final piece of evidence for a return in 244 BC is the state's repossession of allotments, many of which occurred at the end of 244. Three texts from the Petrie papyri (3.104–106, June 243 BC) relate to the repossession of large numbers of *kleroi* in the Fayum in late 244 or early 243 BC. The texts themselves are not standard orders for the repossession of a *kleros* (for one of those, see *P.Lille* 1.14 from 238 BC), but rather, supplementary instructions intended to reconcile recent repossessions with pre-existing sub-leases. The orders were directed to the local nomarch and all follow the same formula: 'After the *kleros* of so-and-so located near such town had been repossessed to the royal account following the planting in the fourth year, the *syngraphophylax* so-and-so has come and presented to us a sub-lease contract negotiated between previously named-cleruch and the farmer so-and-so.' Administrators had transferred *kleroi* to the royal account without first dealing with the farming contracts soldiers had made. Soldiers often made farming contracts, either before going to war or simply to free themselves from the burden of agricultural work. Zenon of Kaunos had run an entire business farming soldiers' allotments.

So *P.Petr.* 3.104–106 were written some months after the repossessions. The 'planting of the fourth year' would have taken place after the flood, so in the last months of 244 BC.

Repossession of military allotments could happen in Ptolemaic Egypt for several reasons in the third century BC, not only in cases of death. There is firm evidence from the 260s BC (presented in the previous chapter) for the repossession of allotments belonging to cleruchs who were still living. That they were still living is proved by the order to ensure the state also repossessed their *stathmoi* (*SB* 6.9454–6). However, there is no evidence to demonstrate that this happened regularly, and most cases of state repossession of *kleroi* arose from the death of the settler soldier. Closer to the Fourth Syrian War, the laws changed to make a transfer to an heir a simpler process, but that law did not exist in the Third Syrian War. The orders were meant to ensure that the harvest – presumably that amount of the harvest that normally went to the cleruch, as well as those paid as taxes, ended up in the royal granaries – was not pocketed by the farmers. The death of the soldiers during the war, however, is the most likely explanation. If the state was simply redistributing land, the time after the planting was terribly inconvenient. Furthermore, the few records that survive in the papyri were parts of a considerably larger file: there were more entries in the same formula beside the ones that survive; that is, the number of allotments repossessed at one time was considerable and affected different classes of soldiers in scattered towns all over the Fayum. After the army's return, one chief order of business would be the management and redistribution of the lands of deceased combatants. If the allotments were not repossessed until the end of 244 BC at the earliest, and spring 243 at the latest, the action came at least a year-and-a-half later than the return of Ptolemy III and part of the army in the spring of 245. This accords with a theorized return of much of the army in 244 BC, and suggests casualty records were not reconciled quickly enough to send repossession orders before the planting season in late 244.

The most significant thing about the three *Petrie* orders is that they point toward the mobilization of the settler army itself. *P.Petr.* 3.104–106 contain ten entries regarding repossessed allotments and their pre-existing farming contracts, but only five of them can be reconstructed well enough to identify the soldiers involved, the classifications of their allotments or their locations in the Fayum. The one entry from 104 is held until last because it is peculiar. The two from 105 concerned the allotments of Kallikles and Lysanias, two men with 24 arouras classed as 'infantry allotments'. The two from 106 concerned the 100-arouras allotment of Lysimachos, undoubtedly a cavalryman, and a '*triakontarouros* allotment' belonging to a [Anti?]genes, undoubtedly another infantryman. All were in different towns across several nomarchies of the Fayum. Given the general prevalence of cavalry in Fayum records, the infantry in these particular records point to their significance both within the settler population in the Fayum and within the army. The previous chapter explored the contingents of 20-arouras veterans and 25-arouras *epigonoi* settled at the conclusion of the Second Syrian War; the *pezoi* (infantry) and 30-arouras settlers in these texts confirm the former two groups were not the first or only infantry settlers in the Fayum. The records may also provide an indication of the combat activities of the phalanx infantry in the Third Syrian War. An important class in Ptolemaic Egypt and the backbone of the Ptolemaic army, the heavy infantry of the phalanx are not represented in great numbers within the papyri, yet if the repossession records are any indication, many mobilized for the campaign. They would have joined Ptolemy, accompanied by elephants, cavalry and siege machines, somewhere in Syria, before proceeding across the Euphrates, where the likes of Kallikles and Lysanias may have fallen in the streets of Babylon, casualties among the hated 'iron-panoplied men' of the Babylonian chronicle.

The one legible order in *P.Petr.* 3.104 concerned the allotment of Alketas, 'one of the prisoners of war from Asia', who had possessed an allotment around the village of Psinharpsenesis. Aside from his identity as a prisoner, the format of the report is very similar to the other records in 104–106. But the case of a prisoner of war with a *kleros* is striking: it resonates with the settlement of prisoners from the Battle of Gaza and with the May 245 BC order to seek 'rehabilitation' of the prisoners who had recently arrived in the Fayum. Was he one of the prisoners from 245 BC or a prisoner from the Second Syrian War? The attempted settlement of prisoners of war was probably commonplace in Ptolemaic history, but it is only securely attested here and in the reign of Ptolemy I. If he was a prisoner from the Second Syrian War, then we may presume he mobilized with the other infantry (his allotment, based on the farmer's rental fee, was between 10 and 30 arouras) and died – or deserted – in Asia. If he was one of the prisoners who arrived in the Fayum in 245 BC, he gained an allotment fairly quickly, but was he dispatched to Asia with reinforcements or should we imagine some other possibility? It may even be possible he was repatriated to Asia as part of diplomacy between Ptolemy III and Seleucus II; that sort of thing is not well attested in the Hellenistic age, but has precedents in the Classical age. However, the peace between the two powers is supposed to have come later, perhaps around 242 BC.

The peace, tentatively dated to the Olympic year 242/241 BC, and the return of a large Ptolemaic army in 244, beg some further consideration of what happened after 244 and how the papyrological evidence relates to the chronology of the war from other evidence. Ptolemy III departed with an initial force in late August or early September 246 BC and probably ordered the main body of the army to meet him in Syria. The king and several bodies of troops returned in about April 245 BC to suppress the rebellion. The army that remained in Syria and Mesopotamia is presumably the force that defeated Seleucus and sent him fleeing to Antioch, then came back to Egypt in spring and summer 244 BC. There were three years of the war left at that point, and Seleucus was able to take the offensive against Xanthippos' force and the garrisons Ptolemy had left in the cities of Syria and Mesopotamia. Perhaps he defeated Xanthippos near Raqqa on the Euphrates in late 244 or early 243 BC. While Seleucus besieged and recovered cities (except Seleukeia-by-the-Sea), did most Ptolemaic activity shift to the Aegean and the burden of fighting it switch to the fleet, local garrisons and local allies?

Papyrological evidence provides several indications for further activity between late 244 BC and the end of the war in late 242 or early 241. A register of horses for the mercenary cavalry (*P.Petr.* 2.35) refers to a decree issued concerning the cavalry who 'had accompanied' someone or something (the object of the participle is missing) 'in the fifth year', 243/242 BC.[37] Other words would more specifically signify a campaign, but 'accompanied' could be used with troops in wartime or peacetime activities.[38] The papyrus records distributions of horses in December–January 243/242 BC and again in August–September 242, so the troops who went somewhere must have done so between June and December 243 or between January and August 242. An unpublished papyrus, *P.Duke. inv.* 706, contains several letters related to the cavalry from spring and summer 242 BC, amid the latter window, which might help clarify military activity in those months. The largest fragment, Fragment 1, contains three columns of text, the first two of which concerned the inspection of cavalry units and their readiness for campaign in the fifth year (thanks to a marginal notation in column A). Column B mentions Phanias and the office of the *epistates* over cavalry, and may have been concerned with ensuring the readiness of the hipparchy of Zoilos. It speaks of dividing the well-equipped from the poorly equipped, sending off the well-equipped and ordering those who failed inspection to remedy their situation. They are not exactly dated, but probably shortly preceded the letters in the third column, which dated from June and July 242 BC, at the start of the sixth regnal year of Ptolemy III.

Fragment 5 dates to Phamenoth or Pharmouthi (approximately May–June), probably of 242 BC. It contains the name of an official, the *strategos* Aphthonetos, governor of the Arsinoite nome, a report about soldier deaths, an order that probably relates to the repossession of allotments by the state and a location: 'in the Thebaid'. The Oxyrhynchites and all points south were considered part of the Thebaid in the middle of the third century BC (e.g., *P.Hib.* 2.262, 240 BC), so the reference could be to the location of some of the dead soldiers' allotments. But it could also indicate where they died, which might mean they died suppressing rebels in southern Egypt. There is little other evidence that suggests serious unrest or violence in the Thebaid in this period, so perhaps it should be set aside.[39] There is also a number mentioned early in the text, 'all 500', which in relation to the other material suggests a contingent of 500 cavalrymen had been dispatched somewhere, and some of them had died. So this text looks back upon a recently completed military mission, while the letters in Fragment 1 A–B anticipated a campaign in the very near future. The nature of military activity in 242 BC cannot be clarified any better, but it is clear that the Ptolemaic military was still active at that date, although probably on a smaller scale. The words from the Book of Daniel may apply here: 'for some years [Ptolemy III] shall refrain from attacking the king of the north. Then the latter shall come into the realm of the king of the south but shall return into his own land.'

The remaining years of possible fighting contain a few sparse references to military activity. There were new cleruchs allotted land in the Arsinoite in Ptolemy's sixth year (242/241 BC) and a group 'after Daisios in year 7', or after September 241 BC (*P.Hib.* 1.82). If there were some significant campaign after the readiness inspections, in the summer of 242 BC, that would help explain the source of veterans for the new settlements in 241. The war had probably ended shortly before these settlements. As we should expect, there is little to suggest military activity in 241 or 240 BC, but some interesting reports in 239 and 238. A military clerk named Artemidoros issued numerous reports of deceased mercenary cavalrymen between December 239 and early 238 BC (*P.Hib.* 1.81, *P.Sorb.* 3.89). (It may be worth reminding the reader here that many of the 'mercenary cavalry' in the Ptolemaic army were military settlers themselves, but were mobilized

Ptolemy III and the Third Syrian War   197

more regularly than the so-called 'settler cavalry' regiments.) Artemidoros was in the office of Stratios, who, given the extent of his authority and the nature of Artemidoros' information, was either *grammateus* (secretary) over all the mercenary cavalry or arch-secretary in the field army. *P.Hib.* 1.81 contained at least three columns of text, but only the middle one largely remains. It contains notifications of six to eight deaths from five different mercenary cavalry hipparchies, all dated between December 239 and February 238 BC. *P.Sorb.* 3.89 was written in early June 238 BC.[40] Unlike the Hibeh papyrus, it is not the death notification but the order for repossession that was generated some time after receipt of the notification. The papyrus reads: 'Ammonios to Aristarchos, greetings. Artemidoros, an aide to Stratios, has written to us concerning the death of one of the men from the mercenary horsemen that have been settled around Pharbaitha: Theodoros son of Phanokles, a Selymbrian, *epilarches* of the men of Eteoneus. Repossess this man's allotment to the crown, and take thought concerning the harvests, in order to secure everything for the crown.' The addressee of the letter, Aristarchos, was one of the Arsinoite nomarchs.[41]

Are the deaths evidence for a military campaign in those years? Chronologically, this would fit with a Ptolemaic campaign in the aftermath of the Battle of Ankyra and the report that Seleucus II had died. The scale of mortality is suggestive of something other than natural deaths: given there were at least two other columns of text in *P.Hib.* 1.81, there were probably at least fifteen deaths from the mercenary cavalry reported through the bureaucracy over a few months. For a population of probably 400–700 troopers, at least 2–4 per cent of them died in the space of a few months, far above normal mortality. Furthermore, the reports came down from the army command to the locality rather than vice versa, which suggests the men were away from their allotments at the time of death. The attested deaths also affected nearly every attested mercenary cavalry hipparchy in the Arsinoite, six in all, which indicates a large mobilization. Meanwhile, as for the Oxyrhynchite cavalry, *P.Strasb.* 7.662 dates to June 239 BC and concerns an official who was overseeing the farmers and police around a hipparch's allotment at Sinaru in the Oxyrhynchites. A hipparch might prove an absentee landlord more often than rank-and-file settlers, but the absence of the unnamed hipparch (possibly Zoilos) and state oversight lends some support to the idea of a mobilization in late spring 239 BC. The campaign that I conjecture they departed on would be the Ptolemaic attacks on Damascus and Orthosia in Syria. It is less likely they could have been involved in the battle alongside Antiochus Hierax at Magnesia about the same time; those troops must have been from the Ptolemaic garrison at Ephesos.

Conclusions

Ptolemy III was joined, probably in Syria, by a substantial portion of the settler army developed by his father and grandfather. Most of Syria submitted without serious resistance, but Ptolemy and his army pushed across the Euphrates into Mesopotamia, where heavy fighting followed in the winter of 246/245 BC. Ptolemy III returned with part of the army in the spring of 245 BC, while a large part of the army remained in Syria or Mesopotamia and defeated Seleucus II in battle before detachments of that army returned to Egypt between spring and autumn 244. What was left of the army in Asia was either defeated by Seleucus II or withdrew when the war finally ended in 242/241 BC. The deaths reported in 239/238 BC may belong to the fighting around Damascus and Orthosia when fighting resumed after the Battle of Ankyra. During the war, the Ptolemaic administrative institutions that helped build and maintain the settler army also maintained the structures of the system in the absence of much of the army. This feat seems to have been managed in spite of a potentially disastrous multi-year agricultural crisis, which contributed to the unrest that forced the return of Ptolemy from Mesopotamia in spring 245 BC.

Although the Ptolemaic army had successfully campaigned in Mesopotamia, it owed much of its early progress to the confusion in the Seleucid realm following the death of Antiochus II and the willingness of some governors, generals, cities and military units to cast their lot with Berenike instead of Laodike. In reality, the weaknesses of the Ptolemaic settler army were demonstrated during the war. It was slow and cumbersome while operating overland far from home and lacked the manpower to assert decisive Ptolemaic control over weakened and disorganized Seleucid regions. It excelled at operations in Koile Syria and along the coastlines of Asia Minor. Ptolemy III would devote time in the remainder of his reign to increasing the organizational efficiency of the army, but would not try to expand it significantly. He may have been confident in both the perpetual disunity of the Seleucid realm and the general reliability of his army and navy for defending the Ptolemaic heartland in Egypt.

At the same time as the Third Syrian War, the First Punic War was drawing to a close. In that war, the two sides – Romans and Carthaginians – mobilized hundreds of thousands of men over twenty-three years of warfare. Although the Seleucids in particular ruled over territories with enormous potential reserves of manpower, they and the Ptolemies mobilized smaller militaries for their war. Through competition for the loyalty (and tax revenues and continued growth) of Greek cities, the two powers effectively forfeited their ability to draw large contingents of soldiers from those cities. Men from those places did serve in the militaries of both kingdoms, but their participation, particularly in the case of Asia Minor, was seldom extensive or systematic. The treaties and decrees passed between kings and cities did not stipulate military service and forged a decisive gap between the Hellenistic kingdoms and the Roman Republic. This resulted from the contingency of each kingdom's power, and their competition against one another for local support. Their largest population base, however, were non-Greeks, and each state seems to have worked actively to circumscribe the military participation of the mass of the population. In the Ptolemaic army, the Egyptians who fought in the Third Syrian War – and many undoubtedly did – were limited to roles in the navy, in a handful of honoured contingents for the Egyptian aristocracy and in general army units where their participation depended on their Hellenization as 'Persians' among the Greek settler class. This difference in manpower reserves would constitute just one of the several decisive distinctions between the Roman Republic and the Hellenistic monarchies, and contributed to the triumph of the one and the demise of the others.

Finally, a word about the Ptolemaic soldier is due here. When we read documentary papyri about soldiers, we mainly find the mundane: harvests and taxes, petty lawsuits and the like. It is easy enough to forget they lived amid the legacies of thousands of years of civilization, sailed past the pyramids and other great ruins along the Nile. The men of the papyri in the decade or so after the Third Syrian War were men who had marched in the streets of Antioch, Babylon or Seleukeia, seen the remnants of those ancient empires, experienced great victories and the plunder of nations before they returned home. Because we find a window into part of their lives through mainly routine things, it is too easy to forget that the Ptolemaic soldiers of this era had also experienced great adventure and perpetrated, witnessed and suffered great violence. The Ptolemaic story is a story of decline, but a telling that begins with a do-nothing army under Ptolemy III desperately needs to be revisited.

Chapter 8

Ptolemy III and the Purported Decline of the Ptolemaic Army

The Ptolemaic military was in a good position at the end of the Third Syrian War. Armed forces had operated successfully on both land and sea, and the agricultural and land tenure system had survived the prolonged absence of many settlers with few signs of trouble. The war ended in more modest gains for the Ptolemaic kingdom than the early going might have suggested, although Seleukeia, Ephesos, Cilicia and Thrace were no mean prizes. It is worth repeating that the entire story might have changed with even an average Nile flood in 246 BC. The Seleucid army did not temper the Ptolemaic advance; unrest in Egypt did. This serves as an excellent reminder for modern historians, and perhaps served a similar lesson in Ptolemaic Egypt, that one of the core missions of the Ptolemaic army was its occupation and pacification of Egypt. The next Syrian War did not come for more than twenty years, and for most of the interim the Seleucid Empire was riven with internal strife: whole satrapies rebelled, the royal brothers ranged forces against one another and Seleucid soldiers killed one another for years on end. For the Fourth Syrian War we possess a detailed narrative in Polybius' *Histories*, which makes for a different approach to the history of that war. It also colours our perception of the inter-war period. Polybius described a kingdom whose military institutions and traditions rapidly deteriorated under the rule of the dissolute Ptolemy IV. The new king's 'chief concern was the idle pomp of royalty' (Plb. 5.34.3). He led the court and army down the same path with him, with terrible consequences: 'not only his Friends, and chief officers, but the whole of the army had laid aside military exercises, and grown corrupt and enervated in idleness' (Just. 30.1.3). Polybius did not say that the decline of Ptolemaic military power and preparedness began under Ptolemy III, but occurred precipitously from the accession of Ptolemy IV in very late 222 or early 221 BC.[1] When war came, Egypt was unprepared, 'so completely had all military preparations been neglected' (Plb. 5.62.8).

Massive military reforms and a heavy reliance on imported Greek military expertise were necessary to rescue the Ptolemaic army from itself and enable it to compete with the resurgent Seleucid army under Antiochus III. How had so much changed in less than a quarter of a century? This chapter seeks to address the activities of the Ptolemaic army between the two wars, and relate the evidence available to historiographies of Ptolemaic Egypt's development in the later third century BC.

Following Polybius, and actually reaching beyond his statements, the period from 242–222 BC has often been reckoned an era of decline for the Ptolemaic military.[2] Bar-Kochva chastened the Ptolemaic establishment: 'The grave mistake of the Ptolemies was in not realizing that availability of Macedonian or European manpower did not by itself guarantee a reasonable military standard in phalanx troops.'[3] It was undoubtedly an era marked by peace. Did the enjoyment of peace correlate to a decline in military readiness, the languishing of a reasonable military standard? Put another way, many historians are suspicious of Polybius' portrayal of Philopator's character, and also question whether one bad king could so quickly ruin an army. If Euergetes' army was ready for war in the late 220's BC, could it truly have been so corrupted by Philopator's manner of rule in just a few years as to necessitate the major reforms Polybius described before Raphia? That would seem unlikely. The natural conclusion, then, has been that Euergetes' army must not have been ready for war either, even before Ptolemy IV got to the throne. The decline narrative goes something like this: under Ptolemy III the army developed a preoccupation with agricultural expansion and neglected military readiness, beating their swords into ploughshares out of confidence in the perpetual weakness of the Seleucid kingdom. Thus the military disarray of Philopator's early years were actually the cumulative effects of twenty years' careless enjoyment of peace and prosperity.

However, perhaps it would be more prudent for us to question the reform narrative and whether Polybius, or his source, might have exaggerated aspects of it. Furthermore, if we were to begin our discussion of the army in Euergetes' post-war reign with the documentary evidence itself, rather than working back from Polybius, we reach very different conclusions. Those twenty years were not a period of inactivity. Instead, Ptolemy reformed the organization of the army, establishing new institutional structures and a model force, completing the work begun under his father and grandfather. The army that accompanied Ptolemy to Asia in the Third Syrian War was the result of piecemeal settlement in the previous generations. The army that Euergetes passed to Philopator was the structured army of an established kingdom, competent for all three of its core missions: projecting and upholding state authority internally, competing internationally in conventional war, and reinforcing the ideology and political balance of the monarchy. The Ptolemaic army also engaged in this period in numerous military actions less than war, which provided opportunities to maintain martial readiness and practice long-distance campaigning. We should thus largely reject the modern scholarly narrative of decline under Ptolemy III, which means two options remain: either Philopator really could undermine military readiness in just a few short years, or the Ptolemaic Reform during the Fourth Syrian War has been exaggerated.

Ptolemaic Military Activity from 242–222 BC

For the remainder of Euergetes' reign, military action may be divided into three categories: military operations in Asia directed against the Seleucids or Seleucid interests, military operations in Europe (and to a lesser degree in Asia) directed against Macedonia, and military expeditions in Africa and the Red Sea directed toward the hunting of elephants. These military activities ranged in scale, and in some cases were conducted wholly through mercenaries or through subsidies to local forces. It is unlikely that any of these necessitated a comprehensive mobilization of the Ptolemaic army. There was no unrest in Cyrenaica in this period, while the king in Meroe was friendly and Hellenizing. For the most part, the twenty years from the end of the Third Syrian War to the death of Ptolemy III was a period of peace, with little to justify a major mobilization.

By comparison, the Seleucid and Antigonid kingdoms were almost constantly at war in the same two decades. The War of the Brothers lasted off and on from about 242 until about 227 BC. In 228 BC, Antiochus Hierax was defeated and fled Asia Minor, first perhaps to Syria for a last try against his brother, then eventually to Thrace, where Ptolemaic forces imprisoned him. In short order he escaped, but was murdered by bandits in the Thracian countryside. Seleucus II died a year later, at about the very end of 226 BC, according to *BCHP* 10, which at least affirms that Seleucus III was definitely king no later than mid-January 225. Seleucus II had been fighting the Parthians, his brother Attalus of Pergamon or other internal unrest since the end of the Third Syrian War, with little or no reprieve. King Attalus of Pergamon had forced Hierax from his Anatolian domains in a series of battles and benefited greatly from the brothers' deaths (he also defeated an army loyal to Seleucus).[4] Antigonus III Doson, king in Macedonia, launched an operation in Caria as well, after Hierax's defeat but while Seleucus II was still alive. He forged an alliance with at least one local dynast, Olympichos, who had formerly been a Seleucid agent.[5] Caria was remote from Pergamon, but that is where Attalus defeated Antiochus in their final battles in 228 BC. In about 223 BC, Seleucus III, barely more than 20 years old, led an army from Syria across the Taurus to wage war on Attalus. Early in the campaign, probably late spring 223 BC, two Galatians in his army assassinated him. The campaign army selected Achaios, a cousin of the dead king, as their new commander, and he conducted a successful campaign against Attalus. Meanwhile, Seleucus' younger brother became king in Mesopotamia and Syria: Antiochus III, known eventually as Antiochus the Great.

Antigonus II Gonatas died in 239 BC, and in the last years of his rule faced opposition from the Achaean League, not only in the Peloponnese but also in central Greece. None of the fighting seems to have involved large-scale campaigns, but comprised many smaller campaigns between regional forces and garrisons.[6] His successor, Demetrius II, ruled until 229 BC and spent most of his reign fighting the same low-intensity conflict with the Achaean League, only he had also to deal with the Aetolian League, and both leagues were backed by Ptolemy III. Demetrius fought a series of minor wars against the Aetolians before suffering a disastrous defeat at the hands of the Dardanians around 230 or 229 BC (Trogus 28). He may have been wounded in that battle, because he died at an early age in 229 BC. His brother Antigonus III reigned during the minority of his son Philip, from 229–221 BC. Early in 229 BC, the Achaeans and others succeeded in purchasing the liberation of Athens for a comparatively paltry 150 talents, a sum contributed by the league and numerous individuals. How much of either the sum or the liberation effort ultimately traced back to Ptolemy III is hard to estimate, but one of the major contributors was a citizen of Seleukeia-in-Piereia, and so plausibly a representative of Ptolemaic benefaction.[7] Polybius identified the leaders of Athenian politics installed after the liberation of the city as friends of Ptolemy (Plb. 5.106.6–8). For the first several years Antigonus III ruled as Philip's guardian rather than king in his own right. In that time he fought a Dardanian incursion and a Thessalian rebellion, a war with the Aetolians over Thessaly, and made the aforementioned campaign to Caria. There is no history of the campaign, but the main result was that the powerful local dynast, Olympichos of Alinda, became an Antigonid partner in Caria, granting the Antigonids a foothold they occasionally employed over the remainder of the third century BC.[8] There is no clear evidence that Antigonus' forces battled Ptolemaic armies in the area, and the campaign was probably very short. Antigonus probably sought to take advantage of Seleucid disarray and tamp the rise of the Attalids as a major power. He faced internal revolt soon after, but emerged from the struggle acclaimed as king, then spent the remainder of his reign fighting the Cleomenic War. He died of an aneurism in battle against the Illyrians in 221 BC (Plb. 2.70.5–6), and Philip V became king, joining two other fairly young, recently crowned kings, Antiochus III (spring–summer 223) and Ptolemy IV (winter 222).

Ptolemy, meanwhile, ruled for approximately twenty years of incredible stability. None of his neighbours posed a threat, so Ptolemaic military activities were strictly elective: adding to the destabilized environments confronting the other major powers. The first action was the campaign after Antiochus Hierax's victory at the Battle of Ankyra in 240 or 239 BC. Rumour had it that Seleucus was dead, and at that time Seleucus' sons were mere toddlers: until Ptolemy heard otherwise, the moment was an opportunity to retry the conquest of Asia. The previous treaty probably could be considered null with Seleucus' apparent death. Ptolemaic campaigns targeted Damascus and Orthosia, border cities of considerable defensive value that, if Eusebius was right in having Ptolemy besiege the two before retreating when Seleucus turned out to be alive, had probably been sacrificed as part of the treaty that ended the Third Syrian War a few years earlier. When Seleucus turned out to be alive, the campaign atrophied quickly, although it does seem likely Ptolemy recovered the two cities. Their earlier treaty was still in effect, and it seems Ptolemy III was unwilling to violate it, despite Seleucus' extreme weakness. Ptolemy's restraint may have helped Seleucus II's branch of the Seleucid dynasty survive. At about the same time, Ptolemaic forces fought alongside Hierax at the Battle of Magnesia, probably against Hierax's former allies. There is no evidence for Ptolemaic action in Asia Minor for some time after that battle, and the campaign in the Levant probably ended in a single campaign season. Furthermore, there is some reason to believe this brief conflict ended with a strong treaty. In 236/235 BC, the Ptolemaic army underwent massive organizational reforms, discussed later in this chapter. A major organizational military reform sounds like the action of a state that had sealed a comfortable peace. This makes the eponymous priest of the previous year, 237/236 BC, interesting: Seleukos, son of Antiochos. The name was shared with Seleucus II, and the pairing of the two names is very poorly attested outside the Seleucid dynasty. Given its rarity, and the priest's appearance right after the fighting at Damascus and Orthosia, some sort of link with the Seleucid Empire seems likely: a high-ranking defector perhaps, or a guest-hostage whose presence in Alexandria helped seal the peace. Either way, peace – for Ptolemy at least – prevailed for nearly fifteen years.

The next Ptolemaic military activities in Asia occurred in the mid-to-late 220s BC, and are not well attested. *P.Haun.* 6, so valuable for the Third Syrian War, hints at Ptolemy's concern with Seleucid developments and the fate of Asia. The entry for Ptolemy III speaks of a 'son, who had laid claim to the affairs of Asia' (υἰον μεταποιησο(μενον) (των) την ἀσιαν πραγμ[άτων]) at some point between Ptolemy's war with Antigonus Doson (see above, about 228 BC) and Ptolemy's death at the very end of 222. Who was this son who sought the mastery of Asia, as Euergetes himself had done at the start of his rule? Another entry in *P.Haun.* 6 is for Ptolemy III's son Magas, who is best known for being assassinated on the orders of his elder brother, Ptolemy IV, in 221 BC. The entry for Magas says that, after the death of Seleucus 'but while his father was still alive', Ptolemy III dispatched Magas to Asia with an army. Chronologically, Magas' campaign in Asia and the bid for power by 'the son' align. This suggests that Ptolemy III tried to position his younger son Magas as a dynast or even a potential claimant to the Seleucid throne, despite his young age, in the late 220s BC.[9] Huss and most others have placed the start of the campaign in 223 BC after the death of Seleucus III. Huss suggested the campaign was in Asia Minor, around the time of Achaios' campaign against Attalus. A campaign in Asia could have taken place anywhere between Cilicia and Ionia, and in truth it is difficult to rule out Syria. A campaign in southern Anatolia would not have necessarily broken any treaties between the two dynasties, since Seleucus II and Seleucus III had not actually held much or any territory south of the Taurus mountains or west of the Cilician plain.

Magas' campaign, somewhere in Asia, contributed to his popularity with the Ptolemaic army, especially among 'the foreign mercenaries and professional contingents' in the garrison at Alexandria, τοὺς ξένους καὶ μισθοφόρους (Plb. 5.36.3). Because of his popularity, his elder brother had him killed a few years later. *P.Haun.* 6 reveals that the assassin was Theodotos the Aetolian, a high-ranking mercenary captain. Theodotos probably entered Ptolemaic service after Antigonus III defeated the Aetolians in Thessaly. Theodotos killed Magas, who was little more than 20 years old, in a bath; because Theodotos was posted in Syria the first time he appears in Polybius' narrative (5.46.1–4) in 220 BC, it is conceivable that was where Magas died as well. Perhaps Magas was even serving as governor of Ptolemaic Syria and Phoenicia, the same position Theodotos held in 220 BC. That does not require that Magas' campaign was in Syria, of course; if the campaign in Asia Minor failed to gain a dynastic-sized foothold, the powerful military-political position in Syria would have been a gleaming consolation prize. It would also have been a suitable place for the only member of the royal family experienced in military operations, in anticipation of future fighting. Magas' campaign may also have involved the capture of Andromachos son of Achaios, uncle to Seleucus II and Antiochus Hierax, brother of their mother Laodike. Writing of events in 222 BC, Polybius could record he had been a prisoner of the Ptolemies at Alexandria for some time (Plb. 4.51.1–4). Andromachos commanded Seleucid forces against Hierax in a campaign in northern Mesopotamia and Armenia during the long War of the Brothers (Polyaenus 4.17.1). His capture during Magas' campaign would fit chronologically, but it also raises all sorts of unanswerable questions about conflict between Seleucid and Ptolemaic forces prior to the start of the Fourth Syrian War.[10] Finally, in *P.Petr.* 3.114 (223/222 BC) we find several men from the mercenary cavalry of Eteoneus were deployed that year, the year of Magas' campaign, but because the document is concerned with taxes, it does not tell us where the cavalrymen went. There is no other papyrological evidence for a campaign, unless the new military settlements measured out in 222 BC were for Magas' veterans (*P.Sorb.* 1.41–55). The chief mystery of the campaign, beyond where it went, is what it accomplished: for it to have so increased Magas' standing among men who included the veterans of the campaign, it must have achieved some success, but there is no evidence for it. Instead, Achaios led a brilliant campaign in 222 BC that shut Attalus, formerly a strong Ptolemaic ally, inside the gates of Pergamon (Plb. 4.48.9–12). If the campaign took place somewhere, almost anywhere in southern Anatolia, like Pamphylia, Pisidia or Cilicia, Magas and Achaios need not have crossed paths. In the absence of new information, the campaign remains shrouded in mystery.

The war with Antigonus is another poorly known aspect of the military ventures of Ptolemy III. The foothold in Thrace gave him a shared border with the Macedonian homeland. *P.Haun.* 6, again, refers to Ptolemaic participation as an ally in the Aetolian League's war with Antigonus. The Aetolians had been fighting the Macedonians practically since Demetrius II came to the throne in 239 BC, so the date of Ptolemaic support for the Aetolians may have predated Antigonus' rule.[11] But in 229–228 BC, the Aetolians invaded Thessaly and roused many Thessalian cities to revolt. *P.Haun.* 6 probably referred to this campaign. Most Ptolemaic involvement in Greece occurred through monetary support, but the papyrus says Ptolemy 'fought alongside' (συνεμαχησεν) the Aetolians against Antigonus. It is unclear how much weight to give to the choice of words, but it is conceivable the Ptolemaic navy, or the Ptolemaic garrison in Thrace, conducted actual military operations in support of the Aetolian War. The Aetolians definitely honoured the royal family for their weighty contributions to the League.[12] Then when the war went poorly, many Aetolian officers and soldiers found ready employment in Ptolemaic Egypt.

Elsewhere in the Aegean, Ptolemaic forces consolidated and expanded their control over newly won territories. One of the biggest prizes of the Third Syrian War, Ephesos, remained a significant Ptolemaic possession for the remainder of the third century BC.[13] Halikarnassos, Samos and numerous other cities were still Ptolemaic, and hosted Ptolemaic garrisons and squadrons of the fleet. Under Ptolemy III, and despite the growing Antigonid hold on the Aegean, the navy was robust and reknowned for its titanic polyremes, like the flagship 'Thirties'. Yet again, their role in military affairs between Hierax's Battle of Magnesia and Magas' theorized campaign in Anatolia is almost completely unknown. Further north, the acquisition of Thrace was one of the largest long-term prizes of the Third Syrian War. On multiple occasions, the large military force posted to Thrace campaigned against invaders, even when the invaders attacked independent but friendly Samothrace rather than Ptolemaic Thrace itself.[14] Military risk was also political opportunity, but Ptolemy III did not engage in truly large-scale interventions to expand Ptolemaic influence in the Greek world. His security and prosperity probably dissuaded him from that sort of effort, despite the opportunities afforded him. Polybius summed up Ptolemaic influence as follows:

> '... masters as they were of Coele-Syria and Cyprus, and their sphere of control also extended over the dynasts of Asia Minor and the islands, since they had the chief cities, strong places and harbors in their hands all along the coast from Pamphylia to the Hellespont and the neighborhood of Lysimacheia; while by their command of Ainos, Maroneia and other cities even more distant, they exercised a supervision over the affairs of Thrace and Macedonia.' (Plb. 5.34.6–7)

The Ptolemaic mixture of strongpoints and soft power made the kingdom the most influential in the Hellenistic world over much of Euergetes' reign, thanks in part to the problems that continually beset the other kingdoms.

Finally, elephant-hunting expeditions functioned as small military campaigns, but did not constitute major tests or exert significant stress upon the settler system. The hunts likely constituted the principal peacetime military activity for Ptolemaic soldiers, although the class of 'mercenary cavalry' (*misthophoroi hippeis*) may have been the primary participants. The Adoulis inscription (*OGIS* 55) establishes that a Ptolemaic elephant corps of some size existed before the Third Syrian War, but historical, archaeological, epigraphical and papyrological evidence confirms the continuation of multiple elephant-hunting campaigns during Euergetes' reign. The founding of several cities on the Red Sea – Berenike upon Deires and Berenike near Saba (Adoulis) – are thought to date from his reign. These settlements facilitated inland expeditions by strengthening Ptolemaic positions along the coast.[15] The hunts may have resumed even before the end of the Third Syrian War. The Adoulis inscription itself may date to 244/243 BC, and its placement far to the south suggests it was set up by an expedition to the area. A papyrus from a settlement near Thebes, *UPZ* 2.157, records compulsory services to the crown, including fourteen Egyptian military men dispatched with an elephant hunt in 242/241 BC. A dedication at Philai, near Aswan, *Thebes à Syene* 309, may belong to the same period; in it, hunters gave thanks for their (and their elephants') safe return.[16] A text from 240 BC ordered pay for mercenaries aboard a ship operating in the Red Sea (*P.Grenf.* 1.9): eighteen rowers and three ship's crew were paid 16.11 drachmas per month, or just over 3 obols per day, and comparing wine rations with pay suggests close to fifty mercenaries were paid 30 drachmas per month. The comparative size of the marine contingent in this small unit suggests they manned a guard station in the Red Sea to facilitate trade or hunting expeditions, and kept a small boat at the station. The strong evidence for elephant hunting and Red Sea activity in the years after the Third Syrian War suggests the elephant corps' performance was promising, but either there were too few elephants to begin with or they suffered too many losses in the fighting.

The evidence for elephant hunts in Euergetes' reign is strongest, however, in his final years. I previously argued that the place-names associated with hunt leaders from Book 16 of Strabo's *Geographica* can be split between Euergetes and Philadelphus. They are arranged north to south, but they are also at least broadly chronological. I suggested that Eumenes was probably the first named hunt leader from Euergetes' reign, and that the following names also belonged to his reign: Pytholaos, Pythangelos, Leon and (initially) Lichas. The most remote hunting ground named in Strabo is that of Charimortos, and he can definitely be dated to the reign of Ptolemy IV (*OGIS* 86, *O.Oslo* 2). The fascinating thing about Eumenes, Pythangelos and Lichas is that they were also eponymous commanders in the Fayum.[17] Only Leon is not easily identified. Eumenes was not only an eponymous commander, but likely the father of the general, governor and elephant-hunter Ptolemaios son of Eumenes, who was prominent in the Thebaid in the reign of Ptolemy V.[18] While Lichas is attested as an eponymous commander as early as 239 BC, he also led his second elephant-hunting expedition around 212–210 (*OGIS* 82), during the reign of Ptolemy IV.

Several papyri from 224–222 BC provide the best evidence about the elephant hunts in the latter part of Euergetes' reign. *Chr.Wilck.* 452 (November 224 BC) is a letter to men at a remote station in the Red Sea, either the hunters themselves or part of a military post established to support the hunts. A new hunting expedition under its *strategos* (general) was heading toward the hunting grounds to succeed the current commander and hunters. The hunters on the new expedition are described as having been drafted, or literally called up for service: ο[ἱ κ]υνηγοὶ ἐπιλελεγμένοι. The men who received the letter had been in dire straits related to food supply ever since an elephant transport being used to carry grain had capsized. The letter mentions that grain transports were coming from Egypt, progressing through the Wadi Tumilat and Heroonpolis/Pithom into the Red Sea, and another elephant transport (laden with grain, presumably) was ready at Berenike. We can infer at least one hunt had taken place in earlier 244 BC, but we do not know the name of either the commander of that hunt or of the hunt that was just departing to take their place. *Chr.Wilck.* 451 (November 223 BC) is a letter from Edfu regarding the preparation of pay for a group of hunters readying to depart on another elephant hunt. The men – 231 of them – were from the command of Andronikos, but the commander of the hunt was Peitholaos, Strabo's Pytholaos, who left his name on two hunting grounds far down the Red Sea and beyond Deire. Andronikos is attested as an eponymous commander of cavalry in *P.Hib.* 2.198 (244 BC); the 231 men could represent the mobilization of his entire hipparchy. Peitholaos may subsequently have been *strategos* of the Herakleopolite nome in 220 BC (*P.Heid.* 6.376). Andronikos may also have been the elephant hunt commander and nome *strategos* attested in 231–229 or 207–205 BC.[19] The papyrus authorized pay for three months spanning the winter of 223/222 BC: 2 talents, 1,860 drachmas; that is, 60 drachmas for the 231 men or 20 drachmas per month. Peitholaos and Andronikos were not the only elephant hunters in 223/222 BC. Mercenary cavalrymen from the eponymous command of 'Pythangelos and Ptolemaios his son' also mobilized for an elephant hunt (*P.Petr.* 3.114) the same year. Because Pythangelos left his name on three stations in the hunting grounds, he very likely led multiple hunts himself. But we might ponder whether his men that year went under his direct command, or like the troops of Andronikos were a portion of the force under Peitholaos.

Elephant-hunting was a prestigious activity for high-ranking Ptolemaic officers. These voyages involved the transportation of small armies of men and materiel, traversed adverse terrain with poor supply, often through the territory of hostile tribes, and covered more than 2,000 miles during the round-trip, further than the campaign of Ptolemy's army in the Third Syrian War. In short, the elephant hunts were essential activities, not only to maintain the Ptolemaic elephant corps but to maintain the logistical and operational readiness of the Ptolemaic army. The elephants were captured for war and killed for ivory, which made the expeditions both strategically significant and lucrative. In 223/222 BC, when men from Pythangelos' command were on an elephant hunt, his daughter held a prestigious priesthood at Alexandria (*SB* 18.14103). Perhaps he led one of his hunting expeditions around 213 BC, when he was himself the eponymous priest at Alexandria (*BGU* 6.1246). The Andronikos who was eponymous priest in 214 BC may have been the mercenary cavalry hipparch and hunt commander mentioned above (*BGU* 10.1944). In 233/222 BC, an unnamed 'son of Leon' held the same priesthood, perhaps either the son of the elephant hunter Leon or, if he bore his father's name, the hunter himself (*P.Cair.Dem.* 2.30604). Charimortos, who led at least one elephant hunt, was never eponymous priest as far as we know, but was a powerful, corrupt member of the court's inner circle (Plb. 18.55.1).

The elephant hunting leaves a few unanswered questions, however. The series of hunts from 225/224 to 223/222 BC and beyond surely contributed to military readiness in the Fourth Syrian War, but for how many commanders and soldiers? It is unclear, for example, whether the 231 troopers of Andronikos' command were the full military complement on Peitholaos' expedition. If so, the four or five hunts from those three years might have only given 1,000 men – mainly mercenary cavalry – a taste of campaigning a few years before Raphia. Is it just a coincidence, then, that the mercenary cavalry performed so well at the battle? If the campaigns were conducted annually while Euergetes was king, several thousand men might get experience of the hunts every decade, which might mark a significant contribution to military readiness. But no evidence has been uncovered for any hunts in 239 and 225 BC. Most likely, Ptolemy III renewed them, or increased the pace, frequency or scale of the hunts, after the death of Seleucus II in anticipation of a coming war. If the expeditions incorporated more military men, such as infantry, their impact on readiness would increase dramatically. After all, we know of the fourteen Egyptian military men from a district around Thebes who were drafted for service on an elephant hunt. Men had to garrison all the waypoints through the desert to the Red Sea and along the Red Sea to the hunting grounds, like the fifty mercenaries and twenty-one boat crew in *P.Grenf.* 1.9. The only strong evidence for multiple units, however, is the possibility that Pythangelos' men accompanied those of Andronikos under Peitholaos in 223/222 BC. Furthermore, those were both cavalry commands.

In conclusion, the Ptolemaic army was not inactive operationally in the twenty years of peace, but the activities of the army seem to have contributed disproportionately to the experience and readiness of its mercenary and semi-professional contingents.

The First Reform of the Army

Ptolemy III did not use his prosperity and security to try to unite the Hellenistic world after withdrawing from the East at the end of the Third Syrian War. He did, however, see his army reformed into an organization befitting an established and powerful kingdom. The army was already large and powerful, but as the product of piecemeal development over nearly a century (since Alexander captured Egypt) it was unnecessarily complex. The reform simplified the structures of the army and adapted its institutions to a theoretical ideal: properly staffed regiments linked to an army corps of the ideal size for royal military actions. It took place, or at least began, in 235 BC.[20] *P.Petr.* 2.16 and 18, from year 12 (236/235 BC), definitely pre-date the reform, while *Chr.Mitt.* 28, from year 15 (233/232), is the earliest definitively dated text that unquestionably identifies cleruchs in reformed units.[21] *P.Petr.* 2.22, however, dated to year 13 (235/234 BC), contains in its second fragment the word ἱππαρχίας (hipparchy) as part of an identification formula for a soldier. While hipparchs are common in the pre-reform papyri, the word 'hipparchy' was never attested in the Fayum until after the reform. Thus the reform seems to have been implemented in 235 BC.[22] In year 13, Sosibios son of Dioskourides, the most famous minister in Ptolemaic history, was eponymous priest of the royal cult at

Alexandria. Sosibios rapidly rose to prominence at the court; it is possible he was involved in this reform, just as he was with the reform before the battle at Raphia, which Polybius described in Book 5 of his *Histories*. The reform was probably meant to organize the army for a new Golden Age of peace, prosperity and power. Yet when war again loomed on the horizon, a new reform was needed.

The reform touched both infantry and cavalry. The reform was the first attempt to bring order, a mixture of accuracy, realism and simplicity, to the Ptolemaic system. The Ptolemies, after the Second and Third Syrian Wars, were no longer highly dependent on new recruits during wartime. The army in 235 BC was an army *of* Ptolemaic Egypt, in that the vast majority of soldiers, aside from the eldest veterans and a handful of recent recruits, had been born in Egypt. With that force, and not reliant on more than the usual bodies of foreign mercenaries to augment them, Ptolemy III had campaigned abroad successfully. There may have been close to 40,000 experienced troops at the time. However, those men were members of scores, possibly hundreds, of eponymous commands, all staffed from the top down, with too many colonels and too few privates. These were, of course, the result of the first Ptolemies' permissive and open-handed recruitment tactics. The reform addressed these sorts of units. The reformed army aimed for a smaller number of fully manned and appropriately officered units. In theory, these would be simpler to administer, train and mobilize for war. The reform produced three tiers of cavalry: the regular settler cavalry in numbered hipparchies, the mercenary cavalry in a smaller number of properly staffed hipparchies, then eventually several additional regiments called the 'ethnic' hipparchies. The reform also addressed the infantry, creating a new, expansive Macedonian infantry class.

The haphazard process of settlement under the first Ptolemies contributed several impediments to the reform, and it is not entirely clear how they were addressed. The first and most obvious is that the reform required quite a lot of demotions, and might also have included seizures of outsized allotments. Just consider the case of the hipparchs Sosillos and Machatas, and their 312 and 314 arouras, respectively (*P.Lille* 1.32 and 34). The documentary evidence is lacking that might show how the state reduced the allotments. Perhaps, to avoid too many offences, the allotments were not reduced in size until the cleruch's death. For example, a papyrus from the first half of the second century BC, *BGU* 14.2423, lists the allotment sizes, in arouras, for thirty-five cavalry settlers from some region of the Fayum. The sizes of their allotments appear in the table opposite:

Allotment Size	Number	Percentage
70-80	2	5.7%
100	22	62.9%
110–120	8	22.9%
180	2	5.7%
220	1	2.8%

Larger allotments like those held by officers still appear, but represent less than 9 per cent of the settler cavalry population, which is fairly close to the expected ratio of officers to the sergeants and regular troopers in a cavalry command.

In addition, there was a pronounced tendency – at least in the Fayum – for Ptolemaic settlers in the same eponymous command to be scattered across a wide area alongside men from multiple other units, rather than concentrated closer together. Perhaps it was not recognized at the time as a bug in the Ptolemaic system, but the dispersion of men from the same unit across a larger area than necessary must have complicated training and mobilization. Even if some in the military command recognized this as a problem, the civil officials who oversaw the settlements would surely have been reluctant to introduce too many shocks to the system. Nonetheless, there is some evidence that the post-reform regiments were less scattered than had been the case before the reform.

The final general concern is the extent of the reform. The reform is most evident in the Fayum: in fact, it is possible to argue that the reform only took place there, and not throughout Egypt. The relative abundance of evidence for the reform in the Arsinoite nome naturally reflects the comparatively large number of texts from the Fayum, as well as the presence there – and nowhere else – of so many settlers of the same classes, especially among the settler and mercenary cavalry. However, that observation does not prove that the reform addressed institutions across Egypt. Several arguments support that conclusion. The infantry reform is particularly helpful. First, the new Macedonian class appears in texts from several other parts of Egypt, not only in the Fayum. Second, the three numbered infantry regiments in the Fayum include the 2nd, 3rd and 7th, necessitating at least four other regiments, which must have been located in other regions. If the infantry reform extended beyond the Fayum, then the cavalry reform presumably did so as well.

The Cavalry: The Numbered Hipparchies

Ptolemaic interest in the further systemization and maintenance of the cavalry is clearly demonstrated in the papyrological record. The cavalry contingents in Ptolemy's army in 240 BC were of several sorts: the royal squadron, attested in a mid-century papyrus and said to have been 700 strong at Raphia;[23] the settler cavalry or *katoikoi hippeis*, well-known from Fayum papyri as the *hekatontarouroi*, 100-aroura cleruchs, because so many held 100 arouras; and the 'mercenary' horse, who often held their own allotments but mobilized on paid service more frequently than the settler cavalry. The reform restructured the settler, or *hekatontarouroi*, cavalry into a core cavalry contingent comprising five numbered hipparchies concentrated in the Arsinoite nome. These divisions did not entirely supplant the previous eponymous command system, which remained the primary system for recording the activities and affairs of Ptolemaic cavalrymen in domestic business. They did, however, provide a clear tactical structure for the Ptolemaic cavalry and removed the effusion of exaggerated ranks.

There were at least five numbered hipparchies at the time of the reform, all of which are attested at some point within the Arsinoite nome. At present, the numbered hipparchies are not attested in other provinces until the second century BC (e.g., *SB* 24.15962, *P.Oxy.* 49.3482, *P.Ryl.* 2.252). By then the numbered hipparchies had grown from five to ten. The Arsinoite nome had become home to Egypt's largest concentration of cavalry through the efforts of the *dioiketes* Apollonios and cavalry secretary Phanias in the 250s BC. *P.Count.* 1 identified a military population with 3,418 adult males in the Arsinoites; they have usually been identified as the 100-arouras cavalry. Clarysse and Thompson suggested the number of them who were actually cleruchs was approximately between 1,000 and 2,000, and much closer to the lower figure (2006: 2: 152). If the hipparchies were about 250 strong, the five hipparchies would have required 1,250 men. This would have required another 1,000 regular cavalry from other regiments and other nomes to fill the ranks at Raphia. If the hipparchies were about 500 strong, as in some of the late Hellenistic tactical manuals, the five hipparchies would have required 2,500 men, far too many for the Arsinoite population to support, and more than the total number of settler cavalry at the Battle of Raphia.

The five hipparchies seem to have been organized across the sub-regions of the Arsinoite nome, although the nature of the distribution or organizational principles used to organize the regiments is not clear at present. Of the five hipparchies, the 1st is quite poorly attested compared to the other four (*SB* 26.16634, *P.Genova* 3.108).[24] It is conceivable that its troopers were actually spread between the Fayum and neighbouring regions, perhaps especially in the direction of Memphis.[25] The distribution of the other four hipparchies, the 2nd to the 5th, suggests at least some attempt to group the cavalry regiments geographically. That might help explain, to some degree, why the eponymous command structure survived the creation of the numbered regiments. Thus, the *CPR XVIII* volume of papyri from Theogonis, a village in the southern region of the Fayum called the precinct of Polemon, is the earliest archive after the reforms. The large majority of the 100-aroura cavalry were from the 5th hipparchy. The few from *CPR XVIII* who were not from the 5th were from the 3rd hipparchy. Many in the 3rd hipparchy were from either the Polemon precinct or the western region of the Fayum, called the precinct of Themistos. Many attested members of the 2nd hipparchy were from the precinct of Herakleides, in the northern Fayum. Most from the 4th hipparchy were also from the precincts of Themistos or Herakleides. The number of officers shrank considerably after the reform: the ranks of chiliarch and pentakosiarch never appear in the numbered hipparchies, and of the handful of officers attested in the papyri, most were simply titled *hyperetes*, 'junior-officers'. The tax records in *P.Petr.* 3.112 include records for dozens of *hekatontarouroi* from the numbered hipparchies, mainly the 3rd and 4th, and include just a handful of *hyperetes*.[26] After the reform, junior officers were less abundant than senior officers were before it.

There were undoubtedly significant numbers of settler cavalry in other nomes as well, but how the military administration categorized them relative to the numbered hipparchies is unclear. Other nomes had fewer cavalry settlers, and probably at most a single hipparchy within the nome. The Oxyrhynchite nome had been home to about half-a-dozen cavalry units a generation earlier, but may have had only one full hipparchy by the time of the reform: the hipparchy of Zoilos. Zoilos' regiment, which eventually passed to the hipparch Philon, was a full regiment itself, and not a component of one of the five hipparchies from the Arsinoite. It is conceivable the regiment of Zoilos and Philon had a number (based on later evidence, perhaps the 8th or 10th), but in the absence of another regiment, the business in the documentary papyri could be conducted without reference to a regimental number. At least one hipparchy was based in the Herakleopolite nome too (*P.Grad.* 5, 230 BC), but the papyrological evidence from that nome is fairly light in the late third century. Eventually, the number of hipparchies grew to ten. In the second century BC, the papyrus *P.Würzb.* 1.4 (142 BC) shows that men from the 8th hipparchy were settled at Philadelpheia in the Fayum, in the precinct of Herakleides. The 8th hipparchy resulted in part from the merger of mercenary cavalry and other cavalry units into the numbered hipparchies in the Fayum, but it also incorporated cavalrymen from the Oxyrhynchites (*SB* 24.15962, 116–107 BC). The 10th hipparchy appears to have been based in the Oxyrhynchites (*P.Oxy.* 49.3482, first century BC). The 7th hipparchy is attested in a single Fayum text from 147 or 136 BC (*BGU* 6.1256). The 6th and 9th hipparchies must have existed as well, but been based in other provinces, and the example of the 8th hipparchy demonstrates that some regiments were based in multiple provinces.

The remaining eponymous commanders for the settler cavalry provide another way of tracking the reform. The numerous eponymous commanders in the 230s and 240s BC contracted dramatically after the reform to eight, among whom three seem to have been commanders of the mercenary cavalry, which was not affected by the reform. The eponymous commanders of the men in the numbered hipparchies were: Onomastos, a former eponymous priest of Alexander; Hippokrates; Ptolemaios son of Nautas, whose father had also been an eponymous commander of cavalry; Ptolemaios son of Eteoneus, whose father remained an eponymous commander of mercenary horse well after the reform; Andriskos, who may have held a command in the first actions of the Third Syrian War; and Menelaos, commander of the elite troops transferred to the Arsinoites from the Hermopolite nome. These five reduced the number of eponymous commanders to the same number as the reform hipparchies. Remarkably, although there were five of each, there was not a complete correlation between eponymous commander and numbered hipparchy. Most of the eponymous commanders were associated with two or even three hipparchies. They were also phased out of use alongside the numbered hipparchies by the end of the Fourth Syrian War. One of the last references to them is *SB* 20.15068 (217 BC).[27] From that document we know that men from the 5th hipparchy and the eponymous command of Ptolemaios son of Nautas participated in the Battle of Raphia. Most likely, nearly all men from all five hipparchies mobilized with the army.

The Mercenary Hipparchies

The mercenary settler cavalry were a large part of the Ptolemaic cavalry population, both in the Fayum and in other parts of Egypt, perhaps especially the Delta (*P.Petr.* 2.31). Because many were classified as officers in their commands, their allotments were often quite large. The reform seems to have put many of them into standardized allotments at 80 arouras, and created a class so named: the *ogdoēkontarouroi* (*P.Genova* 3.108, 229 BC).[28] Only two eponymous commanders of mercenary cavalry are still attested after the reform: Eteoneus and Pythangelos. Eteoneus' son Ptolemaios was one of the eponymous officers in the mercenary horse, while Pythangelos' son Ptolemaios joined him in command of the *misthophoroi* regiment. These hipparchies were consolidated from the far larger number of mercenary cavalry commands in the Fayum in the preceding years. Their regular participation in elephant hunts and other campaigns should have meant they were among the best soldiers in the Ptolemaic army. Eventually, however, many of the 80-aroura cleruchs joined numbered hipparchies, and the mercenary settler cavalry disappeared from the Fayum and many other regions. Fairly soon after the reform, *P.Hamb*. 1.24 (222 BC) has a '100-arouras' cleruch with an 80-arouras allotment; had he transferred units without changing allotment? The same text names six different men from the 2nd hipparchy, but they were split between two different eponymous commanders, including Ptolemaios son of Eteoneus. Could some of the men from his eponymous command have been transfers from the 80-arouras mercenary cavalry? About forty years later, the 80-arouras cavalrymen joined the ranks of the numbered hipparchies *en masse* (*P.Mich*. 3.182, 182 BC). As an example, Jewish 80-aroura cavalry were attested in the 1st hipparchy in 180 BC, under the eponymous commander Dositheos (*P.Tebt*. 3.1.818). The number of mercenary 80-arouras cavalry was fairly significant at one point; Clarysse and Thompson estimated from *P.Count* 1 that there were 400 or more mercenary cavalry in the Fayum (2006: 2: 152). For example, a second-century AD land survey from Philagris, a village in the western Fayum, recorded several dozen 80-aroura allotments in the vicinity of the city (*BGU* 9.1900).

When the 80-aroura cavalry joined the numbered hipparchies officially, in the 180s and 170s BC, it is unclear whether the mercenary settler cavalry units survived. Already in 221 BC, a man could identify himself in a petition to the king as 'the secretary of the mercenary cavalry' in the Arsinoites (*P.Enteux*. 62), suggesting either a joint administrative office for the two hipparchies or a consolidation into a single hipparchy. Eteoneus' command was attested several times that year, but never thereafter, and Pythangelos' command appeared last in 222 BC, in connection with his elephant hunts. The best case for the survival of at least one of these hipparchies is the mercenary settler cavalry of Hippalos who were active in the 180s and 170s BC, with lands in the Fayum but duties often between the Arsinoites and the Thebaid (e.g., *P.Tebt.* 3.2.853, 173 BC). The 80-aroura men who first joined the numbered hipparchies were under another eponymous commander, Galestes, another high-ranking court figure like Hippalos, Eteoneus and Pythangelos. It is conceivable even that both hipparchies survived down to that time, but the evidence is insufficient to give a clear answer. The Fayum evidence puts a lot of emphasis on the 100-aroura cavalry, but the settled mercenary cavalry were a major component of Ptolemaic settlements in other regions. A hipparchy of mercenary cavalry were serving in the Herakleopolite nome in 211 BC (*P.Köln.* 11.448), and it is clear the mercenary cavalry were not done away with across Egypt. Eighty-aroura cavalry are also attested in the Herakleopolites, under an eponymous commander Antimachos (*P.Heid.* 8.417, 190 BC); what is not entirely clear is when or whether these 80-aroura cavalry were eventually transferred into the numbered hipparchies like the 80-aroura cavalry in the Arsinoites. Mercenary cavalry proliferated in the second century BC, but in smaller units and mainly in Upper (southern) Egypt.

The Ethnic Hipparchies

Either as part of the initial regimental reform around 235 BC or as part of an additional move in the next couple of years, the Ptolemaic army created at least five new hipparchies in addition to the other seven present in the Arsinoites. They first appeared in papyri in spring 231 BC (*CPR* 18.10, 18.15). These additional hipparchies are usually called the 'ethnic hipparchies' in scholarship, because they were not numbered but instead bore the name of various nations from the Hellenistic world:

- The Hipparchy of the Macedonians;
- The Hipparchy of the Thessalian and other Greeks;
- The Hipparchy of the Thracians;
- The Hipparchy of the Persians;
- The Hipparchy of the Mysians.[29]

While some scholars have wondered whether the ethnic designations reflected the original ethnicity of the hipparchies, the evidence almost never supports such a link.[30] The earliest known cavalryman in the hipparchy of the Thessalians and other Greeks was a Thracian, and the earliest known cavalryman in the hipparchy of the Persians was a Macedonian. Still, there is an Orontes (an Iranian name) attested among the Persians (*P.UB Trier* SS 77-43). These ethnic incongruities provide good evidence that these hipparchies, though named after ethnic groups, were not truly organized along ethnic divisions originally, and never were.

The men of the ethnic hipparchies received smaller allotments than those in numbered hipparchies or mercenary cavalry: 70 arouras, which gave them the name *hebdomekonterouroi*. Until the appearance of these new hipparchies, 70-aroura allotments were rare in Egypt.[31] Their smaller allotments could reflect either of two things: an expectation of paid service similar to that among the 80-aroura mercenary cavalry, or a lesser military status, perhaps relating to service in a different cavalry role. There is some evidence for the preparation of allotments for the 70-aroura men prior to their arrival.[32] Many of the men in the ethnic hipparchies were receiving settlements up to the start of the Fourth Syrian War. Men from the Thracian hipparchy may be referenced in another mid-220s BC document, which contains details about the management of settler allotments under royal control, including those of several 'Thracians', none of whom had identifiably Thracian names, as well as at least twenty-three men, seemingly Macedonians (*P.Petr.* 2.30.A, 225 BC). Seventy-aroura men were also found in the Oxyrhynchite nome, in small numbers, but with eponymous commanders instead of a hipparchy.[33] From this information, the ethnic hipparchies seem to have first appeared in the late 230s BC as part of the Ptolemaic era of reform under Euergetes, yet most of the evidence for settlement belongs to the second half of the 220s.

The 70-aroura cavalry were introduced to the numbered hipparchies beginning no later than 179 BC, when a 70-arouras cavalryman is attested in the 5th hipparchy (*SB* 22.15213). The same year, other 70-arouras cavalrymen are attested in the eponymous command of Metrophanes and the hipparchy of the Thessalians (*P.Amh.* 2.42, *P.Freib.* 3.36+37). Within a few years, the 70-arouras cavalrymen from the eponymous command of Metrophanes had certainly transferred to the 2nd hipparchy (*P.Amh.* 2.55, 176 or 165 BC; also *SB* 14.12101). Seventy-arouras settlers still appear after this point, but not in large numbers, and the ethnic hipparchies never appeared again. No later than 165 BC, only the numbered hipparchies remained.

The ethnic hipparchies raise five interesting problems and questions, which help address the state of the Ptolemaic cavalry after the reform, not only among these five hipparchies, but as a whole:

1. The 70-aroura men from the Oxyrhynchite nome suggests there were either more than five ethnic hipparchies, or the men from the

hipparchies possessed allotments in multiple nomes, but were based in the Arsinoites. No settler from the Macedonian hipparchy is attested in the Arsinoite nome; perhaps the men in it, like those from the sparsely attested 1st hipparchy, mainly had their allotments in other nomes.

2. What was the total number of hipparchies in the Ptolemaic army in the late third century BC? In the late second century there were at least ten numbered hipparchies for the settler cavalry, a fairly significant number of mercenary cavalry and the royal squadrons. In the third century, after the addition of the ethnic hipparchies, there were *twelve* hipparchies present in the Arsinoite nome alone, including the two mercenary hipparchies. Then there were at least two settler hipparchies and one mercenary hipparchy between the Herakleopolites and Oxyrhynchites, still more men in the south as far as the Hermopolites and even into the Thebaid, as well as other settler and mercenary cavalry in Memphis and the Delta. Not counting the royal squadron of 700, at least 2,300 and more likely 3,300 Ptolemaic cavalry participated at the Battle of Raphia. At approximately 250 men per hipparchy, and assuming one hipparchy was from the Cyrenaica, that army would have required at least eight fully staffed hipparchies on the left wing, and perhaps four to six more completed hipparchies on the right wing. The Arsinoite count is twelve hipparchies, but either they were not all fully staffed or they were not all settled there. Any tally that would go beyond fifteen hipparchies is surely too many, unless many regiments were understrength.

3. Where did the Ptolemies find the men for five new hipparchies in the 230s and 220s BC? Fully staffed, they would have required some 1,250 new cavalrymen. Major recruitment had generally corresponded to demobilization from wars. Yet it had been years since the Third Syrian War ended, and would be years again before the Fourth Syrian War began. Instead, there is a strong possibility the five hipparchies were mainly under-staffed when they were created, drew their personnel from the *epigonoi*, and staffing them may have presented a steady problem. The hipparchies of the Thracians, Persians and Mysians may well have been scrapped to fully staff the first two hipparchies at the time of the Fourth Syrian War: none of the latter three can be confidently identified in papyri after 220 BC (*P.Petr.* 3.112). Thus, with reference to the second point of discussion, the Arsinoite nome cavalry probably fielded eight or nine hipparchies at Raphia: most or all of the men from the five numbered (100-aroura) hipparchies,

Ptolemy III and the Purported Decline of the Ptolemaic Army 221

horsemen equivalent to one or two hipparchies (250–500 troopers) from the ethnic (70-aroura) hipparchies and two mercenary (80-aroura) hipparchies.

4. Were the ethnic hipparchies armed any differently from the other cavalry in the Ptolemaic army? The Thessalians were famed as lancers in the fourth century BC, but by the mid-point of the third century they, the Macedonians and most of the Greek world, including Mysians, seem to have adopted shields in large numbers.[34] Persians had generally used a pair of dual-purpose spears, the *lonchē*. But the use of these would not have been incompatible with a shield. The vast majority of evidence for Ptolemaic cavalry depicts them as unshielded lancers.[35] Evidence for shielded cavalry is comparatively rare.[36] But it is possible the ethnic hipparchies were conceived as a way to begin introducing shields among the Ptolemaic cavalry.

5. Finally, what did it mean that, over time, the 80-aroura and 70-aroura cavalry were enrolled into the numbered hipparchies? They were not enrolled in new, higher numbers only, like the 7th and 8th hipparchies, but also in the 1st, 2nd, 3rd and 5th. There is no case of one in the 4th hipparchy, but this could just be chance in the survival of papyri. There are two possible interpretations. The first is that the manpower of the hipparchies was raised from about 250 troopers to about 500, commensurate with the tactical manuals of the later Hellenistic period onward. The other is that the military defeats, rebellions and waves of unrest in the second century BC steadily eroded the manpower of the 100-aroura cavalry, and other classes were added to the mainstay hipparchies to keep them manned. The evidence is not clear enough to offer a definitive answer, but the latter scenario is more likely in context: a reflection of the decline of the Ptolemaic army in the second century BC.

The Infantry Reform

The military reforms were not restricted to the cavalry. Prior to the reform, the infantry were both far more numerous across Egypt and less organized – at least in the Fayum – than the cavalry. The operations of the phalanx required arraying thousands of men in a close-order formation and orchestrating their movements on the battlefield. Settling the men of a phalanx required surveying and maintaining allotments for thousands of men. The Ptolemies accumulated Macedonian and other infantry from 323–252 BC, and in those seventy years developed the military force that

Ptolemy III deployed to good effect in the Third Syrian War. Papyrological evidence indicates that Euergetes sought to provide equivalent organization for the infantry as that achieved for the cavalry. In one key way, the infantry reform was actually the more meaningful of the two. Out of the mass of ethnicities and mess of settlement patterns that comprised the army and military institutions Ptolemy III inherited, the army Euergetes left at his death featured a large and unified institution on the battlefield and at home in Egypt: the *triakontarouroi Makedones*, unified by ethnicity and organized into numbered regiments, chiliarchies of 1,000 men. The reform had taken place by 232 BC (*CPR* 18.32), and so most likely occurred in conjunction with the cavalry reforms. The 30-aroura Macedonians and their chiliarchies, like the numbered hipparchies, provided a coherent organizational pattern for the infantry that held meaning in war and in domestic affairs. The forging of this class around Macedonian ethnicity created a national body, however imagined it may have been, associated with the throne as the Macedonian people of the Macedonian kings of Egypt.

The infantry of the phalanx were not as prestigious or wealthy as the cavalry and the men of the elite units or the Alexandrian court, and yet they alone were, through the reform, *automatically* styled as Macedonians. This suggests that Ptolemy III sought, in addition to better organizing his army, to shore up his support among the larger infantry class. Doing so countered the political clout of the cavalry and elite units that fed the ranks of the court aristocracy in Alexandria. Therefore the infantry reform served a political purpose, in addition to the military-bureaucratic purposes it and the cavalry reforms fulfilled. When the left wing fell apart at Raphia, the king's appearance among the Macedonians spurred them to victory against the Seleucids' elite Silvershields. When court intrigues nearly ended the dynasty at the end of the third century BC, the stubborn non-cooperation of the Macedonians, who sailed down to Alexandria and encamped at the city during the crisis, preserved the dynasty for several more generations. But when thousands of those same men fell a few years later on the field at Panium, or died in the great Egyptian revolt, their absence permanently weakened and reshaped the Ptolemaic state and army.

The infantry reform collapsed an array of infantry classifications and ethnicities into a single body. The *triakontarouroi*, 30-aroura settlers, existed before the reform, but just one is attested (*P.Petr.* 3.105, 244 BC). The man there, and two other infantrymen classed as *pezoi*, 'foot', all possessed 24 arouras. I have suggested previously that this diversity in classification resulted from different waves of settlement and different origins in service.

Scholars are sometimes cautious about classifying the *triakontarouroi* and similar classes as infantry, but the shared allotment sizes between *pezoi* – definitionally infantry – and *triakontarouroi* demonstrates that the terms were functionally interchangeable in the third century BC. This link is further proven in *P.Petr.* 3.112, an official tax record that referred to the class as the '30-aroura infantry', the τριακονταρούρων πεζῶν. To the *triakontarouroi* and generic *pezoi* we may add the *eikosipentarouroi* (25-aroura) and *eikosiarouroi* (20-aroura) settlers, at least some of the *presbyteroi* (veterans, who also generally possessed 20-arouras) and other eponymous commands of infantry that are more difficult to categorize, like Krateros' command.[37] Their classifications were born out of their sporadic recruitment and local settlement. After the regimental reform, the other categories nearly disappeared. The *eikosiarouroi* were re-established in the second century BC, and a single Macedonian *eikosipentarouros* seems to be attested in a fragmentary text from 222 (*P.Tebt.* 3.1.815). Reclassifying them all as 30-aroura settlers had no impact on their actual holdings: *P.Köln.* 8.345, from 230/229 BC, provides evidence for one of these *triakontarouroi Makedones*, Mikkos, whose *kleros* near Theadelphia in the Fayum was still 25 arouras.[38] The point of the reform was not to undertake the massive administrative task of equalizing small differences in allotment size, but of building a single monolithic institution for the phalanx infantry. Of course few of the men were actually Macedonians, even if they were trained and equipped to serve in the phalanx. While the first two Ptolemies had surely managed to recruit thousands of Macedonians, the so-called 'Macedonian' phalanx of Euergetes must have depended heavily upon a great variety of Greek, Anatolian, Near Eastern and Egyptian soldiers armed and trained in emulation of Alexander's phalanx.

The Macedonian *triakontarouroi* were organized into chiliarchies, regiments of 1,000 men, which were, like the settler hipparchies, assigned numbers. Three of these chiliarchies are attested in the Arsinoite nome. *CPR XVIII* attests two Macedonian *triakontarouroi* in two different regiments in 232/231 BC (*CPR* 18.10 and 32). The 2nd chiliarchy is attested in 18.32, while the 3rd chiliarchy is attested in 18.10. Both Macedonians were, despite their chiliarchies, listed as 'of those without a hegemon'.[39] The editor amended a gap in the text to read hipparchy instead of chiliarchy, but the status 'without a hegemon' was given only to infantry.[40] Cavalry without an eponymous officer were instead described as 'without a hipparch'.[41] Of all the men 'without a hegemon' in the third century BC, only one, in *CPR* 18.19, was not certainly classified as a *triakontarouros*, and the text of *CPR* 18.19 should be amended to read that he, Artabazos, a Macedonian, was a 30-aroura settler.[42] Aside from the 2nd and 3rd, the 7th chiliarchy is attested twice (*P.Petr.* 3.112, 222 BC; *P.Tebt.* 1.137, 218/217 BC). Another Macedonian *triakontarouros* in *CPR* 18.13, Spartakos, was under the hegemony of Nikanor, an infantry officer attested prior to the reform (*P.Petr.* 2.3), and the text is damaged where his numbered regiment would have been recorded.

The presence of at least three regiments of foot in the Fayum raises an important question about infantry settlement in Egypt more generally. First, it should be observed that the presence of the regiments in the Fayum does not mean all 3,000 soldiers held allotments there. Most likely, each had at least a company (256 men and a few officers) in the province, so the 30-aroura Macedonians in the Fayum may have numbered between 750 and 3,000. Most treatments of the Ptolemaic army have understated infantry settlement in the Fayum; infantrymen are attested with less frequency than cavalry, but the existence of three chiliarchies demonstrates the scale of infantry settlement was grander than we have often imagined.[43] It is a little surprising that the 2nd and 3rd chiliarchies were in the Fayum, and not closer to Alexandria in, for example, the Menelaite nome. This may suggest that, as with the cavalry, the locus for the whole regular army had shifted to Middle Egypt. Without knowing how many chiliarchies with which numbers came from the settlers around Memphis and Herakleopolis, it is impossible to speak more clearly. We may at least conclude that the population of infantry cleruchs was larger than often assumed.

The question then is how large Euergetes' Macedonian infantry class actually was. The maximum figure should be the 25,000 regular phalangites at Raphia. More likely, the reform aimed at an 'ideal' phalanx of sixteen chiliarchies. The existence of a 7th chiliarchy suggests at least that many had been organized as regiments and, given the evenness preferred in Greek military organization, an 8th regiment is a plausible minimum. Many of the Macedonians were settled closer to Alexandria and throughout the Delta (e.g., *P.Petr.* 2.31), rather than in the Fayum. Perhaps a future papyrological discovery will identify the home territories of additional regiments, and confirm whether the number of regiments was fully sixteen or closer to eight. If there were eight regiments of settled Macedonians, the army must have depended heavily upon standing regiments of Macedonians, the regular regiments of *misthophoroi* (paid troops, as opposed to *xenoi*, the foreign mercenaries) and levies of *epigonoi* and Alexandrian citizens to extend the phalanx. Evidence for standing units of Macedonians is weak in third-century BC papyri, but second-century papyri include a handful of indicators the Macedonian division by then included both settlers and standing troops.⁴⁴ There is at least one example of an Alexandrian infantry officer and cleruch from after the reform, but his unit, the eponymous command of Strato, was not part of the Macedonians' regimental system (*CPR* 18.20, 231 BC). Unless Strato's unit was part of the 5,000 in the infantry *agema*, then with reference to the Raphia army it must have been classed among the 25,000 in the phalanx or among the 8,000 mercenaries.

The phalanx of 16,000 men, at least half cleruchs, is attractive because it was considered an organizational ideal in the tactical writings of the Hellenistic period.⁴⁵ The tactical manuals that survive today nearly all come from the late Hellenistic period or the Roman era. However, Asklepiodotus and Aelian both insisted that the phalanx of 16,000 was a matter of general consensus among the earlier tactical writers. While modern readers tend to doubt the sway of theory on military practice, we may also see that precisely 16,000 phalangites fought in pivotal battles for both Philip V and Antiochus III in the early second century BC.⁴⁶ This correspondence would be a very strange coincidence, and it is more likely that the grace, precision and decadence of a mathematical ideal really did take hold. The Macedonian successor kingdoms were the most powerful states in the Mediterranean and Near East world, at least in their own self-conception, and their battlefield success depended heavily on the artful, violent coordination of complementary arms. Euergetes, spending his reign reorganizing his army, may have even been the first to pursue an ideal army. During the Diadochi wars there had been no such ideal, and afterwards, for a generation or so, it is doubtful any of the kingdoms possessed the manpower reserves to field 16,000 phalangite regulars, as dependent as they were on mercenaries. Only the Roman victories in the early second century BC would have shattered a link between the ideal and the real, compelling Hellenistic armies to reassess their military organizations.

There are many possible sources for a well-ordered, mathematically ideal army. The genre of mixed mathematical and practical tactical manuals flowered in the late Hellenistic period. The earliest tactical writer was probably Aeneas Tacticus, who wrote in the fourth century BC, but what survives of his work dealt almost exclusively with siegecraft.⁴⁷ Around 300 BC or so, Demetrius of Phalerum, who spent the last years of his career in Alexandria at the court of Ptolemy I, was said to have written a two-book tactical manual (*Diog.Laert.* 5.80). King Pyrrhus of Epirus also wrote a book on tactics. Aelian, in his own *Tactics*, written for Emperor Trajan, noted that another early tactics writer was Kineas of Thessaly, who was Pyrrhus' ambassador to Rome before holding very high rank in the court of Ptolemy II. His work was an epitome of Aeneas (Aelian 1.2). Their rough contemporary Klearchos of Soli spent many years in Seleucid territories and was also said to have written a tactical manual (Arr. *Tactica* 1.1.4). Arrian also mentions a Pausanias and an Evangelos as tactical writers between Klearchos and Polybius. The tactical manual of Evangelos was a favourite of Philopoemen's in the time of his training, the 230s BC (Plut. *Phil.* 4.4). The manual would have chiefly concerned phalanx tactics, based on Plutarch's description of Philopoemen's interaction with the text. Plutarch praised Philopoemen for not focusing on tactical theorems and illustrations, but devising his own adapted conclusions based on each particular piece of ground.[48] Anyone who reads the manuals will see the mathematical influences, but Plutarch's writing made it explicit, talking about theorems and proofs. Polybius' own statements on tactics indicate that the measure of terrain influenced the ideal figure of 16,000 men in a phalanx, and that indeed, in his own day, 16,000 was considered the theoretical ideal: 'One stade will hold, of men properly arrayed in a phalanx, sixteen deep, sixteen-hundred men, and so ten stades are required to hold 16,000' (Plb. 12.9.7).

Later in the third century BC, after Raphia, the numerous *triakontarouroi Makedones* settled in the Oxyrhynchites were always listed without eponymous commander or chiliarchy. Unattested before Raphia, the settlers point to an expansion of the phalanx in the Fourth Syrian War. The infantry phalanx at Raphia was 25,000 strong. An ideal regiment held approximately 1,040 men, counting officers. Two 'wings' of a phalanx, at eight regiments each, would have numbered a little over 16,600. A third wing would have brought the theoretical strength of the phalanx to 24,900, which Polybius' source may have presented as 25,000. The new settlers in the Oxyrhynchites, who were never added to a chiliarchy despite their possession of allotments, might suggest the Ptolemaic army retained the official structure of sixteen regiments and kept the other men, at least some of whom gained allotments after the campaign, as a flexible reserve. The story of their recruitment and settlement, the larger reform of the Ptolemaic army, the creation of a large Egyptian phalanx and the great Battle of Raphia is the subject of the following chapter.

Chapter 9

The Fourth Syrian War and the Battle of Raphia

The Battle of Raphia and the Fourth Syrian War are the fitting capstone to this study of the army and military institutions under the first Ptolemaic kings. In the traditional historiography, influenced heavily by Polybius, Raphia was a fluke. The victory there was a false positive that temporarily broke the trend of decline in Ptolemaic military ability, yet only briefly delayed the inevitable: the loss of Syria and other parts of the Ptolemaic international empire, and the decline of the Ptolemaic state and army into the ranks of lesser powers. This work has attempted to show that the narratives of decline prior to Raphia are errant, dependent on biased traditions that have exerted outsize gravitational pull on the trajectory of modern historians. The story of Raphia and the Fourth Syrian War does fit a line of continuity from the early third century BC, but one of progressive development, reform and competition. And yet, twenty years after the battle, Syria had been lost, along with much of the Mediterranean empire, the Ptolemaic state was in disarray from dynastic turmoil and a dangerous internal revolt, and its military institutions were wracked by economic troubles and wartime casualties. The question for the historian, then, is to discern where the decline began. The Fourth Syrian War and its conduct reveals some of the weaknesses that existed in the Ptolemaic system, but these only began to truly erode the capacities of the Ptolemaic state and army in the aftermath of the war. The success at Raphia built upon decades of Ptolemaic military tradition, not a last-ditch reform authored by brave and virtuous mainland Greeks, as Polybius has it. The trajectory of development in the military and of further accomplishment of its three missions – interstate military competition, contribution to the legitimacy of the monarchy and control of Egypt – was continuing upward. Only the ambitious plans and incompetent follow-through of the post-war period caused the precipitate collapse of all three missions within a narrow chronological frame.

The Fourth Syrian War culminated in the Battle of Raphia in 217 BC and ended during the same summer, but it began four years earlier.[1] The Ptolemaic army took a strong defensive posture when the war began. Defections gave Antiochus III the advantage and paved the way for successes in the middle stages of the war, but the Ptolemaic army defeated the Seleucids at the decisive clash at Raphia. Between the start of the war and Raphia, the main Ptolemaic army was held in reserve. The ancient historical tradition reported that this was because 'the whole of the army had laid aside military exercises, and grown corrupt and enervated in idleness' (Just. 30.1.3). This tradition goes back to Polybius, and to Polybius' source material. A massive reform, overseen by mainland Greeks, prepared the army for battle from 219–217 BC. The possession of *kleroi* and focus on economic affairs in the papyri has often been read as support for the Polybian reform tradition.[2] An examination here will demonstrate the problems with the Polybian tradition. It is not wholly inaccurate, but bent events to fit a narrative where the poor character of the new monarch, Ptolemy IV, and the eventual corruption of his senior advisors correlated to the weakness of military institutions. This makes for a good story, but poor history. The military reforms and other military activities began while Ptolemy III was still alive, and the reason the army left Egypt only in the spring of 217 BC should be sought elsewhere.

The Seleucid Threat

Antiochus III had become king in the summer of 222 BC. Ptolemy III and his advisors must have anticipated the resumption of hostilities between his empire and that of the Seleucids. In considering the possibility, they must have weighed the disparate practical and potential power of the Seleucid army. Aside from the campaign of Ptolemy III's son Magas, which may have targeted the periphery of the Seleucid Empire or territories formerly under Seleucid control, the Ptolemies preferred not to commence hostilities, despite Antiochus' relative weakness. When Antiochus became king, he accepted an arrangement that effectively ceded Asia Minor and the Iranian plateau as viceroyalties to powerful satraps: Achaeus in the west, Molon and Alexander in the east (Plb. 5.40.6). Antiochus was negotiating from a position of weakness at that point: he was young and unproven, the civil wars were barely over and leading veterans from those wars ruled the frontier provinces. The Upper Satrapies, beyond western Iran, were lost to either foreign invasion or independence movements in the 240s and 230s BC. In practical terms, his rule was limited to Syria and Mesopotamia.

Even there, the regent Hermeias and a clique of court officials held significant sway, and Achaeus and Molon commanded a great deal of respect. Finally, a Ptolemaic garrison still held Seleukeia, a day's march from the capital at Antioch. Antiochus would have to prove his military ability eventually, but while Ptolemy III lived, Antiochus must have focused on establishing his power as king.

The primary military calculation that Ptolemys' advisors must have made at the start of their preparations regarded the strength of the Ptolemaic army against that of the Seleucids, and especially the strength of their respective phalanxes. The model army of Euergetes fielded a phalanx likely to have numbered about 16,000 men, to which we may add 5,000 elite infantry from the peltasts and *agema*, the foreign mercenaries (5,000–10,000), the Cyrenaicans (up to 3,000) and a scattering of other troops from Egypt (up to 5,000), which I have previously estimated should have amounted to about 35,000 foot for the royal army in a large-scale mobilization. By most measures, that should have been enough. However, the Seleucid phalanx – just the phalanx – could reach greater numbers, provided Antiochus III could hold his empire together. Bar-Kochva estimated Seleucid phalanx infantry (including the 10,000 elite Silvershields) at near 45,000 at the accession of Antiochus III.[3] There are problems with Bar-Kochva's belief in a fairly static military population, but the order of magnitude seems to be about right. The conclusion is significant: a unified Seleucid Empire could marshal military forces that would rival the massive army Antigonus the One-Eyed once led against Egypt.

The potential size of the Seleucid phalanx, provided Antiochus III could actually mobilize the troops [from the powerful and nearly autonomous satraps] in his east and west, may have inspired the Ptolemaic reforms that began while Ptolemy III was still alive. There is no reference point, prior to the Fourth Syrian War, for a scale of mobilization so high in the Seleucid world. New, more radical mobilization rules must have taken hold in the emergency state that gripped the Seleucid world from Ptolemy III's invasion until Antiochus III fully asserted his authority years after the Fourth Syrian War ended. Aside from its strengths in elephants and cavalry, Seleucus I's army at Ipsos in 301 BC fielded infantry on a scale comparable to Ptolemy I's at Gaza. Seleucus II's royal army suffered a cataclysmic defeat in Galatia early in the War of the Brothers, with casualties estimated at 20,000 and just a handful of survivors. Continued and bloody wars were hardly the recipe for recovering the heavy losses of the Third Syrian War and the slaughter at Ankyra, so a reform granting a Macedonian-like military settler status to a wider section of the population should probably be inferred. Without clear evidence no more can be said, but in sum, it seems the challenges of the era compelled the Seleucids to prioritize an expansion of the military population amid other military efforts. The Seleucid expansion clashed with the popularity of theoretical ideal armies in Macedonia and Ptolemaic Egypt.[4] In that sense, it was a precursor of the Roman challenge to the professional, limited model the Hellenistic kingdoms had adopted.

As an aging Euergetes and the men of his inner circle, such as Sosibios, contemplated the possibility of a new war, they must have become convinced that Seleucid mass posed a threat to the Ptolemaic royal army. The Ptolemies needed either to lower the number of Seleucid phalangites or increase their own dramatically. Because Antiochus was leading from a position of weakness, a natural Ptolemaic strategy was to prevent him from uniting his forces and keep parts of his armies turned against one another. Ptolemaic support for Achaeus – so recently an enemy – in Asia Minor helped ensure that his 6,000-plus heavy infantry were not available to rejoin Antiochus III. Achaeus may also have instigated and certainly supported the subsequent revolt of Kyrrhestai in northern Syria. Antiochus complained about the unabashed Ptolemaic support for rebels (Plb. 5.67.13). Ptolemaic support for the rebellion that broke out in Media in 222 or 221 BC is harder to demonstrate, but Ptolemy IV and Sosibios must have, at minimum, been pleased at the loss of something like 10,000 heavy infantry and thousands of high-quality cavalry and warhorses. The bloody suppression of Molon's revolt in 220 BC restored some of their numbers to Seleucid authority prior to Raphia, but at considerable expense. Their addition was counteracted by the revolt of the Kyrrhestai in northern Syria. Not only did the cities of the region revolt, but the brigade of the phalanx from that region, which Polybius set at 6,000 men (Plb. 5.50.7–8), mutinied against the king at Apameia. One of the king's generals suppressed the army mutiny in a bloody engagement, but the revolt in the region of Kyrrhos continued and must have weakened Seleucid forces available at Raphia.

The considerable real and even larger potential size of the Seleucid phalanx was thus one of the main causes of the Ptolemaic military reform. Antiochus was actually only able to march to the Battle of Raphia in 217 BC with 30,000 phalangites, far short of what watchful Ptolemaic leaders must have feared. The Ptolemaic military reforms aimed at improving both the quality and especially the quantity of battle-ready forces. The Ptolemaic infantry at Raphia numbered 72,000, which suggests the Ptolemies nearly doubled the size of the royal army in preparation for the decisive battle.

Where did the additional 30,000 soldiers come from? Unlike so many other Hellenistic recruitment drives, most of this expansion was not achieved through hiring new mercenaries, although there were a few. The ongoing wars in Greece may have made large hiring drives difficult. Polybius' account emphasized the addition of 20,000 Egyptians trained in the Macedonian manner, but the reform added troops in several components of the army. The reform began while Ptolemy III yet lived, intensified once the war actually began and occurred concurrently with military operations and diplomacy until the climactic struggle at Raphia. The following sections treat the operational and diplomatic history of the conflict down to the spring of 217, then the reform and finally the Battle of Raphia itself.

The Fourth Syrian War from 221 to the start of 217

Antiochus' first attack on Ptolemaic Syria occurred in 221 BC. Ptolemy III died at the end of the previous year, so Ptolemy IV had not been king long. We cannot be certain with the state of the current evidence, but it seems likely that the attack came some time after the assassination of Ptolemy IV's brother Magas. Theodotos the Aetolian, who killed Magas, held command of the Ptolemaic forces that resisted Antiochus in the province of Syria and Phoenicia, and it seems likely he assumed control of that province and its substantial military forces after killing the king's popular brother. In Polybius' narrative, the Seleucid king and his councillors reckoned two things as causes for war: Ptolemy's real or suspected support for Achaeus to declare his independence, and Ptolemy's ῥαθυμία, a character vice involving indifference and laziness (Plb 5.42.4–8). Polybius attempted to reconcile the obvious contradiction in causes by attributing the support of Achaeus to a ruse by one of Antiochus' own ministers. But the mistaken cause is more likely the characterization of Ptolemy IV. Instead, his assassination of his own brother, killed because he possessed more military experience and significant popularity with the professional troops and foreign mercenaries, hinted at Ptolemy's weakness. Ptolemy IV Philopator, at least under the influence of leading men like Sosibios, Ptolemaios son of Chrysermos and other chief advisors in the transition of power, was more inclined toward schemes than indolence, rather like an incompetent case of Machiavelli's prince.

Antiochus launched the attack later in the year. Early in 221 BC he was in Mesopotamia, where he married a Pontic princess, held council about Molon and Egypt, and dispatched forces to Media. Those forces retreated before Molon and all had gone into winter camps by the time Antiochus launched his attack in Syria (Plb. 5.45.5). According to Polybius, Antiochus and his army marshalled at Apameia, near modern Homs, then marched west to Laodicea on the sea to feel out an attack on Ptolemaic Phoenicia. Defences there must have been imposing, because Antiochus and his army then marched back to the east and attempted the Ptolemaic frontier through the Marsyas defile, a highland valley between the imposing Lebanon and Anti-Lebanon ranges now known as the Bekaa. The frontier between Ptolemaic and Seleucid territory lay somewhere in the valley, perhaps in the vicinity of Heliopolis-Baalbek. The main Ptolemaic defences were a little more than a day's march further south, where two garrison-towns, Gerrha and Brochoi, controlled both a narrowing of the valley and arduous roads directly west toward Beirut and east toward Damascus.[5] Much of the valley was wide and in many places a full kilometre above sea level. At Gerrha and Brochoi, the elevation is lower, and until the Middle Ages it was filled with a lake and marshes, which made the 7-mile-wide valley a much narrower passage. Theodotos led the defence at Gerrha and Brochoi, where he fortified the front of the pass and dared Antiochus to attack. Antiochus obliged, but succeeded only in losing men (Plb. 5.46.1–5). The young king soon retreated for the winter and to deal with Molon. The first foray of the Fourth Syrian War had been very short and went in Ptolemy's favour.

The winter of 221/220 BC was filled with intrigues for the Seleucid army. The leading Seleucid generals dispatched against Molon had met with defeat, and Molon had occupied Seleukeia on the Tigris and Babylon in the autumn. Then the army mutinied over pay. The defeat in the Bekaa and the defeats in the East surely contributed to the demand for arrears. When the king's vizier released reserve monies to pay off the troops, they returned to order, except the aforementioned Kyrrhestians. Some 6,000 men left the army camp, perhaps to march home, where the whole region went into revolt. Antiochus spent the campaign season in the East putting down Molon's rebellion, and Achaeus styled himself king and attempted to march into Syria. From the Ptolemaic perspective, the Seleucid state seemed no better off than it had been at the height of the War of the Brothers. That is surely one reason for Ptolemaic inaction in the 220 BC campaign season, although the Ptolemaic court's attempt at supporting rebels failed to achieve its true end when Achaeus turned back from his march before crossing the Taurus. By the start of autumn, the Ptolemaic strategy looked far weaker than it had a few months earlier: Antiochus had defeated Molon, and the mutiny of Achaeus' troops signalled that he threatened to invade

Antiochus' rear in the event of a major war in Syria. The weak, divided, defeated Seleucid state at the end of 221 BC posed a far greater threat at the end of 220.

The year 220 BC was the opportune time for a Ptolemaic counter-attack after the attack in the Marsyas. It quite obviously failed to materialize, but why? At some point during this year's campaign season, Theodotos returned to Alexandria and, according to Polybius (5.61.4), barely escaped with his life. Plutarch's *Cleomenes* points to this time, not long before the Spartan king's death, as when Ptolemy IV spent the campaign season in 'Dionysiac revels' (*Cleom.* 34.2). No papyrological evidence supports any sort of military activity. We might imagine that Theodotos came to Alexandria to urge an attack on Syria. His disappointment and danger mirrored that of Cleomenes at the same time, when a Messenian trader arrived in Alexandria with fine war-horses and Cleomenes told him he would have been better off bringing 'musicians and catamites' (Plut. *Cleom.* 35.2). The year's inaction inconclusively points to Polybius' charge of military unpreparedness, but certainly underscores the weakness in leadership in the Ptolemaic Empire.

The Seleucid Offensive, 219–218 BC

The Fourth Syrian War resumed with Seleucid offensives in 219 BC, the third year of Ptolemy IV's reign. Antiochus opened the year with an attack on Seleukeia, held by Ptolemaic forces since 246 BC. Seleukeia-by-the-Sea had a Ptolemaic garrison and very strong defences. The main city was situated on a steep spur of the southern Amanus mountains, built on terraces ascending to the citadel, which overlooked the sea to the west and the mouth of the Orontes to the south. It required incredible effort to mount an attack on the main city, because its flanks ran across precipices over steep ravines. Much of the population, however, dwelt in what Polybius' history calls the suburb of the city, built up around the harbours by the sea. While the suburb was easier to access, it too was very heavily fortified. Antiochus left one of his leading marshals, Theodotos Hemiolios, with part of the army to watch the approaches toward Apameia from Ptolemaic territory, in case Theodotos the Aetolian led a counter-attack. The army he had with him was large enough to invest the city on every side. Antiochus had successfully purchased some of the junior Ptolemaic officers in the city (Plb. 5.60.2). When his army launched an assault, they did so from all sides, enduring great hazards, to prevent the garrison from bringing aid in the direction of the real assault: the suburb and harbour. There, attacks by land and sea spread out the defenders, as they were across the whole city, and managed to gain a foothold. The junior officers, some of whom held commands in the harbour area, fled to the city and entreated their commandant, Leontios, to negotiate with Antiochus rather than risk the sack of the city (Plb. 5.60.8–10). With stubborn resistance, the siege could have been carried on far longer, but Antiochus received the city of Seleucus I at fairly minimal cost and the Ptolemaic garrison was permitted to leave freely. The surprising element in this episode and the subsequent campaigns is that the powerful Ptolemaic garrison on Cyprus played no role, at least in what survives of Polybius' testimony. The commander at the time was Pelops son of Pelops (*Salamine* XIII 64), from an old aristocratic family with ties to the navy. Part of the attraction of Cyprus was that it provided a powerful base to threaten the flank or rear of any army marching upon Egypt. Forces from Cyprus made useful contributions in later conflicts, but their irrelevance in the Fourth Syrian War underscores some of the incapacities of Ptolemaic strategic leadership.

For Antiochus III, the reconquest of Seleukeia was probably a sufficient feat for the time, and he began preparing for a campaign to deal with Achaeus. The great turning point came at that moment, however, when Theodotos the Aetolian sent Antiochus a letter offering to give up the Ptolemaic province. The last straw for Theodotos may have been the death of Cleomenes of Sparta back in Alexandria. His death is a little difficult to date. News of his death reached Sparta at the start of spring in 219 BC (Plb. 4.35.9), and his demise came soon after Sparta's entry into the Achaean–Aetolian war (Plb. 5.35.2, Plut. *Clem.* 34.1), which points to early winter 219. Cleomenes' men made a vain attempt from their house arrest to raise the Alexandrians in revolt, but succeeded only in slaying a pre-eminent courtier, Ptolemaios son of Chrysermos. He had been eponymous priest of the royal cult in 225/224 BC, and his family was among the most illustrious in Ptolemaic service. When the attempt had failed they committed suicide as a group.

Cleomenes' house arrest and subsequent death may have inspired Theodotos to switch sides, but the truth is that by the time he wrote the letter to Antiochus he was no longer in control of the province. He and his lieutenant Panaitolos had seized upon Ptolemais-Akko and Tyre, respectively, the capital city and one of the greatest cities of the province, and locked themselves within the cities with their supporters. Another Aetolian, Nikolaos, had already taken command of the province. It seems likely Theodotos proposed his plan to the other Aetolian captains among the mercenaries holding Syria and Phoenicia, and Nikolaos refused, putting Theodotos in a more difficult position. Thus, the Ptolemaic forces holding the frontiers were still prepared to resist Antiochus' army and were no longer under Theodotos' command. Their numbers had been reduced, however: Theodotos and Panaitolos surely took some men with them in their sedition, and Nikolaos and a large part of the garrison army diverted to besiege Ptolemais and Tyre, rather than holding the frontiers.

Antiochus' first attack was down the Marsyas again, where a successful assault could give him a march right down the Litani valley to the neighbourhood of Tyre. The path was difficult, but enabled his army to bypass the many fortified cities and narrow passages on the more direct route down the coastline of Phoenicia. His attack began in May or June 219 BC, while Hannibal was still besieging Saguntum in Spain and before Philip V marched into the Peloponnese with his army (Plb. 4.37.4). But Ptolemaic forces were still defending Gerrha and Brochoi, and his plan fell through. He kept most of the army besieging the lines at Gerrha and Brochoi, and with some of his lightest troops – including the Silvershields, the royal peltasts – tried to steal a march and find a different road to link up with Theodotos (Plb. 5.61.7–8). Polybius' account reports that Nikolaos sent men under Lagoras of Crete and Dorymenes of Aetolia to hold passes around Berytos, ancient Beirut (5.61.9). Antiochus' path may have followed rough, steep tracks across the Lebanon near Brochoi, in which case the Ptolemaic defensive line would have been in the mountain gorges east of Beirut. The only other option is that Antiochus went nearly the whole way back to Apameia to take the pass near Arados into Phoenicia; that road is easier, but far longer and ultimately less likely. Antiochus and his picked force succeeded in putting the Ptolemaic defenders to flight near Berytos. Since he camped in the pass to await the rest of his army, which had given up the sieges in Marsyas, Dorymenes and Lagoras may have fled into Berytos. When the full army had gathered, he marched south. He must have bypassed Ptolemaic Sidon to hurry down to Tyre and Ptolemais, where Nikolaos had lifted his sieges. By later summer 219 BC, Antiochus and his field army had linked up with Theodotos and secured the provincial capital at Ptolemais.

The remainder of the campaign was mainly filled with frustration for Antiochus. He entertained the idea of moving rapidly down the coast to attack Egypt, but Ptolemy and the army encamped at Pelusium and prepared to resist a siege (Plb. 5.62.4, *P.Enteux.* 48, *P.Frankf.* 7). This was the point when Antiochus really started to recognize how difficult the conquest of

Syria and Phoenicia would be. According to Polybius, 'visiting one city after another [Antiochus] attempted to gain them either by force or by persuasion. The minor cities were alarmed by his approach and went over to him, but those that relied on their defensive resources and natural strength held out, and he was compelled to waste his time in sitting down before them and besieging them' (Plb. 5.62.5–6). The Ptolemies had fortified dozens of cities in the region, and Nikolaos had ensured that many of them were garrisoned well. The only city the record confirms he besieged was Dura, or Tel Dor, just 23 miles south from Ptolemais, and he broke off the siege of that minor settlement as winter came on (Plb. 5.66.1). The record provides no example of a city that submitted, although one might speculate that Lagoras the Cretan handed over Berytos, since he subsequently entered Seleucid service. Antiochus left Theodotos the Aetolian in charge of Ptolemais and Tyre, and took the rest of his army back into Seleucid territory after agreeing to a four-month truce with Ptolemy.

In the Polybian narrative, Antiochus' successes in 219 BC finally spurred the Ptolemaic military reform. That reform is addressed later in this chapter, but again the Ptolemaic army remained in the confines of Egypt, except for the forces – mainly foreign mercenaries – in the army under Nikolaos. Unless the number of mercenaries serving in Palestine was far larger than anyone has imagined, there was little hope of actually stopping Antiochus' army in a determined campaign. There is little good evidence for the garrison's manpower, but it would be very surprising if, between local settlers and foreign mercenaries, there were more than 10,000. We know, for example, there were at least two mercenary and one settler hipparchies in the region, and so might estimate cavalry forces at about 750, and with a fairly common ten-to-one ratio between foot and horse, the size of the garrison and settler force may have been in the range of 8,250 men.[6] If they had been much larger, surely the Ptolemaic leaders would have preferred to add them to their field force before a major battle rather than spending two years training 20,000 Egyptians for the phalanx. Terrain and fortification clearly served as a force multiplier, and allowed the mercenaries defending the province to slow and dull Antiochus' attacks again and again. Given the military reform narrative, perhaps the Ptolemaic strategy really was simply to slow the pace of Antiochus' advance, permitting time to prepare the field army for battle. Among the units in the camp during the reform were 8,000 mercenary (*misthophoroi*) infantry (Plb. 5.65.4), as well as other mercenary contingents, whose presence with Nikolaos might have stymied the next Seleucid attack in 218 BC. Polybius explained this conservatism as a strategic and diplomatic ruse, intended to lure Antiochus into a false impression that a Ptolemaic main force attack would never come and Ptolemy IV would leave diplomats and mercenaries to settle the war (Plb. 5.63.3). Given how little support the garrison received from Egypt, it is little wonder the Ptolemies suffered defections among mercenary captains left to face the full might of Antiochus' army alone.

The campaign season in 218 BC achieved a dramatic expansion in Seleucid control over Syria and Phoenicia, but no decisive action. Antiochus neglected winter exercises for his army because he did not anticipate serious fighting, while Ptolemy sent a detachment from his fleet and some fresh reinforcements to join Nikolaos (Plb. 5.68.2). The fleet included thirty decked ships, a significant force but hardly a commitment of the main part of the fleet. Its admiral was Perigenes, whom it is tempting to identify with the family of the former admiral Kallikrates of Samos, whose brother Perigenes was also an officer tied to the navy (*IC I* xxii 4A), although Perigenes son of Leontiskos, an Alexandrian, is also a strong possibility (*IG XII⁵* 481). Nikolaos and Perigenes set their main defensive line between Sidon and Berytos, where imposing mountains fall into the sea at Capes Porphyrion and Platanos. Antiochus began his campaign at Arados, around the border of the Seleucid and Ptolemaic provinces at the River Eleutherus. Under Seleucid rule, at least, the provincial border between Syria and Phoenicia and the main province of Syria lay at the Eleutherus. Antiochus and his full army, accompanied by his fleet, marched down the coast, accepting submission from several cities, burning others and probably bypassing some, until he came to Porphyrion, setting the stage for the first engagement of the 218 BC campaign.

The Ptolemaic defences at Porphyrion are another excellent example of the use of fortified terrain as a force multiplier in defensive war. The passage by the sea is very narrow and requires any force heading south to pass westward for nearly a mile beneath the face of a commanding cliff, towering in many places 100 metres above them, before making the turn to the south. East of the passage, a shoulder of Porphyrion projects north and commands the plain 150 metres below. From it to the narrow passage on the western edge of the cape is nearly 1½ miles, and that is where Nikolaos concentrated his forces. The peak of Porphyion was nearly 1½ miles further inland, and comprises several connected heights with elevations of up to about 400 metres. Nikolaos posted a contingent of his forces there to prevent a turning attack. Antiochus launched three divisions of his army at the Ptolemaic defences: one poor division tried to force the passage, another

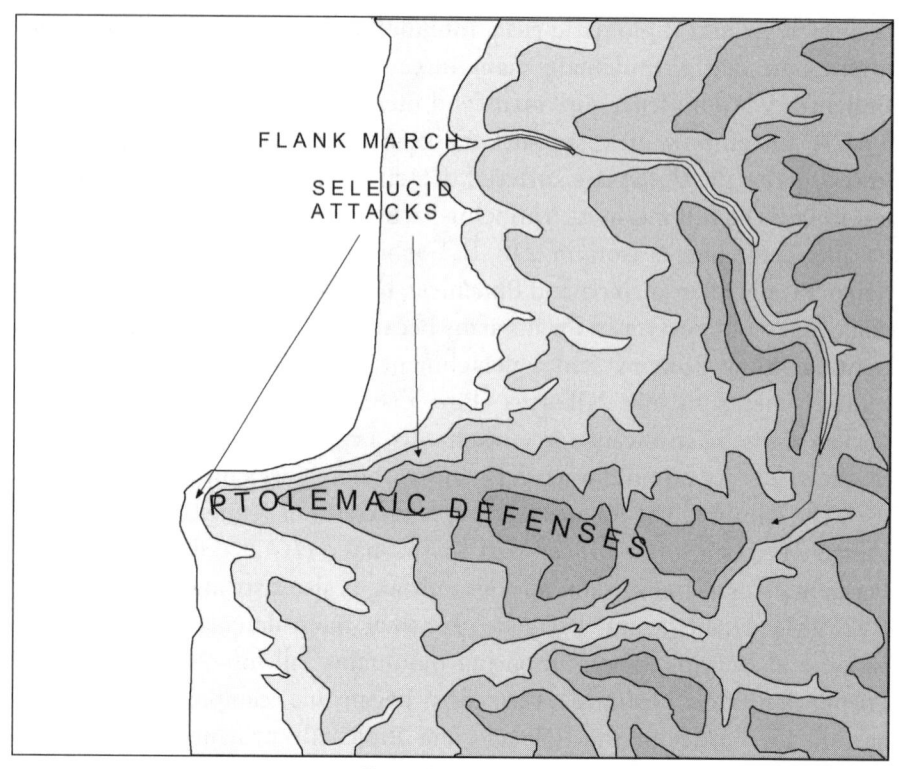

Cape Porphyrion.

attempting to scramble up the gentler slope on the eastern side of the shoulder to attack Nikolaos' right flank on his main line. Neither of these attacks had much hope of success. Theodotos the Aetolian led the third division, which probably advanced by a gorge that empties into the coastal plain 2 miles north of the Ptolemaic position. His troops seem to have mainly been from the Silvershields, and they undertook a 4½-mile turning march to ascend to the peak of Porphyrion. Even there, his troops would have had to attack across a front less than 200 metres wide in order to avoid a steep climb to face the Ptolemaic defenders at the top. The march would have taken hours, during which time the other two divisions waited for orders to attack and were needlessly subjected to missile fire. It seems that Nikolaos was caught by surprise by either Theodotos' manoeuvre or the strength of his force, because he failed to send reinforcements to the peak, where Theodotos' men eventually forced them back (Plb. 5.69.9). Theodotos' turning force then had a commanding position over the remainder of the Ptolemaic forces, and streaming down the slope – they were, after all, far from the main bodies engaged – they routed Nikolaos' army. The Ptolemaic forces retreated toward their secondary lines at Platanos and thence to Sidon, but according to Polybius (5.69.10) they suffered 4,000 killed or captured, which may have represented almost half of Nikolaos' field force.

Antiochus left Nikolaos and his forces inside Sidon and pushed into the interior of the province. Polybius (5.70.3) had him send his fleet 'back' to Tyre, which from the battle at Porphyrion or the encampment at Sidon makes no sense. Instead, Antiochus must have marched down to Ptolemais-Akko. From Ptolemais he marched down the Jezreel Valley toward the region of Galilee. There, he negotiated the surrender of both the Ptolemaic military settlement of Philoteris at Khirbet Kerak, a pretty Greek or Hellenized town by the sea, and the larger city of Scythopolis 16 miles south. These should have been two of the stronger and larger Ptolemaic positions in that region, but many of their men may have been shut up in Sidon with Nikolaos. The main military force in the region was at Mount Tabor, and Antiochus defeated them with a feigned retreat and ambush (Plb. 5.70.6–9). The Ptolemaic defensive strategy was in great danger by that point: the bulk of the force was in Sidon with Nikolaos, and it is unclear if they were able to force the lines to get out of the city until after the Battle of Raphia. Of the units that were left, one leading officer named Keraias and a cavalry commander named Hippolochos deserted to Antiochus, the latter bringing up to 400 cavalrymen with him (Plb. 5.70.10–11). Hippolochos was a Thessalian, and while 400 cavalrymen is a suspiciously large figure and suggests either some exaggeration of the mix of horse and foot or inflating of the number, it is conceivable that he should be identified as Hippolochos son of Alexippos, scion of one of the leading families in Larisa, and indeed in all of Thessaly.[7] He subsequently commanded Antiochus' Greek mercenaries at Raphia (Plb. 5.79.9).

From there, Antiochus pushed his army into the Dekapolis east of the Jordan, which he eventually subjugated. In the process of taking Abila he captured another Ptolemaic battalion, this time under 'Nikias, a friend and relative of Menneas' (Plb. 5.71.2). Polybius wrote the names and the significance of their relation as if the reader would know, which suggests two possibilities. Perhaps Menneas was the dynast of one of the tribal groups in the province, like the Tobiads at Ptolemais-Rabbathammon, or was an ancestor of the Ptolemaios son of Menneas who ruled the Ituraeans of the Marsyas Valley in the first-century BC (Jos. *Ant.* 14.7). The other possibility is that he was a significant Ptolemaic courtier: a Menneas was eponymous priest in 230 BC, and one of the most prominent courtiers of the early second century was Aristomenes son of Menneas. Either way, the regular Ptolemaic forces outside of Sidon were declining considerably as Antiochus defeated or suborned them in detail. Most of the remaining Ptolemaic forces were concentrated at Philadelphia-Rabbathammon, to which Antiochus laid a major and costly siege. Even after divisions of his army under Nikarchos and Theodotos made breaches in the wall, assaults 'night and day' failed to route the hardy Tobiad defenders. Antiochus finally gained the city when he dammed up its underground water supply (Plb. 5.71.4–10). Antiochus left 5,000 Greek mercenaries under Hippolochos to attempt a winter subjugation of Samaria (Plb. 5.72.11–12). His army camped at Ptolemais. By the end of the 218 BC campaign season, Antiochus had taken the Dekapolis, several key positions in Galilee at the junction of the Jordan and Jezreel valleys and much of the Phoenician coast as far south as Ptolemais, with the exception of Sidon. He as yet controlled nothing south of the Jezreel Valley or the territory from Galilee up to the Marsyas and east to Damascus. The Ptolemaic strategy had been costly, made worse by defections, but it had accomplished its purpose.

As spring arrived in 217 BC, it became clear that a major battle finally would take place. Antiochus finally learned that Ptolemy had gathered his full army and was preparing to leave Egypt (Plb. 5.79.3). He concentrated his own forces from their missions around the province, save perhaps a blocking force around Sidon. The remaining Ptolemaic defenders may have gone to Egypt to join the royal army; at least, Antiochus encountered no opposition as he marched down the coastal road from Ptolemais to Gaza, then Raphia. Antiochus had 62,000 foot, 6,000 horse and more than 100 war elephants. Ptolemy had 70,000 foot, 5,000 horse and over seventy war elephants. By late spring, the two armies had inched ever closer to one another along the frontiers of Syria, setting the stage for the great Battle of Raphia. But before getting on to the battle, we must consider the nature of the Ptolemaic reform that, according to Polybius, had taken place from late 219 to early 217 BC.

The Reform of the Ptolemaic Army from Polybian and Papyrological Perspectives

The Polybian reform narrative begins (5.62.7–8) with a statement on the dissolute state of the Ptolemaic military at the onset of the war: 'Ptolemy's obvious duty was to march to the help of his dominions and attack as they had been in such flagrant defiance of treaties, but was too weak to entertain any such project, *so completely had all military preparations been neglected*' (emphasis mine). The army was completely unprepared for war, so diplomatic efforts and a dogged mercenary defence in Syria and Phoenicia had to hold off the Seleucid advance while an army could be prepared. The ensuing reform had six features that can be tested in comparison to documentary papyri. First, the Polybian reform took place from late 219 to early 217 BC. Second, Sosibios and the king's newest favourite, Agathocles, established themselves in the interior, at Memphis, to host diplomatic embassies, and located the army and military reform at Alexandria, where diplomats would not see the great forces being readied (Plb. 5.63.7–8). Third, the heroes of the reform were Greeks from the mainland, 'in whom the spirit of Hellenic martial ardor and resourcefulness was still fresh'.[8] At least two of these, Echekrates and Phoxidas, Polybius recorded as having previously commanded mercenaries in the Antigonid army, while the whole corps of virtuous, experienced officers, all newly arrived in Egypt and as-yet unspoiled by it, included the Cretan Knopias, the Boeotian Sokrates, the Magnesian Eurylochos, the Aspendian Andromachos and the Argive Polykrates. The fourth and fifth features of the reform are the breaking up of the old regiments and formation of new ones, and the organization of those new regiments by age groups and ethnicities. Polybius described it thus:

> 'Taking the troops in hand they got them into shape by correct military methods. First of all they divided them according to their ages and ethnicities, and equipped them with panoplies suitable in each case, paying no attention to the manner in which they had previously been armed. In the next place they organized them as the necessities of the present situation required, breaking up the old regiments and abolishing the existing paymasters' lists, and having effected this, they drilled them, accustoming them not only to the word of command, but to the correct manipulation of their weapons.' (Plb. 5.63.14–64.2).

The sixth feature of the reform was the creation of a new Egyptian corps, armed in the Macedonian fashion and trained to function as heavy phalanx infantry. These were not created by the new officers, but were the brainchild of Sosibios himself. They were 20,000 strong, and thus instrumental in the expansion of the Ptolemaic field army prior to the battle at Raphia. All six of these features require adjustment when put under examination. A reform did happen, but neither when, where or how Polybius described.

The Polybian narrative depicted a languishing military apparatus in the years leading up to 219 BC. The previous chapter already showed that elephant-hunting in particular escalated significantly in the last years of Ptolemy III, while Magas' campaign or campaigns about the same time gave some components of the army Mediterranean operational experience. New military settlements were also undertaken in these same years. Seventy-aroura cavalry from the ethnic hipparchies and 30-aroura infantry received allotments in the Fayum around 222 BC.[9] Individual soldiers were also investing in their readiness in this period. A petition from January 222 BC reports that an officer from the infantry *agema* loaned 150 bronze drachmas to help a young 100-aroura cavalryman pay for '*kataphrakta* and *cheirida*' (*P.Enteux.* 45). We know of cavalrymen purchasing cataphract armour because this particular horseman did not pay the officer back quickly enough. Individual cataphract armour probably does not refer to armament for the horse, but heavy armour for the rider, covering the chest and stomach of course, perhaps the upper legs, and with the addition of lamellar *cheirida*, the arms. It is not customary to think of the Ptolemaic cavalry as including cataphracts; normally considered a Seleucid innovation, we may only surmise *kataphrakta* became a popular element in the Ptolemaic panoply prior to the outbreak of the Fourth Syrian War. Another reference to cataphract armour comes from 218 BC (*P.Enteux.* 32), in which relatives of a deceased cleruch bickered over the value of his cataphract armour, his *subarmalis* (a padded jacket worn beneath the armour) and his military cloak. Not everyone may have been keen for a new war: a recruitment call for police in 221 BC got two Sikyonians from a wealthy family to volunteer, even though most entry-level police were Egyptians. Their haste to join the police suggests things may have changed when Ptolemy IV became king, but the Ptolemaic army was active and expanding up to his coronation.

The Polybian narrative suggests the reform began after Antiochus' successes in the 219 BC campaign season, most of which came fairly late in the summer. But four texts from Genova come from an army camp, and contain requests for rations from groups of 30-aroura Macedonian infantry and cavalry troopers from the 4th hipparchy (*P.Genova* 3.103–106). They all date from May or June 219 BC, but indicate the men had been gathered in the camp since at least April that year. This means some sort of military mobilization had taken place as soon as Antiochus' move toward Seleukeia, and either before or in immediate response to Theodotos' treachery. If this evidence points toward earlier preparation for war, it undermines Polybius' narrative about the reform but actually deepens the criticism of Ptolemaic military leaders, who showed little readiness to take mobilized troops to confront an aggressive enemy. A campaign involving settlers certainly did happen in 219 BC: a 'Persian' in the Fayum filed a complaint against a Thracian cavalryman from the 1st hipparchy who hired him as his batman for the campaign, but did not pay him what was promised (*P.Enteux*. 48). The complaint does not specify the destination, but does state that the mobilization took place at the start of July 219 BC, not long after Antiochus began his attack on Koile Syria.

A study by Fischer-Bovet and Clarysse in 2012 queried specifically the restructuring of regiments in the reform. They found that there is evidence for a reform in the eponymous officers, especially in the cavalry, before the Fourth Syrian War. The old eponymous commanders mainly disappeared and in the Arsinoite nome they were not replaced, and soldiers and administrative records only used their numbered regiments. In the Fayum, all administrative records and most private business or petitions went exclusively by numbered hipparchies starting in 222 BC, the last year of Ptolemy III and first regnal year of Ptolemy IV.[10] There are just two, possibly three, examples attesting eponymous commanders for 100-aroura cavalry in the Arsinoites after 223 BC, all petitions. *P.Enteux*. 16 (221 BC) does not actually include an eponym, but there is a gap between the soldier's name and cavalry regiment large enough to require either an Alexandrian patronymic and deme or an eponymous commander. *P.Enteux*. 22 (218 BC) is a widow's request that her deceased husband's brother-in-law be named as her guardian for legal business. Her use of an eponymous commander is not strong evidence that the eponymous commands were still in normal usage. The last case is *SB* 20.15068 (April 217 BC), a petition to the king from a cavalryman who was at that time already in the king's camp, preparing to march to Raphia. The use of the eponymous commander with regimental number in that papyrus should at least mean that new eponymous commanders had not yet been assigned. It is possible the cavalryman kept the eponymous command in his text for rhetorical flourish, but it is hard to say. If the eponymous commands still existed officially by April 217 BC, then they were not done away with before Raphia at all. To the extent there was a change, it occurred about 222 BC, before the Fourth Syrian War even started.

The Oxyrhynchite hipparchy makes an interesting case for three reasons: the eponymous commander of the unit did change not long before Raphia, from Zoilos to Philon; the hipparchy campaigned in the Fourth Syrian War under its hipparch Philon (*BGU* 10.1905) and fought at the battle of Raphia (*P.Frankf.* 7); and papyri provide the names of fifty or more soldiers from the two units, permitting a study of personnel. Like the changes in the numbered hipparchies, Philon had definitely taken command of the hipparchy well before the Polybian date for the reform, no later than 223/222 BC (*P.Grad.* 8, *P.Hib.* 1.90). Furthermore, the unit's personnel stayed intact after the reform. While Cyrenaians constituted nearly half of the manpower in the hipparchy, they fought alongside Athenians, Thracians, Mysians, Judeans and other soldiers of many diverse origins, both before and after the reform. The lack of a shake-up in personnel points to some of the difficulties in Polybius' narrative: a reform along ethnic lines would have required uprooting men from different parts of Egypt or organizing new military units that stretched across many provinces. One particular document, *P.Frankf.* 7 (217 BC), contains a narrative of the war within one cavalryman's complaint to the king regarding the abuse of his property during the extensive wartime mobilizations. The plaintiff was very likely Eupolis of Athens, a settler attested from 230–212 BC. When the cavalrymen were mobilized, the unit's *logeutai*, who collected taxes from the men in peacetime and facilitated other financial business, also oversaw the management of their allotments. Eupolis, who had been one of the *logeutai* under Zoilos back in 230 BC, accused one of the unit's current *logetuai* of seeking the office 'to avoid campaigning' and abusing it to seize Eupolis' property.[11] This transpired over a period of three years, when the hipparchy mobilized each year and served in the company of the king, first at Pelusium in 219 BC, then in the Boubastite nome in 218 and Syria in 217.[12] We must conclude that, at least among the cavalry, the reform Polybius described grossly exaggerated the extent to which Ptolemaic regiments were broken down and rebuilt.

Another detail in the same papyrus, that the Oxyrhynchite cavalry spent 218 BC around Boubastis, puts another aspect of Polybius' tale in doubt. According to Polybius, the reform took place at Alexandria and embassies were hosted at Memphis. Boubastis is a short journey into the Delta from Memphis. The presence of the cavalry at Boubastis suggests it was the chosen location for training the army, not Alexandria. This makes a lot of sense: Alexandria was a cosmopolitan city, and there would have been little hope Ptolemy could have kept his preparations secret if they were taking place at Alexandria, where traders at least would certainly have noticed 70,000 soldiers encamped beyond the walls. Further evidence that the army was gathering around Memphis and Boubastis is *P.Petr.* 2.20, a text from the last weeks of 218 BC, which concerns the transport of grain for elephants to the vicinity of Memphis. If the elephants were at Memphis, then presumably the army was concentrating there as well, although they did not march for Pelusium until the spring.

In Polybius' narrative, not only were the regiments broken down and reconstituted, but the personnel in them were completely reorganized by age and ethnicity. This implies that the whole military institutions of Ptolemaic Egypt were taken apart down to the level of the individual soldiers. This would mean Macedonians were separated from Thracians, Cretans from other Greeks and Jews from Anatolians, and the new regiments reconstituted among those groups based on age. The addition of ethnically suited panoplies for the new regiments would suggest that true Macedonians served in the phalanx and cavalry, Thessalians in the cavalry, Thracians as peltasts or light cavalry, Cretans as archers, and so on. Even more, the narrative reflects attitudes of Greek exceptionalism, repeats the common refrain of inferior Egyptian and Oriental forces and tells a fanciful story of an ethnographic military reform which should evoke memories of Herodotos' ethnographic catalogue of Xerxes' army[13] or Homer's catalogue of ships.[14] It bears no correlation to the personnel records that survive from Ptolemaic Egypt, where, for example, from 218–210 BC Thracians are identified in Philon's hipparchy (*BGU* 6.1275, 215 BC), the 1st hipparchy (*P.Enteux.* 48, 218 BC) and the 5th hipparchy (*P.Petr.* 3.34, 210 BC).

The military units of the Ptolemaic army remained, with the exception of the phalanx, as diverse as ever as the decisive Battle of Raphia drew closer. The phalanx, comprised largely or even wholly of men who were, in official terms, Macedonians, was only expanded in preparation for the war. New men, some of them verifiably not Macedonians, joined the settler phalanx as Macedonians in the period of reform. Thirty-aroura Macedonians are not attested in the Oxyrhynchite nome until the Fourth Syrian War, but the sudden appearance of them in a dozen different texts suggests they received allotments as part of the reform, even before Raphia. One of these men, Strato son of Stratios, is attested in *BGU* 6.1265 (214/213 BC). In the document, he and his brother leased a *kleros* from a horseman in Philon's hipparchy. His brother, however, was not a Macedonian, but a well-attested Thracian, Aristolochos. Their father, Stratios son of Strato, was also a Thracian, and like Aristolochos a civilian (*P.Hib.* 1.37, 235 BC). It is clear, then, that Strato was born a Thracian, but enrolled in the infantry *as a Macedonian* during the recruitment drive at the start of the Fourth Syrian War. His is the clearest case of the flexibility of the Macedonian military ethnicity. But how common was his situation? Hermias, a 30-aroura Macedonian living in the town of Tholthis, is attested in *BGU* 10.1943 (215/214 BC) and *P.Frankf.* 4 (216/215 BC) leasing out his allotment. But *BGU* 10.1946.15 (213/212 BC) names another man from Tholthis, Agathinos son of Hermias, as a Mytilenian. There is no way to securely identify Agathinos as the son of Hermias, but the Greek community at Tholthis was not very large, and many of the soldiers (like Hermias) and many of the *epigonoi* (like Agathinos) were related. The evidence is inconclusive, but given the case of Strato and the absence of any other Hermias attested in the Oxyrhynchites in the whole third century BC, it is likely that Hermias, too, was given Macedonian ethnic status upon his recruitment into the phalanx.

The phalanx at Raphia had 25,000 men in it. What is not clear is whether all 25,000 of these men were from the settler infantry class, the *triakontarouroi Makedones*. I previously argued for eight to sixteen chiliarchies, based on the appearance of the 7th regiment in records from the Fayum and the prevalence of 16,000 as the ideal size in tactical manuals. The appearance of the Oxyrhynchite infantry suggests they were part of an expansion of the phalanx. The men were not, so long as the archive survives (about 200 BC), incorporated into a numbered regiment. This suggests that, while they received settlements, the army administration chose not to formalize the expanded phalanx corps. At the same time, there are two questions that are difficult to answer. The first is this: did Alexandrian citizens contribute some of the manpower of the phalanx, and if so, did they do so as part of the numbered regiments? Just one of the 30-aroura Macedonians from the Oxyrhynchite nome gave his information in documents with his father's name, a requirement only for Alexandrians serving in the army, which suggests Apollodotos son of Kotys may have been an Alexandrian and a 30-aroura Macedonian (*BGU* 14.2397). One other Alexandrian who was also a Macedonian appears in a text from the Fayum (*P.Enteux.* 88), but his military status is uncertain.

The second question is: where did the semi-professional units serve? Many solders in the Ptolemaic army in Egypt were classed as *misthophoroi*, paid soldiers, even though some of them also had allotments. They were distinct from *xenoi*, foreign soldiers, who fit the more conventional idea of mercenaries. Some 8,000 mercenaries trained for Raphia as a complement to the phalanx. Undoubtedly *xenoi* served in that group of 8,000. The allocation of the *misthophoroi* to the 25,000 or to the 8,000 is less clear. Many Alexandrians served in the *misthophoroi* cavalry, and it seems likely that quite a few also did so in the infantry. Serving infantry units attested within a few years either side of the Fourth Syrian War include the eponymous commands of Endios, with men from Macedon, Thrace and Chalcis; of Agesarchos, attested from a single Alexandrian soldier; of Dionysios, also attested through an Alexandrian; of Kephalon; and of Maraios. Maraios is probably an Oscan name, similar to Marius, which might suggest the command had a large number of Italians in it, but the only soldiers who happen to be attested in papyri were from Chalcedon and Amphipholis.[15] Agesarchos' command was described as being either '*p[ezoi]*' or '*p[eltastai]*', and if the latter reading happened to be correct – it fits the space better – it would be the first mention of the peltasts in the papyri and would strongly suggest the elite unit comprised Alexandrian citizens. Ptolemaios son of Agesarchos was one of the leading courtiers at Alexandria in about 204 BC, which may confirm the importance of Agesarchos' command (Plb. 15.25.14). Dionysios' command, the other that included an Alexandrian, is not conclusively infantry or cavalry. The final conclusion should be this: the 25,000 Greco-Macedonian phalangites at Raphia represented a significant recruitment of new soldiers to augment the *triakontarouroi* Macedonians, and many of the new soldiers were added to that large settler class.

The 30-aroura Macedonians from the Arsinoite were quite active in the war. Their requests for wine rations while at a – or *the* – military camp include the names and often hometowns of nearly twenty infantrymen. The table below presents the information on those men:

The Macedonians from P.Genova 3.103–5

Soldier	Patronymic	Settlement	Nome Province	Papyrus
Spartakos	Ptolemaios	Kerkeesis	Polemon	103
Spokes	-amios	Oxyrhyncha	Polemon	103
Stephanos	Stasikrates	Euhemeria	Themistos	103
Agron	Theodoros	Euhemeria	Themistos	103
Patron	Ptolemaios	Kanopias	Themistos	103
Ptolemaios	Demeas	Kanopias	Themistos	103
Diokles	Moschos	Phnebiesi	Polemon	103
Philippos	Apollonios	Unknown		103
Menandros	Demetrios	Philoteris	Herakleides	104
Philippos	Demetrios	Philoteris	Herakleides	104

Soldier	Patronymic	Settlement	Nome Province	Papyrus
Philotas	Philotas	Arsinoe	Herakleides	104
Nikias	Polemon	Unknown		104
Apollonios	Herakleides	Unknown		104
Amyntas	Amyntas	Unknown		104
Aristomachos	{Missing}	Oxyrhyncha	Polemon	105
Ariston	Theot-?/Theos?	Oxyrhyncha	Polemon	105
Menandros	P-	Gomon	Polemon	105
{Missing}	{Missing}	Gomon	Polemon	105
Aristomachos	Her(-akleides?)	Unknown		105

Where their settlements are known, it shows that seven were from the southern district of Polemon, four from the western district of Themistos and three from the Herakleides district in the centre and north of the Fayum. No later than the time of the war, the 30-aroura Macedonians from the Fayum, although divided between three numbered regiments, had a single administrative office that helped facilitate their needs or the administration of their allotments during war. The clearest insight into that administration, called the *syntaxis* of the 30-aroura Macedonians settled in the Arsinoites, is in the papyrus *P.Lille* 1.4 from 217 BC. It is a docketed collection of correspondence in the office of Lamiskos, one of the officers serving the *syntaxis*. Lamiskos' chief responsibility was agricultural oversight: seed schedules, harvests, dues and the like. He and his superior, Stratokles, who was head of the centralized office, handled all manner of business in 217 BC, especially with the army mobilizing. The soldiers were not present to farm their land and surely many failed to lease it out, so the officers of the *syntaxis* were responsible for handling the harvest in particular for a vast array of non-contiguous smallholdings. Three entries survive in fairly complete state; two of these are death notices for soldiers. One notification came from the office of Marsyas, whom we know from other sources was *archigrammateus* in the royal army, chief administrative officer, reporting the deaths of two Macedonian soldiers a couple of months before the army left for Raphia. The other came from the office of Strato, *grammateus* of the cleruchs for the whole kingdom, and concerned an infantryman who died on about 1 March 217 BC. For kingdom-level officials to notify the local administration of dead cleruchs, the soldiers must have died away from the Fayum, either with the royal army at the training camp or in operations in Syria. There are details missing from Polybius' account of the reforms that might help us make sense of the three dead infantrymen a few months before the army left Pelusium. Were they killed in rigorous training exercises? Or were some Macedonian regiments engaged in combat in Syria the previous year, when according to Polybius they were at the camp? Finally, the message from Strato exhorted the officers of the *syntaxis* to discern whether the dead had sons who could take their places and assume the *kleros* and its management. Strato's exhortation referenced a royal decree on the subject and marks an important turning point in the institutional history of the Ptolemaic army.

The intense additional recruitment in support of the army that fought at Raphia encouraged or perhaps necessitated some new concessions from the state to individual soldiers. *P.Lille* 1.4 provides evidence of a decree that required royal administrators taking possession of a deceased soldier's allotment to register it in the name of their son and successor within a certain number of days.[16] In many cases sons probably did eventually attain their father's allotment, but the new royal decree clearly accelerated that process, signalled the heritability of the *kleros* and began paving the way for the eventual near-privatization of the *kleros*. Another papyrus contains some more details about the royal decree and its new regulations for cleruchs.[17] It includes a list of privileges and obligations tied to being a cleruch. The first surviving line refers to a military uniform and the following line to wages, then regulations about property and slaves; finally, lines 17–22 concern the *kleros* itself: the military settler was encouraged to name his successor and given permission to leave the *kleros* to his successor, but only upon death.[18] Adjusting the property status of allotments should have made military service more appealing, especially where a major battle loomed ahead: soldiers could know, rather than hope, that their family would retain their property if they died.

While thousands of new 30-aroura Macedonians and other new infantry drawn from the *epigonoi* swelled the ranks of the phalanx up to 25,000 men, Polybius put more emphasis, understandably, on Sosibios' novel creation of an Egyptian phalanx with 20,000 *phalangites* (Plb. 5.65.9). Egyptians had played a role in the Macedonian armies of Egypt from the beginning. Six thousand Egyptians learned Greek language and Macedonian military arts in Alexander's Page programme. Thousands of Egyptians fought at Gaza, divided between the missile troops and porters on the one hand, and the battle-line Egyptians on the other, whom I suggest should be identified with graduates of similar training and Hellenizing programmes and with some of the ancestors of third-century 'Persians' in the documentary papyri. Thousands more served in the Ptolemaic navy throughout Ptolemaic history. Ptolemy II raised an elite corps for the palace guard from the elite priestly-military families of the Delta. Nonetheless, the appearance of fully 20,000 Egyptians in a phalanx is striking and poses several key questions. Were the 20,000 *machimoi* other Egyptians, or Hellenized and reclassed as Persians? Were they officered by Greeks or Hellenized Egyptians? And were they settled during or after the war?

Documentary evidence shows there was a substantial shift in the roles of *machimoi* between the mid-third century and the early second century BC. Whether the shift occurred during the Fourth Syrian War or closer to 200 BC is unclear, but some scholars have felt safer with a later date.[19] After reviewing this shift, it will be possible to look at the few documents for the period of the war to consider how the reform related to the observable shift. Before the Fourth Syrian War, many *machimoi* performed paramilitary roles and could be hired by officials for security purposes.[20] There was a sub-class of 5-aroura *machimoi* who may have had some military duties, and their role might have increased under Ptolemy III.[21] In theory other Egyptians, whether or not they were classified as *machimoi* by the Ptolemaic administration, could be mobilized for military duties, such as elephant hunts (*UPZ* 2.157). Second-century BC evidence attests *epilektoi* (picked or elite) *machimoi* beginning about 197 BC, as well a *laarchia*, a unit comprising *machimoi* of multiple classes (*OGIS* 731). The elite sub-unit of *epilektoi* in *OGIS* 731, who served in the palace guard, may have been connected to Ptolemy II's guard unit.[22] No later than the 170s BC there were at least three classes of *machimoi* – the *epilektoi*, 7-aroura and 5-aroura *machimoi* – while by the later second century there were also 10-aroura and cavalry *machimoi*, making a total of five different classes.[23]

Texts from the period of the Fourth Syrian War strongly suggest that the reform significantly altered the military role of some *machimoi* and began including them in the settler system in a more systematic fashion. The first key text is *P.Köln*. 11.452, from October 219 BC and the Herakleopolite nome.[24] In it, the son of Nechthembes, a *pentakosiarch*, or commander of 500 men, wrote to the secretary of the *machimoi* about difficulties with the *kleros* while his father was in Syria. This proves the existence of a larger military apparatus for *machimoi* than had ever been attested before. The existence of the *pentakosiarchy* strongly suggests the reform of the *machimoi* followed the pattern of line infantry units. The settlement of officers may have preceded the settlement of regular soldiers; this was often the case with Greeks as well. More significantly, the letter reveals that Nechthembes was in Syria in late 219 BC. Rather than helping to oversee training of Egyptian recruits in Macedonian military arts, he was leading them in a war zone in a campaign where Polybius' narrative kept the main army in Pelusium. That might suggest Sosibios began the militarization of the *machimoi* earlier, and Nechthembes' was one of the first contingents ready for battle. However, there is a possibility the papyrus actually dates to 202 BC.[25] If so, the dating difficulty dissolves, but the text still amply demonstrates fully militarized *machimoi* in the years after the reforms of the Fourth Syrian War.

The next text, *P.Tebt.* 3.2.884 (spring 210 BC), records a wage distribution (*opsonion*) and personnel roster for the '*machimoi* under Ptolemaios'. Men were paid at the rate of 4 obols per day, on the low side of average among Greek mercenaries in the Hellenistic period, and at least double what most *machimoi* were paid earlier in the century in Ptolemaic Egypt.[26] The personnel roster contains fourteen names, of which the first two and the last are Greek – Ptolemaios twice, Isidoros once – and the rest are Egyptian. The Greek names are dynastic and Egyptian-theophoric, which may suggest they were Hellenized Egyptians. In phalanx files it was customary for the first two men and the last to be a file's senior officers. A file should have sixteen men as its paper strength, but fourteen is a perfectly reasonable actual strength. The presence and organization of men with Greek names in the small unit, and their above-average wages, suggest this, too, is a reference to some of the phalanx *machimoi*.

That leaves the question of settlement, and how the Fourth Syrian War's 20,000 phalanx *machimoi* related to the documentary evidence for the classes of *machimoi* in Ptolemaic Egypt. The best evidence for new settlements about the time of the war, connected to Egyptians but not specifically to *machimoi*, is for 10-aroura allotments. This is surprising, since the 10-aroura *machimoi* are not securely attested again until the later second century BC. However, it is possible that the *epilektoi* and 10-aroura *machimoi* were actually the same classes. The edition of *P.Tebt.* 1.5 (118 BC) separates the two classes, but the papyrus itself supports a reading such as 'the *epilektoi machimoi*, who are 10-aroura'. If the equivalence of the classes is correct, the *epilektoi* are attested at the start of the second century BC and can be connected back to Sosibios' phalanx. Ten-aroura allotments appear in three texts from the period of the Fourth Syrian War. *P.Sorb.* 1.43 (March 219 BC) concerns a dispute over a 10-aroura allotment claimed by an Egyptian, Petōos son of Horus, but apparently impounded by the local police chief. *P.Heid.Dem.inv.* 46, for which Monson suggested a late third-century BC date, mentions one 10-aroura Egyptian, Herieus son of Harmiysis, who was also cultivating some royal land.[27] Finally, *P.Hib.* 2.265, from about 204 BC, refers to at least five 10-aroura *kleroi*, for which four of the cleruchs' names are legible: the Egyptian Imouthes and three men with Greek names, Apollonios, Demetrios and Antigonos. Based on the personnel in the *machimoi* of Ptolemaios, many of the junior officers of the phalangite *machimoi* were either Greeks or, more likely, Hellenized Egyptians. When distributing new 10-aroura allotments, senior and junior officers were probably prioritized over the rank-and-file. If all 20,000 Egyptian *machimoi* were granted 10-aroura allotments in the period of the Fourth Syrian War, it seems very few were in the regions of Middle Egypt where most surviving papyri originated.

The creation of a phalanx of 20,000 Egyptians was a major innovation, attributed to Sosibios, and may have been the decisive addition to the Ptolemaic army at Raphia. Its impacts on *machimoi* institutions back in Egypt are evident, but not at the same scale. This may be explainable through subsequent politics rather than supposing a mistake in Polybius' narrative. For Sosibios and Ptolemy IV, the 20,000 Egyptian pikemen represented untapped potential, a counter to the machinations of Greek mercenary officers like Theodotos the Aetolian (undoubtedly they did not blame themselves for his treachery), and thus a parallel to Alexander's divisive phalanx of 30,000 Iranian *epigonoi*. Alexander's 'successors' outraged his veteran Macedonians. The reception of the Egyptian phalanx by the Greeks of Egypt is harder to gauge. If successful, it could enable aggressive military action abroad due to the far larger population base, and free the military from devoting so much of its resources to a competing mission: the colonization and control of Egypt. But in the years after the battle an Egyptian revolt broke out, which Polybius attributed to the Egyptian military class's experience of victory and dissatisfaction with second-class status in their own country (Plb. 5.107.1–3).[28] Polybius called Sosibios' arming of the Egyptians a 'useful expedient at the time, but a grave mistake for the future'. The problem may not have been with the creation of the Egyptian phalanx, but with an uneven follow-through that eventually provoked the *machimoi* to lead the way in a revolt against Ptolemy.

Now it is possible to review the Polybian narrative of military reform. Polybius' claims about the foreign expertise behind the reform cannot be validated or rejected: only Polykrates of Argos is identifiable outside of Polybius' text. The second-in-command of the Macedonian phalanx, Ptolemaios son of Thraseas, was from an elite Alexandrian family originally from Aspendos, but Polybius' narrative tacitly acknowledged he was not from abroad. There are also some reasons to doubt Andromachos of

Aspendos was a 'newcomer from Greece': so many Aspendians had entered Ptolemaic service over the years (including the Thraseas family), the name was popular among several illustrious families in Ptolemaic Egypt, and while Polybius said he and Polykrates were 'fresh from Greece', Aspendos is far off in the Pamphylian plain. Beyond that, Phoxidas is a *hapax* and the rest are impossible to identify. The table below depicts the results for all six points identified with the reform:

Category	Polybian Narrative	Documentary Evidence
Date	219–217 BC	As early as 223 BC
Location	Alexandria	Bousiris
Officers	Virtuous Mainland Greeks	Some long-serving families among mainland Greeks
Regiments	New Commands	Eponymous Officer shifts between 223 and 219 BC
Organization	By Age & Ethnicity	Continued diversity; no evidence for reorganization; non-Macedonians incorporated into the *triakontarouroi* as Macedonians
Key Addition	20,000 Egyptian phalangites	Increased militarization of *machimoi* and expansion of the *triakontarouroi* Macedonians

Most criticism of Polybius' narrative has been levelled at his description of Seleucid affairs.[29] These critiques do seem to indicate that Polybius' source was neither particularly friendly towards nor well acquainted with affairs at the Seleucid court. At the same time, this review of the evidence also raises significant problems with Polybius' narrative of Ptolemaic affairs. It suggests that Polybius' source material was knowledgeable of Ptolemaic affairs, but interested in heightening the drama of the account by overstating Ptolemaic unpreparedness in practically every facet. To the extent that Polybius described a period, lasting several years, of mobilization and training, his narrative seems to have been adequate. The infantry reforms, however, emphasize a very different story from that of Polybius. The reform relied upon a massive expansion of phalanx manpower, both Egyptian and Macedonian. The major story of Ptolemaic war preparation was not a sweeping ethnographic reorganization of the army, and certainly not the use of blood ethnicity to restructure and homogenize the regiments of the army, but nor was it the revitalization of incompetent soldiers through the hand-holding of valorous Greek aristocrats. The major story was the addition of as many as 30,000 men to the phalanx, and that reform changed the course of the Battle of Raphia.

The Campaign and Battle of Raphia, 217 BC

Polybius (5.79) provides a fairly thorough accounting of the armies on both sides at Raphia. These figures, as the most detailed army list for the Ptolemaic army from any source, and one of the more complete lists for the Seleucid army, have been studied repeatedly.[30] The table below breaks down the two armies at Raphia, using the identifications from chapter 2 of the present study.

In examining these numbers, and especially the differentials, the most striking disparity is in phalanx infantry. The Seleucid army actually outnumbered the Ptolemaic force in every other category, but the Ptolemaic phalanx was very nearly twice as large as the Seleucid phalanx. In thinking about the reform narrative, the size of the phalanx suggests something else: that some number of Syrian and Anatolian military settlers, whom the Ptolemaic army may have fielded as medium or light infantry previously, must have been re-equipped or retrained for service among the heavy infantry of the phalanx. For a pitched battle in the coastal plain of Palestine, a massive phalanx made a lot of sense, and the reforms that helped create such a large phalanx were vindicated by the result of the battle.

The Opening Moves

By late spring, Ptolemy's army had concentrated at Pelusium; Antiochus had learned that Ptolemy was bringing an army into Syria and begun gathering all of his forces too. The addition of 10,000 Arab allies from Hawran helped Antiochus come closer to evening the tally, but as he began to march south from Ptolemais-Akko he may already have known his army was smaller by several thousand men. No doubt many in his force despised the Ptolemaic army for waiting so long to seek battle, and scorned the playboy king Ptolemy. Most of all they probably discounted the value of the Egyptian phalanx. The battle would mark an important test: could Egyptian soldiers kitted with Macedonian equipment go up against Macedonians in battle? Some

The Fourth Syrian War and the Battle of Raphia 255

Military Class	Seleucids	Ptolemies	Ptolemaic +/-
Cavalry	4,000 horse under Antipater 2,000 horse under Themison	700 household cavalry 2,300 settler cavalry 2,000 cavalry: foreign mercenaries, *misthophoroi* settlers and perhaps 70-*aroura* settlers	−1,000 horse
Elite Infantry	10,000 'mostly' *argyraspides*[31]	3,000 royal agema 2,000 peltasts	−5,000 elite infantry
Phalanx Infantry	20,000 phalangites 5,000 *euzonoi* phalangites[32] 5,000 mercenaries	25,000 phalangites, mostly 30-*aroura* Macedonians 20,000 Egyptian phalangites 8,000 mercenaries 3,000 Libyan–Cyrenaican phalangites	+26,000 phalanx infantry
Medium Infantry	10,000 Arab *symmachoi* 5,000 Iranian infantry 1,000 Kardakes[33]	6,000 Galatians and Thracians[34]	−10,000 medium infantry
Light Infantry	2,500 Cretans and Neo-Cretans 2,000 Persian and Agrianian archers 1,000 Thracian *euzonoi*[35] 500 Atropatene *akontistai*[36]	3,000 Cretans and Neo-Cretans	−3,000 light infantry
Elephants	102 elephants	73 elephants	−29 elephants
Total	62,000 foot, 6,000 horse, 102 elephants	70,000 foot, 5,000 horse, 73 elephants	

in the Ptolemaic camp may also have feared the bulk of their advantage – the 20,000 Egyptians – was a paper tiger.

The armies came within sight of one another south-west of the town of Raphia, a few miles south of the city of Gaza. After leaving Pelusium on 13 June, Ptolemy's army encamped on the fifth day about 6 miles from Raphia. Antiochus reached Gaza about the same time, and the next day, as night fell, pitched his camp just a little over a mile from Ptolemy's lines (Plb. 5.80.3–4). A couple of days later, Antiochus moved his camp even closer, to a little more than half a mile from the Ptolemaic camp. This proximity is a little hard to believe, given the sizes of the forces involved. Even a mile apart, the skirmishes and duels that struck up before the day of battle are perfectly comprehensible (Plb. 5.80.7). These skirmishes provided an opportunity for the warriors on both sides to make themselves conspicuous, and hearkened back to archaic Greek traditions of single combat. Some of the skirmishes were between foraging parties, and some were presumably between pickets. Polybius' mention of cavalry missile exchanges and even infantry fights suggests aristocratic duels broke out between young fighters aspiring for glory. The presence of elite troops in these ritualistic combats also explains how Theodotos the Aetolian managed to make an inconspicuous dash through the skirmish lines in an attempt on Ptolemy's life. One day the skirmishes had 'carried close to the Ptolemaic camp' and Theodotos, who was among the skirmishers, noted the location of the royal tent. The next day, Theodotos got inside the camp and sought to find Ptolemy in his tent (Plb. 5.81.4). He failed, but managed to escape. The whole story highlights an aspect of Hellenistic military culture that is often overlooked: the continuation, or rediscovery, of Archaic-era beliefs and practices about individual soldiers performing acts of heroism to demonstrate their courage. Whatever the particular nature of soldierly professionalism in the Hellenistic age, it was at least potentially commensurate with such acts.

The armies encamped and skirmished for five days before the kings committed their forces to battle on 22 June (Plb. 5.82.1). In Polybius, the kings just decide it is the day for battle. However, a little more can be said about this. With 143,000 soldiers and thousands of their attendants on hand, the two concentrated encampments had become, temporarily, one of the larger human settlements in the world. Feeding such a concentration of people, horses and elephants was an incredible challenge. Antigonus' attempt to invade Egypt had failed because he could not manage food supplies well enough for the more than 80,000 men with him. Whatever men had carried with them when they left Pelusium and Ptolemais, they had expended by the time the two sides set up their camps south of Raphia. So for the two massive armies the question had become how long they could maintain their posture in the desert before they suffered a supply problem. Ptolemy was in the better position: the Ptolemaic fleet could ensure transports could reach his forces, and the overland route to Pelusium and all its storehouses was only a little over 100 miles. Antiochus had a more difficult supply position: he controlled Ptolemais and had surely accumulated large harvests from the Jezreel Valley the previous year, but most of the 130 miles between Ptolemais and his camp were not firmly in his hands. His more precarious position might explain his aggressiveness in moving the camp to within a half-mile of Ptolemy's lines. It would not have been inconsistent with Polybius' description of Ptolemy's character if the Egyptian king had waited until Antiochus was forced to withdraw. But after all the work putting the army together, it was time to use it: on 22 June, Ptolemy began leading out his troops, and Antiochus led out his.

Each king positioned himself with his best cavalry and auxiliaries on the western flank of the battlefield. In the centre, the phalanxes faced off, some 45,000 on the Ptolemaic side and 30,000 on the Seleucid. Despite the disparity in size, there is no indication in the text that the Ptolemaic phalanx overlapped the Seleucid one in any significant measure. This suggests that the Ptolemaic army formed up in half-again normal depth, or about twenty-four ranks of men per file. Each king surrounded himself with some of his best cavalry – 3,000 with Ptolemy and 4,000 with Antiochus – the larger part of their war elephants and some of their best infantry. Antiochus put his Cretans, his Greek mercenaries and his 5,000 light-kit (*euzonoi*) phalangites in his right wing, some 12,500 men in total. Ptolemy had his 3,000 Cretans supporting his elephants, then the remainder of the troops on the left wing were all elite Greeks: 5,000 from the peltasts and *agema* and 3,000 Cyrenaicans. All 8,000 may have been, and certainly the latter were, equipped as phalangites. Ptolemy's right wing included 8,000 Greek mercenaries, 6,000 Gauls and Thracians and the remaining 2,000 cavalry, the horse under Echekrates. Antiochus had posted nearly 20,000 auxiliary foot and 2,000 additional cavalry on his left. The western flank and centre were tests of best on best, while the engagement on the eastern flank had more the nature of quality against quantity.

The Battle

The battle began on the western flank, where the kings, the cavalry and the war elephants commenced the engagement. Antiochus' right wing first bested the Ptolemaic left in the clash of elephants, which had such a dramatic effect that much of Ptolemy's left collapsed. Antiochus' attack on the Ptolemaic left exhibited some features of an attempted double-envelopment. The elephant attack drove toward the middle of the Ptolemaic left wing, where the *agema* anchored the left of the line. The Ptolemaic elephants did not fight for long, but fled from the Indian elephants precipitously. The *agema* faced the onslaught of their own fleeing elephants, whose numbers were almost certainly too many to attempt to open channels through which they could pass. The elite guard troops broke. At the same time, Antiochus attacked around the right flank of his elephants with his cavalry against the royal cavalry led by Ptolemy and Polykrates. On the left flank of the elephants, the 10,000 Greek mercenaries and light-kit phalangites attacked the 5,000 peltasts and Cyrenaicans. The latter contingent held their ground, but the peltasts had already broken their formation to avoid some of the routing elephants (Plb. 5.84.9) and were caught out of formation, potentially outflanked by half of the Greek mercenaries. Fairly early in the battle, therefore, the Ptolemaic left wing was either withdrawing or routing.

After a poor start on the western flank, the actions on the eastern flank and then in the centre recovered the day for the Ptolemies. First, Echekrates ordered the infantry, 14,000 professional troops, to charge the auxiliary forces opposite them. Using their dust and the elephants on his front as a screen, he led his cavalry over the dunes that bordered the eastern flank, dashed up to the Seleucid lines, then swept back over the dunes onto the flank and rear of the 2,000 Seleucid cavalry (Plb. 5.85.3). The infantry in the Ptolemaic right wing defeated their enemies in hand-to-hand combat, and together with Echekrates' cavalry pursued their enemy toward Raphia. In the centre, 75,000 phalangites were still standing in ranks and had not yet moved forward for battle. At that point, according to Polybius' source, Ptolemy IV and Arsinoe appeared in the phalanx, the king showing himself to his troops in front of their lines and encouraging them to attack (Plb. 5.85.8). Ptolemy had been with the cavalry on the extreme left of the Ptolemaic army, a mile from the phalanx, and that force was pushed back and parts of it routed. Either the pursuit had streamed toward the centre of the left wing, where the *agema* had retreated and allowed Ptolemy to dash behind the advancing Seleucids with some of his men and seek shelter in the phalanx, or this is a case of Ptolemaic propaganda. Whatever Ptolemy's role, the Ptolemaic phalanx levelled its sarissa pikes and charged. The fight between the Silvershields and Macedonians was fierce and prolonged, but the Seleucid settler phalanx fled soon after they received the Ptolemaic charge, delivered mainly by the Egyptian phalanx under Sosibios' command.

As the dust cleared from the crush of phalanxes, the men from the Ptolemaic right flank were rounding up prisoners from the defeated Seleucid army and pursuing them as far as Gaza. By dusk, the thousands of men retreating and pursuing, withdrawing and regrouping stretched for miles, from the Ptolemaic camp south-west of Raphia to the walls of the town 6 miles away. The right flank of the Seleucid army, composed of crack mercenary contingents, the cavalry and the elephants, withdrew ahead of the Ptolemaic army and mostly intact. Antiochus and his guard cavalry, who had led the right flank in their attack, were well behind the Ptolemaic army when they turned back. As they withdrew north, they must have skirted Ptolemaic forces, perhaps by crossing the dunes and coming closer to the sea. There is a tradition, reported in separate sources, that Antiochus barely evaded capture, losing his diadem and baggage.[37] The Seleucid army huddled inside Raphia for the night and then regrouped at Gaza the next morning, staying there just long enough to recover and bury its many dead under truce. The next day, Antiochus and the army hurried up the coastline toward Syria, stopping only to gather routed soldiers and garrisons along the way. More than 10,000 infantry and 300 cavalry had fallen in the battle, while another 4,000 were captured (Plb. 5.86.5). In all, he lost 20 per cent of his force.[38] Ptolemaic losses were quite heavy among the routed cavalry on the left wing, with 700 dead out of 3,000 men, and another 1,500 were killed in the rest of the army, a loss of just 3 per cent of the force committed to battle. By nightfall on 23 June, the Ptolemaic army, victorious in one of the largest battles of the Hellenistic era, had gathered around Raphia, on the border of Syria. Just two days later, the governor of the Arsinoite nome wrote one of his chief subordinates a letter about exciting news and a sign at the shrine of Dionysios; word of the victory may have travelled very quickly (*P.Enteux*. pglxxxviii). King Ptolemy IV Philopator was delighted with his victory, although shocked perhaps by his harrowing first-hand experience of both a cavalry route and a successful pike push. He gathered his own troops and permitted the Seleucid army to retire before he marched into Syria himself.

The Aftermath

The Ptolemaic army conducted a short campaign in Syria following the triumph at Raphia, before returning home victorious, according to both Polybius and a royal decree from Egypt.[39] The decree was published in November that year, and dates Ptolemy's return to Egypt to 12 October (*Pithom II* 26). Polybius (5.86–87) described a three-month triumphal tour of the reconquered province for purposes of accepting gifts and reaffirming Ptolemaic rule. An inscription from Joppa, halfway between Raphia and Ptolemais, indicates the restoration of royal cult in that city.[40] An inscription from Tyre could relate to the royal visit there. In it, Dorymenes, an Aetolian hipparch in the Syrian garrison under Nikolaos, dedicated spoils from the war.[41] Dorymenes had been defeated at Berytos in 219 BC, and the unsolvable question is whether he participated at Raphia somehow or engaged retreating Seleucid forces after the battle. These visits, along with other visits to cities and temples described in the Raphia decree and historical sources,[42] functioned to restore Ptolemaic power after the Seleucid conquest. There is little indication that force was required at any of these places.

While it is only natural that Ptolemy and his forces would visit the great cities of Phoenicia – Ptolemais-Akko, Sidon and Tyre – and while these visits have the ring of a triumphal tour, there are two indications – neither found in Polybius – that Ptolemy and his army engaged in actions that conform more with a traditional concept of a military campaign. First, a dedication at Laboue in Lebanon, offered on behalf of the royal pair to Sarapis and Isis by the *archigrammateus* of the army, Marsyas, indicates the presence of the king and his army at the northern mouth of the Marsyas Valley, near the Eleutheros river frontier (*SEG* 38.1571). The *archigrammateus* (chief secretary) was one of the highest positions in the military administration. Marsyas also oversaw the casualty notifications during the war.[43] If a senior staff officer was at the frontier with Syria, the king and much of the army surely were as well. He may have been inspired to make the dedication by his presence in the valley called by his own name. Encamped there, about 90 miles from Apameia, the army threatened an invasion of the Seleucid heartland. Polybius (5.87.1) reported that Antiochus feared, unnecessarily, an invasion of Syria. However, their presence there suggests Polybius or his source understated Ptolemaic military activity, and the threat of invasion really did contribute to the treaty that ended the war.

The Ptolemaic priestly decree provides some insight into the activities of the army between the treaty and Ptolemy's return to Egypt. According to the decree:

> 'He then went to the territories of his enemies and caused a fortified camp for his troops to be built, and stayed there as long as he wished. As those who repulsed his enemies wished to fight together with him (?), he spent many days outside that same place. As they did not come again he let his troops loose, so that they plundered their cities. As they were unable to protect their territories they were destroyed. He made it clear to all men that this was the work of the gods / and that it was not good to fight against him. He marched away from that region after he had made himself master in twenty-one days of all their territories, after the acts of treachery which the leaders of the troops had committed.'[44]

The words seem in many places to have been left intentionally vague, but it clearly involved a punitive campaign, twenty-one days long, related to the desertions that occurred during the war.[45] Ptolemy and his army went somewhere and built a camp and plundered settlements. A plausible enemy, given those details, may be the Arab tribes in the vicinity of the Decapolis: many defected to Antiochus' side (Plb. 5.71.1), proved helpful in the Seleucid conquest of the Decapolis (5.71.2) and later contributed 10,000 soldiers to his army at Raphia (5.79.8). The 'acts of treachery' by the 'leaders of the troops' hearkens to the mercenary captains who defected during the war, so the punitive campaign may have been more intense than operations on the frontier of the Dekapolis: cities like Tyre, Scythopolis or Philoteria, or gift estates belonging to dynasts or officers who switched sides, may also have been subjected to plunder because of their roles in the war. This three-week campaign was the last phase of action before he and the army returned home. Because his army did not actually invade Seleucid territory, capturing parts of the Seleucid baggage and plundering the property of traitors comprised the only sources of revenue from the war.

The Ptolemaic victory in the Fourth Syrian War left a sour taste in the mouth of ancient historians, who saw in the outcome a dissatisfying reversal of expectation and a landmark opportunity wasted. Pompeius Trogus, summarized by Justin, judged Ptolemy harshly for defeating his enemy in a grand battle, recovering his territory and making peace: Ptolemy might 'have driven Antiochus from his throne, if he had supported his fortune with suitable spirit' (Just. 30.1.6). Polybius did not state it as strongly, but noted that, for his part, Antiochus III 'seriously feared invasion' and had 'no confidence in his own troops' (Plb. 5.87.1–2). By comparison, it is worth remembering that each of the previous Ptolemaic kings (or in some cases their subordinates) had invaded Syrian territory, so an attack on Apameia would not have been novel. In fact, his reluctance to test his advantage marked a departure from his predecessors, although they had been the most risk averse of the Successors. Worse still, there was no Egyptian revolt or other signal reverse to send him back to Egypt. The Ptolemaic army at Raphia was the pinnacle of developments stretching back to the foundation of the dynasty. The army, developed over a century, put in an exemplary performance at Raphia and could have been deployed as a weapon of conquest against a Seleucid state that, after a couple of years of strength, looked very vulnerable again. Instead, Ptolemy made little use of the army after the conclusion of the campaign, enjoying instead the peace secured on the bloodied sands outside Raphia.

Conclusions

'Wretched Egypt, you are wronged by terrible iniquities wrought against you'

—*The Oracle of the Potter*
Second-century BC anti-Greek apocalyptic literature

The Fourth Syrian War, although it ended in a Ptolemaic victory, dealt a serious blow to Ptolemaic imperial strategy and accelerated several lines of development that contributed to Ptolemaic instability in the later third and especially in the second century BC. In these respects, the aftermath of the Fourth Syrian War makes a reasonable conclusion for this volume. Antiochus' ability to dismantle, by force or coercion, the core of Ptolemy's military forces in the province nearest Egypt illustrated the difficulties of the Ptolemaic system. Theodotos' replacement Nikolaos had commanded a large defensive force in Syria, but he had been unable to hold off Antiochus for very long, particularly after the first reverses. Removed from Alexandria and proximity to the king, the commanders of the garrison units in Syria and Phoenicia lacked the oversight or instilled loyalty that existed closer to the throne. Far too many of the troops in the vital frontier were foreign mercenaries. While the Ptolemaic approach diminished the likelihood of internal rebellion by central authorities, like the satrapal uprisings that wracked the Seleucid kingdom, it also opened the door for Antiochus to bribe away individual units of the Ptolemaic garrison piece by piece. Political competition between the court aristocracy and the commanders of Syria or other foreign possessions like Cyprus only exacerbated the vulnerabilities. Due either to a perception of inevitable defeat, hope of rewards in the camp of Antiochus or fear of Sosibios' clique, commander after commander joined the side of Antiochus. Polybius attributed the defections to the instability and outright perils of the Alexandrian court. Whatever biases may have taken hold in the way Polybius spun his narrative, the record of defections provides a clear indication of the challenges to the stability of the Ptolemaic state and legitimacy of the kingship under Ptolemy IV. The military institutions enabled the Ptolemies to win quite possibly the largest pitched battle of the Hellenistic era, but political corruption rapidly eroded military advantage. Furthermore, as the Ptolemies established the internal networks of settlement to support their enlarged army, their activities created new instabilities within Egypt itself.

To conclude this study, it makes sense to consider what the changes of the Fourth Syrian War, the culmination of long developments and its combination with new designs wrought in Ptolemaic Egypt. The Ptolemaic dynasty was the longest-lived of the Successors, and its entire history cannot be spelled out in a few words here. But as long continuities ran from the first Ptolemies to Raphia, so others pick up in the Fourth Syrian War and run down to the age of Cleopatra. The most important of these new developments was the turbulence of the court, of both the kings and their senior civil and military aristocracy. This is a marked departure from the stability and quality of senior leadership under the first three Ptolemies. The second continuity, not a new development, is the expanding role of Egyptians in the military apparatus. Establishing effective roles for Egyptians in the Ptolemaic army was a concern of the Ptolemies throughout the dynasty, but the manner of Egyptian involvement and its relation to the overall army shifted dramatically because of other factors in the later phase of the dynasty. Third, the army's three missions remained, but in shifted priority. Most importantly, the mission of securing Egypt took precedence after the start of the Great Revolt in about 206 BC, becoming a fight for survival rather than an auxiliary to the economy and secured flank for overseas campaigning. The following pages review the three missions the Ptolemaic army performed under the first four kings, and then consider how the history of the Fourth Syrian War presages the changes of the ensuing generations.

The Army's Three Missions

Interstate Military Competition

The traditional, or conventional, mission was to enforce royal power relative to other entities, either in imperial possessions or interstate warfare. Ptolemaic strategy sprung from the wealth and security of Egypt, and so was conservative rather than bellicose, using limited war or other means to manage potential threats. The first foreign attacker to have some success attacking Egypt itself was Antiochus IV in 169 BC, more than 150 years after the start of the dynasty. The Ptolemaic strategy thus emphasized constant power projection and attentiveness to affairs, with wars that accomplished strategic ends more often than the conquest of new territories (Plb. 5.34). The army and navy performed these functions for the Ptolemies. Despite the Ptolemaic reputation for naval power, the navy had a terrible record in actual naval combat. It was, on the other hand, far better at supporting the Ptolemaic network of fortified possessions all around the Mediterranean and Aegean, as well as the Red Sea and up and down the Nile.

Naval squadrons, allied forces and the Ptolemies' large number of mercenaries conducted a major portion of Ptolemaic military operations throughout the third century BC. Cyprus, battleground and prize in wars with the Antigonids, hosted a large military apparatus under the Ptolemies. This should have meant that any Seleucid king marching south automatically exposed the flank of their army and the Seleukis itself to the naval squadrons and contingents of soldiers on Cyprus. The unexplained and completely inadequate use of Cyprus was, along with the defection of senior mercenary officers, among the greatest failings in the Fourth Syrian War. Prior to that time, while the Ptolemies had lost most of their naval battles, Ptolemaic forces in the empire had accumulated a large number of successes: key contributions to the defence of Rhodes and the acquisition of many of the most important cities in south-western Asia Minor, including Ephesos, off-shore Samos, Halikarnassos, Xanthos and for a time Miletos. Ptolemaic forces helped liberate Athens, failed to bring decisive forces into the Chremonidean War, but enjoyed positive relationships with liberated Athens and most of the Greeks in the late third century BC, which in turn added to Ptolemaic prestige and the third mission of Ptolemaic military forces.

The main army, hosted in Egypt, is the more complicated institution to review. The army, or divisions of it, fought in many wars, but most of its campaigns were quite short affairs. The longest wars for the settler army, the guard regiments and other forces from within Egypt were the Second and Third Syrian Wars, at about four years each. Most others took place in one or two campaign seasons. For the Ptolemaic army, warfare was neither normative nor even routine. Ptolemaic martial restraint helped produce the historiographic tradition, addressed so often in this text, that the army was, by the last quarter of the third century BC, idle and lethargic. The difficulty, however, is this: when the army left Egypt, it was nearly always victorious, from Gaza in 312 BC to Raphia in 217, and in many campaigns in between. Ptolemaic armies fought in Seleucid territory in Syria in the First and Second Syrian Wars, for example, and of course in the Third nearly conquered the heart of the Seleucid Empire. This was despite long gaps between major mobilizations, not only in the years before Raphia, but throughout the Ptolemaic dynasty. Between the effortless conquest of Syria and Phoenicia in 301 BC and the war in Ethiopia, the main army went over two decades without a major mobilization for war. About fifteen years passed between the First and Second Syrian Wars, and close to twenty years between the Third and Fourth Syrian Wars. Neither documentary nor narrative evidence answers this, but we must wonder if routine training and elephant campaigning replaced routine war in Ptolemaic Egypt. If large-scale training did take place under the first four Ptolemies, most of it must have been near Alexandria or at Pelusium, places where large forces regularly concentrated even in peacetime, but documentary evidence is lacking. A relaxed approach to training may have contributed to Polybius' description of Ptolemaic unpreparedness at the start of the Fourth Syrian War. Yet documentary evidence, produced in the preceding chapter, suggests some detachments of settler units – both machimoi and 30-aroura Macedonians – may have actually been involved in the fighting in Syria in the campaigns prior to Raphia.

The Security of Egypt

The army was also an extension and expression of the king's power in areas under Ptolemaic rule, and especially Egypt: the second mission. The use of military settlement not only strengthened Ptolemaic recruitment efforts, which succeeded in establishing a sizeable pool of Greco-Macedonian manpower in Egypt, but also established agents of Ptolemaic military authority up and down Egypt. Military settlements also existed in Syria, Cyprus and Cyrenaica, but most were in Egypt. In addition to military settlements, Greek civilians settled across Egypt to facilitate or profit from the operations of the state, and a fairly small number of forts and garrisons kept the Nile secure. Their presence contributed to security from external threats, but aside from garrisons at Elephantine in the south and Pelusium off the eastern Delta region, the army's role in Egypt was to ensure that the Ptolemaic homeland continued to generate impressive revenues and remained pacific with regard to Ptolemaic authority. The stakes here were high: affluence by default underlay Ptolemaic strategy and the identity of the monarchy, and the possible conquest of the whole Fertile Crescent was thwarted in the Third Syrian War by an Egyptian revolt.

One of the chief difficulties in reviewing this mission is establishing the coercive role of the army. There is at least some sense in which the military settlements helped the Ptolemies occupy and colonize Egypt: the settlers were usually more affluent – often far more – than the Egyptians who dwelt around them, were often better connected to administrative and legal authorities, and as military men constantly represented the potential repressive power of the Ptolemaic state and their own potential for intimidation or violence. After all, it was the absence of the army, combined with successive poor Nile flood cycles, that ignited the revolt in 245 BC. At the same time, this trope could be taken much too far. Fairly light Hellenistic settlement in major Egyptian hubs – places like Thebes in the south, Mendes and Sais in the Delta – were an acknowledgement of Egyptian culture. The lack of meddling, or show of respect, helped secure cooperation from the powerful Egyptian priesthoods and their own military institutions. Meanwhile, one of the major hubs of Hellenistic settlement was in the sparsely populated Fayum, where the Greek population was approximately as large as the citizen population at Alexandria. Their presence turned a backwater into an economic and cultural centre without displacing or treading upon Egyptian traditions and elite families. Thus the Ptolemies attempted to balance catering to both Greek and Egyptian populations in Egypt with practical and coercive concerns about where to find land to settle cleruchs and how to prevent disastrous uprisings by the far larger Egyptian population.

The size and bounty of Egypt facilitated the expansion of the Ptolemaic army, from the company of Friends who came to Egypt with Ptolemy the Satrap to the more than 60,000 Greek and Egyptian non-mercenary troops who fought at Raphia. One-third of those were the much-discussed *machimoi* who fought in the phalanx of Sosibios, but even among the 40,000 Greeks in the army, this project has sought to demonstrate that Hellenized Egyptians and aristocratic Egyptian elites had possessed roles in the army for generations. This estimate for the size of the military population is consistent with other studies of the Ptolemaic army.[1] They were a tiny fraction of the full population of Egypt, some three to four million, but a fairly large part of the total Greek population, which may have been close to 200,000.[2] Among the 40,000, this study has not been able to answer how many possessed land allotments, but with the addition of new settlements during and after the Fourth Syrian War, the number of Greek military settlers probably approached or even surpassed 30,000. As in most previous wars, some captured prisoners were settled after the war.³ Much of our understanding of the settler system derives from the Fayum, where nearly half of all Ptolemaic cavalrymen possessed their allotments, and from mid-second-century BC records about the size of the combined land-holdings of the *katoikoi hippeis*, the class of settler cavalry.⁴ These sources pose a challenge: the usual interpretations offered for them are often on a far different order of magnitude for the size of the settler system than third-century BC evidence tends to indicate. Should historians think of continuity, and revise third-century interpretations, or revisit the later evidence, or emphasize change over time, especially between the late third century and mid-second?

Let us consider this hypothesis: that the late third-century BC Ptolemaic military settler system was a significantly larger presence within Egypt than estimates based off the *katoikoi hippeis* records suggest. Fischer-Bovet's 2014 estimate is the largest to-date, around 7 per cent of cultivable land in Egypt, 1,468km² or 536,000 arouras, derived from three data points.⁵ First, a first-century BC papyrus, *BGU* 8.1760 (51/0 BC) could be read as suggesting the Herakleopolite military settlers (*katoikoi*) – or possessors of *katoikic* land – were responsible for almost 12 per cent of a special levy applied throughout Egypt (Monson, 2012: pp.180–81). Second, she calculated 30 per cent of land in the Arsinoite nome was cleruchic, based off 1,000 100-aroura settlers, 1,000 30-aroura settlers and about 30,000 arouras for other types of settlers to get to that figure.⁶ Third, she conjectured that the same percentage was also a fairly reliable figure for the smaller Herakleopolite nome. If 30 per cent of the Herakleopolite was military settler land, 64,000 arouras or 176km², and 12 per cent of military settler land was in the Herakleopolite, then the total size of settler land was the aforementioned 1,468km². Fischer-Bovet's calculation was significantly larger than previous figures, mainly because it started from census records on settler numbers for the Arsinoite rather than the numbers of allotments or amounts of settler land recorded in surviving papyri.⁷ The latter starting point is more detailed but necessarily incomplete. And if anything, Fischer-Bovet's numbers may still be too small for the third century BC.

The discrepancy between Fischer-Bovet's numbers and some other calculations of settler land in Egypt is only the beginning of a larger problem in talking about Ptolemaic military history. As this volume concludes, it is necessary to say at least a little about this. In contemplating the army's role in the occupation, colonization and cultivation of rich Egypt, the army's presence in the country figures as a prominent metric. Population estimates have posited the Greek population of Egypt was 5–10 per cent of the total population, most of them connected to the settler system, while estimates of the settler system have ranged from 2–7 per cent of the cultivable land. The elite, immigrant, military minority should have certainly controlled a disproportionately large amount of land. The alternative is that the Ptolemaic army, reputed as a settler-based institution in all major works on the subject, was actually a heavily professional force, with a small reserve of settlers and tens of thousands of actively serving troops vastly under-represented in the papyri. If there were, as often posited, something like 30,000 settler families, and 3,000 were the 100-aroura cavalry settlers and the rest held the 24-aroura allotments common among many infantry, the settler system should have had something like 950,000 arouras, or 2,612km^2, which is more than 1,000km^2 larger than Fischer-Bovet's estimate and equivalent to about 13 per cent of the cultivable land in Egypt. Before making a nod toward a possible solution, it is worth exploring where the lower estimates came from.

The problem begins with the cavalry, and especially in the later Ptolemaic era, not covered in this study. The most important text is a petition by the settler cavalry, or *katoikoi hippeis*, from the Herakleopolite nome in Middle Egypt (*P.Lips.* 2.124, 137 BC).[8] From the petition we learn a great deal about a special levy on the cavalry, called the *hippike prosodos*. It was established in 157 BC, imposed on the cavalry settlers of Egypt outside the Thebaid (there were very few cavalry settlers in the Thebaid) and initially pegged at 243,577 artabas of wheat. Furthermore, the in-kind levy was related, at least in theory, to the size of the settler cavalry's land-holdings, chiefly in the form of a *diartabeia*, 2 artabas per aroura of land.[9] This would suggest the *katoikoi hippeis* controlled somewhere in the order of 122,000 arouras in 157 BC. Then the size of the *hippike prosodos* was lowered in 144 BC out of consideration for lands taken away from the cavalry settlers by the crown, so that the new total became 234,777, and in 137 BC the Herakleopolite *katoikoi hippeis* were lobbying to have their component of the total revised downward yet again, to 22,192 artabas instead of 23,864.[10] This implies three important things: first, that the Herakleopolite hipparchy comprised almost exactly one-tenth of the land at issue, which in turn points to ten hipparchies in the settler cavalry. At the time of Raphia, there were, theoretically, ten in the Arsinoite nome alone. Second, it suggests the Herakleopolite cavalry allotments comprised as little as 11,096 arouras. Third, it demonstrates a fairly dramatic decline in cavalry settler land just between 157 and 137 BC, between 3.6 and 10 per cent. A similar text from the Arsinoite nome, *P.Tebt.* 1.99 (also 137 BC), seems to indicate the Arsinoite *katoikoi hippeis* were responsible for about 118,000 artabas out of the *hippike prosodos*, or almost exactly 50 per cent of the total.[11] This suggests that approximately half of the cavalry settler land was in the Fayum, or 59,000 arouras. Finally, *BGU* 8.1760, which provided the figure that in 51 BC about 12 per cent of all the settler land in Egypt was in the Herakleopolite nome, also provides the sum total due from all *katoikoi*, as opposed to the earlier *hippike prosodos*, as 600,000 artabas, in two installments. If treated, like the cavalry tax, as a 2-artabas-per-aroura levy, the tax from 51 BC suggests all settler land throughout Egypt was about 300,000 arouras, 826km^2 or just 4 per cent of the cultivable land. The Herakleopolite portion of the levy, 71,360 artabas, would also point to a total of about 35,680 arouras in that nome, from which something like 11,000 would have been held by the *katoikoi hippeis* from *P.Lips.* 2.124. For the late Ptolemaic army, these numbers work, as shown in the chart below. Eleven thousand arouras for a hipparchy of approximately 250 men comes to an average of 44 arouras per man, quite normal by the second half of the second century BC.[12] The remaining arouras, nearly 25,000, would have sufficed for both the elite guardsmen with land in that nome and the large numbers of paramilitaries, *machimoi*, and few remaining infantry settlers.

Calculations that work for the late Ptolemaic army will not suffice for the third century BC. The evidence on the special tax on the cavalry demonstrates that the amount of land they held was declining over time. Papyri clearly reveal the same thing: the median size of cavalry allotments in the third century BC was 100 arouras; by the late second century it was 40. This was not to increase the size of the cavalry; there is no evidence that would suggest a doubling or more in the number of Ptolemaic cavalry. Documentary evidence, like the Kerkeosiris land surveys, is quite clear that in the late period most cavalry settlers controlled 24–50 arouras instead of 70–100. Experimentation with smaller allotments began in the 180s BC, when veterans who put down an Egyptian revolt in the Thebaid gained 50 arouras instead of 100, then in about 167, after Antiochus IV's invasion was defeated, veterans received mainly 40 arouras.[13] These smaller allotments became the norm for most cavalry between about 151 and 131 BC, especially under the cavalry secretaries Dionysios and Krito; the former was probably the homonymous commander of the Herakleopolite cavalry regiment (*P.Bingen* 35, *P.Köln.* 4.187), and the latter the hipparch of the 1st cavalry regiment (*P.Wuerzb.* 4, *P.Tebt.* 1.61). Similarly, the phalanx declined then disappeared in preference for battalions of standing troops and large numbers of paramilitary police, the former generally

Table 14: Settler Land in the Late Army, from Tax Figures

	Special Tax	Estimated Arouras	Estimated Settlers	Est. Average Allotment
All Settler Land				
Katoikic Levy 51	600,000	300,000	2,500 Horse 16,000 Foot	(See Below) 11.41 Ar.
Cavalry Land				
Hippike Prosodos 157	243,577	121,788.5	2,500	48.72 Ar.
Hippike Prosodos 144	234,777	117,388.5	2,500	46.96 Ar.
Herakleopolite Settler Land				
Katoikic Levy 51	71,360	35,680	1,500	23.78 Ar.
Hippike Prosodos 157 (est)	24,744	12,372	250	49.49 Ar.
Hippike Prosodos 144	23,864	11,932	250	47.73 Ar.
Hippike Prosodos 137	22,192	11,096	250	44.38 Ar.
Arsinoite Settler Land				
Hippike Prosodos 144–138	118,078	59,039	1,250	47.23 Ar.
Hippike Prosodos 137	118,556	59,278	1,250	47.42 Ar.

without allotments and the latter with small ones, mostly just 10 arouras. The median infantry allotment of the early period was 2.4 times larger than the median allotment in the late period; likewise, the median cavalry allotment was 2.5 times larger. Applied as a rough metric, this suggests the late third-century BC military settlers controlled about 2.5 times more land, some 750,000 arouras, just over 2,000km^2, and just over 10 per cent of the cultivable land in Egypt. The settler population probably did not change a great deal, but the area of settlement declined dramatically from its peak around the time of the battle at Raphia.

Military settlement at this approximate magnitude – three-quarters of a million arouras, or 2,000km^2 – can be defended through a reconsideration of the calculations introduced previously by Fischer-Bovet. Her calculation estimated the percentage of cleruchic land in the Fayum in proportion to the percentage in the Herakleopolite, which at least in 51 BC was approximately 12 per cent of the cleruchic land in Egypt. The first figure to revise for making a late third-century BC estimate is the percentage of military settler land in the Arsinoite nome, the Fayum. Fischer-Bovet's calculation granted 1,000 100-aroura settlers, about 1,000 30-aroura settlers and about 30,000 other settler arouras, for a total of 163,000 arouras. The first figure derives from *P.Count* 1's 3,418 adult males in the households of the 100-aroura cleruchs, which the editors suggested related to 1,068 or more actual settlers.[14] Monson previously estimated land for the same number of 30-aroura infantry settlers, and Fischer-Bovet added the rest to meet a threshold at 30 per cent to get closer to the 34–40 per cent settler land in village land surveys studied by Monson.[15] The 1,000 or so infantry settlers may be on the right order of magnitude (I suggested between 750 and 1,500 previously in this work), but the 100-aroura settlers, from five hipparchies, should have been closer to 1,280, an addition of 28,000 arouras. Instead of arbitrarily adding arouras to reach 30 per cent of the Fayum, we should instead just account for the other settlers attested in the nome. Her tally excluded the *misthophoroi* cavalry, made little accommodation for the larger allotments possessed by officers and left out the settlement of the ethnic hipparchies, which almost certainly occurred after the record in *P.Count* 1 was made (probably between 251 and 243 BC). Clarysse and Thompson estimated 400–750 mercenary cavalry were in the Fayum; whether they were all settled, or their officers foremost, is unclear.[16] Documentary evidence at least shows that many were also settled.[17] Because of the generous size of allotments for officers (130–400 arouras) and their over-representation in the *misthophoroi*, the conservative approach here is to just take the figure of 400 cavalrymen at 80 arouras, or 32,000 arouras.[18] Although there were five ethnic hipparchies, this study has previously suggested only 400–500 were ever settled. Four hundred cavalrymen at 70 arouras would add 28,000. In all, this adds 88,000 arouras to Fischer-Bovet's figures, for 220,040 arouras, 606km^2 and 40.4 per cent of Fayum land. By counting from bodies of troops and their allotment sizes and the percentage of settler land in actual Arsinoite land surveys, it makes sense to run the same calculation at 40 per cent for a projected late third-century BC range. This is even more justified in comparison to evidence from the Herakleopolite and neighbouring nomes in the middle Nile valley, where our limited evidence gives examples of 48–60 per cent settler land, so I add a range up to 48 per cent to set a theoretical maximum.[19] At 40–48 per cent of cultivable land, the Herakleopolite *katoikoi* figure becomes 85,000–102,000 arouras, 234–281km^2, and since they also controlled 12 per cent of all settler land, it adjusts the amount of settler land to 715,000–850,000 arouras or 1,968–2,341km^2, approximately 10–11.7 per cent of all cultivable land in Egypt. Any attempts to identify the size of the cleruchic system, in the absence of more evidence, will be methodologically problematic, but previous studies, by relying so heavily on material compiled after dramatic changes in the late Ptolemaic army, have almost certainly set the range too low.

The recategorization or repurposing of military settler land in later Ptolemaic history suggests two conclusions about the Ptolemaic military's relationship with the land and with the state apparatus. The Ptolemaic state eventually determined that it no longer needed, militarily or agriculturally, to expand the settler system or even maintain the gratuitously large allotments many third-century BC settlers had enjoyed. The first conclusion is that the larger allotments limited state income and ceased to be useful for land recovery, which is why the state impounded and confiscated uncultivated land from cleruchs. The Herakleopolite Land Registers (*BGU XIV*) contain many examples of infantry-sized allotments possessed by police or administrators or in private possession. *BGU* 14.2437, for example, includes several Greeks with private land measuring 24, 25, 20 and 30 arouras – suspiciously aligning with traditional sizes for infantry allotments – three *ephodoi* (mounted police) with 24-aroura allotments and four administrators with 20, 24 and 30-aroura allotments. The second conclusion is that the continued occupation and pacification of Egypt required more paid service from soldiers instead of distributed settlement. This justified smaller allotments, the expansion of standing regiments or longer duty rotations for settler regiments, and the Ptolemaic state's willingness to permit cleruch families to dispose of some of their properties. This was due mainly to the Great Revolt and subsequent shift in the nature of this second mission, an important part of the changing fortunes of the dynasty, addressed in more detail below.

The Army of a Dynasty

Thirdly and finally, the army was part of the cultural-political project that was the Ptolemaic dynasty. The traditional model of Hellenistic monarchy called for kings to forge and sustain their legitimacy through military prowess and spear-won land. Ptolemy I redefined the cultural sense of 'spear-won' land when he reckoned his successful defences of Egypt as affirming his 'conquest' of the satrapy-turned-kingdom. The Ptolemies continued this tactic of doing traditional things in novel ways with gusto to create a strategy for forging a Macedonian monarchy in Egypt. In much the same way, Ptolemy I came to Egypt with an aristocracy but no army. The first two Ptolemies heavily prioritized and privileged their aristocracy and their officer class. This is evident enough in the proliferation of commands and overrepresentation of rank, still evident into the reign of Ptolemy III. The exaggeration seems to have worked well enough: the court of Ptolemy II was the place to be for enterprising Greeks; the strategy built up the ranks of the royal family's 'Friends' and by the time of the Second Syrian War had produced a sufficient population boom in Egypt for Ptolemy II to conscript large numbers of Greeks from within Egypt. During and after the war, thousands were settled on allotments of their own within Egypt, mostly in the Fayum, as 25-aroura *epigonoi* or 100-aroura *neaniskoi*. This moment from the Second Syrian War is pivotal for understanding the relation of army and dynasty: it signalled an initial independence from the mercenary market. The Ptolemaic army continued to use mercenaries, but under Ptolemy III and Ptolemy IV (despite Polybius' narrative of Raphia) the Ptolemies' reliance on mercenaries declined precipitously. The ability to mobilize from within Egypt an army of sufficient size and quality to win wars abroad made the Ptolemaic kingdom truly independent.

After securing the aristocratic cohort and the rank-and-file population, under Ptolemy III the mission transitioned from recruiting and retaining to maintaining and refining. Euergetes had a successful operational record, a little more impressive than the short, sharp demonstrations of prowess that had sufficed for his father. Moreover, following his military reforms, he was king over a robust settler system and a regimented army, capped off with his phalanx of Macedonians. Less evident than we would wish in papyri, a Macedonian phalanx was necessary for a Macedonian monarchy. The previous study suggested settler land in Egypt peaked between 715,000–850,000 arouras, after adjusting Fischer-Bovet's model. It also estimated that, after accounting for some 3,000 settler cavalry, 415,000–550,000 arouras remained for other cavalry and the infantry. If the entirety was devoted to Macedonian settlers at an average of 24 arouras, 17,000–23,000 could have been accommodated. But the actual distribution of allotments was assuredly far more complex: there were non-Macedonian infantry settlers, like Cretans (*P.Köln.* 5.218, a 30-aroura settler) and Galatians (Plb. 5.65.10), mercenary infantry (*P.Petr.* 2.31) and however many men from the infantry agema had allotments in the country. For these reasons it seems likely the 30-aroura Macedonian class was limited to about eight to twelve regiments, except possibly after Raphia. Nonetheless, it also sustained a larger expansion of the ostensibly Macedonian population by passing their martial pseudo-ethnic on to their children. The phalanx Macedonians and the Alexandrian and Macedonian men in the agema (whether or not they comprised the entire agema) powerfully reinforced the Macedonian identity of the monarchy.

The cultivation of a large and influential aristocracy at court was one of the defining features of the Ptolemaic dynasty from the start, but is also implicated in the causes of Ptolemaic decline during and after the reign of Ptolemy IV. Competition for influence at court also caused infighting in the court of Antiochus III, but helped produce assassinations, defections and attempted coups, often with devastating impact, in the Ptolemaic sphere. No fewer than seven high-ranking military commanders went over to Antiochus between the start of the Fourth Syrian War and the start of the Fifth Syrian War in about 202 BC.[20] The last of these, Ptolemaios son of Thraseas, was scion of a leading Alexandrian family and one of Ptolemy's marshals at Raphia. As governor of Ptolemaic Syria, his defection signalled the depth of internal divisions in the Alexandrian aristocracy and practically assured Antiochus' conquest of the province.[21] The Ptolemies' loss was Antiochus III's gain, as many of the seven played prominent roles in Antiochus' successful conquests in the following decades. Sosibios, Agathokles and, until his death, Ptolemaios son of Chrysermos seem to have led the divisive clique in Ptolemy IV's reign. The latter fell in the desperate uprising of Cleomenes III of Sparta, the first fell at the hand of Agathokles around 204 or 203 BC and Agathokles fell in a furious and bloody intrigue that accompanied the fight for regency during Ptolemy V's boyhood.

Dynastic turbulence and aristocratic infighting are the earliest markers of decline for the Ptolemaic state. It is fairly easy to imagine that the state's difficulties and a steep military decline went hand in hand, although the relationship is undoubtedly more complex. Infighting between courtiers reportedly politicized the army over time. At first this had a positive outcome: the courtier Agathokles conspired to seize Ptolemy V's regency and may have planned to usurp the throne itself, but the Macedonian division (*systema* – Plb. 15.26.9) of the army acted decisively, and largely independently, to overthrow Agathokles and invite the commander of the field force at Pelusium, Tlepolemos, to assume the regency. Several regents advised the boy king, nearly all military men, and amid the rotating courtiers the mercenary general Skopas of Aetolia attempted yet another coup. Polybius visited Alexandria in the middle of the second century BC, and afterwards described the mercenaries of the garrison as 'a numerous, rough, and uncultivated set, it being an ancient practice there to maintain a foreign armed force, which owing to the weakness of the kings had learnt rather to rule than to obey' (Plb. 34.14.3). Even later, Caesar described the political role of the Ptolemaic field army in similar terms: 'These men had been in the habit of demanding for execution the Friends of the princes, of plundering the property of the rich, of besetting the king's palace to secure an increase of pay, of driving one man from the throne and summoning another to fill it, after an ancient custom of the Alexandrian army' (BC 3.110). Political infighting steadily politicized elements of the army, not as backers of the Macedonian dynasty and a counter-balance to the aristocracy, as at first, but as agents of their own interests.

The aristocracy, and particularly Sosibios, played an important role in the final important shift that began under Ptolemy IV. By the waning decades of the third century BC, it was evident the great clash in the Western Mediterranean between Rome and Carthage in the Second Punic War and the continuous replenishment of armies in the Seleucid civil wars presaged a decisive challenge to the golden age of the Ptolemaic army. To an outside observer or modern historian, Roman mobilization posed a critical threat to the Hellenistic military model. Pyrrhus had labelled the Romans a hydra, marvelling at their ability to replace losses. While he trusted in his professional troops to beat the Roman citizen militia head-to-head, he came to dread the losses the Roman system inflicted, losses he could not easily make up. Decades later, the Roman legions had grown more efficient and no less resilient. Sosibios' grand plan, which began with the reforms before Raphia, seems to have been to militarize the Egyptian population.

After Raphia, the king and the court credited Sarapis and Isis with a divine intervention that led to the Ptolemaic victory, a propagandistic step toward more strongly forging a syncretic Greco-Egyptian state.[22] Unless the Ptolemaic army could draw reliably on its enormous Egyptian population, it had little hope of sustaining a military competition with such a large pool of martial manpower. Unless the Ptolemies could strengthen the Egyptian aspects of the dynasty's legitimacy and incorporate Egyptians into their military classes, threats of revolt and unrest would linger during any significant military mobilization, military crisis or prolonged absence of the settler population from the country. The Egyptian performance at Raphia, in particular, signalled such a plan could work, at least on the battlefield. With Egypt secure and thousands of Egyptians serving in the front lines of the army, the Ptolemies could turn their attentions directly to the Mediterranean world and the great power competition brewing within it.

The stable militarization of the *machimoi* would have restored the Ptolemies' ability to mobilize from within Egypt an army of sufficient size and quality to win wars abroad, even against the new powerhouses of the Western Mediterranean. New settlements of Greeks or new waves of Greek immigration were probably insufficient. The Ptolemies had already drawn very heavily upon their Greek population: most estimates of the adult male Greek population of Egypt have reckoned between 50,000 and 90,000. Not all of these would have been military-age or able to serve, but most or nearly all who were – some 40,000 – were at Raphia. Rome survived astounding losses at Cannae the year after Raphia; the Greek population of Egypt could not have done the same. If the new Greek settlements during and after the war took root and their families prospered, the next Ptolemaic kings might be able to wage war at such a large scale with less risk of a total demographic disaster. But that would take time. Instead, a Cannae-like disaster struck Egypt in 200 BC at the Battle of Panion, with profound consequences. Thus an increased militarization of the Egyptian population was the obvious way to secure a larger pool of martial manpower.

The true militarization of the *machimoi* and other Egyptians was a massive undertaking. The early, fantastic success at Raphia disguised the complexity of the full effort. The Ptolemies had incorporated elements of Egyptian monarchies since the dynasty's inception. Just as Macedonian soldiers reflected and affirmed the Macedonian character of the monarchy, so Egyptian soldiers and benefactions and appeals to Egyptian temples or priesthoods forged associations with the Pharaohs of Dynastic Egypt. And yet, prior to the reign of Ptolemy IV, most Egyptians' only possible contact with military service was if they were conscripted for service as rowers in the navy. Even the Egyptian military classes – aside from a small number of elites and a larger number of Hellenized Egyptians counted as Greeks or 'Persians' – were restricted to paramilitary, police and auxiliary functions. In the years after the war, Sosibios and Agathokles acquired large gift estates, Sosibios in part of the Herakleopolite nome and Agathokles in the Thebaid in Upper Egypt.[23] While these gift estates provided additional income for the king's top ministers, they also, like other gift estates, could help facilitate eventual military settlements, like the *dioikēsis* of Simaristos, or advance land reclamation projects that would facilitate military settlement in adjoining territory, like the *dōrea* of Apollonios in the Fayum. Agathokles was an infamously imprudent and intemperate court favourite, and so the natural choice for a huge tract of land near Thebes, where, until then, the traditional Egyptian temples and local institutions had enjoyed a great deal of independence. While some phalangite *machimoi* probably served in standing roles after Raphia, most were undoubtedly demobilized. In time, Sosibios' plan seems to have been to apportion a larger number of 10-aroura allotments, treating the Egyptian population, or at least the *machimoi*, much like the smaller Greek population, with a mix of standing units, settlers and a conscription pool.

The arming of the Egyptians as phalangites culminated in Ptolemaic decline rather than ascension, chiefly because it contributed to the devastating Great Revolt. The new Egyptian military class instigated and sustained the rebellion, which first erupted in serious violence around 206 BC and was finally suppressed in different parts of Egypt between 186 and 182. Polybius condemned the decision to arm them in Book 5 (5.107.2), saying Ptolemy and his advisors 'took a step which was of great service for the time, but which was a mistake as regards the future'. The problem was not a myopic concern with expedience; the problem was overconfidence in attaining their objective. The *machimoi* were the bottom of the military population prior to the reform, and there is little evidence after Raphia to suggest that ever changed. The 10-aroura allotments, while double the standard *machimoi* holdings, were still less than half the size of most Greek infantry allotments. Even the captured prisoners settled after the war received 16-aroura allotments.[24] Worse still, generalizing from the little evidence available, the 10-aroura allotments generally went to Hellenized soldiers first. Ptolemy IV also distributed a bonus after the Fourth Syrian War. According to the Raphia decree, it was 300,000 chrysoi, or gold staters, enough for four coins for every soldier, equivalent to 80 silver drachmas.²⁵ However, the primary gold coin from the Raphia period was actually a 5-stater coin, the mnaieion, worth 100 drachmas, which suggests some bonuses were far larger (see plate 1 fig. 1d). But bonuses for officers, cavalrymen and possibly Greeks would have been greater than those for the Egyptians, who then demobilized into a long and frustrating waiting game.²⁶ Before the revolt truly began, Ptolemaic administrators could note increasing incidences of desertion among the *machimoi*, many of whom were abandoning posts and disappearing (*P. Tebt.* 3.1.703). They returned eventually as the leaders of the dangerous Egyptian revolt.

Aimed at securing Egypt, empowering competition abroad and strengthening the Ptolemaic dynasty's association with the traditional institutions of Egypt, the arming of the *machimoi* led to the opposite effects. After the Great Revolt ended, the state redistributed large numbers of 10-aroura allotments to police and paramilitaries. Many of them were Hellenized Egyptians, or from the larger Hellenized milieu of Egypt. The same was true for large numbers of *ephodoi*, mounted police, who received infantry allotments left vacant after the great defeat at Panion and the bloodshed of a twenty-year rebellion. Sosibios, and I suspect Ptolemy III as well, must have imagined the settler Macedonians and pike-wielding Egyptians would be the core of the state for generations. The settler systems built for each were heavily cannibalized for police forces just a few decades after Raphia. In the end the revolt actually did lead to greater roles and higher profiles for Egyptians in the military establishment, both as *machimoi* and 'Persian' *misthophoroi*, paid troops. By the later second century BC, Egyptians, Hellenized or not, almost certainly comprised the majority of the army's personnel, the distinctions between Egyptians and Greeks within the military milieu blurred at an accelerating pace and growing numbers of Egyptians held very high military commands. As for the missions of the Ptolemaic army, the weight of effort shifted heavily toward that of occupying a restive Egypt, and international competition or forging a Macedonian people and kingdom in Egypt – two missions and ideas so central to the history of the third-century BC Ptolemaic army – were afterthoughts, fading rapidly into the sands of Egypt like the ruins of the kingdoms of old.

Notes

Introduction

1. Antigonus had 88,000 outside Pelusium (Diod. 20.73.2), and 80,000 at Ipsos, where the combined armies of Seleucus and Lysimachus were 74,500 (Plut. *Dem.* 28.6). Antiochus may have had 72,000 at Magnesia (Livy 37.37), although the contingent lists suggest a force in the range of 52,000–63,000, and a similar-sized force at Panium, where he avenged his defeat at Raphia.
2. The triumvirs may have had nineteen legions and 20,000 cavalry at Philippi (Appian *BC* 4.108), but Appian also used 20,000 for the total number of cavalry they raised for the war (4.113), so some exaggeration could be involved. The Liberators had nineteen understrength legions at Philippi, plus auxiliaries, and 13,000 cavalry, quite possibly near or more than 100,000 in all (Appian *BC* 4.88, 108). Polybius estimated 86,000 Romans at Cannae (3.113), although Livy (22.36) expressed some scepticism toward the largest figures. Velleius Paterculus claimed Gnaeus Pompeius had 75,000 soldiers in a battle near Asculum in the Social War (2.21.1), but Appian's account does not accord with nearly so many (*BC* 1.47.1). The Populares faction may have fielded 70,000 at the Colline Gate in 82 BC (Eutrop. 5.17), although Paterculus claims they were only 40,000 (2.27.1). Seventy thousand is popularly cited for the Vitellian army at Bedriacum, but that was the initial size of the armies of Vitellius' lieutenants, and both had been attrited or posted detachments elsewhere over lengthy campaigns leading up to First Bedriacum.
3. Chief works include: Fischer-Bovet 2014, Scheuble-Reiter 2012, Sekunda 2001, Van 't Dack 1988, Uebel 1968, Launey 1949-50, Lesquier 1911. Nearly all of these works are heavily documentary, oriented toward cataloguing personnel and institutions or offering social history of the army. Most scholarly studies with an operational angle have been conducted in articles and chapters by Peremans (mostly French), Winnicki (German), and most recently by Hauben (mostly

naval). Fischer-Bovet's and Scheuble-Reiter's recent monographs, on the army and society, and on the settler cavalry, represent major updates to the field, mostly as institutional or social history. There have been a number of significant new works in the later Ptolemaic period (after 200 BC), but these are not covered in this work.

4. Hölbl 2001, Huss 2001, and Manning 2010 are the most comprehensive monographs on the dynasty; works like Bingen 2007, Lewis 2001, Crawford 1971 are excellent entry points to varied aspects of Ptolemaic history; on the rulers covered here, see Worthington 2016 on Ptolemy I, the essays in McKechnie and Guillaume 2008 on Ptolemy II; many important contributions reflecting the expansion of papyrological work and its application to history lay in or sprang from the essays in Maehler and Strocka 1978; on the phenomenon of the Syrian Wars, so important to 3rd century Ptolemaic history, see Heinen 1984 and Grainger 2010. As for the narrative of glory-then-decline, it is evident in all the older works, e.g. Mahaffy 1895, Bevan 1927; in the present generation the narrative has shifted: the link between Egyptians and decline is rejected, but the narrative regarding decline itself has been put to little scrutiny (see e.g., Fischer-Bovet 2015), aside from Huss's revisionist history of Ptolemy IV (1976). Major new analytical works based on new editions of papyri are still coming out, see recently, e.g., Clarysse and Thompson 2006, or Christensen, Thompson, and Vandorpe 2017.

5. On the Ptolemaic economy, especially in Egypt, we have recent and excellent contributions in Monson 2012 and Manning 2003 and 2007, and comparative Seleucid material in Aperghis 2004 and Le Rider and Callatay 2006. Préaux's 1939 study (English 1979) is classic; for the monetary side of the economy see Cadell and Le Rider 1997, Reden 2007.

6. The place of Egyptian soldiers in Ptolemaic military history is the most important historiographic development of the past fifty years. Documentary evidence, both in papyri and in Egyptian temple statues and inscriptions, has demonstrated the military role of the Egyptian aristocracy (e.g., Peremans 1977 and 1978, Quaegebeur 1979, Thiers 1995, Lloyd 2002) or Egyptian contributions to naval affairs (Van 't Dack and Hauben 1978, Fischer-Bovet 2016), while studies of the *machimoi*, the traditionally Egyptian rank-and-file, revealed men with Greek names among their number (e.g. Winnicki 1985, Clarysse 1985, Van 't Dack 1992, Fischer-Bovet 2013), and demotic studies revealed

categories of non-Greek soldiers previously unknown (e.g., Winnicki 1977, Vleeming 1985, La'Da 2007, Vandorpe 2008). This evidence has sometimes produced a corrective project privileging Egyptian contributions with modern sensibilities: uncovering and ennobling Egyptian military service, identifying Egyptian cultural influence on the Ptolemies, exploring multiculturalism and eschewing nationalistic or ethnic explanations for divisions in Egypt.

7. The use of papyri in Egypt and of ancient accounts and inscription and coinage in the Ptolemaic empire tends to reinforce separate treatments, but even Polybius wrote of the the Ptolemaic overseas holdings in a different way than he wrote of Egypt. Bagnall 1976 is still the most comprehensive work but nearly half a century later needs an update; similarly for Huss 1976. Modern contributions, not in monograph form, include Marquaille 2008, Meadows 2012, and many of the contributions in Buraselis, Stefanou and Thompson 2013.

8. For the Hellenistic military tradition, many works are available: Hamilton 2001 and Chaniotis 2005 are good starting points, illustrative of the social and cultural interests of Hellenistic military history (hardly just a Ptolemaic phenomenon); see Sekunda 2008, De Souza 2008 for more conventional studies, and Matthew 2015 on the Hellenistic phalanx. The Antigonid Macedonian dynasty has the strongest influence on the larger field, represented by the signal contributions of Hatzopoulos 1996 and 2001, two studies of the Antigonid state and its army, or Bar-Kochva 1976 on the Seleucid army. Many works now nearly a century old, e.g., Griffith 1935 and Tarn 1930, still contain some important contributions.

9. On Hellenistic kingship and warfare, Austin's 1986 essay has been very influential, as has Eckstein's 2005 monograph describing endemic warfare in the Hellenistic world; see also Mehl 1980, Buraselis 1982, Hammond 1988, Billows 1995, Virgilio 2003. On Ptolemaic kingship, the main works to consult are Hazzard 2000, Samuel 1993, Mooren 1977; on the Ptolemaic monarchy as a cultural project, see Erskine 1995, and for Egyptian elements, see e.g. Clarysse 2000.

Chapter 1: The Ptolemaic Army at Raphia

1. Polybius 15.27.6 and later in the same narrative, and *P.Mich.inv.* 6648.
2. On the settler cavalry, see in particular, Scheuble-Reiter 2014, Fischer-Bovet 2014: pp.125–33; see Bingen 2007: pp.132–40 for the settler

cavalry in late Ptolemaic Egypt, with some useful references to long tradition.
3. Hatzopoulos and Juhel (2009: 423–37) suggested a much earlier date for the introduction of cavalry shields, in the late fourth or early third century BC, contingent on accepting their reconstruction of the date and identification of a shield on the funerary monument of Nikanor son of Herakleides (Kilkis Mus. inv. 2315) from Gephyra in Macedonia. For the larger question of Hellenistic cavalry shields, see Nefedkin 2009: pp.356–66.
4. Spyridakis 1977: pp.299–307.
5. Griffith 1935: pp. 119 and 144 n.2, where Griffith notes the idea came from Tarn.
6. *Thess.Mnemeia* 119, 8, *SEG* 53: 523. The painted stele is on display in the Volos archaeological museum. This could be the 'Cretan shield' from Plb. 10.29.6.
7. Sekunda 2007: pp.343–44; see e.g. the treaty between Hierapytna and Rhodes, *Syll.*^{3} 581, Austin 2006, no.113.
8. Casson 1993, Burstein 2008; Cobb 2016 and Charles 2007 suggest some were Indian elephants taken in the Third Syrian War, which is a possibility. The Ptolemies gained many elephants from their wars in Syria, and not only from Red Sea hunts.
9. Markle 1978, Hammond 1980, Matthew 2015, and on elite phalanx units, Foulon 1996 and Hatzopoulos 2001: pp. 56-73.
10. For example, the Macedonian Sogenes was a *chiliarch* in the command of Endios, perhaps an infantry unit in the Oxyrhynchite nome or several neighbouring nomes.

Chapter 2: Ptolemy the Satrap, Ptolemy the King

1. *Suda* B'147.2.
2. Ptolemy's acclamation was also associated with his successful intervention in the defence of Rhodes against Demetrius the Besieger from 305–304 BC (Zenon of Rhodes, FGrH 523.2; see for example Gruen 1985), but that occasion is more plausibly and better attested as the source for Ptolemy's cognomen Soter, 'Saviour', awarded to him by the Rhodians (Diod. 20.100.3–4; Paus. 1.8.6).
3. Seibert 1969: p.11 n. 33, Berve 1926: p.106 n. 3.
4. Arrian 3.30.5. Diodorus 17.83.8 and Curtius 7.5.19–26 do not mention Ptolemy's role. This has led to broad criticism of Ptolemy's own history,

upon which Arrian relied; see Roisman 1984 for a more sanguine study of Ptolemy's reliability.
5. Cohen 2006: p.366. Antioch near Daphne's were 112x58m, Laodicea by the sea's were 112x57m and Apameia on the Axios's were 107x54m, while Alexandria's have been measured at 310x277m.
6. Fraser 1996: pp.214–16. The antiquity of the name is suggested by a papyrus (*BGU* 4.1121) from 5 BC that refers to properties in the Alexandrian suburb of Arsinois, 'which is also called "of Eurylochos"'.
7. Bosworth (1980–1995: 1.275) suggested they were conscripted from Persian and other military settlers in Egypt itself, but this would be a hastily raised and suspect army after Alexander took such care over other dispositions in Egypt. But at that stage in Arrian's history of Alexander's campaign, *xenoi* seems always to refer to the mercenaries serving in his campaign army.
8. On this passage and its interpretation, see Hammond 1990 and 1996; on the Royal Pages, see Strootman 2014: pp.136–44, Billows 1997: pp.246–50.
9. On the Caro-Memphites and Helleno-Memphites, who hundreds of years earlier provided bodyguards for Late Dynastic Pharaohs, see *PSI* 5.531, Thompson 1988: pp.88–99.
10. On the *epigonoi*, see Olbrycht 2015.
11. Hammond 1996: p.106.
12. Litvinenko 2001: pp.813–20, Meeus 2015: pp.146–65.
13. Billows 1995: pp.191–92, esp. n. 21, Bosworth 2002: p.84, Roisman 2012: pp.93–95. Most historians have estimated 12,000–15,000 Macedonians in the army after Alexander's death, with 30,000 *Epigonoi* Persians, about 20,000 skirmisher troops and at least another 20,000 auxiliaries of various sorts, or nearly 90,000 in all. More than half could have been distributed to the satraps and generals and kept Perdiccas' royal army at a manageable 40,000. Surprisingly, none of these estimates consider the number of Macedonian cavalry with Perdiccas.
14. Hdt. 2.161–63, Diod. 1.68.1–2 for Apries' Greeks, Diod. 11.71.3–6 and 74.3 for Inaros, Diod. 15.92.2–3 for Teos, Diod. 16.47.6 for Nectanebo. On mercenary service in pre-Ptolemaic Egypt, see Kaplan 2003, Fischer-Bovet 2014: pp.18–27, and Rop 2019. Eumenes managed to hire 10,000 foot and 2,000 horse in short order in 318 BC (Diod. 18.61.4–5).
15. Fischer-Bovet 2014: pp. 37–43, Winnicki 1977: p.268.
16. Winnicki 1985: p.48. For an even dimmer view of the Egyptian contribution, see Lesquier 1911: pp.2–10, 43–44. For elites in the early

Ptolemaic army, including two descendants of the pharaoh Nectanebo, see as well the overview in Moyer 2011: pp.87-91.
17. Kuhrt 2013: pp.458–59, and Tresson 1931.
18. Upper Egypt: Dietze 2000, Thiers 1995; Delta: Redon 2014; the Eastern desert roads to the Red Sea: Redon 2018.
19. Cairo JE 46341; Thiers 1995: doc. 4; Fischer-Bovet 2014: p.265.
20. Cohen, 2006: pp. 393–94, Mueller 2006: pp.143–45.
21. Bagnall 1976: pp.34–35.
22. Hammond 1996: pp.108–09. The *melophoroi*, Apple-Bearers, drawn from Persian aristocracy, are likely identical to the 1,000 Persian hypaspists raised up by Alexander in 324 BC (Arr. 7.11.3, Diod. 17.110.1).
23. Ancient sources: Arrian *Met'A* 1.24, Diod. 18.25.3–4, Just. 13.6, Plut. *Eum.* 5.1. For that war, see Anson 2014: pp.57–82, Billows 1997: pp.64–80, Romm 2011: pp.99–125, Waterfield 2011: pp.57–68, and much of Grainger 2019.
24. Eumenes had about 20,000 foot and 5,000 horse, but the vast majority of the latter were raised among the Cappadocians rather than handed over from the Royal Army (Diod. 18.30.5). Attalus had 16,000 foot and 1,000 horse when he faced Antigonus later, but 6,000 of them were Pisidians whom he may have recruited in Pisidia and not from the royal army, and some of the other troops presumably joined his army after Perdiccas' defeat (Diod. 18.45.1). Dokimos was forced to carry out a military campaign to wrest Babylonia from Archon, the previous satrap (*Met'A* 24.3–5), so he must have had several thousand men with him, aside from the distinguished Macedonians.
25. For secondary sources on Perdiccas' campaign, see Molina 2018, Worthington 2016: pp.95–99, Anson 2014: pp.68–70, Roisman 2014, Romm 2011: pp.163–67.
26. Diod. 15.42.1–3 on Nectanebo I's additional engineering works at Pelusium to aid in defence of Egypt against Persian invasion *c*. 373 BC, and 16.46.6–9 on the canal works around Pelusium during Nectanebo II's defence in 343.
27. The Late Ptolemaic Defenna 'gladius' seems to assure the military occupation of Daphne (Defenna) in the later second or first centuries BC, if not earlier.
28. Engels 1980: pp.154–56.
29. Hoffmeier and Abd El-Maksoud 2003: pp.169–70, fig. 1.
30. Redon 2014: pp.51–52.

31. There are several other pre-Ptolemaic fortified places between these and Pelusium. Tell El-Herr has good evidence for early Ptolemaic or even Alexandrian occupation, but is on the eastern edge of the paleo-lagoon, and does not fit the Diodoran narrative. It is also only 5 miles from and within line of sight of Pelusium.
32. The 'hypaspists' at the Fort of Camels, Anson 1988: pp.131–33, Roisman 2012: pp.99–100, Bosworth 2002: pp.82–83 for a shield-bearing role rather than hypaspists, often rejected since; see Roisman *ibid.* n.37 for citations of places where Alexander used hypaspists for wall assaults, and there are many more comparable places in the record.
33. Front. *Strat.* 4.20, Polyaenus 4.19.
34. On *andreia*, see Rosen and Sluiter 2003; on its connection to Hellenistic kingship, see Billows 1997: pp.323–24. On spear-won land, see Mehl 1980/81: pp.173–212 and Hammond 1988: pp.382–91. In the historiography of Ptolemy I, there are basically two main camps. One, typified by Seibert 1969, describes Ptolemy's defensive imperialism, an Egypt-centric foreign policy little concerned with conquest. The other, typified by Meeus 2015, sees Ptolemy, like Alexander's other Marshals, aimed at universal dominion. Seibert saw Ptolemy as practically craven; Worthington (2016: pp.85-86) sees him as shrewd and ambitious.
35. Eusebius 114.3; Bevan 1927: p.24 followed the Eusebian date, Bouché-Leclerq 1903: pp.50–52 preferred 312 BC, and more recently Bar-Kochva 2010: pp.76–77 argued for 302.

Chapter 3: The Antigonid Wars, 315–285 BC

1. The inscription is SEG 9.1, with 18.726. On the constitution, see Fraser 1958: pp.120–27; Bagnall 1976: pp.28–29; for a translation of 9.1, see Austin 2006: doc. 29. Ptolemy's Cyrenean constitution is given multiple dates; the aftermath of the revolt seems more likely than 321 BC.
2. On the chronology of the war from 313–311 BC, see Hauben 1973. See also Winnicki 1989 and 1991a, Billows 1990: pp.109-34, Anson 2006, Meeus 2012 and 2015, Worthington 2016: pp.147–64.
3. Diod. 19.80.4: ἔχων πεζοὺς μὲν μυρίους ὀκτακισχιλίους, ἱππεῖς δὲ τετρακισχιλίους, ὧν ἦσαν οἱ μὲν Μακεδόνες, οἱ δὲ μισθοφόροι, Αἰγυπτίων δὲ πλῆθος, τὸ μὲν κομίζον βέλη καὶ τὴν ἄλλην παρασκευήν, τὸ δὲ καθωπλισμένον καὶ πρὸς μάχην χρήσιμον.

4. Implied in modern translations of Diodorus; see also Griffith 1935: p.109, Devine 1984: p.35.
5. Diod. 19.85.4: ὁ δὲ Πτολεμαῖος τοὺς μὲν ἁλόντας στρατιώτας ἀποστείλας εἰς Αἴγυπτον προσέταξεν ἐπὶ τὰς νομαρχίας διελεῖν.
6. Garlan 1999: pp.223–24; Bagnall 1976: pp.88–91. On the larger campaign see Hauben 2014, Billows 1990: pp.143-45. Worthington 2016: 147-54 sees in the campaign a bid for the Macedonian throne from the outset.
7. Plut. *Dem.* 16.1 and Diod. 20.49.3 confirm the sixty ships. Plut. *Dem.* 16.4 gives Menelaus 12,000 infantry and 1,200 cavalry to surrender at the end of the campaign (suspiciously correspondent figures), while Diod. 20.47.4 has Menelaus previously losing 4,000 out of 12,800 when he gave battle to Demetrius by land. On the Cyprus campaign and Battle of Salamis, see Hauben 1976, Worthington 2016: pp.157-60. The Egyptian role in the Cyprus campaign (true as well for Ptolemy and many of his best troops) was primarily naval. On Egyptians as rowers, crew, and marines in the Ptolemaic navy, see Van 't Dack and Hauben 1978.
8. 16,000 infantry and 600 cavalry were recorded on Antigonid rosters after being enrolled from the captives on Cyprus (Diod. 20.53.1). Whether these included the 8,000 from the fleet is unclear. Plutarch records that Demetrius' own announcement to his father recorded '12,800 prisoners of war' (*Dem.* 17.5).
9. Gruen 1985: pp.253–58 & 267 n. 37, suggests that Ptolemy assumed the kingship in spring 304 BC, following the defeat of Demetrius I at Rhodes; Samuel 1962: pp.8–10, placed the accession in 305/304 as well. The Parian Marble is *IG XII^5* 444.
10. *Lindos* 99, D.101.
11. Jones 1971: p.99; Will 1979: 1.140; Meadows 2006: pp.460–61.
12. *P.Cair.Zen.* 1.59003, *P.Count* 26, *P.Lille* 1.5, *P.Tebt.* 3.1.818.
13. Unless he was the same Philippos the Macedonian who was governor of Lycia in the autumn of 281 BC (Robert 1966: pp.53–58; see Meadows and Thonemann 2013 for discussion of that text).
14. Diodorus 21.1.5; Appian, *Syrian Wars* 55; Polybius 5.67.
15. Diod. 20.76.7.
16. Shear 1978: pp.61–73; Shear identifies the conquest of Tyre as having taken place between November 288 and November 287 BC based on numismatic evidence, and would prefer a date closer to November 288 because of the size of the Ptolemaic fleet operating in the Aegean.

Chapter 4: Origins of Soldiers in the Ptolemaic Army

1. e.g., Delia 1988: pp.287–88, Rathbone 1990: p.120.
2. The *Gerousia Acts* papyrus (*P.Yale* 2.107, line 15) is discussed at Rostovtzeff 1941: pp.1138–39 and Gambetti 2009: pp.94–105.
3. Fraser 1972: II.172.
4. Scheidel 2004: p.31.
5. Manning 2010: p.139.
6. Coale & Demeny West Model Level 4 is the leading favourite, and I am using the growth rate with that model from Bagnall and Frier 1994: p.100. In truth, which life table we use matters very little for the calculation of later teens relative to military-age males.
7. Clarysse 1998: pp.7–10.
8. Several appear in the *Petrie Wills*, and others are scattered through papyri. Not all are recognized as Alexandrians in their original editions, e.g., *P.Tebt.* 3.1.815, Fragment 5, lines 10–27, contains a lease by Tryphon son of Anaximenes, a cleruch, whom the editors incorrectly identified as a member of the *epigone* because of his patronymic. Because he was a cleruch he was, by definition, not of the *epigone*, and while the papyrus is too damaged to confirm his Alexandrian deme, he was almost certainly an Alexandrian.
9. *SEG* 25.916, *IG* XII3 466, 1296.
10. See *P.Tebt.* 3.1.815, *P.Mich.* 1.66. The others were from Thrace, Samos, Epeiros and Achaia. *P.Petr.* 2 18 probably provides the ethnic for a ninth member of the unit, a Heraklean.
11. Josephus dated this to Alexander's reign in *Against Apion* 2.35–36 and *Jewish War* 2.488, but to the reign of Ptolemy I in *Antiquities of the Jews* 12.8.
12. Kasher 1978; the figure of 30,000 comes from the *Letter of Aristeas* 13, but the *Letter* was composed under a pseudonym for Jewish propaganda purposes in the second century BC, thus exaggeration should be expected. Pseudo-Hecataeus, quoted in Josephus' *Antiquities*, provides the 'tens of thousands' of Jews taken to Egypt under the first Ptolemy, and in *Against Apion* 2.4 Josephus quotes him regarding their use as soldiers there.
13. *P.Enteux.* 23 (218 BC) references a Jewish *politikon* or civic body, probably in the Arsinoite nome, while the Jewish *politeuma* in the Herakleopolite nome is known from an entire archive of second-century documents (*P.Polit.Iud.*, Cowey and Maresch 2001, Kasher 2002).

14. Turner 1974.
15. Clarysse, Martin, and Thompson 2014. Frame 5 of the text includes records for probably six to eight settler cavalry, twenty-eight to forty infantry settlers and then three apparent infantry from the command of Timotheos, all with patronymics, a sign they were citizens, presumably of the much closer Ptolemais rather than remote Alexandria.
16. Uebel 1968 contains a compendium of soldiers and their ethnics, the *Prosopographia Ptolemaica* (Peremans and Van 't Dack 1950–81) an even more exhaustive prosopography organized in different volumes by ethnics, offices or ranks, and La'da 2002 contains a trove of material on the Greek ethnics of Ptolemaic Egypt; additionally, see Bagnall 1984, Clarysse 1985 and 1998, Anagnostou-Canas 1989, O'Neil 2006, Stefanou 2013 and Fischer-Bovet 2011 and 2014: pp.169–77.
17. O'Neil 2006; Fischer-Bovet 2014: pp.169–77, Sanger 2015.
18. Launey 1949–50: pp.1079–80 (my translation); for general discussion, see pp.1064–85.
19. The *politeuma* at Alexandria is the main object of discussion here, although it is known better from the *Letter of Aristeas* than from documentary sources; documentary evidence is better for its analogue in the Herakleopolite nome of Middle Egypt, for which see Cowey and Maresch 2001, *P.Polit.Iud.* There was also a Jewish *politeuma* at Berenice in Cyrenaica. For the Judean population in Egypt, see Capponi 2017, Honigman 2002, Kasher 1985, Zuckerman 1989, and Murray 1967. On the Idumaean *politeuma*, see Thompson 1984.
20. *SEG* II 871.
21. *SB* I 1106, see Van 't Dack 1988: pp.85–95.
22. Abd El-Fattah, Abd El-Maksoud and Carrez-Maratray 2014: pp.149–77.
23. New Paphos: *SEG* 13.573, 587; Old Paphos: the mini-volume of inscriptions in *ABSA 56* 1961.
24. From Crete: *I.Cr. IV* 195 (all Egyptian); Thera: *IG XII^3* 327, 466. *OGIS* 102, from Alexandria, also refers to the soldiers and Egyptian *machimoi* at several garrisons in the Aegean.
25. Rey-Coquais 1976: pp.51–60 and 1978: pp.313–25, and Cohen 2006: pp.124–26.
26. This is approximately the consensus taking shape in the scholarly community, see for example Fischer-Bovet 2013: pp.209–36.
27. Sources for *machimoi* as escorts, staff, or similar to police: *P.Hib.* 1.41 (261 BC), *P.Hib.* 2.248 (*c.* 250 BC), *P.Col.* 4.77 (*c.* 245 BC), *P.Zen.*

Pestm. 49 (244 BC), *SB* 22.15237 (*c.* 240s BC), *P.Grenf.* 14 (233 BC), *SB* 16.12468 (third century BC), *P.Lille* 1.25 (third century BC).

28. In addition to the inscriptions mentioned in the previous section, *UPZ* 1.110 contains a reference to naval *machimoi*. *SEG* 8.714 is a dedication at Thebes by the Greek leaders of a religious association of *machimoi* stationed on the island of Thera.
29. Derchain 1986.
30. Klotz 2009: p.302. See also Quack 2008: pp.277–78 and Fischer-Bovet 2014: p.162.
31. Also *ṯz.n=f* as 'collected' rather than 'levied' or 'raised', *tp.w=sn* as 'leaders' rather than 'officers', and *ḥwn.w nfr.w* as 'good youths' is a phrase that almost always has a military context and should be analogous to a royal page programme or *ephebeia* cadet system. Klotz translates *ḏȝm.w=f* as 'troops'.
32. Early editions of the stele avoided this difficulty, filling a lacuna at the end of the line to read 'sons of Mendes' rather than 'sons of Egypt'. This resolves the difficulty immediately and sensibly, but subsequent examinations of the text (see Maulenaere 1976) have largely assured that *[tȝ]-mry*, 'the Beautiful Land', i.e. Egypt, is the correct reading.
33. The main works are Pestman 1963, Oates 1963, Bresciani 1972, Goudriaan 1988: pp.18–20, Vandersleyen 1988, La'da 1997: pp.187–89 and Vandorpe 2008.
34. For the most important recent coverage, see Clarysse and Thompson 2006, Vandorpe 2008, Fischer-Bovet 2014: pp.186–87.
35. Fischer-Bovet 2014: pp.186–87, Vandorpe 2008: pp.87–109, Clarysse and Thompson 2006: p.159. Some have suggested they were actual Persians or Greek soldiers from the Persian Empire's garrisons in Egypt, most famously Hammond 1996: pp.108–09, who suggested that they were the descendants of the thousand Apple-bearers in Alexander's funeral guard. On the demotic terms used to designate Persian and other Egyptian soldiers, see Winnicki 1986, Vleeming 1985, La'da 2007.
36. *Pros.Ptol.* (PP) 1972, 2027, 2084, 2092, 2150, 2176.
37. *P.Sorb.* 3.73, *P.Hib.* 1.112, *PSI* 5.513.
38. *P.Mich.* 18.781 lists nine Persian cleruchs, at least one of whom seems likely to be an infantryman, although all may be. After that, *P.Hels.* 1.16 (163 BC) identifies a Persian infantry cleruch. Persian soldiers in Upper Egypt, who were generally paid soldiers rather than cleruchs, are commonplace after the Ptolemaic reconquest of the Thebaid in 186 BC.

Chapter 5: The Age of Midas, Part I

1. Livy, *Per.* 14; Justin 18.2.9; Dion. Hal. 20.14; Zonarus 8.6.11. Livy is most important for dating the embassy to 273 BC; the others show that the Romans sent ambassadors to Alexandria.
2. Theocritus *Idyll* 15.6 on the men of Alexandria: παντᾷ κρηπῖδες, παντᾷ χλαμυδηφόροι ἄνδρες, 'all boots and military cloaks', *Idyll* 14.58–59 on the desirability of mercenary service with Ptolemy: Αἰσχίνα. εἰ δ' οὕτως ἄρα τοι δοκεῖ ὥστ' ἀποδαμεῖν,μισθοδότας Πτολεμαῖος ἐλευθέρῳ οἷος ἄριστος. *Idyll* 17.88–92 on the conquest and recruitment of southern Asia Minor: Παμφύλοισί τε πᾶσι καὶ αἰχμηταῖς Κιλίκεσσι σαμαίνει, Λυκίοις τε φιλοπτολέμοισί τε Καρσί καὶ νάσοις Κυκλάδεσσιν, and 17.93–94 on the impressive army of the king: πολλοὶ δ' ἱππῆες, πολλοὶ δέ μιν ἀσπιδιῶται χαλκῷ μαρμαίροντι σεσαγμένοι ἀμφαγέρονται.
3. Callixenus, *FGrH* 3, 2.385–86: Πεζοὶ μὲν ἐς πέντε μυριάδας καὶ ἑπτακισχιλίους καὶ ἑξακοσίους, ἱππεῖς δὲ δισμύριοι τρισχίλιοι διακόσιοι. On the Procession, which occurred in 274 or 270 BC, see Foertmeyer 1988, Rice 1983, Walbank 1996, Thompson 2000, Johstono 2018.
4. Gaza: Diod. 19.80.4, including the retinue of Seleucus and mercenary horse; Raphia: Plb. 5.79.2, including 2,000 mercenary cavalry.
5. Just. 17.2.14: Ptolemeus, *cui nulla dilationis ex infirmitate uirium* ('Ptolemy, who could not claim lack of forces as an excuse').
6. The key discussions on this conquest are Meadows 2006, 2012 and 2013.
7. Tarn 1926, Will 1979: 1.139–44, Huss 2001: pp.261–62, Meadows 2012: pp.117–18.
8. *SB* 3.6134, see Fischer-Bovet 2014: p.262 for discussion and additional sources.
9. Burstein 2008: pp.139–40, Dietze 1994, Török 1997 and 2009.
10. Dates in the Pithom stele are a subject of some debate, because it is unclear whether the stele definitively uses dates from Ptolemy II's coregency with his father or counts years from the beginning of his sole rule; it could even use both inconsistently. Ptolemy used coregency regnal years in the Macedonian calendar from a very early point, but there is a good bit of evidence some Egyptian dates were based on Ptolemy's accession to sole rule. The prevailing view is that the Pithom stele uses years from the coregency (Samuel 1962: pp.26–27, 68–74), although for the opposing view see Hazzard 2000: pp.89–90.

11. The spelling in the stele defies a conclusive statement. But on the point, see Winnicki 1990, who reviews the evidence and favours Palestine, similarly Lorton 1971, Thiers 2007.
12. The royal couple were deified as the Theoi Philadelphoi, the sibling-loving gods, no later than 272 BC, based on their incorporation that year into the royal cult. Hazzard (*ibid.*) employed the cult reform and the presence of the queen in the Pithom stele to argue that the Pithom stele's year 14 refers to 272/271 BC rather than 274/273. Changing the dating method for the Pithom stele in this way baldly contradicts the information in Pausanias.
13. Sachs and Hunger 1988, no. -273B. See the tablet and its translation at < http://cgeh.nl/cgeh/translation-astronomical-diary.htm>. See also Van der Spek 1993.
14. *TAM V,2* 881 and *Erythrai* 18 both record Seleucid activity, and strongly suggest the local presence of the king, in 276/275 and 275/274 BC, respectively. The latter text also makes mention of Seleucid naval forces.
15. On the revolt, see *OGIS* 219 and Memnon (*FGrH* 434) 9.1. On the comparatively light army Antiochus commanded in Asia Minor (the heavy phalanx was drawn largely from settlers in the Seleukis), see Lucian, *Zeuxis* 8. It is also possible he had recently fought the Elephant Battle against the Galatians, in which he was wounded in the neck and presumably laid up for some time (OGIS 220). On Antiochus' war with the Galatians, see Wörrle 1975, Çoskun 2012.
16. Bar-Kochva 1976: pp.78–79. Bar-Kochva and Tarn (1926) connected Ptolemy's campaign with the revolt in the Seleukis, but this produces incredible chronological difficulties Bar-Kochva ignored and which did not apply for Tarn because the Babylonian chronicles were not yet reliably dated.
17. Historiography of the Chremonidean War is far more extensive than the ancient source material. Leading studies include Launey 1945: pp.35–39, Heinen 1972: pp.92–213, Habicht 1992, O'Neil 2008: pp.71–87 and Hauben 2013: pp.39–65.
18. Casson 1971, Tarn 1930, Murray 2012.
19. Hauben 1970 and 2013: pp.39–65.
20. Gill 2007: pp.60–61, Bagnall 1976: p.135, Cohen 1995: p.125.
21. For a review of the inscriptional evidence for the base-founding campaign, see Hauben 2013: pp.54–60.
22. Ps-Aristeus 180–81 also contains a memory of a celebrated but unnamed Ptolemaic victory over the fleet of Antigonus. So even Kos, though

more famous, seems not to have been a decisive battle or the only one of the conflict. Chronology in Ps-Aristeus is famously fraught, so it is impossible to date the battle (Demetrius of Phalerum is alive, Arsinoe II is married to Ptolemy II and still living, and the High Priest is Eleazar; none of the three referents overlapped at all). Scholars have reckoned the fight at Kos to either an early date (262–261) or a late (257–256), with more evidence needed to resolve the date; see Peremans 1939, Momigliano and Fraser 1950, Buraselis 1982: pp. 141-50, Hammond and Walbank 1988: pp. 595-99, Reger 1994: 39–41.

23. Ath. 5.209e; Paus. 1.29.1 mentions an 'undefeated "nine"' that Antigonus dedicated at Delos. Tarn 1930: pp.212–18 and Casson 1971: p.139 suggested these ships were the same.
24. For the economic angle on elephant hunts, see Burstein 1996. On the elephant hunts in general, see Casson 1993 and Cobb 2016.
25. Will 1979: 1.234–61, Heinen in *CAH VII¹*: 412–19. The war ended in 253 BC; see Clarysse 1980: pp.83–89.
26. Front. *Strat.* 3.2.11; Habicht 1957: p.220 made the astute observation on Sa[m]iorum, endorsed as well by Bagnall 1976: p.81.
27. It has been very widely assumed that Ptolemaic control over Ephesos extended back into the period after the First Syrian War, but all of the evidence that grounded this assumption relies on associating 'Ptolemy the Son' (of Lysimachus) with the Ptolemy who was at Ephesos and slain by Thracian mercenaries, which has been disproven satisfactorily. Nonetheless it is often stated, wrongly, that Ptolemy II controlled Ephesos from about 268 BC until the Second Syrian War, see Huss 1998 and Gygax 2002.
28. Segre 1938: pp.181–208; Bagnall 1976: pp.106–09; Billows 1995: pp.101–03.
29. *Lindos* 99.C.98–103, translated in Burstein 1985: pp.60–62.
30. Badoud 2014: pp.116–19. See also the Delian reference to a peace treaty in 255 BC, *IG XI* 2.116, cf. Reger 1994: p.44.
31. See Blumel 1992 for the Kildaran inscription indicative of his military position in southern Asia Minor at the outset of the Third Syrian War, when he was simultaneously eponymous priest. For the trierarch Xanthippos, see Bagnall 1971.
32. Barbantani 2010: pp.72–102; Strobel 1996: pp.125–26.
33. Jones and Habicht 1989; Cohen 1995: pp.363–64; Sosin 1997.
34. Davesne and Yenisoganci 1992; Grainger 2014: p.172; Aperghis 2006: p.204.
35. Clarysse 2007; Winnicki 1991b.

36. The other potential referent for 'the boy' is Ptolemy Andromachou, a bastard son of Ptolemy II who was eponymous priest in 251/250 BC and held several military commands in the Third Syrian War. But his birth is usually reckoned around 268 or later, which would make him much too young.

Chapter 6: The Age of Midas II: The Settlements

1. Diod. 20.47.4: διὰ τὸ τὰς ἀποσκευὰς ἐν Αἰγύπτῳ καταλελοιπέναι παρὰ Πτολεμαίῳ, cf. Chapter 2.
2. These texts date between 311/310 and 284/283 BC, many of them focused on Temnite families, but business dealings and witness lists provide a window into the ethnic background of the community.
3. See in particular *P.Hib.* 1.84 (=*Chr.Mitt.* 131), from 285/284 BC.
4. From *P.Hamb.* 2.168: [οἱ μὲ]ν στρατιῶται ἀπογραφέσθωσαν τά τε ὀνόματα [αὐτ]ῶν καὶ τὰς πατρίδας καὶ ἐξ ὧν ἂν ταγμάτων ὦσιν [καὶ ἃ]ς ἂν ἔχωσιν ἐπιφοράς.
5. We only can say that it doesn't date to Ptolemy II's 7th regnal year, 279/278 BC (counting the years from his co-rule with his father), because the eponymous priest is listed in the Hibeh text and for the 7th year in *P.Yale* 1.27, but no other is known until the 12th year, 274/273.
6. See discussion in Van 't Dack 1988: pp.103–23, Kramer *CPR XVIII* 74–78, Bagnall 1969, and Fischer-Bovet and Clarysse 2012: pp.29–34.
7. To these we might add the mercenary cavalry of Ptolemaios son of Spinther, Eupolemos and Demeas, but none is securely attested at the same dates.
8. Clarysse, Thompson and Capron 2011: p.51.
9. The chief text on the estate of Apollonios and career of Zenon is still Rostovtzeff 1922, but see Bingen 2006: pp.229–39 for a study of the administration of the estate in its early years, before Zenon took over, and Kloppenborg (2006: pp. 285–292, 355–442) on aspects of managing the estate and Zenon's other endeavours.
10. Irrigation infrastructure was top priority in the Fayum, as demonstrated by the activity of the architect Kleon (see *P.Petr.* 2.13 in particular), and the activities of Apollonios' agents within his estate (*P.Lille* 1, *PSI* 486 and 488, *P.Cair.Zen.* 1.59109), see also *P.Petr.* 2.42 and 3.39 in other parts of the Fayum. See Rostovtzeff 1922: pp.60–64.
11. See Rostovtzeff 1922: pp.136–39 and Lesquier 1911: pp.202–05.

12. *P.Genova* 4.137 dates to 258/257 BC, may relate to business in the Fayum, and mentions two cleruchs and 50 artabas of wheat for seed grain between them. *P.Cair.Zen.* 2.59207 is from 255/254, and refers to at least two cleruchs who had been settled in somewhere near Philadelpheia.
13. See also *PSI* 8.976; Scheuble-Reiter 2014: p.39 reckoned Neoptolemos one of the cavalry settlers, but it is equally likely he was among the infantry; see also Clarysse 1988.
14. Meyer 1900: pp.73–75 read the status of second-century BC *epigonoi* units into the third century, as privileged active-duty units of the main army. Lesquier 1911: pp.52–55 and Scholl 1987: pp.111–15 considered the *epigonoi* active-duty soldiers as well, but sons of cleruchs, who eventually succeeded to the place of their fathers. The analysis by La'da 1997: p.569 is probably the best thus far: the *epigonoi* and *tes epigones* were equivalent groups, sons of soldier-settlers and themselves eligible for military service, though he expresses doubt about the conditions for conscription and allowed that some were active duty soldiers. Clarysse and Thompson 2006: p.464 suggest that the *epigonoi* provided much of the Ptolemaic infantry, while cleruchs provided mostly cavalry. See as well Fischer-Bovet 2014: pp.177–87.
15. This name does not appear in a papyrus until the Fourth Syrian War, which has led to some speculation that Ibion was not settled until nearer that date. The reform that folded the 25-aroura class into the 30-aroura class around 235 BC suggests the Ibion settlement predated the reform.

Chapter 7: Ptolemy III and the Third Syrian War

1. *P.Col.* 4.89.6–7: εἰς τὴν ἀνάδωσιν τῶν στρατιωτῶν.
2. Heinen 1984: pp.420–21; for variant narratives of the war, see Will 1979: i.259ff, Hauben 1990: pp.29–37, Altenmueller 2010: pp.27–44, Grainger 2010: pp.153–70 and 2014: pp.186–99, and Çoskun 2018. For the surrounding problems of Ptolemaic chronology and the war, see: Hölbl 1994: pp.46–50, Gygax 2000: pp.353–66 and 2002: pp.49–56, Huss 1998: pp.229–50 and 2001: pp.338–54, and Tunny 2000: pp.83–92.
3. Çoskun 2018 and Grainger 2014: pp.186–99 are the two most important recent accounts of this war. Çoskun's new chronology, which places the War of the Brothers prior to most of the Third Syrian War, should be rejected on any number of counts, but the simplest is that it provides

no avenue for Seleucus to be present in Sardis or Ephesos about the time the war began, where he received embassies from Ionian cities and minted coins in his name.
4. Just. 27.2.11–12; Plut. *Mor.* 489A-B, 508D-E; Polyaenus *Strat.* 4.9.6, 8.61.
5. Polyaenus 4.15.1, Grainger 2009: pp.247–49.
6. Many scholars have pointed to a Babylonian tablet, *MMA* 86.11.299, as evidence Laodike was still alive in 236 BC, but the references to Laodike in the tablet are uniformly to actions of hers when she was still Antiochus II's queen. There is no particular reason to feel confident she outlived 245 BC.
7. Antigonus' festivals were not necessarily related to the victory at Andros; his reverence for the Saviour Gods and Pan hearkens to his victory over Gauls at Lysimacheia, as argued cogently by Champion 2005. In favour of the link between the festivals and the battle at Andros, see Reger 1994: pp.43–46, Hammond and Walbank 1988: pp.587–99 and Buraselis 1982: pp.141–47.
8. Segre 1944: p.274; Huss 1976, Huss 1977, Bulow-Jacobsen 1977, Schwartz 1978, Oikonomides 1978 and Habicht 1980.
9. See discussion, for example, in Buraselis 1982: pp.124–41, Kosmetatou 2004: pp.18–36, and Ogden 2008: pp.353–85.
10. On Ptolemaios Andromachou, Ptolemy the Son, Ptolemy of Ephesos and Ptolemy son of Lysimachus, and the confusion arising from varying ways of identifying two near contemporaries who both held command at Ephesos a decade apart, see Tunny 2000: pp.83–92 for overview and further reading, as well as Holleaux 1921, Huss 1998: pp.242–44, Bagnall 1976: pp.169–70, Grainger 2010: p.167 and Hammond and Walbank 1988: p.592.
11. Oikonomides 1978 very plausibly reconstructs the last line as dating the death of Ptolemy III to the Athenian archon Euxenos. Lines 18–21 refer to Ptolemy's role in the Aitolian-Macedonian war, for which see Schwartz 1978.
12. Piejko 1990, 'Episodes from the Third Syrian War in a Gurob Papyrus, 246 BC', AfP 36: pp.13–27.
13. ἤδη 20 ἡλίου περὶ καταφορὰν ὄντος εἰσέλθομεν εὐθέω[ς] 21 πρὸς τὴν ἀδελφὴν καὶ μετὰ ταῦτα πρὸς τῶ[ι] 22 πράσσειν τι τῶν χρησίμων ἐγινόμεθα
14. Altenmueller 2010: p.31, Huss 2001: p.345.
15. Burstein 2016, Altenmuller 2010, El-Masry *et. al.* 2012.

16. Van der Spek 1997/98: pp.167–75. Many of the texts discussed in this section are being actively edited on the internet at <www.livius.org/sources/content/mesopotamian-chronicles-content/>.
17. <https://www.livius.org/sources/content/mesopotamian-chronicles-content/bchp-11-invasion-of-ptolemy-iii-chronicle/>. Official publication is anticipated in 2020. On the text, see Clanciers 2012 and some discussion in Burstein 2016.
18. The text, on obv. 3, 7–8, refers to a city, Seleukeia, the royal city located on the Euphrates and on the Royal Canal. Other Babylonian texts refer to this city, and were it not for the reference to the Euphrates, it would easily be thought the city of Seleukeia-on-the-Tigris, which truly was a royal city, complete with a royal residence and also on the Royal Canal. The Royal Canal connected the Tigris and the Euphrates, the former at Seleukeia, the latter several miles north of Babylon, near Sippar. Line 4 refers specifically to the presence of Ptolemy outside Babylon.
19. Preliminary edition at <https://www.livius.org/sources/content/mesopotamian-chronicles-content/bchp-10-seleucid-accessions-chronicle/>.
20. Potts 2017.
21. Much has at times been made of an Uruk document dated by Seleucus II from 11 July 245 BC. It is at least the earliest documentary text dated by that king, but it is clear he was recognized as the true king in Mesopotamia from August 246, and thus there is little reason to grant it particular weight.
22. Cohen 2013: p.77. The date is based on the first year of the 134th Olympiad, as found in the *Chronicon Pascale*.
23. Blumel, AE 20 1992, pp.127–33; *SEG* 42.994; *BE* 94, 528.
24. Crampa 1969: p.82ff; Habicht 1972: pp.144–47. See *I.Labr.* 3, a letter from Philip V, for a description of Olympichos' status under Seleucus II. See also Walbank 1942, Virgilio 2001 and Isager and Karlsson 2008 for more on the career of Olympichos.
25. Ma 2002: p.44. We might add to this the decree from Smyrna (see next note), which certainly resulted from multiple embassies to the king (*cf.* the example of the Samians), who lobbied the Seleucids before rejoining the Ptolemies, or Miletos, which seems also to have lobbied Seleucus for grants and privileges in exchange for loyalty (*RC* 22, *OGIS* 227). Miletos had been taken by Antiochus II and must have either fallen back to Ptolemy III earlier in the war or been at risk of doing so.

26. In addition to the locations mentioned above, Larisa and Lebedos were renamed as new Ptolemaic settlements and unpublished inscriptions Bagnall 1976: pp.169-70, 175 indicate that Kolophon, Teos and Ephesos were all captured by Ptolemaic forces during the Third Syrian War. For a review of the scattered evidence, see Bagnall 1976: pp.159–60, Cohen 1995: pp.157–58, 188–90 and Ma 2002: p.45.
27. *IG* XII.8.156 for Hippomedon, as well as the comment of Teles in *Of Exiles*, Hense, p. 23. The decree for Epinikos has been partially published in multiple works, but see especially Gauthier 1979 and further commentary in Bagnall 1976: pp.160–65, Ma 2002: p.45 and Pritchett V.342.
28. Rigsby 1996.
29. Tarn 1928: p.717, Rostovtzeff 1941: I.414. Will 1979: I.225 suggests that court intrigues provided '*un prétexte à justifier une retraite honorable*'.
30. Droysen 1877: p.403, Edgar 1931: p.7.
31. Mahaffy 1895: pp.202–05.
32. Huss 1978: pp.151–56) has laid out both the historiography of the revolt and suggested the reading of the papyrus that describes the revolt. His reading has since been accepted by later writers; the plates accompanying Bulow-Jacobsen 1977 confirm the reading.
33. Manning *et. al.* 2017 provide evidence for a series of poor inundations, potentially resulting from volcanic activity, in the 240s BC that could match well with the reconstruction offered here.
34. Tax receipts from the Thebaid, a region closely associated with later revolts, exhibit no irregularities in the 240s BC that might indicate a rebellion.
35. *P.Enteux* 48 (217 BC), *P.Frankf.* 7 (215 BC), *P.Genova* 3.103–6 (219/218 BC), *P.Tebt.* 1.137 (217 BC) and *SB* 12.11061 (218 BC) all either discuss activities at or originated from military camps, or refer to leases related to military campaigns. In the second century BC, when most campaigns were in Egypt proper, references to camps and leases of land before deployments are even more common.
36. The royal half-*kleros* was used in later years as a sort of absentee management system, but for individual cleruchs. See, e.g., *P.Enteux.* 55, the complaint of an 80-arouras cavalryman against a Macedonian infantryman, arising from the handling of his affairs after the infantryman had rented the cavalryman's royal hemi-kleros while he was in Alexandria and absent from his land for a prolonged period.
37. *P.Petr.* 2.35.A3.1: ἐπιστολὴν προσῆλθεν πρὸς τοὺ[ς](*) ἵππους [-ca.?- τ]ῶν ἐν τῶι ε (ἔτει) παραγεγονότων. Tantalizing, but inconclusive, are

the characters to the left of ἐπιστολὴν, 'Syr', a possible reference to Syria itself.
38. *Chr.Wilck.* 452, on an elephant hunt; *P.Lond.* 7.1938 and *P.Cair. Zen.* 2.59175, conveyance of troops in Egypt during the Second Syrian War
39. A work record from the Perithebaid in 242/241 BC (*UPZ* 2.157) includes a categorized status list for 282 men, which noted that thirty-seven men were registered as fugitives and fifty-three older men were registered as guards for the dikes and canals.
40. It is mistakenly read as a status transfer in Lewis 2001: p.164, a mercenary becoming a cleruch and receiving an allotment.
41. On this nomarch, see Clarysse 1974. For his initial role overseeing the allotment of *hekatontarouroi* in the *epoikion* of Metrodoros, see *P.Lille* 1.12, where his role in overseeing transfers of grain to the royal granaries is also mentioned as in *P.Lille* 1.13 (244/243 BC). He is identified as a *nomarches* over a region with cavalry settlement at *P.Petr.* 2.39a 19–20, cf. *P.Petr.* 2.37 and *PSI* 4.399 and others. For his involvement in irrigation, see the section above on evidence for the insurrection.

Chapter 8: Ptolemy III and the Purported Decline of the Ptolemaic Army

1. The latest papyrus dated to Ptolemy III's reign is *P.Sorb.* 1.48, dated early January 221 BC, while the first to Ptolemy IV is *P.Enteux.* 83, dated to late February 221, with a less securely dated reference to year 1 of Ptolemy IV also including a date near mid-January 221.
2. Van 't Dack (1988: p.33) pinpoints the reign of Euergetes as the beginning of the decline of the Ptolemaic army. He and Lesquier located the dissolution of their military quality in the economic emphasis built into the cleruchic system.
3. Bar-Kochva 1976: p.48.
4. *OGIS* 273–279, Hansen 1937, Heinen in *CAH* VII.1, 1984: pp.428–32.
5. For the career of Olympichos, see the Labraunda inscriptions and discussion in Crampa 1969, Isager and Karlson 2008, and overviews in LaBuff 2015: pp.35–40 and Chrubasik 2016: pp.58–59.
6. For example, the main military engagement of the period was the Achaean defeat at Phylakia in Arcadia, but Demetrius II was not present personally, and rumours grossly exaggerated the size and decisiveness of the engagement (Plut. *Arat.* 34.2–3).

7. Habicht 1997: pp.173–78 questioned Ptolemaic involvement, but Ptolemaic subsidies and Ptolemaic agents almost certainly played a role, even if the decision was not Ptolemy III's; Paus. 2.8.6, Plut. *Arat.* 34.5–6, *IG 2² 1.786, IG 2³* 1.1160, *IG 2³* 1.1140.
8. For discussion of the campaign, see Walbank 1942, Habicht 1972 and Hammond and Walbank III.343–44.
9. Huss 1977, Habicht 1980: p.4.
10. On the capture, see Huss 1977: p.192. It is also conceivable Pergamene forces captured Andromachos and sent him to Alexandria in 223 BC or earlier (Will 1979: pp.313-14).
11. Grainger 2006: p.219 dated the start of the Aetolian involvement in Demetrius' wars with the Achaean League in 236 BC, Larsen 1975 and Scholten 2000: pp.132-52 to 238 BC.
12. Ptolemaic involvement is confirmed by an honorific dedication at Thermon in Aetolia, *IG IX,1²* 1.56. Its presence in the Aetolian capital makes most sense within the context of Ptolemaic assistance. The Aetolians also named a new settlement in honour of Ptolemy (Cohen 1995: pp.33–34).
13. Bagnall 1976: pp.170–71, 211 Whatever may have transpired during the revolt of the Thracian mercenaries, Ephesos was later used as a royal mint for Ptolemy III, the only royal mint outside Egypt in the second century BC, and was not taken by Seleucid forces until the Fifth Syrian War (Porphyry, 11.15–16).
14. See the preceding chapter, n.27 for references.
15. Cohen 2006: pp.305–44 and Mueller 2006: pp.152–56.
16. [Ἴσιδ]ι Σαράπιδι Ἁρποχρ[ά]τη[ι Ἄ]μμωνι θεοῖς Σωτῆρσιν ὑπὲρ [τ]ῆς τῶν ἐλεφάντων σωτηρίας; for the date in the early part of Euergetes' reign, see Bingen 2006: p.34. *P.Grenf.* 1.9 (240 BC) should also relate to the elephant hunts in those years.
17. *P.Hib.* 1.81, *P.Petr.2* 3 and 6, *P.Petr.* 3.21.
18. *OGIS* 99, *Thebes a Syene* 314.
19. *Pan du Desert* 2 and *P.Grad.* 1.
20. Kramer 1991: pp.79–80 presented an argument for a date around 235 BC as part of the edition of the Theogonis papyri, with their many mentions of the numbered hipparchies, in *CPR* XVIII.
21. It mentions Sosos, of Kos, a 100-arouras man of the 5th hipparchy. *P.Heid.* 6.383 was redated to 234 BC in Fischer-Bovet and Clarysse 2012b, which would make that text the earliest case. It too refers to two men from the 5th hipparchy.

22. The first fragment has, however, the last mention in a papyrus of the eponymous command of Lichas. The reform was either instituted shortly after that text but before the next fragment, or Lichas' command was a mercenary command, so that the reform did not immediately impact his unit. At least two pre-reform eponymous commands survived the reform because their mercenary cavalry were not absorbed by the new regimental structure: Pythangelos and Eteoneus.
23. See *SB* 16.12221 and Straus 1983.
24. Also in the second century: *P.Monts.Roca* 4.76 (183/182 BC), *P.Giss.* 2 (173 BC) and *P.Würzb.* 4 (142 BC).
25. See *PSI* 8.976 for cavalry settlement in the Aphroditopolite, and *P.Hib.* 2.198.Fr1, *P.Cair.Zen.* 3.59325 and *P.Lond.* 7.2015 for the Memphite.
26. Of the *hyperetes*, only one seems to have possessed an allotment larger than 100 arouras, Philoxenos of the 5th hipparchy, who possessed, according to his *chomatikon* tax, a per-arouras tax, 255.
27. The chief outlier is *P.Petr.* 2.47 (209 BC), which mentions several men in the 2nd hipparchy and eponymous command of [Hippo]krates, who had not been attested in a papyrus since 224 BC. Most of the dating formula exists in the text, so it is unlikely to be dated incorrectly; it could have read, e.g., [Poly]krates.
28. Clarysse 2004: p.27, the 80-arouras cavalryman Demetrios son of Asklepiades, Persian. Other early examples include *P.Enteux.* 8 and *P.Petr.* 3.112, both from 221 BC.
29. Scheuble-Reiter 2012: pp.65–71, Fischer-Bovet 2014: pp.125–33, with Scheuble-Reiter 2014 on *P.UB Trier* SS 77-43.
30. Fischer-Bovet 2014: p.113, Kramer 1991: pp.79–80.
31. Two Thracian cleruchs near Memphis, *P.Cair.Zen.* 1.59001 (274 BC) are the earliest; the only other before the reform is a Lykian cleruch in the Fayum, *P.Zen.Pestm.* 20 (252 BC).
32. *P.Hamb.* 3.202 (220s BC) has an Egyptian family farming a 70-arouras plot of land around Techtho Nesos, perhaps in a temporary role prior to the assumption of the *kleros* by a soldier.
33. *BGU* 10:1959 – Ptolemaios, a Bithynian, in the eponymous command of Nikomedes in 215/214 BC.
34. The Thessalian cavalry were famed in the fourth century BC as lancers, but in the third century, cavalry across Greece were adopting large shields and carrying throwing spears or javelins as often as lances; see Nefedkin 2009. The many funerary stelai from Bithynia and Mysia

depict an identical shift in panoply in those regions as well; see Post 2010. Thracians likely followed a similar trajectory, although that is more difficult to confirm.
35. For unshielded cavalry, see Brown 1957: nos 16, 21 and 34, just a few examples of many.
36. Both shielded and unshielded cavalry terracottas are known from Ptolemaic Cyprus, for which, see Young 1955: nos 2032, 2214 and 2935. Evidence for shielded cavalry in Egypt itself is rare; the only evidence of which I am aware is a terracotta figurine depicting Bes on horseback, with an aspis, for which see Török 1995, no. 19.
37. Krateros' command appeared in the Herakleopolite and Arsinoite nomes, included two attested Macedonians, a Mesembrian and Pisidian, and is not attested after the reform; see *P.Lille* 1.27, 234 BC, *P.Hib.* 2.267, *P.Stras.* 7.642, P.Köln. 16.642. The last also gives us the infantry command of Pleistarchos, with attested officers from Elis and Macedon.
38. See also *P.Petr.* 3.112, section D, for two more men from the *triakontarouroi Makedones* who actually held 25 arouras.
39. Lines 7–8: τῶν οὔπω ὑπὸ ἡγεμόνα.
40. Van 't Dack 1993.
41. See, for example, *CPR* 18.18.382, *P.Cair.Zen.* 3.59340.19 and *P.Petr.* 2.1.85, 2.16.47.
42. The latest Ptolemaic soldier described as lacking a hegemon is in *SB* 5.7632, a *taktomisthos* (paid soldier) from Larissa, in 159 BC.
43. Most recently, see Fischer-Bovet 2014: pp.208–09, as well as Clarysse and Thompson 2006: 2.153. Monson 2012: p.89 gave a higher-range estimate of a little more than 1,000 men on about 32,000 arouras.
44. BGU 20.2840 (200 BC, or more likely 176) identifies a troop of *pezoi hypaithroi*, encamped infantry, part of the *Makedonikon*, the division of Macedonians, in the Herakleopolite nome. They numbered almost 200 men, three-quarters of a *taxis* by the Ptolemaic system. See also *P.Tebt.* 3.1.722, *P.Tebt.* 3.2.856 (171 BC).
45. Wheeler 2004: pp.313n.25, 336–43; cf. Devine 1989 and 1995, Sekunda 2001: pp.125–34; Wrightson 2015: pp. 87–89.
46. At Cynoscephelae, Livy 33.4, and Magnesia, Livy 37.40 and Appian *Syriaca* 32.
47. The first several chapters of the edited volume by Pretzler and Barley 2018 contain helpful material on Aeneas.
48. Plut.*Phil.* 4.5: καὶ γὰρ τῶν τακτικῶν θεωρημάτων, τὰς ἐπὶ τοῖς πινακίοις διαγραφὰς ἐῶν χαίρειν, ἐπὶ τῶν τόπων αὐτῶν ἐλάμβανεν ἔλεγχον καὶ

μελέτην ἐποιεῖτο, χωρίων συγκλινίας καὶ πεδίων ἀποκοπὰς καὶ ὅσα περὶ ῥείθροις ἢ τάφροις ἢ στενωποῖς πάθη καὶ σχήματα διασπωμένης καὶ πάλιν συστελλομένης φάλαγγος ἐπισκοπῶν αὐτὸς πρὸς αὑτὸν ἐν ταῖς ὁδοιπορίαις, καὶ τοῖς μεθ' ἑαυτοῦ προβάλλων. Loeb translation: 'Indeed, he would ignore the charts and diagrams for the illustration of tactical principles, and get his proofs and make his studies on the ground itself. The ways in which places slope to meet one another, and level plains come to an abrupt end, and all the vicissitudes and shapes of a phalanx when it is elongated and contracted again in the vicinity of ravines or ditches or narrow defiles, these he would investigate by himself as he wandered about, and discuss them with his companions.'

Chapter 9: The Fourth Syrian War and the Battle of Raphia

1. Griffith 1935, pp.118–25; Heinen in *CAH* VII.12 1984, pp.433–42; Hölbl 2001, pp.129–32; Huss 2001, pp.386–404; Fischer-Bovet and Clarysse 2012.
2. History of the Ptolemaic state has rejected one part of the narrative of Ptolemaic decline, and embraced the other. That part which falls to Polybius' bias against Egyptian culture is rejected, see Fischer-Bovet 2015, Walbank 2002: pp.53–69, 193–211, and the tenor of recent major studies like Manning 2010 and Monson 2012. That part which falls to the Ptolemaic army, tied to a conviction that *kleroi* weakened the army, still stands: Van 't Dack 1988: p.33, Fischer-Bovet 2014: pp.45, 56, 86–87, and Grainger 2015: p.72.
3. Bar-Kochva 1976: pp.40–45; the figures are not incredibly consistent: it is seems likely the citizens of Seleukeia were included in his tally, for example, despite living under Ptolemaic rule at the time.
4. And even in the Seleucid world, where Antiochus III eventually fielded a phalanx of 16,000 professional Macedonian soldiers at Magnesia in 190 BC.
5. Locating Gerrha and Brochoi has been the subject of considerable discussion, much of it collected in Cohen 2006: pp.103–04, 240–41.
6. Dorymenes of Aetolia was a mercenary hipparch (*SEG VII* 326), as was, it seems, Hippolochos of Thessaly (Plb. 5.70.11), and a unit of settler cavalry is attested in the command of Toubias at Philadelphia-Rabbathammon and the Sidonian hipparch Libanos' tomb at Maresha in Idumaea has been published.

7. Alexippos was one of the leading men of Larisa at the time of the Fourth Syrian War (*IG IX,2* 517), and Hippolochos son of Alexippos had taken his place by the early second century BC (*IG X,2* 506), then was elected to lead the Thessalians several times between 182 and 178 BC. If they are one and the same men, Hippolochos was quite a young *condotierre* or quite an old president; but his contemporary Polykrates of Argos had a similar length of career.
8. Plb. 5.64.5: συνήθεις δ' ἀκμὴν ὄντες ταῖς Ἑλληνικαῖς ὁρμαῖς καὶ ταῖς ἑκάστων ἐπινοίαις.
9. *P.Sorb.* 1.41, April 222 BC, *P.Sorb.* 3.106, 222 BC, *P.Enteux.* 63, 222-218, *P.Enteux.* 11, 221 BC
10. *P.Enteux.* 45 (222 BC), *Chr.Wilck.* 337 (222/221), *P.Enteux.* 36 (221), *P.Enteux.* 91 (221), *P.Petr.* 3.112 (221/210), *P.Sorb.* 3.108 (220 or 219), *P.Genova* 3.106 (219), *P.Enteux.* 48 (early 218, ref. 219 events), *P.Enteux.* 52 (early 218).
11. Line 4: ἵνα μὴ στρατεύσηται.
12. Lines 9–12: ἐγὼ δ' ἐν ἐκείνοις τοῖς χρόνοις [οὐκ ἔλαβον ἐ]κφόριον τοῦ κ[λ]ήρου ἀλλ' ἢ ὀλ(ύρας) ἀ(ρτάβας) 500 κα[ὶ τοῦ] 3 (ἔτους) εἰς Πη[λούσιον καὶ τ]οῦ 4 εἰς τὸν Βουβαστίτην καὶ τοῦ 5 ἐπὶ Συρίαν [συνεστρατευσ]άμην σαι.
13. *Histories* 7.61–80.
14. *Iliad* 2.494–759.
15. Endios: *BGU* 6.1266, *P.Grad.* 10; Hagesarchos: *P.Petr.2* 24; Dionysios: *P.Enteux.* 85 (this command is least reliably identified as infantry); Kephalon: *P.Enteux.* 92; Maraios: *P.Petr.* 2.47.
16. *P.Lille* 4, lines 30–33: κατέχειν τὸν κλῆρ[ο]ν ἐν τῶι βασιλικῶι σὺν τοῖς \ἐκ τοῦ/ ἐνεστηκότος σπόρο[υ] ἐκφορίοις ἕως τοῦ, ἐὰν ὑπάρχωσιν αὐτῶι υἱοί, ἐπιγραφῆναι ἐν ταῖς κατὰ τὸ πρόσταγμα ἡμέραις.
17. *SB* 20.14656. This document is undated, but since it contains clauses related to the aforementioned decree, it must be later than the decree. But the letter forms support for a third-century BC date. It is safe to date it generally to the reign of Philopator.
18. Lines 17–19: περὶ τοῦ κλήρου· οὐκ ἀξιοῖ ἐπιγραφῆναι αὐτῶι τ[ὸν] κλῆρον ἕως ἂν ζῆις· ἐὰν δέ τι ἀνθρώπινον, κα[τα]λείψεις αὐτῶι.
19. Peremans and Van 't Dack 1959: pp.xix–xx; Fischer-Bovet 2014: pp.161–66.
20. For example, *P.Yale* 1.33 (253 BC) refers to a contingent of *machimoi* dispatched under their captain Bithelminis to the lower (northern)

parts of the Herakleopolite to provide security for harvesters in that region. *P.Hib*.1.41 (*c*. 261 BC) also mentions a contingent of *machimoi* dispatched to the lower Herakleopolite as an escort for a *dokimastes* travelling with a large sum of money. Individual *machimoi* could be hired out as assistants (P.Grenf. 14a.21–23, 233 BC): Ἀριμούθηι τῶι μισθωτῶν μαχίμωι, cf. *P.Köln*. 8.346.r.16–19, v.14–16, 49–50. They often served in functions comparable to *phylakitai* (police), see *P.Hib*. 2.248. Fr3.8–10, where both a *machimos* and *phylakites* are given duties related to the business of an *oikonomos* (*c*. 250 BC), *SB* 22.15237.3–4, where three *machimoi* arrest and hold a man at the orders of a *sitologos* (grain official) in about 242 BC, and *P.Zen.Pestm*. 49.19–23 (244 BC).

21. *P.Petr*. 3.100, which probably dates to the 240s BC, includes seven *pentarouroi machimoi*. Fischer-Bovet 2014: p.162 followed Lesquier 1911: p.298 in identifying two Greek property managers or farmers with the *pentarouroi*, but all of the allotments were in the name of Egyptians. See also *P.Petr*. 2.39 (246/245 BC), *CPR* 18.3 (231 BC) and *P.Grad*. 12 (229 BC).
22. Mendes stele (*I.Cairo* 22181); see Thiers 2007: pp.64–65, Clarysse 2007: pp.201–06, Derchain 1986: pp.203–04, Winnicki 1985: p.49, n.41, De Meulenaere and MacKay 1976: p.175 and Sethe 1904: p.42.
23. For the earlier period, see *P.Mich*. 3.190 (172 BC) and *UPZ* 2.110 (164 BC); for the later see *P.Tebt*. 1.5 (118 BC) and *P.Haun*. 4.70 (119/118 BC).
24. An alternative date for this papyrus is 202 BC, with small implications for the conclusions here.
25. It dates to the very beginning of a 4th regnal year in the late third century BC; more likely it is 219, but it could be 202.
26. For 1 obol, see *P.Lille* 1.58, 2 obols, see *P.Lille* 1.25. For 4-obol mercenaries in Alexander's day, Turner 1975.
27. Monson 2014: pp.229, 235.
28. *P.Tebt*. 3.1.703 also links the *machimoi* to the start of unrest in Egypt, as does the Rosetta decree. On the revolt, see McGing 1997 and Johstono 2016.
29. Bar Kochva 1976: pp.128–29 collects much of the literature on this point, and evaluates several of the suggested sources: Zenon of Rhodes and Ptolemaios of Megalopolis (Jacoby, *FrGH* 2.B.4) chief among them; Bar-Kochva prefers the latter because he wrote a pro-Ptolemaic yet anti-Philopator history, plus Polybius' professed disdain for Zenon's battle narratives.

30. Fischer-Bovet 2014: pp.151–52, Peremans 1951, Bar-Kochva 1976: pp.48–51, 129–35, Aperghis 2004: pp.191–93.
31. These should likely be identified with the 'picked men armed in the Macedonian manner' at 5.82.2 (τοὺς ἐπιλέκτους τοὺς εἰς τὸν Μακεδονικὸν τρόπον καθωπλισμένους), the 'picked men of the Syrians' at 5.85.10 (ἐπίλεκτοι τῶν Συριακῶν), and the 'men called up from the entire kingdom' at 5.79.2 (ἐκλελεγμένοι τῆς βασιλείας, καθωπλισμένοι δ' εἰς τὸν Μακεδονικὸν τρόπον).
32. Polybius identified these 5,000 – a mix of Cilicians, Dahae and Carmanians, commanded by a Macedonian, Byttakos – as euzonoi, or light troops, at 5.79.3, but 'armed in the Macedonian manner' at 5.82.10. Their placement in the battle between the Greek mercenaries and the argyraspides should weaken any doubts that they were not phalangites. Their diverse origins suggest the Seleucids continued some use of the Diadochi armies' pa*ntodapoi*.
33. Bar-Kochva 1976: p.50 identified these as light troops, but the grammar does not require this. Instead it is quite plausible that these were Median thureophoroi, trained and commanded by a Galatian, who fought for Molon in the previous war (Plb. 5.53.8).
34. Galatian settlers are rare in the papyri, but inscriptions and burial monuments in particular indicate that large numbers lived around Alexandria, cf. Brown 1957: nos 3, 7–10.
35. Polybius placed 3,000 euzonoi on the left flank of the Seleucid army under the command of Menedemus (5.82.10), but Menedemus commanded 4,000 Persian, Agrianian and Thracian troops in the initial army list (5.79.6).
36. Here I follow the suggestion of Bar-Kochva (1976: p.50) that they are Ludim from Atropatene, since Lydia was under Achaeus' control.
37. See Porphyry (*FGrH* 260 44). This claim was originally made in the surviving demotic portion of the Raphia Decree found on Pithom II: 13–14, Thissen 1966: p.19.
38. Porphyry (*FGrH* 260 44) claimed Antiochus lost almost his entire army.
39. For discussion of these, see Walbank 1957: pp.610–13 and Thissen 1966: pp.19, 60–63. For a translation of the demotic text, see Austin 2006: no.276. For the incomplete Greek fragments of this text, see *SB* 5.7172 and *SEG* 8.467. Like the other Ptolemaic decrees published after priestly synods, it was published in several languages, but little survives of the Greek version, while the Demotic is largely complete.

40. *SEG* 20.467. See also Lifschitz 1962: pp.82–84 and Huss 1977: pp.131–40.
41. *SEG* 7.326. The restoration of Nikolaos is uncertain, but in the context, likely. βασιλεῖ [Πτολεμαίωι]
τῶι ἐγ βασιλ[έως Πτολεμαίου] καὶ Βερενίκη[ς, θεῶν Εὐεργε]τῶν, θεῶι Φ[ιλοπάτορι] Δορυμέν[ης τοῦ δεῖνος] Αἰτωλὸς [τῶν περὶ Νικόλ] αον ἱππά[ρχης δυνά[μεων (?)] τὰ [ὅπλα (?)].
42. Plb. 5.86.8–11, Pithom II:14–23, and is the setting for *3 Maccabees* 1.6–10. The *3 Maccabees* text includes several intriguingly accurate details, though much of it must be taken as fantastical. For example, the *Philos* of Ptolemy who saved the king from Theodotos the Aetolian's assassination attempt (known from Plb. 5.81) is given as Dositheos son of Drimylos by *3 Maccabees*, and in no other source, and indeed Dositheos was one of the Friends of the king, and had been eponymous priest in the 25th year of Euergetes (223/222 BC).
43. *P.Lille.* 1.4.2–4. For a similar military position (in the Seleucid army), see *SEG* 19.904.5–6.
44. Pithom II: 23–25. The translation is from Austin 2006, no.276, pp.481–84.
45. Thissen 1966: pp.60–63, Heinen in *CAH VII²* 1: 437–38, Winnicki 2001: pp.133–45.

Conclusions

1. See Fischer-Bovet 2014: pp.57–75 for a review of the literature, and several hypothetical models of military and total population size.
2. See Rathbone 1990: p.123, Schiedel 2001: pp.220–23 and Manning 2003: pp.47–49, all of which hover around four million, and see Clarysse and Thompson 2006: 2:101, for a model based off the Fayum with a lower total. Two hundred thousand represents about 5 per cent of the population, but several estimates have been closer to 300,000.
3. The settlement of prisoners following the war further expanded the settler system. A report in *P.Lille* 1.3, from 216 BC, indicates (lines 64–69) that perhaps eleven prisoners-of-war had been assigned to allotments of roughly 16 arouras apiece following the war. Another document contains a complaint that three prisoners-of-war were stealing olive oil produce and selling it as their own (*P.Köln.* 6.261).
4. Lesquier 1911, Uebel 1968, Christensen 2002, Clarysse and Thompson 2006, Monson 2012 and Fischer-Bovet 2014.
5. Fischer-Bovet 2014: pp.204–09.

6. For estimates of the size of the Arsinoite nome, see Clarysse and Thompson 2006: p.90. The Edfu temple gives 9,000,000 arouras as the ideal capacity of Egypt, but modern estimates place the total close to 20,000 km^2 or 7,258,000 arouras. See Rathbone 1990: pp.109–15, Scheidel 2001: pp.92–93, Manning 2003: pp.48–49 and Fischer-Bovet 2014: pp.202–10
7. The main estimate scholars have followed or responded to was Christensen's 2002 dissertation on the Apollonopolite (Edfu) land surveys, which drew on material in Uebel's and Lesquier's earlier studies of the cleruchs; on the text, see now Christensen, Thompson and Vandrope 2017, and historical discussion pp.36–48.
8. Duttenhöfer 2002, Monson 2012: pp.176–82 and Scheuble-Reiter 2012: pp.246–49.
9. The few surviving payment records on the *diartabeia* suggest many men contributed far less than 2 artabas per aroura (*P.Tebt.* 1.99, fr. C). Some of these underpayments may explain the steep Arsinoite arrears (in 137 BC they owed almost 1.5 times the total levy in arrears, reflecting an average 14 per cent underpayment per year). Another payment type used in the cavalry levy, the *epigraphē*, seems to have been taken at 1 artaba per two planted arouras (*SB* 18.13095, 142 BC), far less than the theoretical levy. This suggests the official *diartabeia* may have been inaccurate, and the state actually imposed a lower total.
10. Note, however, that some of these included men who were transferred to other parts of the *katoikoi* or to other regiments within the *katoikoi hippeis*, so only some of the lost land left the *katoikoi* system entirely.
11. Monson 2012: pp.180–82 calculated closer to one-quarter, but the text fairly clearly notes 340,000 (actually 342,989) in arrears and 461,000 (actually 461,067 or 461,545, contingent on the addition of some mounted police (*ephodoi*) to the *katoikoi hippeis*) as a new total. That alone suggests the total for year 33 was a little over 118,000. Sums paid and to-be-paid for the year 33 dues should be added together, not overwritten, to make 55,840 and 62,654, the full sum.
12. Similarly, 234,777 artabas for all the *katoikoi hippeis*, divided by approximately 2,500 cavalrymen and the *diartabeia*, yields an average of 47 arouras per cavalrymen.
13. *P.Tebt.* 1.79 (about 148 BC) contains records of two such settlements.
14. Clarysse and Thompson 2006: II.152, up to about 2,000.
15. Monson 2012: pp.89–92.
16. Clarysse and Thompson 2006: II.152, up to 759.

17. *P.Petr.* 3.112, and fairly recently, Clarysse and Thompson 2009 published a tax record (*P.Sorb.* inv.371) with dyke tax receipts for allotments with 381, 334.5, 325, 248, 196.5, 196.5, 156, 156, 130.5, 130.5, 130.5, 119.25 and 118.5 arouras of cultivable land. The editors (2009: pp.251–52, notes on lines 29 and 48–50) suggested, based on the irregular allotments, the lands had been purchased privately and were not allotments; however, the sizes are not random and after the four largest the rest all repeat. The allotments should be related to officer ranks rather than private acquisitions.
18. The *P.Sorb.* inv.371 record includes 2,622.75 arouras from just thirteen cavalrymen, most of whom were, one presumes, officers. Eighty-aroura allotments are lacking in that text, which includes tax receipts from 235 BC and earlier. Those may have been measured out after the reform in 235.
19. *BGU* 6.1216 (about 110 BC), from the Aphroditopolite nome, just north of the Herakleopolite, may point to 39.5–48 per cent settler land (4,265 arouras), contingent on how the amount of royal land is read in the text. *P.Giss* 1.60 (early second century AD), likewise from the Aphroditopolite, gives an example that may be 60 per cent (2,980 arouras). The 48 per cent from the Herakleopolite Land Registers (*BGU XIV*) is calculated by Monson 2012: p.85.
20. Theodotos and Panaitolos at the start, Hippolochos, Keraias and perhaps Lagoras during the conquest of central Koile Syria, and presumably Nikolaos at some point after the war.
21. *OGIS* 230; see Gera 1987 and Piejko 1991.
22. Bricault 1999.
23. *BGU* 6.1415, *O.Strasb.* 1.294 and *O.Wilb.* 2 all provide evidence for the large gift estate of Agathokles south of Thebes, between Thebes and Hermonthis. See *P.Tebt.* 3.2.860 for the gift estate of Sosibios, which still contained over 1,000 arouras in the middle of the second century.
24. This depends on accepting the consensus that the *Asiageneis* in Ptolemaic texts were settled prisoners; see Uebel, nos 650–59 and Clarysse 2008: p.59.
25. *CM* 31088, *SEG* 8.467, lines 20–22. *3 Maccabees* 1.4 records a tradition Queen Arsinoe promised the soldiers at Raphia 2 *mnai* (200 drachmas in silver) apiece for victory in the crisis of the battle. See also Huss 1976: pp.81–82.
26. See calculations of several ways to attempt to square the *mnaieion* with the *chrysoi* and the donative in Olivier and Lorber 2013: pp.102–07.

Bibliography

Abd El-Fattah, A., Abd El-Maksoud, M. and Carrez-Maratray, J.-Y. (2014), 'Deux inscriptions grecques du *Boubasteion* d'Alexandrie', *AncSoc* 44, pp.149–77.
Altenmüller, H. (2010), 'Bemerkungen zum Ostfeldzug Ptolemaios' III. Nach Babylon und in die Susiana im Jahre 246/245', in J.C. Fincke (ed.), *Festschrift für Gernot Wilhelm anlässlich seines 65. Geburtstages am 28. Januar 2010* (Winona Lake, IN: Eisenbrauns), pp.27–44.
Anderson, J.K. (1967), 'Shields of Eight Palms' Width', *California Studies in Classical Antiquity* 9, pp.1–6.
Anson, E.M. (1988), 'Antigonus, the Satrap of Phrygia', *Historia* 37.4, pp.471–77.
_____ (2006), 'The Chronology of the Third Diadoch War', *Phoenix* 60.3–4, pp.226–35.
_____ (2014), *Alexander's Heirs: The Age of the Successors* (New York: Wiley-Blackwell).
Anagnostou-Canas, B. (1989), 'Rapports de dépendance coloniale dans l'Égypte ptolémaïque: I. L'appareil militaire', *BIDR* 3 série 31–32, pp.151–236.
Aperghis, G.G. (2004), *The Seleukid Royal Economy: the finances and financial administration of the Seleucid empire* (Cambridge: Cambridge University Press).
Austin, M.M. (1986), 'Hellenistic kings, war, and the economy', *CQ* 36, pp.450–66.
_____ (2006), *The Hellenistic world from Alexander to the Roman conquest: a selection of ancient sources in translation*, 2nd ed. (Cambridge: Cambridge University Press).
Badoud, N. (2014), 'Rhodes et les Cyclades à l'époque hellénistique', in G. Bonnin and E. Le Quéré (eds), *Pouvoirs, îles et mer. Formes et modalités de l'hégémonie dans les Cyclades antiques (VIIe s. a.C.- IIIe s. p.C.)*; Ausonius Scripta Antiqua 64 (Bordeaux: De Boccard), pp.115–29.

Bagnall, R.S. (1969), 'Some Notes on P. Hibeh 198', *BASP* 6, pp.73–118.
_____ (1971), 'The Ptolemaic Trierarchs', *Chronique d'Égypte* 46, pp.356–62.
_____ (1976), *The Administration of the Ptolemaic possessions outside Egypt*, Columbia studies in the classical tradition 4 (Leiden: E.J. Brill).
_____ (1984), 'The Origins of Ptolemaic Cleruchs', *BASP* 21, pp.7–20.
Bagnall, R.S. and Derow, P. (2004), *The Hellenistic Period: historical sources in translation*, 2nd ed. (Oxford: Blackwell).
Bagnall, R.S. and Frier, B. (1994), *The Demography of Roman Egypt* (Cambridge: Cambridge University Press).
Bar-Kochva, B. (1976), *The Seleucid army: organization and tactics in the great campaigns* (Cambridge: Cambridge University Press).
_____ (2010), *The Image of the Jews in Greek Literature: The Hellenistic Period*, Hellenistic Culture and Society 51 (Berkeley: UC Press).
Barbantani, S. (2010), 'The Glory of the Spear: a powerful symbol in Hellenistic poetry and art; the case of Neoptolemus (of Tlos?) and other Ptolemaic epigrams', *Studi Classici e Orientali* 53, pp.67–138.
Bernand, É. (1969), *Inscriptions métriques de l'Egypte gréco-romaine. Recherches sur la poésie épigrammatique des grecs en Egypte*, Annales littéraires de l'Université de Besançon 98 (Paris: Belles Lettres).
Berve, H. (1926), *Das Alexanderreich auf prosopographischer Grundlage* (Munich: Beck).
Bevan, E. (1927), *The House of Ptolemy* (London: Methuen).
Billows, R.A. (1995), *Kings and Colonists: aspects of Macedonian imperialism*, Columbia studies in the classical tradition 22 (Leiden: Brill).
_____ (1997), *Antigonos the One-Eyed and the Creation of the Hellenistic State* (Berkeley: University of California Press).
Bingen, J. (2007), *Hellenistic Egypt: Monarchy, Society, Economy, Culture*, Hellenistic Culture and Society 49 (Berkeley: University of California Press).
Blümel, W. (1992), 'Brief des ptolemaïscher Minister Tlepolemos an die Stadt Kildara in Karien', *EA* 20, pp.127–33.
Bosworth, A.B. (1980/1995), *A Historical Commentary on Arrian's History of Alexander*, 2 vols (Oxford: Oxford University Press).
_____ (2002), *The Legacy of Alexander: Politics, Warfare, and Propaganda Under the Successors* (Oxford: Oxford University Press).
Bouche-Leclerq, A. (1903–07), *Histoire des Lagides*, 4 vols (Paris: Ernest Leroux).
Breccia, E. (1907), 'La Necropoli de l'Ibrahimieh', *BSAA* 9, pp.35–86.

_____ (1912), *Catalogue Général des Antiquités Égyptiennes (Musée d'Alexandrine) I: La Necropoli di Sciatbi* (Le Caire: Imprimerie de l'Institut Français d'Archéologie Orientale).
Bresciani, E. (1972), 'Annotazioni demotiche ai "Persai tes epigones"', *La Parola del passato* 142/144, pp.123–28.
Bricault, L. (1999), 'Isis et Sarapis sauveurs de Ptolémée IV à Raphia', *Chronique d'Égypte* 74, pp.334–43.
Brown, S. (1957), *Ptolemaic Paintings and Mosaics and the Alexandrian style*, Monographs on archaeology and the fine arts 6 (Cambridge, MA: Archaeological Institute of America).
Bülow-Jacobsen, A. (1979), 'P. Haun 6. An Inspection of the Original', *ZPE* 36, pp.91–100.
Buraselis, K. (1982), *Das hellenistische Makedonien und die Ägäis* (Munich: Beck).
_____ (2013), 'Ptolemaic Grain, Seaways and Power', in K. Buraselis, M. Stefanou and D.J. Thompson (eds), pp.97–107.
Buraselis, K., Stefanou, M. and Thompson, D.J. (eds) (2013), *The Ptolemies, the Sea, and the Nile. Studies in Waterborne Power* (Cambridge, Cambridge UP).
Burstein, S.M. (1985), *The Hellenistic Age from the Battle of Ipsos to the Death of Kleopatra VII*, Translated Documents of Greece and Rome 3 (Cambridge: Cambridge UP).
_____ (1996), 'Ivory and Ptolemaic Exploration of the Red Sea. The Missing Factor', *Topoi* 6.2, pp.799–807.
_____ (2008), 'Elephants for Ptolemy II: Ptolemaic Policy in Nubia in the Third Century BC', in P. McKechnie and P. Guillaume (eds), *Ptolemy Philadelphus and his World* (Leiden: Brill), pp.135–48.
_____ (2016), 'Ptolemy III and the Dream of Reuniting Alexander's Empire', *AHB* 31, pp.77–86.
Cadell, H. and Le Rider, G. (1997), *Prix de blé et numéraire dans l'Egypte lagide de 305 à 173*, Papyrologica Bruxellensia 30 (Brussels: Fondation égyptologique Reine Élisabeth).
Capponi, L. (2017), 'Deserving the Court's Trust: Jews in Ptolemaic Egypt', in A. Erskine, L. Llewelyn-Jones and S. Wallace (eds), *The Hellenistic Court. Monarchic Power and Elite Society from Alexander to Cleopatra* (Swansea: Classical Press of Wales), pp.343–58.
Casson, L. (1971), *Ships and Seamanship in the Ancient World* (Princeton: Princeton UP).
_____ (1993), 'A Petrie Papyrus and the Battle of Raphia', *BASP* 30, pp.87–92.

Chaniotis, A. (2005), *War in the Hellenistic World: A Social and Cultural History*, Ancient World at War (Oxford: Blackwell).

Charles, M. (2007), 'Elephants at Raphia: Reinterpreting Polybius 5.84–5', *CQ* 57.1, pp.306–11.

Christensen, T. (2002), 'P. Haun. Inv. 407 and cleruchs in the Edfu Nome', in K. Vandorpe and W. Clarysse (eds), *Edfu, an Egyptian Provincial Capital in the Ptolemaic Period: Brussels, 3 September 2001* (Brussels: Koninklijke Vlaamse Academie van Belgie voor Wetenschappen en Kunsten), pp.11–16.

Christensen, T., Thompson, D.J. and Vandorpe, K. (2017), *Land and Taxes in Ptolemaic Egypt: An Edition, Translation and Commentary for the Edfu Land Survey (P. Haun. IV 70)* (Cambridge: Cambridge UP).

Chrubasik, B. (2016), *Kings and Usurpers in the Seleukid Empire: The Men who would be King* (Oxford: Oxford UP).

Clanciers, P. (2012), '"Le *Rab Sikkati*" de Babylone contre 'l'homme de renom venu d'Égypte': la Troisième Guerre Syrienne dans les rues de Babylone', in P. Goukowsky and C. Feyel (eds), *Folia Graeca. In honorem Edouard Will: Historica* (Nancy: ADRA), pp.9–31.

Clarysse, W. (1974), 'The Nomarchs Abat[--] and Aristarchos', *ZPE* 13, p.84.

_____ (1980), 'A Royal Visit to Memphis and the End of the Second Syrian War', in D.J. Crawford, J. Quaegebeur and W. Clarysse (eds), pp.83–89.

_____ (1985), 'Greeks and Egyptians in the Ptolemaic Army and Administration', *Aegyptus* 65, pp.57–66.

_____ (1991), *The Petrie Papyri. Second Edition 1: The Wills*, Collectanea Hellenistica 2 (Brussels: Koninklijke Academie voor Wetenschappen, Letteren en Schone Kunsten van Belgie).

_____ (1998), 'Ethnic Diversity and Dialect among the Greeks of Hellenistic Egypt', in A.M.F.W. Verhoogt and S.P. Vleeming (eds), *The Two Faces of Graeco-Roman Egypt*, Papyrologica Lugduno-Batava 30 (Boston: E.J. Brill), pp.1–13.

_____ (2000), 'Ptolémées et temples', in D. Valbelle and J. LeClant (eds), *Le décret de Memphis. Colloque de la Fondation Singer-Polignac à l'occasion de la celebration du bicentenaire de la découverte de la Pierre de Rosette* (Paris), pp.51–65.

_____ (2004), 'Prosopographica', *JJP* 34, pp.27–31.

_____ (2007), 'A Royal Journey in the Delta in 257 BC and the Date of the Mendes Stele', *Chronique d'Egypte* 82, pp.201–06.

_____ (2008), 'Graeco-Roman Oxyrhyncha, A Village in the Arsinoite Nome', in S. Lippert and M. Schentuleit (eds), *Graeco-Roman Fayum – Texts and Archaeology. Proceedings of the Third International Fayum Symposion, Freudenstadt, May 29–June 1, 2007* (Wiesbaden: Harassowitz), pp.55–73.

Clarysse, W., Martin, C.J. and Thompson, D.J. (2014), 'A Demotic Tax List from the Thebaid', in A.M. Dodson, J.J. Johnston and W. Monkhouse (eds), *A Good Scribe and an Exceedingly Wise Man: Studies in Honour of W.J. Tait*, GHP Egyptology 21 (London: Golden House), pp.25–56.

Clarysse, W. and Thompson, D.J. (2006), *Counting the People in Hellenistic Egypt*, 2 vols (Cambridge: Cambridge University Press).

Clarysse, W., Thompson, D.J. and Capron, L. (2011), 'An early Ptolemaic bank register from the Arsinoite nome revised', *APF* 57.1, pp.35–54.

Clarysse, W. and van der Veken, G. (1983), *The Eponymous Priests of Ptolemaic Egypt* (Leiden: E.J. Brill).

Cobb, M. (2016), 'The Decline of Ptolemaic Elephant-Hunting: An Analysis of the Contributory Factors', *Greece & Rome* 63.2, pp.192–204.

Cohen, G.M. (1995), *The Hellenistic Settlements in Europe, the Islands, and Asia Minor* (Berkeley: University of California Press).

_____ (2006), *The Hellenistic Settlements in Syria, the Red Sea basin, and North Africa* (Berkeley: University of California Press).

_____ (2013), *The Hellenistic Settlement in the East from Armenia and Mesopotamia to Bactria and India* (Berkeley: University of California Press).

Çoskun, A. (2012), 'Deconstructing a Myth of Seleucid History: the So-Called "Elephant Victory" over the Galatians Revisited', *Phoenix* 66.1–2, pp.57–73.

_____ (2018), 'The War of Brothers, the Third Syrian War, and the Battle of Ankyra (246–241 BC): a Re-Appraisal', in K. Erickson (ed), *The Seleukid Empire, 281–222 BC. War within the Family* (Swansea: Classical Press of Wales), pp.197–252.

Cowey, J.M.S. and Maresch, K. (2001), *Urkunden des Politeuma der Juden von Herakleopolis (144/3–133/2 v. Chr.) (P.Polit.Iud.)*, Papyrologica Coloniensia 29 (Wiesbaden: Westdeutscher Verlag).

Crampa, J. (1969), *Labraunda, vol. III, part 1: The Greek Inscriptions, 1–12: The Period of Olympichus* (Lund: Gleerup).

Crawford, D.J. (1971), *Kerkeosiris: an Egyptian village in the Ptolemaic period* (Cambridge: Cambridge UP).

Criscuolo, L. (1981), 'Orphanoi e orphanoi kleroi: nuovi aspetti dell'evoluzione del diritto cleruchico', *Proceedings of the Sixteenth International Congress of Papyrology*, pp.259–65.

Davesne, A. and Yenisoganci, V. (1992), 'Les Ptolémées en Séleucide: le trésor d'Hüseyinli', *Revue Numismatique* 34, pp.23–36.

De Meulenaere, H. and MacKay, P. (1976), *Mendes II* (Warminster: Aris & Phillips).

De Souza, P. (2008), 'Military Forces: Naval Forces', in P. Sabin, H. van Wees and M. Whitby (eds), *The Cambridge History of Greek and Roman Warfare, Volume I: Greece, the Hellenistic World, and the Rise of Rome* (Cambridge), pp.357–66.

Delia, D. (1988), 'The Population of Roman Alexandria', *TAPA* 118, pp.275–92.

Derchain, P. (1986), 'La garde "égyptienne" de Ptolémée II', *ZPE* 65, pp.203–04.

Devine, A.M. (1984), 'Diodorus' Account of the Battle of Gaza', *Acta Classica* 27, pp.31–40.

──── (1989), 'Aelian's manual of Hellenistic military tactics', *The Ancient World* 19, pp.31–64.

──── (1995), 'Polybius' lost *Tactica*: the ultimate source for the tactical manuals of Asclepiodotus, Aelian, and Arrian?', *AHB* 9, pp.40–44.

Dietze, G. (1994), 'Philae und die Dodekaschoinos in ptolemäischer Zeit. Ein Beitrag zur Frage ptolemäischer Präsenz in Grenzland zwischen Ägypten und Afrika an Hand der architektonischen und epigraphischen Quellen', *AncSoc* 25, pp.63–110.

──── (2000), 'Temples and Soldiers in Southern Ptolemaic Egypt. Some Epigraphic Evidence', in L. Mooren (ed.), pp.77–89.

Droysen, J.-G. (1877), *Geschichte des Hellenismus*, 3 vols (Basel: B. Schwabe).

Duttenhöfer, R. (2002), *Griechische Urkunden der Papyrussammlung zu Leipzig (P. Lips. II)*, APF Beiheft 10 (Munich: K.G. Saur).

Edgar, C.C. (1931), *Zenon Papyri in the University of Michigan Collection. [Michigan Papyri I]* (Ann Arbor: University of Michigan).

El-Masry, Y., Altenmüller, H. and Thissen, H.J. (2012), *Das Synodaldekret von Alexandria aus dem Jahre 243 v. Chr.*, SAK Beiheft 11 (Hamburg: Buske).

Engels, D.W. (1980), *Alexander the Great and the logistics of the Macedonian Army* (Berkeley: University of California Press).

Erickson, K. (ed.) (2018), *The Seleukid Empire, 281–222 BC. War within the Family* (Swansea: Classical Press of Wales), pp.197–252.

Erskine, A. (1995), 'Culture and Power in Ptolemaic Egypt: The Museum and Library of Alexandria', *Greece & Rome* 42.1, pp.38–48.

Fischer-Bovet, C. (2011), 'Counting the Greeks in Egypt. Immigration in the First Century of Ptolemaic Rule', in C. Holleran and A. Pudsey (eds), *Demography and the Graeco-Roman World. New Insights and Approaches* (Cambridge: Cambridge UP).

_____ (2013), 'Egyptian Warriors: The *Machimoi* of Herodotus and the Ptolemaic Army', *CQ* 63, pp.209–36.

_____ (2014), *Army and Society in Ptolemaic Egypt*, Armies of the Ancient World 1 (Cambridge: Cambridge UP).

_____ (2015), 'A challenge to the concept of decline for understanding Hellenistic Egypt. From Polybius to the twenty- first century', *Topoi. Orient – Occident* 20, pp.209–37.

_____ (2016). 'Les Égyptiens dans les forces armées de terre et de mer sous les trois premiers Lagides', in T. Derda, A. Łajtar and J. Urbanik (eds), *Proceedings of the 27th International Congress of Papyrology Warsaw, 29 July – 3 August 2013* (Warsaw: Univ. of Warsaw), pp.1669–79.

Fischer-Bovet, C. and Clarysse, W. (2012), 'A military reform before the battle of Raphia?', *APF* 58.1, pp.26–35.

_____ (2012b), 'Silver and bronze standards and the date of P. Heid. VI 383', *APF* 58.1, pp.36–42.

Foertmeyer, V. (1988), 'The Dating of the Pompe of Ptolemy II Philadelphus', *Historia* 37.1, pp.90–104.

Foulon, E. (1996), '*hypaspistes, peltastes, chrysaspides, argyraspides, chalkaspides*', *REA* 98, pp.53–63.

Fraser, P.M. (1958), 'A Ptolemaic Inscription from Thera', *JEA* 44.1, pp.99–100.

_____ (1972), *Ptolemaic Alexandria*, 3 vols (Oxford: Clarendon Press).

_____ (1996), *Cities of Alexander the Great* (Oxford: Clarendon Press).

Gambetti, S. (2009), *The Alexandrian Riots of 38 C.E. and the Persecution of the Jews. A Historical Reconstruction* (Leiden: Brill).

Garlan, Y. (1999), *La Guerre dans l'antiquité*, 3rd ed. (Paris: Nathan Université).

Gauthier, P. (1979), 'EXAGOGH SITOU: Samothrace, Hippomédon, et les Lagides', *Historia* 28.1, pp.76–89.

Gera, D. (1987), 'Ptolemy son of Thraseas and the Fifth Syrian War', *Anc. Soc.* 18, pp.63–73.

Geraci, G. (1979), 'La "basilike ile" macedone e l'esercito dei primi Tolemei', *Aegyptus* 59:1–2, pp.8–24.

Gill, D.W.J. (2007), 'Arsinoe in the Peloponnese: The Ptolemaic Base on the Methana Peninsula', in T. Schneider and K. Szpawkowska (eds), *Egyptian Stories: A British Egyptological Tribute to Alan B. Lloyd* (Munster), pp.87–110.

Goudriaan, K. (1988), *Ethnicity in Ptolemaic Egypt*, Dutch monographs on ancient history and archaeology 5 (Amsterdam: J.C. Gieben).

Grainger, J.D. (1999), *The League of the Aitolians*, Mnemosyne suppl. 200 (Leiden: Brill).

――― (2009), *The Cities of Pamphylia* (Oxford: Oxbow).

――― (2010), *The Syrian Wars*, Mnemosyne suppl. 320 (Leiden: Brill).

――― (2014), *The Rise of the Seleucid Empire (323–223 BC)* (Barnsley: Pen & Sword).

――― (2015), *The Seleucid Empire of Antiochus III (223–187 BC)* (Barnsley: Pen & Sword).

――― (2019), *Antipater's Dynasty* (Barnsley: Pen & Sword).

Griffith, G.T. (1935), *The Mercenaries of the Hellenistic World* (Cambridge: Cambridge University Press).

Gruen, E.S. (1985), 'The Coronation of the Diadochi', in J.W. Eadie and J. Ober (eds), *The Craft of the Ancient Historian: Essays in Honor of Martin Ostwald* (Lanham: Univ. Press of America), pp.253–71.

Gygax, M.D. (2000), 'Ptolemaios, Bruder des Ptolemaios III. Euergetes, und Mylasa: Bemerkungen zu *I. Labraunda* Nr. 3.', *Chiron* 30, pp.353–66.

――― (2002), 'Zum Mitregenten des Ptolemaios II. Philadelphos', *Historia* 51.1, pp.49–56.

Habicht, C. (1957). 'Samische Volksbeschlüsse der hellenistischen Zeit.', *AM* 72, pp.152–274.

――― (1972), 'Review of J. Crampa, *Labraunda III.1: The Greek Inscriptions*', *Gnomon* 44, pp.162–70.

――― (1980), 'Bemerkungen zum P. Haun. 6', *ZPE* 39, pp.1–5.

――― (1992)' 'Athens and the Ptolemies', *Classical Antiquity* 11.1, pp.68–90.

――― (1997), *Athens from Alexander to Antony*. trans. D. Lucas (Cambridge, MA: Harvard UP).

Hamilton, C. (2001), 'The Hellenistic World', in K.A. Raaflaub and N. Rosenstein (eds), *War and Society in the Ancient and Medieval Worlds* (Cambridge, MA: Harvard UP), pp.163–91.

Hammond, N.G.L. (1980), 'Training in the Use of a Sarissa and its Effect in Battle, 359–333 B.C.', *Antichthon* 14, pp.53–63.

_____ (1988), 'The King and the Land in the Macedonian Kingdom', *CQ* 38, pp.382–94.

_____ (1990), 'Royal Pages, Personal Pages, and Boys Trained in the Macedonian Manner during the period of the Temenid Monarchy', *Historia* 39.3, pp.261–90.

_____ (1996), 'Alexander's non-European troops and Ptolemy I's use of such troops', *BASP* 33, pp.99–109.

Hammond, N.G.L. and Walbank, F.W. (1988)' *A History of Macedonia: 336–167 B.C.*, 3 vols (Oxford: Clarendon Press).

Hansen, E.V. (1937), 'The great victory monument of Attalus I', *AJA* 41.1, pp.52–55.

Hatzopoulos, M.B. (1996), *Macedonian Institutions under the Kings*, 2 vols, MELETHMATA 22 (Athens and Paris: Diffusion de Boccard).

_____ (2001), *L'Organization de l'armee Macedonienne sous les Antigonides: problemes anciens et documents nouveaux*, MELETHMATA 30 (Athens and Paris: Diffusion de Boccard).

Hatzopoulos, M.B. and Juhel, P. (2009), 'Four Hellenistic Funerary Stelae from Gephyra, Macedonia', *AJA* 113.3, pp.423–37.

Hauben, H. (1970), *Callicrates of Samos. A Contribution to the Study of the Ptolemaic Admiralty*, Studia Hellenistica 18 (Leuven: Leuvense Universitaire Uitgaven).

_____ (1973), ;On the Chronology of the Years 313–311 B.C.', *American Journal of Philology* 94.3, pp.256–67.

_____ (1976), 'Fleet Strength at the Battle of Salamis (306 B.C.)', *Chiron* 6, pp.1–5.

_____ (1990), 'L'expédition de Ptolémée III en Orient et la sédition domestique de 245 av. J.-C. Quelques mises au point', *APF* 36, pp.29–37.

_____ (2013), 'Callicrates of Samos and Patroclus of Macedon, Champions of Ptolemaic Thalassocracy', in K. Buraselis, M. Stefanou and D.J. Thompson (eds), pp.39–65.

_____ (2014), 'Ptolemy's Grand Tour', in H. Hauben and A. Meeus (eds), *The Age of the Successors and the Creation of the Hellenistic Kingdoms (323–276 B.C.)*, Studia Hellenistica 53 (Leuven: Peeters), pp.235–62.

Hazzard, R.A. (2000), *Imagination of a Monarchy: Studies in Ptolemaic Propaganda*, Phoenix, suppl. 37 (Toronto: University of Toronto Press).

Heinen, H. (1972), *Untersuchungen zur Hellenistischen Geschichte des 3. Jh. v. Chr. Zur Geschichte der Zeit des Ptolemaios Keraunos und zum Chremonideischen Krieg*, Historia Einzelschriften 20 (Wiesbaden: Steiner).

_____ (1984), 'The Syrian-Egyptian Wars and the New Kingdoms of Asia Minor', in *CAH 7.1²*, pp.412–45.

Hoffmeier, J. and Abd El-Maksoud, M. (2003), 'A New Military Site on "The Ways of Horus" – Tell El-Borg 1999–2001: A Prelminary Report', *JEA* 89.1, pp.169–97.

Hölbl, G. (2001), *History of the Ptolemaic Empire* (New York: Routledge).

Holleaux, M. (1921), 'Ptolemaios Epigonos', *JHS* 41.2, pp.183–98.

Honigman, S. (2002), 'The Jewish *Politeuma* at Heracleopolis', *SCI* 21, pp.251–66.

Huss, W. (1976), *Untersuchungen zur Aussenpolitik Ptolemaios IV*, Münchener Beiträge zur Papyrusforschung und antiken Rechtsgeschichte 69 (Munich: C.H. Beck).

_____ (1977), 'Eine Ptolemaische Expedition Nach Kleinasien', *Anc.Soc.* 8, pp.187–93.

_____ (1978), 'Eine Revolte der Ägypter in der Zeit des 3. Syrischen Kriegs', *Aegyptus* 58.1–2, pp.151–56.

_____ (1998), ‚Ptolemaios der Sohn', *ZPE* 121, pp.229–50.

_____ (2001), *Ägypten in hellenistischer Zeit 332-30 v. Chr.* (Munich: Beck).

Isager, S. and Karlsson, L. (2008), 'A New Inscription from Labraunda: Honorary Decree for Olympichos: *I.Labraunda* no. 134', *Epigraphica Anatolica* 41, pp.39–52.

Johstono, P. (2016), 'Insurgency in Ptolemaic Egypt', in T. Howe and L.L. Brice (eds), *Brill's Companion to Insurgency and Terrorism in the Ancient Mediterranean World* (Leiden: Brill), pp.183–215.

_____ (2018), 'The Grand Procession, Galatersieg, and Ptolemaic Kingship', in F. Pownall and T. Howe (eds), *Ancient Macedonians in the Greek and Roman Sources* (Swansea: Classical Press of Wales), pp.181–200.

Jones, A.H.M. (1971), *The Cities of the eastern Roman provinces* (Oxford: Oxford UP).

Jones, C.P. and Habicht, C. (1989), 'A Hellenistic Inscription from Arsinoe in Cilicia', *Phoenix* 43.4, pp.317–46.

Kaplan, P. (2003), 'Cross-cultural Contacts among Mercenary Communities in Saite and Persian Egypt', *MHR* 18.1, pp.1–31.

Kasher, A. (1978), 'First Jewish Military Units in Ptolemaic Egypt', *Journal for the Study of Judaism* 9.1, pp.57–67.

_____ (1985) *The Jews in Hellenistic and Roman Egypt: The Struggle for Equal Rights* (Tübingen: Mohr Siebeck).

_____ (2002), 'Review of J. Cowey and K. Maresch, *Urkunden des Politeuma der Juden von Herakleopolis*', *Jewish Quarterly Review* 93, pp.257–68.

Kloppenborg, J. (2006), *Tenants in the Vineyard: Ideology, Economics, and Agrarian Conflict in Jewish Palestine* (Tübingen: Mohr Siebeck).

Klotz, D. (2009), 'The statue of the dioikêtês Harbechi/Archibios. Nelson-Atkins Museum of Art 47–112', *BIAO* 109, pp.281–310.

Kosmetatou, E. (2004), 'Bilistiche and the quasi-institutional status of Ptolemaic royal mistress', *APF* 50, pp.18–36.

Kramer, B. (1991), *Griechische Texte XVIII: das Vertragsregister von Theogenis*, Corpus Papyrorum Rainieri Archeducis Austriae 18 (Vienna: Verlag Brüder Hollinek).

Kuhrt, A. (2013), *The Persian Empire: A Corpus of Sources from the Achaemenid Period* (New York: Routledge).

La'da, C.A. (1997), 'Who were those "of the Epigone"?', in B. Kramer, W. Luppe and H. Maehler (eds), *Akten des 21. Internationalen Papyrologenkongresses, Berlin, 13.–19.8.1995* (Stuttgart: Archiv für Papyrusforschung und verwandte Gebiete 3.1), pp.563–69.

_____ (2002), *Prosopographia Ptolemaica X: Foreign ethnics in Hellenistic Egypt*, Studia Hellenistica 38 (Leuven: Peeters).

_____ (2007), 'The meaning of the Demotic designations *rmt Pr-iy-lq*, *rmt Yb*, and *rmt Swn*', in J. Froesen, T. Purola, and E. Salmenkivi (eds), *Proceedings of the 24th International Congress of Papyrology Helsinki, 1–7 August 2004* (Helsinki: CHL, II), pp.369–80.

LaBuff, J. (2015), *Polis Expansion and Elite Power in Hellenistic Karia* (Lexington).

Larsen, J.A.O. (1970), 'The Aetolian-Achaean Alliance of ca. 238–220 B.C.', *CPh* 70.3, pp.159–72.

Launey, M. (1945), 'L'Exécution de Sotadès et l'Expédition de Patroklos dans la mer Égée (266 av. J.-C.)', *REA* 47.1–2, pp.33–45.

_____ (1949–50), *Recherches sur les armées hellénistiques*, 2 vols (Paris: De Boccard).

Le Rider, G. and Callatay, F. d. (2006), *Les Séleucides et les Ptolémées: l'héritage monétaire et financier d'Alexandre le grand* (Monaco: Rocher).

Lesquier, J. (1911), *Les institutions militaires de l'Egypte sous les Lagides* (Paris: Ernest Leroux).

Lewis, N. (2001), *Greeks in Ptolemaic Egypt. Case Studies in the Social History of the Hellenistic World*, 2nd ed., Classics in Papyrology 2 (Oakville, CT: American Society of Papyrologists).

Liampi, K. (1998), *Der Makedonische Schild* (Bonn: Habelt).
Lifschitz, B. (1962), 'Papyrus grecs du désert de Juda', *Aegyptus* 42, pp.240–56.
Litvinenko, Y. (2001), 'Sostratus of Cnidus, Satrap Ptolemy, and the Capture of Memphis', in I. Andorlini *et. al.* (eds), *Atti del XXII Congresso Internazionale di Papirologia. Firenze, 23–29 agosto 1998* (Florence), pp.813–20.
Lloyd, A.B. (2002), 'The Egyptian Elite in the Early Ptolemaic Period: Some Hieroglyphic Evidence', in D. Ogden (ed.), *The Hellenistic World: New Perspectives* (London: Duckworth), pp.117–36.
Lorton, D. (1971), 'The Supposed Expedition of Ptolemy II to Persia', *JEA* 57, pp.160–64.
Ma, J. (2002), *Antiochos III and the Cities of Western Asia Minor* (Oxford: Oxford University Press).
Maehler, H. and Strocka, V.M. (eds) (1978), *Das Ptolemäische Ägypten: Akten d. internat. Symposions, 27.–29. September 1976 in Berlin* (Mainz: von Zabern).
Mahaffy, J.P. (1895), *The Empire of the Ptolemies* (London: Macmillan).
Manning, J.G. (2003), *Land and Power in Ptolemaic Egypt: the structure of land tenure* (Cambridge: Cambridge University Press).
_____ (2007), 'The Ptolemaic Economy', in I. Morris, W. Scheidel and R. Saller (eds), *Cambridge Economic History of the Graeco-Roman World* (Cambridge: Cambridge University Press), pp.435–59.
_____ (2010), *The Last Pharaohs: Egypt Under the Ptolemies, 305–30 B.C.* (Princeton: Princeton University Press).
Manning, J.G. *et. al.* (2017), 'Volcanic suppression of Nile summer flooding triggers revolt and constrains interstate conflict in ancient Egypt', *Nature Communications* 8.1, pp.1–9.
Markle, M.M. (1978), 'Use of the Macedonian Sarissa by Philip and Alexander of Macedon', *AJA* 82, pp.483–97.
Marquaille, C. (2008), 'The Foreign Policy of Ptolemy II', in P. McKechnie and P. Guillaume (eds), pp.39–64.
Matthew, C. (2015), *An Invincible Beast: Understanding the Hellenistic Pike Phalanx in Action* (Barnsley: Pen & Sword).
McGing, B. (1997), 'Revolt Egyptian Style: Internal Opposition to Ptolemaic Rule', *APF* 43, pp.273–314.
McKechnie, P. and Guillaume, P. (eds) (2008), *Ptolemy II Philadelphus and his World*, Mnemosyne Supplement 300 (Leiden: Brill).

Meadows, A. (2006), 'The Ptolemaic Annexation of Lycia: SEG 27.929', in K. Dörtlük *et. al.* (eds), *The IIIrd Symposium on Lycia, 07–10 November 2005, Antalya. Symposium Proceedings*, 2 vols (Antalya: Suna & İnan Kıraç Enstitüsü), pp.459–70.

_____ (2012), '*Deditio in Fidem*: The Ptolemaic Conquest of Asia Minor', in C. Smith and L. Yarrow (eds), *Imperialism, Cultural Politics, and Polybius* (Oxford: Oxford UP), pp.113–33.

_____ (2013), 'The Ptolemaic League of Islanders', in K. Buraselis, M. Stefanou and D.J. Thompson (eds), pp.19–38.

Meadows, A. and Thonemann, P. (2013), 'The Ptolemaic Administration of Pamphylia', *ZPE* 186, pp.223–26.

Meeus, A. (2012), 'Diodorus and the Chronology of the Third Diadoch War', *Phoenix* 66, pp.74–96.

_____ (2014), 'The Territorial Ambitions of Ptolemy I', in H. Hauben and A. Meeus (eds), *The Age of the Successors and the Creation of the Hellenistic Kingdoms (323–276 B.C.)*, Studia Hellenistica 53 (Leuven: Peeters), pp.263–306.

_____ (2015) 'The Career of Sostratos of Knidos: Politics, Diplomacy, and the Alexandrian Building Programme in the Early Hellenistic Period', in E. Garvin, T. Howe and G. Wrightson (eds), *Greece, Macedon, and Persia: Studies in Social, Political, and Military History* (Oxford: Oxbow), pp.143–71.

Mehl, A. (1980/81), '*Doriktêtos Chora*. Kritische Bemerkungen zum "Speererwerb" in Politik und Völkerrecht der hellenistischen Epoche', *AncSoc* 11/12, pp.173–212.

Meyer, P.M. (1900), *Das Heerwesen der Ptolemäer und Römer in Ägypten* (Leipzig: Teubner).

Molina, I. (2018), 'Death on the Nile. The murder of Perdiccas and the river crossing in Ancient Macedonia', *Karanos* 18, pp.87–106.

Momigliano, A. and Fraser, P. (1950), 'A New Date for the Battle of Andros? A Discussion', *CQ* 44.3–4, pp.107–18.

Monson, A. (2012), *From the Ptolemies to the Romans. Political and Economic Change in Egypt* (Cambridge: Cambridge UP).

_____ (2014), 'Landholders, Rents, and Crops in a Ptolemaic Village: P. Heid. Dem. inv. 46', in A.M. Dodson, J.J. Johnston and W. Monkhouse (eds), *A Good Scribe and an Exceedingly Wise Man: Studies in Honour of W.J. Tait*, GHP Egyptology 21 (London: Golden House), pp.229–40.

_____ (2016), 'Harvest Taxes on Cleruchic land in the third century BCE', in T. Derda, A. Łajtar and J. Urbanik (eds), *Proceedings of the*

27th International Congress of Papyrology (Journal of Juristic Papyrology Suppl. 28) (Warsaw: Univ. of Warsaw), pp.1615–631.

Mooren, L. (1975), *The Aulic Titulature in Ptolemaic Egypt: introduction and prosopography* (Brussels: Paleis der Academiën).

———— (1977), *La hiérarchie de cour ptolémaïque: contribution à l'étude des institutions et des classes dirigeantes à l'époque hellénistique*, Studia Hellenistica 23 (Leuven: Peeters).

Moyer, I.S. (2011), *Egypt and the Limits of Hellenism* (Cambridge: Cambridge UP).

Mueller, K. (2006), *Settlements of the Ptolemies: city foundations and new settlement in the Hellenistic world*, Studia Hellenistica 43 (Leuven: Peeters).

Müller, W.M. (1920), *Egyptological Researches III: The Bilingual Decrees of Philae* (Washington, D.C.: Carnegie Institution of Washington).

Murray, O. (1967), 'Aristeas and Ptolemaic kingship', *JTS* 18.2, pp.337–71.

Murray, W.M. (2012), *The Age of Titans: The Rise and Fall of the Great Hellenistic Navies* (Oxford: Oxford UP).

Nachtergael, G. (1977), *Les Galates en Grèce et les Sôtéria de Delphes: recherches d'histoire et d'épigraphie hellénistiques* (Brussels: Palais des académies).

Nefedkin, A.K. (2009), 'On the origin of Greek cavalry shields in the Hellenistic period', *Klio* 91.2, pp.356–66.

O'Neil, J. (2006), 'Places and Origin of the Officials of Ptolemaic Egypt', *Historia* 55, pp.16–25.

———— (2008), 'A Re-Examination of the Chremonidean War', in P. McKechnie and P. Guillaume (eds), pp.65–89.

Oates, J.F. (1963), 'The Status Designation: Persēs tēs epigonēs', *Yale Classical Studies* 18, pp.1–129.

Ogden, D. (2008), 'Bilistiche and the Prominence of Courtesans in the Ptolemaic Tradition', in P. McKechnie and P. Guillaume (eds), pp.353–85.

Oikonomides, A.N. (1978), 'P. Haun. 6 and Euxenos the Athenian Eponymous Archon of 222/1 B.C.', *ZPE* 32, pp.85–86.

———— (1984), 'The Death of Ptolemy "The Son" at Ephesos and P. Bouriant 6', *ZPE* 56, pp.148–50.

Olbrycht, M. (2015), 'The Epigonoi – The Iranian Phalanx of Alexander the Great', in W. Heckel, S. Müller and G. Wrightson (eds), *The Many Faces of War in the Ancient World* (Newcastle: Cambridge Scholars), pp.196–212.

Olivier, J. and Lorber, C. (2013), 'Three Gold Coinages of Third Century Ptolemaic Egypt', *RBN* 159, pp.49–150.

Peremans, W. (1939), 'La date de la bataille navale de Cos', *L'Antiquité Classique* 8.2, pp.401–08.

―――― (1951), 'Notes sur la bataille de Raphia', *Aegyptus* 31, pp.214–22.

―――― (1975), 'Ptolémée IV et les Egyptiens', in J. Bingen *et. al.* (eds), *Le Monde Grec. Pensée, littérature, histoire, documents. Hommages à Claire Préaux (*Brussels: Editions de l'Universite de Bruxelles), pp.393–402.

―――― (1977), 'Un groupe d'officiers dans l'armée des Lagides. Recherches Anthroponomiques', *Anc.Soc.* 8, pp.175–85.

―――― (1978), 'Les Indigènes Égyptiens dans l'Armée de Terre des Lagides. Recherches Anthroponomiques', *Anc.Soc.* 9, pp.83–100.

Peremans, W. and Van 't Dack, E. (1959), 'Notes sur quelques Prêtres Éponymes d'Égypte Ptolémaïque', *Historia* 8.2, pp.165–73.

―――― (1950–81), *Prosopographia Ptolemaica*, Studia Hellenistica 6, 8, 11–13, 17, 20–21, 25 (Leuven: Peeters).

Pestman, P.W. (1963), 'A proposito dei documenti di Pathyris: II. Persai tès epigonès', *Aegyptus* 43, pp.15–53.

Piejko, F. (1990), 'Episodes from the Third Syrian War in a Gurob Papyrus, 246 B.C.', *APF* 36, pp.13–27.

―――― (1991), 'Decree of the Ionian League in Honor of Antiochus I, ca. 267–262 B.C.', *Phoenix* 45.2, pp.126–47.

Potts, D.T. (2017), 'Appointment in Apollonia', *Anabasis* 8, pp.71–89.

Préaux, C. (1978), *Le monde hellénistique: la Grèce et l'Orient de la mort d'Alexandre à la conquête romaine de la Grèce, 323-146 av. J.-C.*, 2 vols (Paris: Presses universitaires de France).

―――― (1979), *L'Économie royale des Lagides*, 2nd ed (New York: Arno Press).

Pretzler, M. and Barley N. (eds) (2018), *Brill's Companion to Aineias Tacticus* (Leiden: Brill).

Pritchett, W.K. (1991), *The Greek State at War, Part V* (Berkeley: UC Press).

Quack, J. (2008), 'Innovations in Ancient Garb? Hieroglyphic Texts from the Time of Ptolemy Philadelphus', in P. McKechnie and P. Guillaume (eds), *Ptolemy Philadelphus and his World* (Leiden: Brill), pp.275–90.

Quaegebeur, J. (1979), 'Documents égyptiens et rôle économique du clergé en Égypte hellénistique', in E. Lipinsky (ed.), *State and Temple Economy in the Ancient Near East, Proceedings of the international conference*(Leuven: Departement Oriëntalistiek), pp.707–29.

Rathbone, D.W. (1990), 'Villages, Land and Population in Graeco-Roman Egypt', *Proceedings of the Cambridge Philological Society* 216, pp.103–42.

Reden, S. v. (2007), *Money in Ptolemaic Egypt: from the Macedonian conquest to the end of the third century B.C.* (Cambridge: Cambridge University Press).

Redon, B. (2014), 'Le maillage militaire du Delta égyptien sous les Lagides', in A.-E. Veïsse and S. Wackenier (eds), *L'armée en Égypte aux époques perse, ptolémaïque et romaine* (Geneva: Droz), pp.45–80.

_____ (2018), 'The Control of the Eastern Desert by the Ptolemies: New Archaeological Data', in J.-P. Brun, Th. Faucher, B. Redon and S. Sidebotham (eds), *The Eastern Desert of Egypt during the Greco-Roman Period: Archaeological Reports* (Paris: Collège de France), pp.1–21.

Reger, G. (1994), 'The Political History of the Kyklades, 260–200 BC', *Historia* 43, pp.32–69.

Rey-Coquais, J.-P. (1976), 'Inscription découverte à Ras Ibn Hani', *AAAS* 26, pp.51–60.

_____ (1978), ‚Inscription grecque découverte a Ras Ibn Hani: stèle de mercenaires lagides sur la côte syrienne', *Syria* 55, pp.313–25.

Rice, E.E. (1983), *The Grand Procession of Ptolemy Philadelphus* (Oxford: Oxford Classical and Philosophical Monographs).

Rigsby, K.J. (1996), *Asylia: Territorial Inviolability in the Hellenistic World*, Hellenistic Culture and Society 22 (Berkeley: University of California Press).

Robert, L. (1966), *Documents de l'Asie mineure mé ridionale: Inscriptions, monnaies et gé ographie* (Geneva: Droz).

Roisman, J. (1984), 'Ptolemy and His Rivals in His History of Alexander the Great', *CQ* 34, pp.373–85.

_____ (2012), *Alexander's Veterans and the Early Wars of the Successors* (Austin: UT Press).

_____ (2014), 'Perdikkas' Invasion of Egypt', in H. Hauben and A. Meeus (eds), *The Age of the Successors and the Creation of the Hellenistic Kingdoms (323–276 B.C.)*, Studia Hellenistica 53 (Leuven: Peeters), pp.455–74.

Romm, J. (2011), *Ghost on the Throne: The Death of Alexander the Great and the Bloody Fight for His Empire* (New York: Alfred A. Knopf).

Rop, J. (2019), *Greek Military Service in the Ancient Near East, 401–330 BCE* (Cambridge: Cambridge UP).

Rosen, R.M. and Sluiter, I. (2003), *Andreia: studies in manliness and courage in classical antiquity* (Leiden: Brill).

Rostovtzeff, M.I. (1922), *A Large Estate in Egypt in the Third Century B.C.: A study in economic history* (Madison: University of Wisconsin Studies in the Social Sciences and History 6).

_____ (1941), *The Social & Economic History of the Hellenistic World*, 2 vols (Oxford: Clarendon).
Sabin, P., Whitby, M. and van Wees, H. (eds) (2007), *The Cambridge History of Greek and Roman Warfare. Volume 1, Greece, the Hellenistic World, and the Rise of Rome* (Cambridge: Cambridge University Press).
Sachs, A.J. and Hunger, H. (1988–2006), *Astronomical Diaries and Related Texts from Babylon*, 5 vols (Vienna: Verlag der Österreichischen Akademie der Wissenschaften).
Samuel, A.E. (1962), *Ptolemaic Chronology* (Munich: C.H. Beck).
_____ (1993), 'The Ptolemies and the Ideology of Kingship', in P. Green (ed.), *Hellenistic History and Culture* (Berkley, CA: UC Press), pp.168–204.
Scheidel, W. (2001), *Death on the Nile: disease and demography of Roman Egypt*, Mnemosyne supplements 228 (Leiden: E.J. Brill).
_____ (2004), 'Creating a metropolis: a comparative demographic perspective', in W.V. Harris and G. Ruffini (eds), *Ancient Alexandria between Egypt and Greece* (Leiden: Brill), pp.1–31.
Scheuble-Reiter, S. (2012), *Die Katökenreiter im ptolemäischen Ägypten*, Vestigia 64 (Munich: Beck).
_____ (2014), 'Fragmente mit nummerierten und ethnischen Hipparchien (P.UB Trier S 77-43)', *APF* 60, pp.263–72.
Scholl, R. (1987), 'Epigonoi', *ZPE* 67, pp.111–15.
Scholten, J. (2000), *The Politics of Plunder: Aitolians and the Koinon in the Early Hellenistic Era, 279–217 B.C.*, Hellenistic Culture and Society 24 (Berkelely: University of California Press).
Schwartz, J. (1978), 'Athenes et l'Étolie dans la politique lagide (à la lumiere du P. Haun. 6)', *ZPE* 30, pp.95–100.
Segre, M. (1938), 'Iscrizioni di Licia, I, Tolomeo de Telmesso', *Clara Rhodos* 9, pp.190–207.
Seibert, J. (1969), *Untersuchungen zur Geschichte Ptolemaios I* (Munich: Beck).
Sekunda, N. (2001), *Hellenistic Infantry Reform in the 160s BC* (Lodz: Oficyna Naukowa MS).
_____ (2008), 'Military Forces: Land Forces', in P. Sabin, H. van Wees and M. Whitby (eds), *The Cambridge History of Greek and Roman Warfare, Volume I: Greece, the Hellenistic World, and the Rise of Rome* (Cambridge), pp.325–56.
Sethe, K. (1904), *Hieroglyphische urkunden der griechisch-römischen zeit* (Leipzig: J.C. Hinrichs).

Shear, T.L. (1978), *Kallias of Sphettos and the Revolt of Athens in 286 B.C.*, Hesperia Suppl. 17 (Princeton: ASCSA).

Sosin, J.D. (1997), 'P. Duk. Inv. 677: Aetos, from Arsinoite Strategos to Eponymous Priest', *ZPE* 116, pp.141–56.

Spyridakis, S. (1977), *Ptolemaic Itanos and Hellenistic Crete* (Berkeley: University of California Press).

Stefanou, M. (2013), 'Waterborne Recruits: The Military Settlers of Ptolemaic Egypt', in K. Buraselis, M. Stefanou and D.J. Thompson (eds), pp.108–31.

Strobel, K. (1996), *Die Galater* (Berlin: Akademie Verlag).

Strootman, R. (2014), *Courts and Elites in the Hellenistic Empires: The Near East After the Achaemenids, c. 330 to 30 BCE* (Edinburgh: Edinburgh UP).

Tarn, W.W. (1913), *Antigonos Gonatas* (Oxford: Clarendon Press).

_____ (1926), 'The First Syrian War', *JHS* 46.2, pp.155–62.

_____ (1928), 'The Struggle of Egypt against Syria and Macedonia', in J.B. Bury, S.A. Cook and F.E. Adcock (eds), *Cambridge Ancient History*, vol. *VII*, pp.699–731.

_____ (1930), *Hellenistic Military and Naval Developments* (Cambridge: Cambridge University Press).

Thiers, C. (1995), 'Civils et militaires dans les temples. Occupation illicite et expulsion', *BIFAO* 95, pp.493–516.

_____ (2007), *Ptolémée Philadelphe et les prêtres d'Atoum de Tjékou: nouvelle edition commentée de la 'stele de Pithom' (CGC 22183)*, Orientalia Monspeliensia 17 (Montpellier: Université Paul Valéry).

Thissen, H.-J. (1966), 'Studien zum Raphiadecret', *Beitrage zur Klassischen Philologie* 23, pp.67–71.

Thompson, D.J. (1984), 'The Idumaeans of Memphis and the Ptolemaic Politeumata', in M. Manfredi (ed.), *Atti del XVII Congresso internazionale de papirologia. Napoli, 19–26 maggio 1983* (Naples: Centro internazionale per lo studio dei papyri ercolanesi), pp.1069–75.

_____ (1988), *Memphis under the Ptolemies* (Princeton: Princeton University Press).

_____ (2000), 'Philadelphus' Procession: Dynastic Power in a Mediterranean Context', in L. Mooren (ed.), *Politics, Administration, and Society in the Hellenistic and Roman* World (Leuven), pp.365–88.

Török, L. (1995), *Hellenistic and Roman Terracottas from Egypt*, Bibliotheca Archaeologica 15 (Rome: L'Erma di Bretschneider).

_____ (1997), *The Kingdom of Kush: Handbook of the Napatan-Meriotic Civilization* (Leiden: Brill).

_____ (2009), *Between Two Worlds: The Frontier Region between Ancient Nubia and Egypt 3700 BC–500 AD* (Leiden: Brill).
Tresson, J. (1931), 'La Stele de Naples', *BIFAO* 30, pp.368–91.
Tunny, J.A. (2000), 'Ptolemy "The Son" Reconsidered: Are There Too Many Ptolemies?', *ZPE* 131, pp.83–92.
Turner, E.G. (1974), 'A Commander-in-Chief's Order from Saqqara', *JEA* 60, pp.239–42.
_____ (1975), 'Four obols a day men at Saqqara', in J. Bingen, G. Cambrier and G. Nachtergael (eds), *La monde grec. Pensée, littérature, histoire et documents. Hommages à Claire Préaux* (Brussels), pp.353–57.
Uebel, F. (1968), *Die Kleruchen Ägyptens unter den ersten sechs Ptolemäern* (Berlin: Akademie-Verlag).
Van der Spek, R.J. (1993), 'The Astronomical Diaries as a source for Achaemenid and Seleucid History', *Bibliotheca Orientalis* 50, pp.91–101.
_____ (1997/98), 'New Evidence from the Babylonian Astronomical Diaries concerning Seleucid and Arsacid History', *Archiv für Orientforschung* 44/45, pp.168–75.
Van 't Dack, E. (1977), 'Sur l'évolution des institutions militaires lagides', in *Armées et fiscalité dans le monde antique. Actes du colloque national, Paris, 14–16 octobre 1976* (Paris), pp.77–105 (= Van 't Dack, 1988, pp.47–64).
_____ (1983), 'La collégialité dans les commandements éponymes de l'armée lagide', *Chronique d'Égypte* 60, pp.379–92 (=Van 't Dack, 1988, pp.103–23).
_____ (1988), *Ptolemaica Selecta: Études sur l'armée et l'administration lagides*, Studia Hellenistica 29 (Leuven: Peeters).
_____ (1992), 'L'armée de terre Lagide: reflet d'un monde multiculturel?', in J.H. Johnson (ed.), *Life in a multi-cultural society: Egypt from Cambyses to Constantine and beyond*, SAOC 51 (Chicago: Oriental Institute), pp.327–41.
_____ (1993), 'Les triacontaroures du Corpus P. Raineri XVIII, Griechische Texte XIII', *JJP* 23, pp.163–67.
Van 't Dack, E. and Hauben, H. (1978), 'L'apport égyptien à l'armée navale lagide', in H. Maehler and V.M. Strocka (eds), *Das Ptolemäische Ägypten: Akten d. internat. Symposions, 27.–29. September 1976 in Berlin* (Mainz: P. von Zabern), pp.59–93.
Van 't Dack, E., Van Dessel, P. and Van Gucht, W. (eds) (1983), *Egypt and the Hellenistic World: Proceedings of the International Colloquium, Leuven, 24–26 May 1982*, Studia Hellenistica 27 (Leuven: Peeters).

Vandersleyen, C. (1988), 'Suggestion sur l'origine des "Persai, tes epigones"', in *Proceedings of the XVIII International Congress of Papyrology* (Athens, II), pp.191–201.

Vandorpe, K. (2000), 'The Ptolemaic *epigraphe* or harvest tax (*shemu*', *APF* 46, pp.167–232.

_____ (2008), 'Persian Soldiers and Persians of the Epigone, Social mobility of soldiers-herdsmen in Upper Egypt', *APF* 54, pp.87–108.

Virgilio, B. (2001), 'Roi, cite et temple dans les inscriptions de Labraunda', *REA* 103, pp.429–42.

_____ (2003), *Lancia, diadema e porpora. Il re e la regalità ellenisticai*, 2nd ed., Studi Ellenistici 14 (Pisa: Giardini Editori e Stampatori).

Vleeming, S.P. (1985), 'The reading of the title "man receiving pay"', in P.W. Pestman (ed.), *Textes et étudesde papyrology grecque, démotique et copte*, Papyrologica Lugduno-Batava 23 (Leiden), pp.204–07.

Walbank, F.W. (1942), 'Olympichos of Alinda and the Carian Expedition of Antigonus Doson', *JHS* 62, pp.8–13.

_____ (1957), *A Historical Commentary on Polybius, vol. 1* (Oxford: Clarendon Press).

_____ (1993), *The Hellenistic World*, 2nd ed. (Cambridge, MA: Harvard University Press).

_____ (1996), 'Two Hellenistic Processions', *Scripta Classica Israelica* 15, pp.119–30.

_____ (2002), *Polybius, Rome, and the Hellenistic World: essays and reflections* (Cambridge: Cambridge University Press).

Walbank, F.W. et. al. (eds) (1984), *Cambridge Ancient History, Vol. VII.1: The Hellenistic World* (Cambridge: Cambridge UP).

Waterfield, R. (2011), *Dividing the Spoils: The War for Alexander the Great's Empire* (Oxford: Oxford UP).

Welles, C.B. (1970), *Alexander and the Hellenistic world* (Toronto: A.M. Hakkert).

_____ (1974), *Royal Correspondence in the Hellenistic period: a study in Greek epigraphy* (Chicago: Ares).

Wheeler, E. (2004), 'The Legion as Phalanx in the Late Empire, Part I', in Y. Le Bohec and C. Wolff (eds), *L'armée romaine de Dioclétien à Valentinien I* (Lyon), pp.309–58.

Wilcken, U. (1912), *Grundzüge und Chrestomathie der Papyruskunde, Bd. I, Historischer Teil* (Leipzig: Teubner).

Will, E. (1979), *Histoire politique du monde hellénistique*, 2nd ed., 2 vols (Nancy: Presses universitaires de Nancy).

Winnicki, J.K. (1977), 'Die Kalasirier der spätdynastischen und der ptolemäischen Zeit. Zu einem Problem der Ägyptischen heeresgeschichte', *Historia* 26, pp.257–68.

———— (1985), 'Die Ägypter und das Ptolemäerheer', *Aegyptus* 65, pp.41–55.

———— (1989), 'Militäroperationen von Ptolemaios I. und Seleukos I. in Syrien in den Jahren 312-311 v. Chr. (I)', *Anc.Soc.* 20, pp.55–92.

———— (1990), 'Bericht von einem Feldzug des Ptolemaios Philadelphos in der Pithom-Stele', *JJurP* 20, pp.157–67.

———— (1991a), 'Militäroperationen von Ptolemaios I. und Seleukos I. in Syrien in den Jahren 312–311 v. Chr. (II)', *Anc.Soc.* 22, pp.147–201.

———— (1991b), 'Der zweite syrische Krieg im Lichte des demotischen Karnak-Ostrakons und der griechischen Papyri des Zenon-Archivs', *JJurP* 21, pp.87–104.

———— (2001), 'Die letzten Ereignisse des vierten syrischen Krieges: Eine Neudeutung des Raphiadekrets', *JJurP* 31, pp.133–45.

Wörrle, M. (1975)' 'Antiochos I, Achaios der Ältere und die Galaten', *Chiron* 5, pp.59–87.

Worthington, I. (2016), *Ptolemy I: King and Pharaoh of Egypt* (Oxford: Oxford UP).

Wrightson, G. (2015), 'To Use or Not to Use: The Practical and Historical Reliability of Asclepiodotus's "Philosophical" Tactical Manual', in G. Lee, H. Whittaker and G. Wrightson (eds), *Ancient Warfare: Introducing Current Research* (Newcastle-upon-Tyne: Cambridge Scholars), pp.65–93.

Yardley, J.C. and Heckel, W. (1997), *Justin, Epitome of the Philippic History of Pompeius Trogus, vol. 1: books 11–12: Alexander the Great* (Oxford: Oxford University Press).

Young, J. and Young, S.H. (1955), *Terracotta Figurines from Kourion in Cyprus* (Philadelphia: Penn Press).

Zuckerman, C. (1989), 'Hellenistic Politeumata and the Jews. A Reconsideration', *SCI* 8–9, pp.171–85.

Index of Personal Names

Achaeus, Seleucid dynast, 203–206, 228–34
Adaios, dynast, 168–9
Aetos son of Apollonios, courtier, 133–4, 189
Agatharchides, historian, 116–18
Agathokles, courtier, 241, 275–8, 310 n.23
Agesarchos, eponymous commander, 247
Alexander III of Macedon, 18–23, 45–6
   and dispositions of Egypt, 23–8, 79–81
   body of, 34–6
Alexandros, eponymous commander, 89–90, 139–40
Amadokos, son of Satokos, 152–3
Andriskos, eponymous commander, 216
Andromachos, (1) husband of Bilistiche, 171–2, (2) son of Achaios, 168, 206, (3) of Aspendos, 252–3
Antigonus I the One-Eyed, 18–19, 42–8, 62–5, 68
   Ekregma conference, 48
   Skepsis treaty, 57
Antigonus II Gonatas, 72, 116, 124–8, 168–70
Antigonus III Doson, 202–205

Antiochos, courtiers and eponyms, incl. 'The Cretan' son of Kratidas, and son of Kebbas, 134, 151, 165
Antiochus I Soter, 119–21
Antiochus II Theos, 130–2, 135–6, 163, 175
   assassination of, 162, 179
Antiochus Hierax, 165–7
   aided by Ptolemaic troops, 168, 185
Antiochus III the Great, 228–40, 254–60, 275
Apollonides, *nomarch*, 147–50
Apollonios the *dioiketes*, 147, 153–6, 214
Arrhidaios, 34–5, 42
Arsinoe I, wife of Ptolemy II, 121
Arsinoe II, sister and wife of Ptolemy II, 119–25, 129, 135
Arsinoe III, sister and wife of Ptolemy IV, 258
Attalus I of Pergamon, 168, 202–206

Berenike I, 122
Berenike II, daughter of Magas I, 162, 171, 177–8
Berenike *Phernophoros*, daughter of Ptolemy II, marriage to Antiochus II, 130

role in Third Syrian War, 164, 173–6, 186
Bion of Cyprus, on Meroe, 118

Callimachus, court poet, 120, 162, 171
Cassander I, 44–5, 65
Chremonides of Athens, 132
Chrysermos, courtier, 152–3
Cleomenes of Naucratis, 25–8, 31
III, of Sparta, 233–4

Demeas, hipparch, 140, 144, 152
Demetrius I the Besieger, 29, 51–5, 59–68, 72–3
Demetrius II, 203
Dionysios, eponymous commander, 247
    possible link to D. 'the Thracian', 2
Djedhor, priest, 30–1
Dorymenes, hipparch, 235, 260, 304 n.6

Endios, eponymous commander, 247
Eteoneus, (1) eponymous commander, 16, 140–5, 192, 216–18, (2) son of Eteoneus, eponymous priest, 140
Eumedes, general and elephant hunter, founder of Ptolemais Theron and perhaps Berenike Troglodytike, 128–9
Eumenes, (1) of Cardia, 23, 36, 42–5, (2) elephant hunter and eponymous commander, 16, 129, 144, 208–209, (3) E. I of Pergamon, 168

Eupolemos, hipparch, 143–4
Eurylochos, (1) of Magnesia, 241, (2) of Alexandria, 24

Glaukon of Athens, 132–4

Hippalos, courtier, 217–18
Hippodamos, military settler administrator, 147–50
Hippolochos of Thessaly, 239–40, 304 n.6, 305 n.7
Hippomedon of Sparta, governor of Thrace, 185, 299 n.27

Kallias of Sphettos, commandant at Andros, 72–3
Kallikrates, son of Boiskos, admiral and courtier, 125–31
Kineas, son of Alketas, courtier, 152, 225–6

Laodike, Seleucid queen, 162, 169, 179, 185, 297 n.6
Leonides, courtier, 57–8, 71, 133–4
Lykophron, eponymous commander, 101, 151–2
Lysimachus I, 47, 58, 65, 70–2, 109–11, 114

Magas, (1) stepson of Ptolemy I and king of Cyrene, 70, revolt by, 119–21, father of Berenike II, 162, (2) son of Ptolemy III and Berenike II, 205–207, 228, 231
Marsyas, army secretary, 248, 260
Menelaos, eponymous commander, 78, 159, 216
Menelaus, brother of Ptolemy I, 48, 60, 78

Index of Personal Names   335

Molon, Seleucid satrap, 228–33
Myrmidon, commander, 48

Neoptolemos son of Kraisos, courtier, 133–4
Nikolaos of Aetolia, 234–9, 260

Olympichos, dynast, 184, 202–204
Ophellas, commander, 27, 31–4, 49–50

Patroklos, son of Patron, admiral, 125–30
Pelops, (1) son of Alexandros, courtier, 128, (2) son of Pelops, 234
Perdiccas, 27–9, 34–42
Pertaios, Elephantine commander, 117
Phanias, cavalry secretary, 155–9, 190–1, 195, 214
Philinos son of Philotimos, eponymous commander, 135
Philokles, admiral and king of Sidon, 71–3, 114–15, 133
Philon, hipparch, 90, 140, 215, 243–5
Phoxidas of Achaea, 241, 253
Pleistarchos, son of Antipater, 70–1
Polemaios, nephew of Antigonus I, 57–9
Polykleitos, admiral, 48
Polykrates of Argos, 241, 252–3, 258
Polyperchon, 44, 57
Ptolemaios (1) called son of Andromachos, 169, 171–2, 295 n.36, 297 n.10, (2) son of Chrysermos, 231, 234, 275, (3) son of Eteoneus, 216–17, (4), son of Eumenes, 209, (5) son of Nautas, 141, 216, (6) son of Pythangelos, 210, 217, (7), son of Spinther, 295 n.7, (8), son of Thraseas, 252, 275
Ptolemy I Soter, 18–23
  brigade commands under Alexander, 21–2
  monomachy, 22–3
  acquisition of Egypt, 28–30, 34–5
  defeat of Perdiccas, 37–42
  Cyprus campaign, 43–4
  Cyrene settlement, 49–50
  at Gaza, 54–5
  settlements, 56–7
  in the Aegean, 58–9
  at Salamis, 61
  defending Pelusium and acclamation, 63–4
  Rhodes and Soter, 67–8
  reconquest of Cyprus, 70–1
  transition to Ptolemy II and service in guards, 113–14
Ptolemy II Philadelphus, 114
  in Meroe, 116–18
  Anatolian conquests, 119
  marriage to Arsinoe II, 119–20
  Syrian campaigns, 120–2
  Grand Procession, 122–3
  elephant expeditions, 128
  visiting temples, 135
  military settlements, 139–41, 160–1
  games at Memphis, 152
Ptolemy Keraunos, 109, 114–16
Ptolemy 'the Son', 128–31, 135

Ptolemy III Euergetes, 135–6, 162–66
  in Third Syrian War, 171–8, 195–8
  in Mesopotamia, 179
  strategy, 201–205
  elephant hunts, 210–11
  reform, 211–12, 221–2, 274–5
Ptolemy IV Philopator, 200–202, 252, 254–64, 276–8
Pyrrhus of Epirus, 23, 72, 110–13, 152, 225–6
Pythangelos, eponymous commander, elephant hunter, 16, 144, 208–11, 217–18

Satyros, explorer, 128–9
Seleucus I Nikator, 23, 47–8, 54–7, 65, 68–70, 109–14
Seleucus II Kallinikos, 162–70, 182–6, 195, 202
Seleucus III, 202–205
Simaristos, *dioikesis* of, 150–3
Sokrates of Boeotia, 241
Somtutefnakht, 30–1, 103
Sophron (Opron), 168–72, 185
Sosibios, courtier, 211–12, 230–1, 241–2, 249–52, 275–9
Sostratos of Knidos, engineer and courtier, 28, 72
Spinther, hipparch, 134, 146–7

Theocritus, court poet, 111, 114, 118–19
Theodotos the Aetolian, 205–206, 231–6
  at Cape Porphyrion, 238–9
  attempt to assassinate Ptolemy, 256
Thraseas son of Aetos, courtier, 134, 252–3
Timarchos, commander and tyrant, 131
Tlepolemos son of Artapatos, 133, 184
  homonymous grandson, 276

Xanthippos, trierarch and courtier, 132–3
  in Mesopotamia, 165, 172–3, 181–3

Zenon of Kaunos, 135–6, 147, 153–7
Zielas, king of Bithynia, 168, 185
Zoilos, hipparch, 140, 190–1, 195–7, 215

General Index

Adoulis inscription, 175–7
Aetolian War with Antigonus III, 203–207
Alexandria, 29–30
　foundation of, and Rhakotis, 24–6
　attractive for immigrants, 35, 67
　citizens of, 74–7
　military contributions, 77–80, 86–8, 225
　lands of, 78–9
　garrison of, 80–1
Alexandrian Synod Decree, 177–8
allotments, 138–42, 148–9
　of cavalry, 5, 142–7, 159–60
　of infantry, 13, 157–9
　of *machimoi*, 13, 101
　of officers, 79, 86–7, 145–6
　as rewards, 141–5
　of police, 103, 270, 279
　of prisoners, 138, 194
　heritability of, 149–51, 189, 249
　measurement of, 154–6
　preparation of land for, 150–4
　repossession of, 145–50, 192–4,
　subletting of, 156–7, 192, 245
　taxation of, 145, 189
　temporary administration of (*hemikleroi*), 190–1
　see also military settlers

Andros, capture and garrisoning of, 59, 72, 125
　battle of, 168–72
Ankara, battle of, 166–7, 229–30
Antioch (Syria), 9, 85
　and Daphne raid, 134–5
　and 3rd Syrian War, 164–5, 173–5
Apameia-on-the-Orontes,
　Ptolemaic raid against, 122
　site of army revolt, 230
Aphroditopolite nome, 156, 310 n.19
Apollonia–Sittake, *see* Sittake, 182–3
Apollonopolis Magna (Edfu), 151, 187, 209
armour, 4–16, 180
　helmets, 131
　kasai, felt, 117
　kataphrakta, 242
　see also shields, weapons
army, Ptolemaic, 29, 70, 201–202, 229, 265–75
　size of, 45–6, 62, 111–13, 229, 255
　regiments (*tagmata*), 140–1
　training of, 266–7
　strategy for developing, 108, 274

see also infantry, cavalry, elite regiments, military settlers
Seleucid, size of, 228–31, 257
Arsinoe–Methana, 125
Arsinoite nome (the Fayum), 83–9, 153–60, 213–24, 267–73
  see also allotments, military settlers
Athribis, Athribite nome, 31, 135, 160
association (*koinon* or *politeuma*), of soldiers, often on ethnic lines, 95–8

Babylon, battle of, 179–82
Babylonian chronicles and diaries, 37, 121, 167, 178–83
Berenike in Cyrenaica, 91
  Troglodytica, on the Red Sea, 209
  upon Deires, 208
  near Saba (Adoulis), 208
Boubastis, Boubastite nome, 244–5
Bousiris, Bousirite nome, 79

Camels Fort, battle of, 38–41
Canopus decree, 177–8
Carian War, 114–16
cavalry, cavalry regiments (hipparchies), 219–21
  weaponry of, 5–7
  numbered hipparchies, 214–16
  'ethnic' hipparchies, 218–19
  mercenary hipparchies, 15–17, 143–4, 216–18
  katoikoi hippeis, 268–70
  cavalry tax (*hippike prosodos*), 270–3
Chremonidean War, 123–8

Cilicia, Mallus, 50–1
  Rough Cilicia, 119
cleruchs (military settlers), 138, 148, 156–60, 211–14, 224–5
  origins of, 81–100
  mobilizations of, 160–1, 187–94
  anticipation of war, 242
  regulations and privileges, 248–9
  see also allotments, army, infantry, cavalry
commanders, eponymous, 140–2, 192, 209–10, 214–16
  over-representation of officers, 143–7, 212
  hipparchs, 142–5, 212
  cavalry chiliarchs, 139–44
  infantry chiliarchies, 156, 222–4
Crete, Ptolemaic naval basing, 98, 126
  Cretan (and neo-Cretan) soldiers, 7–8, 66, 71, 80, 92–8, 245, 255, 275
Cyprus, conquest of, 43–4, 60–2, 70–2
  garrisons of, 97–9
  naval power, 124, 264–5
  irrelevance in Fourth Syrian War, 233–4
Cyrene, Cyrenaica, 31–4, 49–50, 70, 119–21
  major source of settlers, 10, 49, 80, 90–1
  military contributions, 10, 222, 229, 258

Damascus, 34, 43, 167–8, 198
Daphne, near Antioch, 134–5, 164
  Tapanhes (Tel Defenna), 39

decline, of Ptolemaic army, 199–202, 227, 275–8
   in cavalry settler land, 269–72
dekarouroi, esp. *machimoi*, 251–2, 278–9
Delta, Nile region, military settlements in, 33, 96, 160, 216, 224
   Egyptian soldiers from, 99, 103–104, 250
Diadochi Wars,
   First, 36–42
   Second, 42–5
   Third, 50–9
   Fourth, 59–64
dioiketes (financial minister), 147, 214
   see also Apollonios

Egyptians, 13, 30, 46, 277–9
   in the military, 52–3, 100–107
   as officers, 250–1
   Hellenization, 94–5, 199
   priesthoods, 31, 103–104, 117, 120, 267
   and policing, 102
   kalasiries, 101–103
   as labour, 156–7
   in Sosibius' phalanx, 249–56, 259
   see also machimoi
Elephantine, 69–70, 81, 102, 118, 266
elephants, 8, 112, 118, 176, 194
   hunts, 128–30, 150–1, 208–11
   at Gaza, 53–4
   Seleucid, 121–2
   at Raphia, 257–8
   in the Great Procession, 123
   seized in invasions of Syria, 176–7
elite regiments, 64, 114
   cavalry (*agema*, veteran *agema*, *peri aulēn*, royal squadron), 3–5, 190
   foot (*agema*, hypaspists, peltasts), 8–10, 67, 172, 182, 225, 242
   Egyptian, 103–105, 251
   ethnic character of, 80, 87–8
   settlement of, 4, 9, 78, 81, 89
epigones, epigonoi (civilian relatives of cleruchs), 12–13, 130, 157–8
   in Greek population, 91–2, 94
   Persian, 106–107
   25-aroura *e*. from 2nd Syrian War, 136–7, 154–6
   4th Syrian War, 224, 246–9
Ephesos, 131–2, 169–72, 197–8, 207, 265
Erythrai in Ionia, 47–8
   and Galatians, 116
Ethiopian War, 116–18, 120, 123
ethnic (*patris*, homeland), 74, 139
   of Ptolemaic settler population, 82–95
   constructed, 82
   Macedonian, 91, 245–6
   Persian, 105–107

Fayum, *see* Arsinoite nome
First Punic War, 166, 198–9
Friends (*Philoi*), 27–9, 38–40, 49–51, 64, 81
   officers and dynasts, 131–3
   eponymous commanders, 140
   supporters of Ptolemy IV, 200

Galatians, invasion of, 115–16
  mercenaries of Ptolemy II, 120
  in fight at Megara, 127
  in Ptolemaic army, 275
garrisons, in Egypt, 13–14, 266
  by Alexander, 24–25
  at Andros, 72
  Thera, 78
  Alexandria, 80
  Cyprus, 97–9
  Elephantine, 117
  Samos, 131
  in Third Syrian War, 172–4
  in the Aegean, 207
  Seleukeia, 233–4
Gaza, battle of, 51–5
Gerrha, in the Bekaa, 232, 235
gift estates (*doreai*), 147, 153–4, 261, 278
grammateus (secretary), 196–7
  of cleruchs, 249
  of the army (*archigrammateus*), 249, 260

Halikarnassos, 114–15, 132, 207, 265
Heliopolis, Heliopolite nome, 39, 160
Herakleans, 85–6
Herakleopolis, Herakleopolite nome, 4, 6
  military settlers in, 268–71, 273
  elite Egyptians, 30, 250
  Judeans, 95
  hipparchy of, 89–90, 93, 215, 220
Hermopolis, Hermopolite nome, 78, 97, 150–1, 159, 216
Heroonpolis (Pithom), 121–2
hipparchy, hipparchies, *see* cavalry

infantry, 7–15, 52–3, 255
  as settlers, 156–9
  light, 13, 21–2, 102, 254
  heavy/phalanx, 10–15, 193–4, 221–5, 245–50
    ideal size of 225–6
    Macedonian character of, 221–2
  medium, 14–15, 254–55
  see also mercenaries

Judeans/Jews, in Alexandria, 79–80
  as Macedonians, 79–80
  and Cleomenes of Naucratis, 31
  deportation to Egypt, 56, 138
  in the Ptolemaic army, 79–80, 88
  and the commander Ananias, 67
  politeuma of, 95

Kallinikon (Raqqa), 195
katoikoi, *see* cleruchs
kingship, Ptolemaic, 263–4
  and acclamation, 64–5
  and military action, 227, 274
  spear-won land, 19, 42, 64
kleroi, *see* allotments
klerouchoi, *see* cleruchs
Kos, 58–9
  battle of, 127
Kyroupedion, battle of, 114

Laodikeia (in Syria), 173–4
Laodikeian War, 169–70, 185
Leontopolis, Leontopolite nome, 160
Libya, Libyans in Ptolemaic army, 90, 105, 151
  and Cyrenaican Greeks, 10, 50

Lycia, 58–9
  soldiers and officers from, 71, 92–3, 98, 133–4

Macedonians, in Ptolemaic army, 9–13
  military pseudo-ethnic, 82, 91, 94–5, 106, 222
  esp. *triakontarouroi Makedones*, 222–4
machimoi, 100–103
  early roles, 305 n.20
  epilektoi, 104–105
  allotments of, 250–2, 306 n.21
  and Raphia reform, 249–53
  and revolt, 277–9
Marsyas (Bekaa), 232–3, 235, 239–40, 260
Memphis, Memphite nome, 25, 35
  Perdiccan invasion, 38–41
  use for accession ceremonies, 135
  military settlers in, 81, 141, 151–3, 158–9, 215, 224
  Raphia reform, 244–5
Mendes, Mendesian nome, Mendes stele, 103–105, 267
Menelaite nome, 78–9, 224
mercenaries (*xenoi, misthophoroi*), 14–17, 69, 80, 110
  in Ptolemy I's army, 29–30, 46, 52–3
  Raphia reform, 224–5, 246–7
  (1) *misthophoroi*, paid or standing regiments, 9, 142–5, 160, 196–7, 209–11, 216–18
  (2) *xenoi* foreign mercenaries, 111–12, 117–23, 134–6, 188, 205, 231, 236
  sources of, 82–3, 92–3, 98–100

becoming cleruchs, 146–7, 151–2, 192
Meroe, 81
  kings of, 202
  Ptolemaic campaigns, 116–18
  Meroitic/Nubian soldiers in Ptolemaic service, 107
  see also Ethiopian War
Miletos, 114–16, 127–8, 130–2, 265
military reforms, Arsinoite settlement, 153–9
  of Ptolemy III, 211–26
  before Raphia, 240–54
military settlements,
  administration of, 147–59, 190–1, 248–9
  total size of, 267–74
  see also allotments, cavalry, infantry
mobilization,
  for elephant hunts, 196–7
  for liturgy, 138, 160
  for war, 274–7
  demobilization, 278–9

Napata, 117–18
navy, 43–4, 124–8, 265
  polyremes in, 60–1, 124, 132, 207
  Egyptians in, 13, 30, 76, 102, 199, 277–8, 291 n.28
  operations, 57–9, 62–3, 72–3, 119, 132, 135, 169, 173–6, 237
  ports/basing for, 66–7, 70, 115, 207
  admirals, 71, 125, 132
neaniskoi (young recruits), 154–9
Nile River,
  floods/inundations, 177–8, 186–7, 267

tie to volcanic activity, 299 n.33
riverine fleet and fortifications,
  39, 63–4, 124, 265–6
connection to Red Sea, 128
role in military operations, 28,
  37–41, 62–3, 120
nomarchs, 148–50, 187, 191–4,
  300 n.14

Oxyrhynchite nome,
  administrators in, 147–51, 197
  hipparchy of, 90–2, 190–1, 243–4
  esp. Cyreneans in, 33–4, 140
  many hipparchies, 151, 159–60,
    215–16, 219–20
  introduction of Macedonian
    infantry, 91, 226, 246

Pages, Royal,
  of Alexander, 27
  of the Ptolemies, 76–7
  Egyptian, 46, 104–105
  Alexander's *Epigonoi*, 26–9
Pamphylia, 48, 71, 114, 175–6
  Pamphylian soldiers, esp.
    Aspendians, 71, 92–5,
    133–4, 252–3
Pelusium, 37–8
  Pelusiac branch of the Nile,
    39–41
  Antigonid invasion, 62–4
  garrison and settlers, 81
  and Fourth Syrian War, 235,
    244–5, 256
Persians, (1) of Persia, 30, 177,
  184, 218, (2) of Alexander
  (the Epigonoi), 26–7, 46,
  (3) military pseudo-ethnic
  for Hellenized non-Greeks,
  esp. Egyptians, 80, 82, 94–7,
  104–107, 151, 199, 243,
  249–50, 278
phalanx, 10–12
  ideal size of, 225–6
  Macedonians in, 222
  combats of, 257–9
  see also infantry, heavy
Phoenicia, *see* Syria and Phoenicia
Pithom Stele, 118–22, 128
population,
  of Alexandria, 75–7
  of Greeks in Egypt, 267–8,
    308 n.1–2
  of settler class, 267–9
  of Ptolemaic military, 93–5, 277
Porphyrion, battle of, 237–9
presbyteroi, veterans, 154–5,
  158–9, 223
priesthoods, eponymous,
  of Alexander and the royal cult,
    77–8, 129, 132–4, 140, 210
  Egyptian, 31, 103–104, 117, 120,
    177, 267
prisoners, of war and as settlers,
  138, 188–9, 194, 278
private land, 249, 273
Ptolemais Hermiou, 69, 81
  Theron, 128–9
  near Barke, 33, 80
  Akko, 134, 234–5, 239–40,
    254, 257
  Rabbath-ammon, 239–40

Raphia, battle of, 254–9
reforms, and Arsinoite settlement,
  136–7, 153–60, 274
  of Ptolemy III, 213–24
  and Fourth Syrian War, 240–54

Revolt,
    of Timarchus and Ptolemy
        the Son, 131
    of the Seleukis, 122
    Third Syrian War, 172, 177–8,
        186–8, 196, 266–7
    of the Kyrrhestians, 230
    after Raphia/Great Revolt, 252,
        262, 278–9
Rhodes, siege of, 65–8
    alliance with Antigonus I, 48
    naming Soter, 67–8
    war and peace with
        Ptolemies, 132

Salamis (Cyprus), 43–4, 97–9, 135
    siege and naval battle of, 60–2
Samos, 114–15, 207
    Ptolemaic base, 99–100, 128, 265
    source of Ptolemaic officers,
        77–8, 237
    seizure by Timarchos, 131
    in Syrian Wars, 132
Seleukeia, by the Sea, 163,
        174–5, 203, 233–4
    on the Euphrates (Sippar),
        179–82
    on the Tigris, 9, 181–2, 232
Seleukis, campaigns in, 179, 183
    Ptolemaic conquest of, 174–5
    rebellions of, 122, 230
shields,
    thureos, oval 'Galatian' shield,
        13–14, 122–3, 307 n.33
    aspis, 15, 132
    Macedonian pelte, 10–12,
        111, 119
    cavalry shields, 6–7, 221, 284 n.3
Smyrna, 183–4

stathmos (quarters), 148–9, 155, 193
strategos (nome governor), 96, 129,
        196, 209, 259
strategy, 264–6
    prudence, 23, 68
    indirect approach, 47–8, 55–6
    projecting power, 70–1
    thalassocracy, 123–4
    incoherence of, 128
    Berenike ruse, 184
    and manpower limitations, 198–9
    against Antiochus III, 230
    to defend Syria, 239–40
    to militarize Egyptians, 276–8
Syene (Aswan), *see* Elephantine,
        Thebaid
Syria and Phoenicia, 1, 134, 260–1
    frontiers of, 136, 167, 198,
        232–7, 260
    campaigns in, 43, 47–8, 135–6,
        146–7, 234–40
    conquest of, 56, 70–2
    garrison of, 47, 134, 236
    naval contributions, 43, 47

tactics, manuals and writers of, 214,
        221, 225–6
temples, Egyptian, 30–1, 118,
        277–8, 282 n.6
    plunder from 165
    refuge in, 156–7
    recovery of relics from the East,
        177, 189
    and Babylon fighting, 181
Thebaid (Upper Egypt),
    temples of, 118
    settlers in, 69–70, 81,
        148–51, 187
    military role of, 111, 129

gift-estates in, 278
see also Ptolemais Hermiou, Elephantine
Thrace,
   conquest of, 168–71, 185, 2062–07
   Thracian soldiers, 15, 90–4, 151–2, 172, 219

War of the Brothers, 166–8, 202–203
War of the Syrian Succession, 114–16
weapons, 4–15, 52–5, 221, 259
   pike (sarissa), 10–12
   Galatian and Thracian swords, 15